The History of the White Star Line

Robin Gardiner

Ian ✦ Allan
PUBLISHING

First published in hardback 2001
First published in paperback

ISBN (10) 0 7110 3170 3
ISBN (13) 978 0 7110 3170 8

Published by Ian Allan Publishing

an imprint of Ian Allan Publishing Ltd, Hersham, Surrey KT12 4RG.
Printed by Ian Allan Printing Ltd, Hersham, Surrey KT12 4RG.

Code: 0609/B2

Visit the Ian Allan Publishing website at: www.ianallanpublishing.com

Contents

Foreword

Thanks to a very efficient effort by succeeding owners of the White Star Company to obliterate all trace of the firm's activities, precious little of the line's archive remains in existence. For much of the earlier history we are forced to rely on old newspapers and entries in registers. Nevertheless, much of the effort to obscure the past comes to naught because the White Star Line, down the years, touched many other people and organisations.

The White Star Line had two distinct, and separate, incarnations. In its first it was a sailing ship line, specialising in the transportation of emigrants to America and Australia, while also trading with the Orient and both North and South America. Although the line was relatively successful at this stage it was not exceptional, and its story could be that of almost any other contemporary. In its second incarnation the line gained a new prominence, becoming one of the world's most successful steamship lines, then specialising in the North Atlantic trade, although its other activities continued unabated. Of all the other shipping lines of the late 19th and early 20th centuries possibly only Cunard compares to White Star.

As in any successful enterprise, throughout its history the White Star Line was continuously changing and evolving. When it stopped evolving it began to die.

Unfortunately, little in the way of records or company archives is still available for a number of reasons, not least among these being the cold-blooded attempt by the Cunard Line to eradicate all trace of its old rival after the two lines were merged, and when Cunard took over completely a few years later. As a result of this destruction of what would now be seen as important historical documents it is no simple matter to reconstruct the history of White Star, and there must inevitably be gaps and inaccuracies in any such reconstruction. Newspapers in the 19th century, as now, are not notable for the exactitude of their reporting even when they are given reasonable information in the first place. When they are given somewhat dubious information then what appears in print might bear little or no resemblance to the truth. Nevertheless, as surviving newspaper articles and advertisements are virtually all that appears to remain as a record of the activities of the White Star Line during the latter half of the 19th century, we are obliged to use them. Some of the more obvious items of misinformation can be corrected by referring to such reliable sources as *Lloyd's Register*, and in some cases harbour records.

In recent years information regarding at least a small part of the White Star Line's archive appears to have come to light. Various tales of what became of this material have circulated over the years, most of them without foundation. We know that much of the archive was destroyed in the 1930s on Cunard instructions, but not all of it. Other material was supposedly ruined in 1940 and 1941 when the Luftwaffe bombed Liverpool, hitting the old White Star offices at 30 James Street. While it is true that the Germans did bomb Liverpool, and that they did hit the White Star building, the purpose-built offices and their contents were not destroyed. Incendiary bombs slightly damaged the roof, as can be seen by comparing modern photographs to ones taken before 1939.

It would appear that tons of paper relating to the White Star Line were removed from the damaged building to a warehouse for safekeeping. These papers were never returned to their old hiding place but remained in the damp, decaying, rat-infested warehouse for about 30 years. During that time the material, stored in wooden crates and reinforced cardboard boxes, was regularly seen by security guards patrolling the premises. What became of it then is shrouded in mystery, although there is no clear reason why it should be.

It would seem that the archive material was still in the Liverpool warehouse in the late 1960s, still in its crates, some of which were actually marked 'White Star Line'. Then, as far as we have been able to discover, it was decided by those who had custody of this material that it should be destroyed. In the early 1970s a huge amount of this paper was transported to a paper mill at Warrington. The transportation of this material could hardly have been less secret, and between 20 and 30 tons of it was stacked in the open at the mill, the stack of paper reaching as high as the eaves of the mill building.

In one of those curious twists of fate that ruin the best laid plans, the manager of the mill was called away to London soon after the archive was supposedly pulped. While he was on the train heading for the capital he met the curator of a museum not far from Warrington and, during the conversation, mentioned the archive, and how reluctant he had been to destroy so important a record. It seemed that 'that was that' and the archive had gone for ever. Then, a few years later, odd snippets of information began to come to light, and isolated documents started to come up for auction. This raised the possibility that perhaps the mill manager had managed to save some of the archive, or the people who had been responsible for its safekeeping, and who had sent so much to be destroyed, had not sent it all to the mill after all.

Further enquiries were put in train and these turned up the road haulage company who had transported the archive from Liverpool to Warrington. Regrettably their records did not go back far enough to provide any details, just a few memories, but it did confirm the existence of the paperwork in the early 1970s. In addition to the boxes and crates, the archive material was described by at least one witness, quite independently, as containing enormous ledgers with invoices and receipts pasted in, next to the entries relating to them.

Then came what looked like a breakthrough. One of those security guards who had patrolled the warehouse where the archive material had been stored came forward. Thirty years had passed since he last saw the White Star Line crates and he was no longer even sure which building he had guarded, but he could tell us that it was definitely one of three or four. As luck would have it, all of the buildings had survived and been modernised. The ex-patrol man could remember who his employers had been, and that it was they, he believed, who were responsible for the archive's long sojourn in the decaying warehouse: the Liverpool Museum Service.

We wrote to the museum asking for confirmation of the one-time existence of the White Star material, and that they had once used the premises in question as a storage facility. They appeared to have no record of the warehouse or its contents, and could not tell exactly which building was concerned. In fact they denied ever having a storage facility at all in the Dingle Dock Road, as it is known locally. After having had the existence of the old shipping line records confirmed by three entirely separate and unrelated sources this singular lack of information from the museum seemed curious.

The next step was, obviously, to determine exactly which of the three or four buildings tentatively identified by the security guard was the right one. The guard went back to Liverpool and retraced his old route along the road where the buildings stood. The area had changed considerably since he had last seen it, but there was enough remaining for him to be almost certain which warehouse he had once patrolled. To reinforce his memory he photographed all of the buildings he thought might be the one in question, allowing us to place them exactly on a map of Liverpool; this gave us the addresses. Consultation with a late 1960s *Kelly's Street Directory* quickly provided the names of the companies that occupied the buildings at the relevant time. Two of them turned out to have been used as depositories during the period in which we were interested. Liverpool Corporation were then asked which of the buildings had been used as a storage facility by the museum since World War 2. They could not identify the correct building, but they did confirm that the Museum Service had used a number of temporary storage facilities throughout the city, although they did not seem to know just where.

Then we contacted, with the aid of an estate agent, the present-day owners and occupiers of the warehouses we were interested in, with surprising results. The present owners of the building identified by the guard as being almost certainly the one he had patrolled, confirmed the existence of old papers relating to the emigrant traffic from Liverpool in the third quarter of the 19th century, a time when the White Star Line was engaged in just that business. It seems that, when the present owners took over the building, it was in dire need of renovation. During those renovations some old papers came to light, stuffed into cracks in the wall and so forth. Most, but not all, of the papers recovered had been handed to the Liverpool Museum Service (where they seem to have disappeared once again). Copies of what remained in the owner's possession were obtained. One was a government booklet of 1863 specifying what must be provided by shipowners for the use of emigrants aboard ship – clear evidence that the warehouse had once been used for the storage of papers relating to a shipping line engaged in the emigrant trade. A request to the Liverpool Museum Service asking for a sight of the other material discovered in the warehouse renovation has, at the time of writing, been ignored for three months. Just about all museums have vast amounts of material stored away from the public gaze in basements and other storage facilities. Much of this stored material is not even catalogued; even the museums themselves don't know what they have got. No doubt, in the fullness of time, the documents discovered during the warehouse refurbishment will reappear.

Even while these enquiries were ongoing new information regarding the fate of at least some of the material that had found its way to the Warrington paper mill reached us, from a source we had been in contact with for a number of years. Our museum curator, who had already been a mine of information, suddenly recalled being told that quite a lot of the material, instead of being pulped, had been put into a shipping container. He did not know where it had gone from there.

Shortly after hearing of this container full of paperwork which had disappeared almost 30 years before, we began to notice what seemed to be White Star archive material coming onto the open market. A fair proportion of this material was being marketed by anonymous vendors. At the same time information that could only have come from official White Star passenger and crew lists began to circulate. Those responsible for the release of this information refused to reveal their sources, which makes their data of dubious value. However, checking the data with our own sources showed it to be accurate in most cases.

Since the White Star Line was a major shipping line with agents and offices scattered around the world it follows that the company's paperwork would also be well distributed and could come to light in various ways. Although the company's head office was in Liverpool, White Star later operated predominantly out of Southampton, with its other major transatlantic terminal at New York. Such mundane items as passenger lists must have been available to the American office, probably before a ship left England. It should come as no surprise therefore to discover that passenger lists do exist in America. What is curious, however, is the secrecy that surrounds the source of this material.

When the Cunard Line set about eliminating the records of its old rivals perhaps it included those in America, and those from all the other branch offices, which would have been readily available to them then. In that case it is quite possible that the only quantity of historic White Star documents that survived the purge were those lying forgotten in the basement of the office building in James Street, Liverpool. Clearly, nobody attached any importance to those documents when they were rescued from the damaged offices or they would have been found a better home than a run-down warehouse. Still, this perceived unimportance may have been the reason the material survived for as long as it did.

Only with the tremendous revival of interest in the White Star Line in the late 1950s and early 60s, generated by Walter Lord's book on the loss of the *Titanic*, and the film *A Night to Remember*, did the real value of the archive material become apparent. Had the documents been destroyed before the reawakening of interest in the White Star Line, in an effort to save space and reduce overheads, then it might have been understandable. Should valuable documentation on the line have been destroyed, and on possibly *Titanic* itself, in the late 1960s or early 70s, when interest in the line was already intense and growing daily, it would beggar belief. By that time societies dedicated to remembering the *Titanic*, and researching every aspect of the ship and the line she served, were springing up all over the place.

Then, as now, museums all over the world must have been inundated with requests for information on the line. No doubt they would all have been only too happy to take a part of the material rotting in Liverpool, which would at least have ensured its survival, and availability to public scrutiny. Instead, the vast majority of White Star material known to exist is in the hands of private collectors, or acquisitive societies, who are prepared to pay large sums of money for anything relating to the line.

We can only hope that some of the material from the Liverpool warehouse still exists, perhaps in a shipping container or museum storeroom somewhere. If it does, it may solve some of the puzzles that remain in the White Star history or at least fill in a few gaps in our knowledge. In the meantime the search for whatever else remains of the White Star Line's archive continues.

Ship Names and Tonnages

White Star reused a number of older ship's names for new vessels at various times. Whenever confusion might arise these are distinguished in the text as in the following example: *Adriatic¹* (launched 1871, scrapped 1899) and *Adriatic²* (entered service 1907, scrapped 1934).

All ship tonnages are given as gross register except where noted, where they follow format in which they are listed in the records. Other measurements likewise follow the format in which they are listed in the records.

Acknowledgements

I would like to express my gratitude to all of those authors and reporters, far too many to name here, whose works over more than a century provided such a wealth of information.

Further information was provided by the Guildhall Library, Lloyds' Register, Lloyds' List, the BBC, the Memorial University of Newfoundland, the National Maritime Museum, Liverpool Record Office and Liverpool Leisure Services Directorate.

I would like to list here individuals who found the time to take an interest in this project, and took the trouble to seek out pieces of White Star's history that might otherwise have been lost. These include: Mr T. Aldridge, Debbie Beavis, Steve Hall, Peter Dawson, P. Ludlow, Ian Fryer, John Soloman, Roy Backhouse, Kenneth Mallin and John Anstee. Thanks to Professor Roy Storer who provided a previously unpublished photograph taken aboard *Olympic*.

Special thanks to Robert McDougall for his unstinting help identifying certain buildings in Liverpool, for access to his extensive archive and research material, and in particular his collection of maritime photographs and postcards.

Chapter 1

1820-1853

Befoie we even begin the story of the White Star Line perhaps we should learn a little of the men behind it. The first of these were John Pilkington and Henry Threlfall Wilson. John Pilkington, the son of sea captain and businessman Christopher Pilkington, was born in Liverpool in 1820. Henry Threlfall Wilson, the son of John Wilson, an emigration agent of 74 Waterloo Road, Liverpool, was born three years later, in 1823. Just 20 years on, Pilkington & Wilson were to form a partnership that would give birth to one of the most famous shipping lines of all time: White Star.

In the very same year that Henry Wilson entered upon the world's stage James Baines was born at 85 Duke Street, Liverpool, on 26 October 1823. James Baines was to become the owner, and was probably the founder, of the Black Ball Line, which was inextricably bound up with the White Star Line in its early days. Although they were competitors in a cut-throat market, the two shipping lines would charter one another's vessels at times, allow ships belonging to one to sail under the flag of the other, and even share ships between them when both house flags would fly from the masthead. Because of this intermingling of resources during the early years of both lines it is worth while looking at all of the players in the drama relatively closely.

It might be of interest to some to learn that the popular television series *The Onedin Line* not only had a foundation in fact but was actually based on the history of the Black Ball Line, with James Baines the model for James Onedin, so anybody who saw the series will have some idea of the sort of people involved in the earlier parts of this story.

William Baines, James's father, died on 17 June 1829 at the early age of 37. He was a successful sugar refiner, a trade that occupied a substantial part of Liverpool's economy at the time, and he owned more than one refinery. Mary Baines, William's wife, was also in business and manufactured confectionery, which she sold from her own shop in Duke Street. It would be difficult to imagine two businesses that complemented one another more, and both thrived. Perhaps not a marriage made in heaven but certainly a very practical and successful one.

Shortly before he died William and Mary had opened a boarding house in what was then the very fashionable Rathbone Street. Probably for economic reasons, after William's death Mary, a daughter and three sons, moved into the boarding house rather than continuing to run it from the Duke Street residence.

While the Baines family were living at Rathbone Street they took in a paying guest, John Grant Morris. Morris was then a mere coal merchant's junior clerk but he had ambitions. One of these objectives was to marry James Baines' sister Mary. (Not his mother — it pays to keep these things clear.) The marriage took place at Trinity Church, Liverpool, in August 1835, and it was to have a profound influence on the fortunes of the Black Ball and White Star lines more than a quarter of a century later.

In the period between his marriage and the 1860s, John Morris opened his own coal business and made a fortune. The ambitious Morris even became Lord Mayor of Liverpool in the fullness of time. Long before then Mary Baines senior became the toast of Liverpool when, in 1837, she was appointed Confectioner to Her Royal Highness Princess Victoria. Clearly, the Baines family were doing well, and they were destined to do better still.

In the same year that Mary Baines won her appointment to the Princess, very soon to be Queen Victoria, when James Baines was 14 years old, his mother apprenticed him to a local engineer. The employment did not suit the young Baines at all because he was extremely averse to getting his hands dirty and, anyway it entailed his getting up at what he considered to be an ungodly hour. He did not outstay his welcome. Shortly afterwards he went to work for his uncle Richard, an established shipbroker, at 2 Wellington Buildings, Poole Lane.

Another major player in the history of the White Star Line, Thomas Henry Ismay, was born at Maryport, at the mouth of the River Ellen, in Cumberland, in the year that Queen Victoria ascended the throne. The Queen outlived Ismay by only two years, and because the whole of his life was spent under that one monarch he is oft-times described as the most 'Victorian' of the great shipowners. Because T. H. Ismay was to have such a tremendous effect on the development of the White Star Line perhaps we should take a short look at his family history in order possibly to understand him a little better, as to many people T. H. Ismay was the White Star Line.

Maryport was built on the property of Humphrey Senhouse and named after his wife. During its early years in the 18th century the town's economy was based on coal mining, and the building of small ships to transport the coal, mostly to Ireland. The Ismay family had moved to Maryport from Uldale, a hamlet some 12 miles away where they had been small farmers. T. H. Ismay's grandfather, Henry, had been born in Maryport in 1777, as had his father, Joseph Ismay, who was a successful local shipbuilder, so there had been an Ismay in Maryport almost from its beginning. There were three shipyards in the town in the late 18th century, including that of the elder Ismay, and one which was owned by Joseph Middleton.

Joseph Middleton was a fairly typical example of the shipbuilder of his day inasmuch as he did not only build ships for other people but also built a small fleet for himself. Henry Ismay was the captain of one of Middleton's ships, and in 1800 he married the yard owner's eldest daughter, Charlotte. Their second son, Thomas worked as a foreman shipwright in the yard, which had now passed to his uncle, Isaac Middleton. When Henry Ismay retired from the sea he took on a small grocery shop in Maryport High Street, and moved in with his wife and young Thomas.

Thomas Ismay lived with his parents until he married Mary Sealby, the daughter of another High Street resident, John Sealby, who described himself as a 'gentleman'. The couple moved into one of a row of tiny cottages in what was known as Whillan's Yard. It was here that Thomas Henry Ismay was born in 1837. Three sisters were born over the next four years, and by the end of that time the diminutive house was getting more than a little crowded, so the whole lot of them moved to a larger dwelling, Ropery House. Their new home's unusual name came from the fact that all of the ropes to be used in the shipyards were laid out outside it. In 1847 T. H. Ismay's brother John Sealby Ismay was born.

Sometime roundabout, or shortly after, the birth of T. H. Ismay his father started in business on his own account as a timber merchant, shipbroker and builder. He had shares in four vessels trading out of Maryport and began to have dealings with another firm of shipbrokers, Imrie Tomlinson, who were to have more than a little effect on the career of his eldest son. On 11 July 1840 they wrote to Joseph Ismay, Thomas senior's brother, and apparently business partner.

The letter concerned the late arrival of Ismay's vessel *Middleton*, under the command of Captain White, which Imrie Tomlinson thought might have been delayed by northerly gales, despite another ship which had departed after her having arrived home on time. The shipbrokers suggested that the *Middleton*, which was a new ship at the time, should be seasoned by a trip to the River Plate and back. They would be quite happy to arrange such a voyage. In the meantime the ship was ordered to London to operate out of that port for a while. As well as the trip to the River Plate, Imrie Tomlinson also offered Ismay's ship a round trip to Barbary, carrying coal on the outward voyage and sugar on the return. The shippers of the coal were prepared to pay £3 10s (£3.50) a ton to the shipowners, a fair price in 1840. There was a problem, which the shipbrokers pointed out, in that acceptance of the cargo of coal and sugar might delay or prevent the *Middleton's* change of port from Liverpool to London. As a third alternative they offered Joseph Ismay the opportunity of using his vessel as a mail packet to Rio de Janeiro for a return of about £525. Evidently, the Ismay family was on fairly good terms with the well-established shipbrokers, to such an extent that Imrie Tomlinson was prepared to offer friendly advice.

Throughout his early childhood T. H. Ismay was continually exposed to the world of shipping in general, and shipbuilding in particular. He would spend hours standing on the shore, watching the ships and talking to the sailors. When he was not watching ships he was carving models of them out of wood with his penknife. It should come as no surprise to learn that T. H. Ismay, as he grew older, envisaged a future for himself in maritime commerce. Little could he have known in those early days just what an impression he was going to make on that world.

T. H. Ismay's parents were determined that he should have as good an education as his standing in the community, as the son of a successful shipbuilder and property owner, demanded. When he left the local school at the age of 12, in 1849 they promptly packed him off to Croft House School, at Brampton, near Carlisle. Croft House was, at that time, one of the best boarding schools in the country and attracted pupils from all over the north of England, Scotland and Ireland. More than half a century later Clement Jones, who was at school with Ismay, wrote this of him:

'Fifty years ago Thomas Henry Ismay was, along with myself and many others, a pupil at Croft House under the late Mr Coulthard. Survivors of that company will remember well the dark complexioned lad with dark piercing eyes, whose hobby was the sea, whose ambition was a seafaring life, and who never seemed so happy as when engaged in fashioning a miniature sailing vessel with pocket knife out of a block of wood, rigging it with masts and sails, all according to the orthodox rig of its class, and then sailing them on the pond at Irthington.'

Jones also described how the young T. H. Ismay was very good at sports, taking a particular interest in cricket. It was during his stay at Croft House that Thomas Ismay acquired his love of what was then popularly known as 'the weed'. He became convinced that tobacco was one of the perks of life at sea, and the habit of chewing it earned him the nickname 'Baccy Ismay', which followed him throughout his life.

Thomas's period at Croft House was not entirely a happy one, however. When he had been at the school for just a year his father suddenly died, at the relatively early age of 46.

Isaac Middleton, Thomas's great-uncle, took the boy's future in hand and arranged for him, on the completion of his schooling, to be apprenticed to his own agent, the shipbrokers Imrie Tomlinson. As we have seen, Joseph Ismay also had regular, and apparently friendly, dealings with the Liverpool-based shipbrokers, which must have helped in securing a position for Thomas Henry with the company. For the time being Thomas continued at Croft House, although his learning took a distinctly maritime turn when he added navigation to his course of studies.

By the time he was 20 years old, in 1843, James Baines was already representing himself as a gentleman, of 1 Rathbone Street. He had a certain amount of justification in thus describing himself as his family was now successfully involved in sugar refining, confectionery, boarding house, and shipbroking businesses. In 1845 Baines took on a partner, John Hamilton, and they set themselves up in business as merchants and shipbrokers. The partnership did not last and later in the year James ditched Hamilton and joined forces with John Carter. The partnership of Carter and Baines took offices at 3 India Buildings and set about building its business.

At the very same time that James Baines was setting himself up, John Pilkington and Henry Threlfall Wilson were doing exactly the same thing. It seems that the young Henry Wilson, who had been an apprentice in the office of what was known in the 20th century as T. & J. Harrison, but was just Thomas Harrison in 1845, decided to go into a shipbroking partnership with Pilkington. The partnership would be known as Pilkington & Wilson and took offices in Prince's Buildings, 26 North John Street, just a short walk from James Baines' offices. The elements that would culminate in the White Star Line were already beginning to come together.

By 1846 Carter and Baines owned three ships: the 421-ton *Charles Brownell*, built in 1846 at Pwllheli, North Wales; the 351-ton barque *General Sale*, built in 1843 at Sunderland; and the 744-ton barque *Sisters*. The partners traded their small fleet around the Horn to Valparaiso and China while acting as shipbrokers for vessels trading with the New World and the Middle East.

In the same year Pilkington & Wilson advertised the first sailing of a vessel for which they, as agents, had procured a cargo, the small brig *Elizabeth*. The ship sailed for Canada on 26 February 1846. During the next two years they also acted as agents for the *Desdemona* and the *Thomas H. Perkins*, the first emigrant ships to be loaded by the partners. The vessels carried their human cargoes, seeking a better life, to America, establishing important contacts there that would stand the embryo White Star Line in good stead in later years.

Some time in 1847 Isaac Chambers, one-time flour dealer of Burlington Street and latterly a corn broker of Juvenal Street, retired from business and moved away from Liverpool, to Ulcoats, near Egremont in Cumberland. Isaac had long been interested in the shipping business and now, with a certain amount of time to indulge that interest, he began to invest quite a substantial amount of his money in Pilkington & Wilson's business venture. As a result of the interest Isaac Chambers was showing in his business, close ties grew up between Henry Wilson and the Chambers family.

Perhaps because of a genuine fondness, or perhaps because of a desire to cement a bond between the Chambers family fortune and his own expanding enterprise, Henry Wilson married Isaac Chambers' eldest daughter Anne on 5 September 1848. Whatever his reasons, Wilson had united two families that in a very few years would both be major shareholders in White Star. With the passage of time the connection between the families would become even closer.

In the spring of 1848, at Altcar, James Baines married Anne Brown, the daughter of the late John Brown of Netherton. A notice of the wedding appeared in the local press on 4 May 1848. The newlyweds set up home in Holly Street, Fairfield.

In 1849 Pilkington & Wilson bought their first ship, the 879-ton *Iowa*, which had been built specially for them at St John, New Brunswick, Canada, for the then princely sum of £8,500. Even though they were already advertising passages to New York, New Orleans, Charleston and Boston, the *Iowa*, as the first vessel actually owned by Pilkington & Wilson, has a unique place in history. With her first advertised sailing to Boston on 28 June 1849 the *Iowa* became the first vessel of the White Star Line, and was probably the first ship to sail under the house flag, a five-pointed white star on a red burgee.

In 1849 James Baines dissolved the partnership with John Carter and set up on his own as a shipbroker and sugar refiner, having taken on what had been his father's refinery at 6 Jackson Lane. His mother had found a partner of her own in the shape of a Mr Rigby and was running another refinery, under the title Rigby and Baines, at Belle Vale, Derby Road, as well as the confectionery and boarding house businesses.

Sometime round about 1850 John Pilkington bought a second vessel for the White Star Line, to trade with Valparaiso. She was the ten-year-old *Windsor Castle*, built by G. Black & Co of Quebec. Command of the *Windsor Castle* was given to Captain T. Rogers. Even as Pilkington & Wilson were setting their sights on the South American trade routes, events on the far side of the world were already shaping their business future.

Edmund Hammond Hargrave returned to his adopted country, Australia, from the United States in January 1851. In 1832 the 16-year-old Hargrave had decided to leave his native England and seek his fortune in the antipodes. Fortune, however, was not yet ready to smile on the young immigrant and for years he tried one way or another to earn a respectable living, without any conspicuous success. Then, in 1849 came word that gold had been found in California. Edmund Hargrave boarded a vessel and set off for the gold-fields. After spending more than a year of hopeful searching he had still not 'struck it rich' and began to believe that he just might do better at home. During the journey back to Australia Hargrave made no secret of his intention to seek gold there. He later wrote, 'I made known to my friends and companions my confident expectations on the subject. One and all, however, derided me, and treated my views and opinions as those of a madman.'

Hargrave left Sydney on 5 February 1851 to pursue his quest. He may not have discovered gold in California but he had certainly learned a useful amount about how to go searching for it. His plan was to cross the Blue Mountains on horseback and work his way north-westwards. After a couple of months he arrived in the Bathurst area of New South Wales, where his belief, so derided by his companions on the voyage from California to Sydney, was rewarded when he discovered a rich source of the precious mineral. The *Sydney Morning Herald* announced the find on 15 May 1851 and the Great Australian Gold Rush had begun.

Within a month more than 10,000 men had made their way to Bathurst, and many, many more were on their way. Meanwhile, in Liverpool, certain shipowners were realising that there was money to be made carrying prospectors and the supplies they would undoubtedly need to within striking distance of the goldfields. Until now the great majority of the Australian emigrant trade had been handled by Gibbs, Bright & Co, James M. Walthew, and Henry Fox's The Liverpool Australian Line of Packets. (Henry Fox also acted as the Liverpool agent for the Colonisation Assurance Corporation.)

Gibbs, Bright & Co was an established merchant partnership that had been set up in 1825 at 22 Water Street, Liverpool. Over the years it had moved the centre of its operations, first to Oldhall Street, and then to Bretherton Buildings, North John Street. George Gibbs was a London merchant when the partnership with Robert Bright, of Bristol, was formed. Both men, with George Gibbs' brother Henry, were directors of the Great Western Steam Ship Company, and were also involved in the construction of the Bristol and London Railway, with the great, if perhaps slightly over-ambitious, Isambard Kingdom Brunel.

Gibbs and Bright initially acted as the Liverpool agents for the Great Western Steam Ship Company, but soon set up their own shipping line, the Eagle. When, a little later, the exodus to Australia was at its height and the Eagle and Black Ball lines had joined forces in competition with the rapidly growing White Star Line, Gibbs, Bright played their ace card by buying the Brunel-designed *Great Britain*, the most famous and successful ship ever used in the Australian emigrant trade, from the Great Western Steam Ship Company for £18,000.

Although news of the Australian gold strike had reached Liverpool by October 1851, Henry Fox failed to mention it in an advertisement he placed in the local paper on the 10th of that month. His advertisement, on behalf of the Colonisation Assurance Corporation, showing that an emigrant ship was leaving Liverpool on 30 October, read:

'To small farmers, agricultural labourers, and servants of every kind, carpenters, bricklayers, masons, blacksmiths, wheelwrights, and mechanics generally. And the families of these; and to female domestic servants, this corporation offers passages at £6 for each adult, but by this ship only.'

There was no mention of any concessionary fares for gold miners and prospectors.

At the same time as Henry Fox and the Colonisation Assurance Corporation were advertising for settlers to open up the young country, Gibbs Bright was appealing to a slightly different type of emigrant. They were advertising the next departure of the *Gibson Craig*, which would be sailing for Sydney, being careful to mention that Sydney was the nearest port to the newly discovered goldfields.

Gibbs Bright had read the situation correctly and young adventurers, anxious to try their luck, flocked to purchase passage on the vessel. It did not take the other shipowners and brokers long to see which way the wind was blowing, and they, too, were soon including the diggings among the attractions offered by Australia in their advertisements. However, despite the best efforts of the other Liverpool lines involved in the Australian emigrant trade, Gibbs Bright had stolen a march on them, and was determined to hold on to it. Until 1851 most of the trade with Australia had been carried out by shipping lines operated out of London, but now they were being challenged. As ever more prospectors clamoured for a place on a ship bound for the new Eldorado, the Gibbs Bright fleet of clippers grew steadily.

By 1851 James Baines had moved both house and office. He was now living at 19 Upper Canning Street and running his business affairs from the Commercial Bank Building at 6 Cook Street. He owned three ships by this time: the *Maria*, the *Express*, and a 421-ton barque named *Cleopatra*, built in 1848 at Parrsboro', Nova Scotia. He had given command of this last vessel to Captain James Nichol Forbes, who was to become the Black Ball Line's most famous commander.

Gibbs Bright was advertising the sailing of three vessels for Australia by January 1852, the *Salacia*, *Petrel* and *Falcon*, but it seems unlikely that the *Falcon* departed with the other two ships as she was advertised again in April as sailing on the 25th of that month.

By February 1852 reports were reaching Liverpool that the number of men digging for gold around Bathurst, New South Wales, had risen to more than 40,000. Many of these reports were exaggerated and described how once poor men were becoming wealthy overnight, without effort. Of course, some prospectors did become immensely wealthy, but they were in the minority. Most scratched a meagre living, at best. One of those at the diggings described his best ever day by saying that he collected about £3 worth of gold, but only by digging a hole 6ft deep. Another, whose account appeared in the *Liverpool Mercury* on 7 February 1852, described the gold- field in more glowing terms:

'This is the El Dorado of the World. Money is actually so plentiful here that men do not know how to get rid of it. You will laugh when I tell you as a matter of fact that two men, at a Public house in Melbourne, destroyed two ten pound notes after this fashion: one put a ten pound note between bread and butter and ate it, remarking that he was rather fond of a rich sandwich: the other lighted his pipe with the note. These are not singular instances. Men that never were worth £5 in their lives are now possessed of fortunes, and the yoke is burdensome, and they scatter the money like chaff. The whole country for hundreds of miles is one immense gold field.'

Undeterred by the 'burden' of immense wealth, the steady flow of adventurers bound for the Australian gold diggings grew into a flood. Liverpool was full to bursting with would-be gold miners. There were simply too many emigrants for the existing shipping lines already carrying them to cope with, so lines that had hitherto sailed on different routes transferred vessels, and new companies were set up and began advertising passages.

Another company, J. S. de Wolf, which had been set up in 1840 by Canadians John Starr and James Ratchford de Wolf, to trade between Nova Scotia and Liverpool, promptly made the move into the Australian trade. By 2 April 1852 the local papers were advertising their *Geelong* as a fine clipper, about to depart for the gold-fields. However, despite the sudden dramatic growth in competition Gibbs Bright, with more vessels employed on the run than any other owner or broker, was still maintaining its lead.

By early April 1852 there was a certain amount of consternation amongst the shipowners and brokers of Liverpool. It was all well and good sending ever growing numbers of emigrants to seek their fortunes in the Australian gold-fields but growing numbers of sailors were also deciding that gold prospecting might offer a better life than the one they were used to. More and more of them were deserting their ships and heading inland. This somewhat farcical situation had become so acute that ships were unable to return to Britain because masters could not muster a crew for them.

Even the masters themselves were not always able to resist the easy profits that might be made from the gold seekers. Some smaller vessels, instead of off-loading their passengers at Sydney and returning to Britain for more, were taking people upriver toward the mines, for an extra remuneration of course. The would-be gold miners were prepared to pay well for any means of transport that would get them to the mines faster than on foot or horseback. An example of this impatience, and a captain's readiness to exploit it, is the

Sea Queen. She had already begun loading in preparation for her return to London when her captain had the cargo removed so that he could take passengers upriver instead.

On Friday 14 May 1852 an advertisement appeared in the shipping sections of the Liverpool press announcing the New Liverpool, Line of Australian Packets. There was a noticeable similarity in the name of the new line to that of Henry Fox & Co's line, which had been established in 1829. Although the new line was a separate entity to any of the shipping lines already mentioned, it shared at least some familiar names among its managers in John Pilkington, Henry Threlfall Wilson and James Baines. The ships they advertised were the *Maria*, *Bhurtpoor*, *Northumberland*, and *Argo*. It was intended that the new line would operate exclusively on the run from Liverpool to Port Phillip and Sydney. Here, for the first time we see James Baines & Co acting in concert with Pilkington & Wilson. In later years they were to become implacable rivals.

The policy of using their own ships where possible but chartering one from another owner whenever demand required, which both Baines and Pilkington & Wilson had regularly practised, was carried over into the new venture. The *Argo* and *Northumberland* were both chartered, although Baines was to buy the *Northumberland* a couple of years later.

The *Maria*, a 1,014-ton vessel, was built in 1851 by T. Oliver and Co of Quebec for Captain James Nichol Forbes, who it will be recalled was a master for James Baines. In January 1852 Baines and Thomas Miller MacKay, who was to become his partner, bought the ship from Forbes, thus making this the first ship of the Baines MacKay partnership.

Less than a week after the New Liverpool Line's first advertisement another similar one appeared. There was an extra ship named in this second advertisement, the frigate-built *Marco Polo*, due to sail on 21 June. Demonstrating a genius for catching the public imagination, which would remain with White Star throughout its existence, the partnership advertised the 2^1/$_2$-thousand-ton *Marco Polo* as the largest vessel ever to sail from Liverpool. They also claimed that the vessel was expected to sail as fast as any ship afloat, had splendid accommodations, and, rather ominously, carried two surgeons.

The *Marco Polo* was an impressive vessel for her time at 185ft long and 38ft in the beam. She had been built by James Smith at Courtney Bay, New Brunswick, in 1851. Smith had not designed the vessel as a passenger ship at all, but had intended that she be used in the timber trade; consequently she was not, in the conventional sense of the word, beautiful, being shaped more like a box than anything else. There was a small river running through Smith's yard and it was his practice, in an age when ships were more usually launched sideways, to launch new ships stern first into this river. The *Marco Polo* was launched in this manner, on an ebbing tide. Instead of drifting into midstream and stopping, she backed straight across the river and ran aground on the far side. As the tide ebbed the grounded ship gently fell over onto her side. It took a fortnight to refloat her. Luckily the vessel was undamaged by her unusual launching and was completed and put to work.

To begin with James Smith retained ownership of the *Marco Polo* and put her under the command of Captain Amos Crosby of Yarmouth, Nova Scotia. Her first voyage was to Liverpool, loaded with timber, where Smith hoped to sell both cargo and ship. Nobody in Liverpool was interested in purchasing the homely *Marco Polo* so her Liverpool agents, Stitt, Coubrough & Stitt, sent her to Mobile for a load of cotton. On her return in early May 1852 they again tried to sell her, and this time they found a buyer in the shape of James Baines, and his partner T. M. MacKay.

Baines and MacKay bought 28 shares each of the 64 on offer. Captain Forbes, who was to be her captain, bought the remaining eight. The new owners spent a small fortune in fitting the ship out as a passenger vessel, and she was described by the *Illustrated London News*:

'The poop was used as a ladies' cabin, and on deck, forward of the poop, was the dining saloon. The ceiling of the saloon was in maple and the pilasters were panelled with highly ornamented and silvered glass, coins of various countries being a feature of the decorations. Between each pilaster was a circular aperture, about six feet in circumference, for light and ventilation. Over each aperture was placed a sheet of plate glass with a painted picturesque view in the centre, enclosed in a framework of foliage and scroll of opaque colours and gold. The whole panels were brought out slightly by a rim of perforated zinc so that the air was freely admitted, as well as light being diffused over the whole.

'The saloon doors were panelled in stained glass, bearing figures of commerce and industry from the designs of Mr Frank Howard. In the centre of the saloon was a table of thick plate glass, which had the advantage of giving light to the dormitories below. The upholstery was in embossed crimson velvet. The berths were ranged in the 'tween decks in separate state rooms and had circular glass ports of effective construction.'

Captain James Nichol Forbes had been born in 1821, in Aberdeen, and was known as 'Aberdeen' Forbes when he took command of the *Marco Polo*. He was the son of a prominent advocate and had gone to sea at the age of 12, in vessels that traded across the North Atlantic between Aberdeen and Canada. He had soon worked his way up to mate and then to captain. The fact that shipowners were often obliged to settle issues in the courts meant that Forbes' family connections wouldn't have held him back too much in his chosen career. Even at school he had shown a natural ability in navigation, and this ability stood him in good stead when making the fast passages for which he was to become world famous.

A hard, if particularly efficient, master, Forbes is best remembered as 'Bully' Forbes, an unlikely sobriquet for a man that was only 5ft 7in in height. However, his appearance may well have been made more intimidating by a large scar over his right eye. His position as ship's master would most certainly have made him more intimidating than any other single aspect, and it would have given him every opportunity to exercise any inclination toward bullying he might experience.

Even though engaged in their joint venture, the New Liverpool, Line of Australian Packets, both the White Star and Black Ball lines had their own businesses to look after. On 1 June 1852 Pilkington & Wilson placed a notice in the Liverpool papers advertising the projected sailing days of their fleet of six White Star vessels engaged in the Australian emigrant trade. They were:

The *Ellen*, a 397-ton barque built in 1834 at New Brunswick. White Star advertised this tiny vessel, first on 1 June 1852 as a ship of 1,600 tons, under the command of Captain Phillips, bound for Port Phillip, Australia, on 20 June, and then on 23 July 1852, as a 1,800-tonner bound for Australia under the command of Captain Leighton. It would appear that as early as 1852 Messrs Pilkington & Wilson were not above a little misrepresentation if it suited their purposes.

The *Earl of Derby*, a 1,047-ton wooden ship built in 1851 at Quebec. Chartered from Moore & Co of Liverpool she sailed for Melbourne on 5 July 1852, under the command of Captain Tweedie. Without stepping even slightly out of character Pilkington & Wilson advertised this vessel, on 1 June, as being of 2,000 tons.

The *Phoenix*, an 801-ton wooden ship built in 1851 by J. Fisher at St John. Chartered, probably from Maggee & Co of Liverpool, she sailed for Sydney on 20 July 1852, under the command of Captain Soley. *Phoenix* appeared on the 1 June advertisement, in customary Pilkington & Wilson/White Star style, as a 1,700-ton vessel. Later in the year she supposedly also sailed to New Zealand, under the same commander.

The *Dundonald*, a 1,142-ton wooden ship built in 1849 at St John, New Brunswick. Chartered from Wright & Co of St John she sailed from Liverpool for Geelong and Port Phillip on 5 August 1852, under the command of Captain Gilles. She appeared in the 1 June advertisement as a vessel of 2,000 tons.

The *Bhurtpoor*, a 978-ton wooden ship built by W. & R. Wright at St John, New Brunswick, in 1851 for Pilkington & Wilson. Originally intended for the Australian run, the plan was that Captain George Bainbridge would take the ship from Liverpool to Port Phillip or Sydney on 15 or 20 August, under the flag of the New Liverpool, Line of Australian Packets, but the voyage was cancelled. As usual with White Star's optimistic sizing, the vessel was advertised on 1 June as being of 1,900 tons. Instead of going to the antipodes the ship sailed for New Orleans but was wrecked on the Irish coast near Wexford on 18 September 1852. Probably the first example of a White Star ship failing to complete its maiden voyage for the line, but by no means the last.

The *Blanche*, a 966-ton wooden ship built in 1850 at St John, New Brunswick. Chartered from Brown & Co of Liverpool she sailed from Liverpool for Port Phillip on 25 August 1852, under the command of Captain G. Rudolph. The *Blanche* was advertised on 1 June as being a 1,800-ton vessel sailing for Sydney on 5 September.

Beneath the list of ships, their capacity, captains, destinations and projected sailing dates, the 1 June advertisement had the legend:

'The above are A.1. fast-sailing clipper-built ships, commanded by men of great experience, who will take every precaution to promote the health and comfort of passengers during the voyage. Each vessel will likewise carry a surgeon.

For further particulars apply to
PILKINGTON & WILSON
Commercial Building,
Water Street,
Liverpool.'

For use on the Atlantic routes H. T. Wilson also ordered a 733-ton wooden ship from New Brunswick. The *Jesse Munn* was built in 1852 and although she was partly owned by Wilson himself (56 shares) and partly by her master Captain J. Duckett (8 shares), she was probably intended for White Star service.

Despite there being more prospective passengers than they could hope to handle in the near future, competition between shipping lines endeavouring to win emigrants to Australia had become ferocious by the middle of 1852. Some lines were prepared to go to ridiculous lengths to attract passengers away from their competitors. Henry Fox was working with

Vianna, Jones and Chapple to establish the 'Line of Screw Steamers from Liverpool to Australia'. At least two of their vessels, the *Osmanlia* and the *Rattler*, being of only 500 tons, would have been too small to carry enough coal to make such voyages. Their other two ships, being larger, might have been capable of making the journey, provided that suitable coaling stations could be arranged along the way, but a successful steamship line was still some way away in the future.

Gibbs Bright was still in the fight and was spending a small fortune in refitting the *Great Britain* after buying it for £18,000. It cost more than £15,000 to alter the rigging and hull, and yet a further £6,000 was spent on a new engine designed to run at a pressure of 10lb/sq in instead of 4lb used by the original engine. The appearance of the ship had been dramatically altered by reducing the number of masts from four to three. *Great Britain's* owners believed that the vessel, with her new modifications, would be able to make the run to Australia in 56 days. Eventually they would be proved correct, but not before the vessel's rigging and sails had been altered yet again. (*Great Britain* is being restored and preserved at Bristol, where she was built, and is the sole survivor of her type.)

The refitted *Great Britain*, at 3,500 tons one of the world's largest vessels and a thousand tons bigger than the previous largest ship ever to leave Liverpool, weighed anchor at 3pm on Saturday 21 August 1852. Watched by thousands of spectators she made her way slowly down the River Mersey at the start of her first voyage for the Eagle Line. Her decks were crowded with passengers who had paid more than 70 guineas (£73.50) for a first-class ticket in the aft saloon, 40 guineas (£42) in the forward saloon, and 25 guineas (£26.25) for a second-class ticket. Both first and second class would have the benefit of the surgeon and the services of stewards. However, second-class passengers were required to supply their own beds, linen and blankets. There was 1,400 tons of coal in her bunkers, more than she would normally have required for the voyage, much of which would be made under sail.

Despite what was believed to be an abundance of coal, her owners, who were careful men, had arranged for the *Great Britain* to stop off at the Cape of Good Hope to pick up more, along with some livestock. Unfortunately the ship ran into a severe gale and had to proceed for most of the early part of the voyage using only her steam engine. On 23 September she was accordingly obliged to put into St Helena to refuel, where she remained for several days before proceeding to Cape Town. *Great Britain* left Cape Town on 17 October and arrived in Port Phillip on 14 November. Six days later she arrived at Sydney to an uproarious welcome, and anchored next to the 699-ton P&O steamer *Chusan*, which did nothing to play down the impressive dimensions of Brunel's design. Luckily for the other lines engaged in the Australian trade there were so many people wanting to emigrate to Australia that there were more than enough to go around.

Pilkington & Wilson/White Star was still trading with the Americas in 1852 when it bought the *Colonist* specifically for that purpose. Peculiarly, although the partnership's main efforts seem to have been directed toward the Australian trade, it tended to charter vessels for this route rather than buy them.

In 1852 a new name appears in the story of the White Star Line, that of another member of the Chambers family, John. The company bought, with a little assistance from him, the 1,195-ton wooden ship *Fitzjames*. The *Fitzjames* was registered as a White Star ship and put to work on the Atlantic routes. The burgeoning White Star Line also bought the five-year-old, 1,331-ton wooden ship *David Cannon* in 1852, for the Atlantic trade. As usual at this period in the line's history, the ship had not been built in the British Isles but by

W. & R. Wright at St John. For some reason never explained it appears to have been a policy of the White Star Line at that time not to buy ships built in Britain, if they could avoid it. In the same year, for service on the antipodean run, they chartered the *Tantivy* and the *Lady Russel*.

Continuing the company policy of chartering for the Australian trade, rather than buying vessels, the *Agnes* was chartered from Hanmer & Co of Liverpool. She sailed from Liverpool for Australia in January 1852, but with only a small number of passengers aboard despite the huge numbers of people trying to reach the new Australian gold-fields.

The White Star Line might be growing but there was no shortage of competition. Gibbs Bright's *Great Britain* left Australia, bound for Liverpool, in January 1853 with a full cargo, a considerable amount of gold and a great many passengers. The time taken on the voyage was a little disappointing so on her return it was decided to alter her sail layout again, this time to ship rig. Her initial trip to the antipodes had taken 81 days; under her new rig she cut that time to between 55 and 64 days for most of her voyages over the next 20 years. Some masters seem to have been able to get a better performance from a ship than others, and on *Great Britain's* return from Liverpool after her first voyage as a full rigged ship Captain Gray had taken over command of the vessel. The combination was just about unbeatable and *Great Britain* was to prove the most successful of all the ships engaged in the Australian emigrant trade.

On 18 March 1853 White Star advertised two chartered vessels bound for Australia within the next couple of weeks. One was the new clipper *Lochiel*, and the other was the splendid new coppered and copper-fastened *North Atlantic*. The *North Atlantic*, which was to sail for Australia on 24 March 1853 had been built expressly as a passenger vessel, at a time when most passenger ships were converted merchantmen, and was fitted with, 'every modern improvement to render her a desirable conveyance. Intending emigrants are respectfully requested to inspect her accommodations. The poop berths are of a superior class, and worthy of the notice of those who look for comfort on the voyage at a moderate rate of fare.'

White Star was so confident of the sailing abilities of the *North Atlantic* that it advertised her as an ideal way of transporting goods intended for an early market. It also believed that the ship was suited to the transportation of gold and other precious metals, and was not backward in saying so. For the coming voyage the *North Atlantic's* cargo would be restricted to fine goods, obviously to save weight, and only a limited number of passengers would be carried for the same reason.

Throughout most of 1853 White Star continued the rent rather than buy policy, sending no fewer than five chartered ships to Australia on its own behalf. They were the *Defense*, *Mooresfort*, *Tasmania*, *Mobile* and *Earl of Derby*. A sixth chartered vessel, the *Marion Moore*, also sailed for New South Wales in 1853, but under the flags of both the White Star and Black Ball lines, yet another example of collaboration between the two companies, although they were supposedly direct competitors. A possible seventh charter was the *Ellen*, which according to *Lloyd's List* was owned by H. T. Wilson as distinct from the partnership, and voyaging to Prince Edward Island. It would seem that the driving force behind some of White Star's possibly less than entirely honest stunts may have been H. T. Wilson who, as we will see, appears at times to have been running an entirely different company from within the parent line.

On 21 December 1853 James Chambers, the eldest son of Isaac Chambers, married Henry Wilson's youngest sister, Jane Grey Wilson. With Chambers' money invested in the company, and now with the close marital relationship between himself and Wilson it could only be a matter of time before James Chambers became a partner in the White Star Line.

In 1853, at the age of 16, somewhat older than usual for those days, Thomas Henry Ismay left Croft House School. Soon after this he started his apprenticeship, which had been arranged three years before, with the Imrie Tomlinson partnership at its Liverpool offices at 13 Rumford Street. He turned out to be a thoroughly satisfactory employee and soon built himself a good reputation with the local merchants for the efficiency with which he dealt with their affairs. Ismay stayed with the shipbrokers for three years, until he had completed his indentures. While he was there he met William Imrie, the son of the senior partner in the firm, who was the same age as himself and was also serving his apprenticeship with the company.

In 1856, once he had discharged his obligation to Imrie Tomlinson, and made a lifelong friend of the young William Imrie, with whom he would later go into partnership, Ismay decided to broaden his horizons. He determined to discover if life at sea was what he had always imagined, so he arranged with Jackson & Co of Maryport to sail, as supercargo, on their 352-ton barque *Charles Jackson* to Chile, by way of Cape Horn.

Towards the end of 1853 Pilkington & Wilson were preparing to unveil their latest spectacular development, the iron ship *Tayleur*. Soon after the ship was launched White Star began to place its usual pretentious advertisements in the local Liverpool press. Not untypically the partners claimed that their vessel was 'superior to any ship hitherto despatched to the Australian colonies'. Not content with such general claims for their newest vessel they went on to say,

'This truly splendid vessel, just launched, and the largest merchantman ever built in England, will undoubtedly prove to be the fastest of the Australian fleet, as she has been constructed expressly with the object of attaining the very highest rate of speed. Her vast dimensions enable the owners to provide passenger accommodation not to be met with in any vessel afloat. Thorough ventilation has been secured and by means of ports, of which she has one at every seven feet, and numerous skylights, the passenger deck is perfectly lighted at every part.'

The partners had clearly forgotten all about Gibbs Bright's *Great Britain*, which was at least as fast as *Tayleur* and more than half as large again.

The claims appearing in the advertisement are not wholly dissimilar to those made for another record-breaking White Star vessel, 59 years later. There is also a passing similarity in the fates of the two ships. None the less it is quite clear from the 1853 advertisement that Pilkington & Wilson expected the *Tayleur* to bring a new eminence to the line.

Chapter 2

1854-1855

In 1854 the White Star Line was still owned by Pilkington & Wilson but now they were engaged, for the main part, in carrying prospectors, their equipment and provisions to Australia, though they maintained their interest in the Atlantic trade. As well as taking prospectors out to Australia there was money to be made bringing home the gold that a few of those prospectors discovered.

Throughout 1854 the White Star fleet grew enormously. Over the 12-month period Pilkington & Wilson bought no less than eight new ships for the line: the *Red Jacket*, *Mermaid*, *Golden Era*, *Emma*, *Arabian*, *Shalimar*, *Annie Wilson* and the line's flagship *White Star*. Obviously the partners would have had to borrow heavily to finance this scale of expansion, but equally obviously the moneylenders considered them to be a good risk, because the money was made available. Even though it was buying ships as fast as it possibly could, White Star was still obliged to charter vessels in order to meet the demand for passage, vessels such as the *Albatross*, and the *Blue Jacket*, which it would later buy.

The cholera epidemic which swept Europe and was to spread to the allied armies camped in the Crimea, where it accounted for more lives than the conflict itself, sets 1854 apart from most other years. In Liverpool, it was already widespread when on 14 January the Black Ball Line's 1,168-ton clipper *Conway* attempted to set sail for Australia, where the scourge was eagerly awaited!

Only a few days out, beset by disease and bad weather, the vessel was obliged to abandon the passage and put in to the Clyde, seeking succour. Understandably the local people at first resisted the suggestion that more than 400 potential cholera carriers be distributed amongst them. Not exactly overjoyed at the prospect of having those aboard *Conway* landed so that the ship could be cleaned and fumigated, they refused to allow them to leave the ship. However, eventually the passengers were taken ashore and the vessel was cleansed, but not before 24 of the 445 aboard had died of the disease. A month after the ship had left her home port, on 15 February, the surviving emigrants were reboarded and the ship prepared to resume her interrupted journey. As if the voyage was not ill-starred enough, before the *Conway* could weigh anchor, a mutiny broke out amongst the crew and the vessel was delayed yet again. Finally, on 12 March 1854, the *Conway* left the Clyde and headed for Australia.

The *Tayleur*, as usual with ships used by White Star for the Australian emigrant trade, actually belonged to somebody else, this time Moore & Co, who had purchased the vessel specifically to charter it to the White Star Line. She was a 1,997-ton iron ship built in 1853 by Mr Tayleur, who bashfully named the ship after himself. The *Tayleur* was amongst the biggest merchant sailing ships to have been built in England at the time. *Tayleur* departed Liverpool for Melbourne at midday on Thursday 19 January 1854, being towed out of harbour by the steam tug *Victory*. In command of the vessel was Captain Noble, who had formerly commanded the Moore & Co clipper *Australia*.

Captain Noble had been recommended to Moore by Captain Towson, the Head Examiner of Masters and Mates at Liverpool, and on that recommendation had been given command of the *Australia*. Moore & Co was more than satisfied with Noble's performance aboard the *Australia*. He had taken the ship from Liverpool to Melbourne and landed both passengers and cargo in good condition. Leaving Melbourne he next called at Amoy and picked up a cargo for the West Indies, which he duly delivered. Then he sailed to New Orleans to collect a cargo for Liverpool, which he delivered to that port only a couple of days over 13 months after leaving. It was this outstanding feat of seamanship which earned Captain Noble command of the new *Tayleur*.

Although the owners had selected a competent captain, and we must assume competent officers, for the *Tayleur*, the crew were a very different matter. There was a high proportion of Chinese and Lascars (as sailors from the East Indies were then known) among the crew, many of whom were not fully trained seamen at all, and who spoke little English. The language barrier, of course, meant that these crew members couldn't understand the orders issued by Captain Noble and his officers. Had the weather been favourable all might have been well, giving these inexperienced seamen a chance to learn their business and what action was required in response to orders, but the weather was not favourable.

After nightfall on 19 January the wind began to strengthen and the ship made little headway. Overnight, and throughout the following day, conditions deteriorated and the passengers began to become alarmed at the obvious inexperience of the crew. Because of the thick weather no observations could be made either that night or the next day and consequently the officers began to lose track of exactly where they were. By the following morning, Saturday 21 January, the wind was rising to gale force and a heavy sea was running.

It was the custom then for a captain in doubt about his whereabouts or the conditions his vessel was facing to press on at top speed. True to type, although he had no real idea of where he was, Captain Noble kept the *Tayleur* under full sail until about 11.30am when he ordered a course change of 2 points (22.5°) to windward. About half an hour later the bow lookout cried out 'Breakers on the starboard bow.' The helm was put hard a-starboard and the head sails were let go in a desperate attempt to avoid the rocks ahead. It was no good, and the *Tayleur* smashed into 'The Nose' of Lambay Island, about 5 miles north-east of Malahide Point, County Dublin, Ireland. A large wave lifted the ship on to the rocks and brought her down with a crash, only for a second wave to repeat the procedure moments later, this time turning the stricken vessel until she was broadside to the island. The *Tayleur* began to sink by the stern and frightened passengers streamed up from below on to the wind- and wave-swept decks. Women with small children and babies lay on the deck screaming for help while male passengers carried some of the youngsters towards what they hoped was safety.

The stern of the ship swung around, close to the rocks, and a cook's assistant, two Lascars and three seamen managed to jump to safety. A spar and a rope were got across the gap between the stern section of the vessel and the rocks, and with the aid of this makeshift bridge many more passengers and crew were saved, chiefly by the exertions of a couple of young male passengers. Very few, if any, people escaped from the sinking clipper by way of the bow. Those that tried were caught by the waves and dashed to pieces on the rocky shore. A first-class passenger left the following graphic account of the disaster.

'Amongst some of the earliest of the females who attempted to get on shore were some young Irish women. Most of them had lost their hold of the rope, and fell into the sea. The doctor of the ship, a most noble fellow, struggled hard to save his wife and child, he had succeeded in getting about half-way to the shore on a rope – holding his child by his clothes in his teeth – but just then the ship lurched outwards, by which the rope was dragged from the hands of those who held it on the lower rocks, and was held only by those above, thus running him high in the air, so that the brave fellow could not drop on the rock. Word was now given to lower the rope gently; but those who held it above let it go by the run, and the poor fellow, with his child, was buried in the waves; but in a short time he appeared above the water, manfully battling with the waves and the portions of the wreck that now floated above him. He at length swam to a ladder hanging by a rope alongside the ship, and got upon it. After he had been there a minute or two his wife floated close to him; he immediately took hold of her, and dragged her on the ladder, tenderly parting the hair from her face, and appeared to be encouraging her; but in another minute she was washed from his hold and sank almost immediately. He then got up again into the ship and tried to get his wife on shore, but they both perished. He deserved a better fate!

'The scene was now most truly awful. The most desperate struggles for life were made by the wretched passengers; great numbers of women jumped overboard, in the vain hope of reaching land; and the ropes were crowded by hundreds who, in their eagerness, terror, and confusion, frustrated each other's efforts for self-preservation. Many of the females would get half-way, and then become unable to proceed further; and, after clinging to the rope for a short time, would be forced from their hold by those who came after them. Three women only, out of 200, were saved. One of those had got part of the way across when her legs fell, and she hung some time by her two hands over the foaming waves; her husband then came on the rope, and managed to assist her to the shore. Two men came on shore with children tied to their backs; but of the whole who fell in to the water not above five were saved. I saw one fine girl, who, after falling from the rope, managed to get hold of another one, which was hanging from the side of the ship, and which she held on to for more than a quarter of an hour, the sea every moment dashing her against the side of the ship; but it was impossible for us to lend her any assistance. Some of us got a spar out, by which several got on shore; but it soon broke; and now might be seen hundreds hanging to the bulwarks of the ship, each struggling to get on shore. I saw one young woman hanging on the middle of the rope for some time by her two hands, but those pushing to get on shore soon sent her to her doom.

'The ship's stern now began to sink; the ship made a lurch, and all the ropes were snapped asunder. The scene was now most harrowing. Every wave washed off scores at a time – we could see them struggle for a moment, then tossing their arms, sink to rise no more. At length the whole of the ship sunk under water. There was a fearful struggle for a moment, and all, except two who were in the rigging, were gone. The coast-guard who had been apprised of the wreck, now came up; but all they could do was attempt to save the two who were in the rigging. They managed to get a line to one of them, by fastening two lines, at the end of each of which there was a piece of wood, to a single line, and guiding it from the rock to the spot where the poor fellow was, so that he could reach it. Then they dragged him ashore. There was one fine young man left on the top, but they could not reach him, and when he saw them going away his cries were heartrending. About two o'clock the next morning the coast-guard managed to reach him, after he had been in the top fourteen hours; you may fancy the poor fellow's joy at his deliverance. We found we were on Lambay Island, three miles from Rush, and about thirteen miles from Dublin.'

When the survivors were counted it was found that there were about 250 of them, which meant that 420 had perished; there were only three females and two children. Still, it could have been worse. Captain Noble, who is somewhat doubtfully recorded as being the last man to leave the ship, had managed to make his way ashore, accompanied by his first and third mates. The second mate, along with the surgeon who we already know about, lost their lives, probably in attempting to save others.

With the *Tayleur* the White Star Line had begun a tradition that it would probably have rather not; that of holding the record for the worst shipping disaster to date. The loss of the *Tayleur* was a severe blow to the White Star Line, but not as severe a blow as it was to the ship's owners and the 420 souls who went down with her.

However, the company was nothing if not resilient and within days was advertising the departure of another fine clipper bound for the antipodes, the *Golden Era*, which it had only bought in January 1854. Command was given to Captain J. T. Pray. Despite the fact that the vessel had not before sailed to Australia, the White Star Line, never backward when it came to stretching the truth a little, advertised her as, 'one of the fastest of the Australian fleet'. As usual, in its publicity announcement the line described the vessel as having a saloon fitted with every regard for comfort. Perhaps not quite so usually the advertisement also pointed out that, 'the rates of passage fare will be found extremely moderate, and the accommodation most desirable' in the poop and deck house. Other than noting that third-class accommodation was well ventilated and that there was a great height between decks, it did not warrant advertising space at all.

During January 1854 competition on the emigrant trade route was growing ever more ferocious. Gibbs Bright was advertising the *Eagle*, named after its own line, which was leaving for Port Phillip and Sydney in January. No secret was made of the fact that Sydney was the nearest major port to the gold diggings. In the preceding couple of years the *Eagle* had made some fast runs between Liverpool and Australia. In 1852 she had travelled from Melbourne to her home port in 76 days, and the following year she had sailed from Liverpool to Melbourne in 78 days and back again in 82 days.

But by far the greatest competitor White Star faced in the Australian trade at this time was James Baines' Black Ball Line. At the same time as Pilkington & Wilson were advertising the *Golden Era,* James Baines was promoting his 'celebrated clipper' the *Indian Queen*, which was also heading for Melbourne and Port Phillip. Baines had another ace or two, or four, up his sleeve, which would lead to a policy being adopted by White Star that would culminate over half a century into the future with the *Olympic* Class ships.

On 3 January 1854 the *Lightning*, a 2,083-ton, 243ft-long, American clipper with a striking figurehead of a young woman with flowing blonde hair and a golden thunderbolt in her outstretched hand, was launched at Donald Mackay's yard in Boston, for the Black Ball Line, who had paid about £30,000 for her. Command of the new vessel was given to Captain Forbes, and for the trip from Boston to Liverpool he would have the assistance of the builder's brother, Captain Laughlan Mackay.

The new ship left Boston on Saturday 18 February 1854. 'She left a wake straight as an arrow, and this was the only mark of her progress. There was a slight swell, and as she rose, one could see the arc of her forefoot rise gently over the seas as she increased her speed,' wrote a reporter from the *Boston Atlas*.

Despite strong gales, which tore away her fore topsail and a jib, the *Lightning* made 18–18.5kt, covering 436 miles in one day's run and breaking all records for sailing ships. She completed the voyage in 13 days and 20 hours. It would be more than another 30 years before a steamship bettered her distance for a single day's run, but a mere matter of weeks before another clipper did so. Once in Liverpool the ship had another £2,000 spent on her in decoration and furnishings – and the *Lightning* was but the first of four such 'Yankee Clippers' to be built, in rapid succession, by Mackay for James Baines.

As the Liverpool winter slowly drew to a close Pilkington & Wilson were not sitting idly by and allowing Baines to have it all his own way, as an advertisement in the *Liverpool Mercury* of 10 March 1854 shows:

"WHITE STAR" LINE OF AUSTRALIAN PACKETS

To be despatched early in April

Will be fully armed, and carry bullion safes.

FOR MELBOURNE

Loading at Wellington Dock, the celebrated new American Clipper Ship

RED JACKET

2,430 tons register

This ship, so justly celebrated for her unprecedented passage from New York to Liverpool of thirteen days two hours, and for her remarkable run of 417 miles in 24 hours, has just been purchased to form one of the packets of this line, going direct for Melbourne and back. Shippers will find this vessel in all respects worthy of their attention for goods intended for an early market, as she may reasonably be expected to make faster passages than any steamer running from England to Australia. Special arrangements will be made to forfeit £2 per ton freight if the passage is not made under 65 days.

The rates of freight, cabin passage (for which accommodations are both commodious and elegant), or second cabin, can be obtained on application to the owners,

PILKINGTON & WILSON

No goods will be received at the ship without a written order from the office.

Late in 1853, or early in 1854, Pilkington & Wilson bought the *Red Jacket*, which was of a type known as an extreme clipper ship, for the then very expensive price of £30,000, the same amount that Baines had paid for the *Lightning*. The *Red Jacket* had been designed by Samuel H. Pook for Secombe, Taylor & Co of Boston whose intention was to trade her around the Cape to California. The ship, which was launched on 2 November 1853, was 251ft 2in long by 44ft in the beam and 31ft deep (depth of hold), quite a considerable vessel of the period. Called after Sagoyewatha, a chief of the Native American Seneca tribe, the new ship was named *Red Jacket*, because as a boy he always wore a jacket of that colour. The ship's figurehead was a carving of this famous Indian, complete with red jacket with a large, five-pointed, white star on the breast; the same emblem that appeared on the line's house flag.

Between 11 and 23 January *Red Jacket* made the North Atlantic crossing from west to east. In command was Captain Asa Eldridge, late of the Dramatic Line's packet *Roscious*.

Captain Eldridge was soon to be given command of the Collins Line steamer *Pacific*, which left Liverpool for New York on 23 January 1856, and was never seen again. On her best day of the passage the *Red Jacket* covered 413 miles and on her worst only 106. She completed the voyage in a magnificent 13 days, 1 hour and 25 minutes; a sailing ship record which I believe stands to the present time.

As a White Star ship *Red Jacket* sailed from Liverpool for Melbourne on 4 May 1854, arriving on 12 July having taken only 67 days and 13 hours on the passage. Under the command of Captain Samuel Reid the ship had, on 6 July, almost equalled her one day North Atlantic record when she covered 400 miles. Whether or not White Star made good on its publicity and forfeited £2 per ton on the ship's cargo, because she had not completed the voyage in less than the advertised 65 days, does not appear to be recorded.

Red Jacket had met another White Star clipper, the *Mermaid*, off Oporto. *Mermaid* was making the same voyage as *Red Jacket* but with nowhere near her turn of speed. She left Liverpool the day before *Red Jacket*, 3 May, and arrived at Melbourne 6½ days later than her stablemate, having taken over 74 days to do what *Red Jacket* had managed in 67½. On the return voyage, which began on 3 August, *Red Jacket* rounded Cape Horn a mere 20 days out of Melbourne and crossed the Equator only 21 days later, completing the voyage in 73 days. However, she would never again make such speedy passages. Between 20 September and 4 December 1855, under the command of Captain Millward, she took 75 days to complete a passage from Liverpool to Melbourne. For the return leg she left Melbourne on 12 January 1856 and arrived in Liverpool on 8 April having taken 86 days. The next outward voyage, between 20 May and 13 August, took 85 days.

Pilkington & Wilson had purchased the *Mermaid* early in 1854, for the then considerable sum of £14,850, although it was less than half what they paid for *Red Jacket*. After all, there had never been any doubt as to which of the two vessels would be the faster sailer, and this would have been reflected in the price. White Star Line bought the new vessel to complement *Red Jacket* on the Australia and New Zealand routes and her first master was Captain Samuel Reid, who owned 8 shares in the vessel. *Mermaid* would remain with White Star until 1867 and in that 13-year period was commanded by a succession of captains, notably Captains Reid, E. Devey and Rose.

The departure of *Mermaid* and *Red Jacket* within days of each other had aroused the interest of the *Mercury*, which carried an article on 5 May 1854:

'DEPARTURE OF THE *MERMAID* FOR MELBOURNE.
The fine clipper-ship belonging to Messrs Pilkington & Wilson's "White Star Line", was cleared by the government officers on Monday, and seldom has an emigrant vessel been submitted to their inspection more perfect in all her appointments, with a finer crew and officers on board, and a more satisfied body of passengers. The latter number 398 adults in the saloons and between decks, and ten in the best cabin.'

The article went on to sing the praises of the emigrants, many of whom were Cornish miners who would bring their long years of experience in tin and copper mining to bear on the problems of removing gold from the Australian fields. Of course, not all of the passengers aboard were planning to dig for gold. There was a large proportion of tradesmen, their families and children, making the trip as well, who would prove to be of value to the young country in the coming years.

In the same newspaper the sailing of the *Red Jacket* the day before also received a mention.

'The clipper *Red Jacket*, which, from her build, and her first performance in the voyage from New York to this port, may be expected to prove herself the crack Australian ship of the "White Star Line", passed a highly satisfactory inspection on Wednesday, and went to sea yesterday. Nothing could be more beautiful than the order of her arrangements throughout, which reflect the highest credit upon her liberal owners, Messrs Pilkington & Wilson, as well as upon her commander Captain Reed, and the very effective staff who have superintended her loading and fitting-up.'

On this trip *Red Jacket* carried no steerage passengers whatsoever, but only a few first-class and a majority of second-class travellers. The bulk of those who had booked passage aboard the pride of the White Star fleet were artisans such as engineers and joiners, who could comfortably expect to make a good living in Australia. Along with her complement of passengers and crew the *Red Jacket* carried a large consignment of mail, much of it duplicates of despatches sent earlier on the *Great Britain*.

The article went on to say,

'As a proof of the high estimation in which the "White Star Line" is now held by the public, we are informed that since the 17th March last the number of passengers despatched by their vessels has been 1,367. At the very time that the *Red Jacket* was going down the river applications for berths on board her were pouring into the office; and, already, their next ship, the *Fitzjames*, is one third full.'

The *Fitzjames* was not quite the crowd-puller that the line wanted. She had been transferred to the Australian run for the one trip to Melbourne in 1854, under the command of Captain Alex Lowe. Then she was put to whatever other work the company could find for her, until 1866.

In 1854 Pilkington & Wilson bought the *Shalimar*, a wooden clipper ship built for them by J. Nevins of St John, New Brunswick. One of the most famous clipper ships of the line, *Shalimar* made many voyages to Australia and New Zealand during her time with the White Star Line under various masters. She was commanded in turn by Captains Duckett, Amos Robertson, J. R. Brown, Allen and Deighton. This fine vessel was taken over by the Royal Bank of Liverpool in 1867, as we shall see.

Although it was now the proud owner of some of the finest vessels afloat, White Star still felt the need to charter ships from other lines. In 1854 White Star chartered the *Moira*. She sailed for Australia on 27 January 1854 under the command of Captain S. Smart. Then the *Lochiel*, under the command of Captain Thomas Rogers, was again chartered from Jardine & Co of Liverpool.

On 27 February 1854 the British and French governments sent a diplomatic note to the Russians demanding that they withdraw their forces which had invaded Turkey. The Russians ignored the note, forcing the British and French to consider stronger action. Four weeks later, on 28 March 1854, the British and French declared war on Russia. The Crimean War had begun, and with war came the government's need to transport thousands of troops, horses, guns and all the other paraphernalia required by the army to fight in a foreign land. Amongst the vessels soon to be chartered by the British Government were at least part of the White Star fleet.

Some time in 1854 Pilkington & Wilson bought a new 1,155-ton wooden ship built that year at Boston, Massachusetts, the very aptly named *Mystery*. The careers of few White Star vessels can be completely reconstructed, but even amongst such elusive company *Mystery* stands out. Nothing is known of the vessel from the time she entered service until she suddenly, and briefly, reappears nine years later, to make just one voyage for the line before vanishing again.

June 1854 brought its drawbacks to the line when the seven-year-old *David Cannon*, which had been bought by White Star just the year before, was wrecked on Big Dover Head, near Halifax, Nova Scotia, not far from where she had been built. The ship had been purchased for use in the North Atlantic trade, which was the partners' customary practice at the time.

When the *Iowa*, the first White Star ship, returned from Australia in 1854 she was promptly sold to J. Steel & Co of Liverpool. On her next voyage to the antipodes, under her new owners, she disappeared without trace.

Despite these minor setbacks the line continued to expand, buying more and more ships, such as the *Emma*, which it purchased with the financial assistance of others. Unusually for the line, which preferred to use chartered vessels for the purpose, she was put to work on the Liverpool–Melbourne route for two years, under the command of Captain E. Underwood.

In 1854 White Star also bought the *Arabian*, specially for the emigrant trade. Despite her being a purpose-built vessel, her first owner, Thomas Edward Millidge, had put her to the Indian trade and she completed her first voyage by making the homeward passage from Bombay in 105 days. For the voyage the vessel had been dramatically overloaded, to the point where she drew 21ft of water instead of the 17ft that was her designed draught. Even so grossly over-laden the *Arabian* had completed that homeward voyage at least 10 days faster than the sprightliest of her competitors, and closer to 30 days faster than the usual run-of-the-mill ship. White Star was convinced that the *Arabian* would perform even better if she was not so heavily loaded, which she wouldn't be when carrying passengers, as was intended, rather than heavy cargo. Consequently, Pilkington and Wilson each bought 32 shares in this vessel, in June 1854, for £14,100, and took delivery later in the year. They gave command of the new vessel to Captain Duckett, who was very experienced in sailing the eastern seas.

Being purpose-built, the *Arabian* was fitted out accordingly, with a first-class promenade to her large poop cabin, which extended the full width of the ship. The state cabin, on the main deck, which could accommodate only a limited number of special first-class passengers, was panelled in red velvet, set in white and gold. There were four frosted glass windows in the stern, which diffused the light, and beneath them was a green velvet covered sofa. The rudder housing, which occupied a part of the room, was boxed in with mirrors, an unusual practice. The vessel was fitted with no less than seven WCs, four of them for the exclusive use of the ladies.

The less affluent first-class and other passengers were carried in the between-decks accommodation which was extraordinarily spacious, being 166ft by 32ft, and almost 8ft from deck to deckhead, with portholes all along the sides providing light and ventilation to every berth. The passenger areas were also lit and ventilated from on deck, a practice being adopted by all White Star vessels. The crew quarters were, as usual, in the forecastle, the wettest and most uncomfortable part of the ship. However, the location of the crew's accommodation did mean that they were, in their off duty moments, kept well away from the fare-paying passengers, something that the owners no doubt found reassuring. Put on the Liverpool to Melbourne route, the *Arabian* worked for 13 years under Captains Millward, Ballantyne, M. Gandy and Davison.

In the same year the rapidly expanding White Star Line bought the *Annie Wilson* (probably named after H. T. Wilson's wife or daughter). Under the command of Captain Edward Langley she worked on the Liverpool–Australia route until about 1859.

Even though they were now buying ships for the Australian trade, Pilkington & Wilson were still finding it necessary to hire vessels from other owners in 1854. They chartered the *Golconda* from Anthony & Co of Liverpool. She sailed under the command of Captain Kerr. The *Anne Chambers* may well have not been a White Star vessel, when she was advertised as sailing as one, for Australia, under the command of Captain Robertson in July 1854. At the time John Chambers, the vessel's owner, was already a major shareholder in White Star and would, on Pilkington's retirement three years later, take over his position as a partner in the company. The *Anne Chambers* was named after John's daughter.

On 15 September 1854 the following advertisement appeared in the Liverpool press:

"WHITE STAR"

LINE OF AUSTRALIAN PACKETS

Sailing regularly between
LIVERPOOL AND MELBOURNE

Passengers and luggage for Melbourne landed at the Wharf free, and those booked for Sydney, Geelong, Adelaide, and Launceston are forwarded at ship's expense. Return tickets issued at half-fares to all except Cabin Passengers for the homeward passage, as per circular. The ships which compose the 'White Star' line are new and first rate clippers, constructed by the most celebrated builders expressly for the conveyance of passengers, and fitted up with every convenience for that business, in which alone they are intended to be employed. They are owned by the proprietors of the line; and passengers may therefore depend upon their being more liberally found in all requisite stores, and efficiently officered, and manned, than in the case with ships not regularly in the trade.

FOR MELBOURNE

Ships	Captains	Tons	To sail
Golconda	Kerr	3,000	Sept 25
Shalimar (New)	Duckett	3,600	Oct 16
Annie Wilson	Brown	3,000	Oct 30
Golden Era	Peat	3,500	Nov 15
Red Jacket (New)	Reed	4,000	Nov 30
Blue Jacket (New)	Millward	4,500	Dec 15
Mermaid (New)	Devey	3,800	Dec 30
	1855		
White Star (New)	O'Halloran	4,000	Jan 15
Arabian	Ballantyne	2,500	Jan 30
Emma	Underwood	2,500	Feb 15
Fitzjames	Hamilton	3,000	March 1

33

The above ships carry surgeons and chaplains, the provisions are of the finest quality, and duly inspected by the Government surveyors. Money orders granted on the agents abroad, free of charge.

For freight and passage apply to the owners,

PILKINGTON & WILSON, Water Street, Liverpool

Agents in Melbourne – Childwell, Train and Co.'

As usual with White Star advertising of this period the truth had been stretched a little. Despite the line's claim to owning all of the vessels listed, the *Golconda* was certainly chartered, the *Annie Wilson* was probably chartered, and the *Blue Jacket* is a spectacular source of confusion, there apparently being two vessels of this name, both of which sailed under the White Star flag.

The 1,790-ton *Blue Jacket*[1] was built in 1854 by Robert E. Jackson of East Boston to the order of Messrs Charles R. Green & Co of New York. Like *Red Jacket*, she was an extreme clipper (a vessel where everything had been designed to give her the greatest possible speed) built of fir and white oak with copper and iron fastenings. *Blue Jacket* was just over 208ft long and 41½ft in the beam, with an 80ft poop and 8ft between decks. She was an exceptionally fast ship and made her maiden voyage across the Atlantic, from Boston to Liverpool, in just 12 days. Her first British owner was Captain J. J. Frost of London, who also commanded her. Realising that there was more business to be done in Liverpool than in London, despite his connection with the English capital, Frost chose to bring his ship to the Mersey. This vessel would appear to be the *Blue Jacket* that was advertised as sailing for the White Star Line in May and December 1854.

Also in 1854 a second wooden vessel, of 2,340 tons, was built as the '*Blue Jacket*', by W. & R. Wright at St John, New Brunswick for White Star. Pilkington & Wilson owned 43 shares in this, the then flagship of the line, while Richard Wright held the remaining 21. This '*Blue Jacket*' was, it seems, listed to sail under her original name for Australia in January 1855 under the command of Captain O'Halloran, but her name was changed to *White Star* before she left Liverpool. *White Star* made many voyages to the Australian continent in 1855–7 under the command of Captains W. R. and J. R. Brown. On her maiden voyage across the Atlantic, from New Brunswick to Liverpool, although heavily laden with a full cargo of timber, and beating against strong headwinds, she made the crossing in 15 days, arriving at Liverpool on 1 December 1854, under the command of Captain Thomas Kerr. Once there, at what was to be her home port, she was refitted ready to take her place in the emigrant trade.

Sailing to the antipodes had its risks, as the Land and Emigration Commissioners report for the year 1854 clearly shows. It should be remembered that 420 of those lost were from the single disaster to the White Star's *Tayleur*. Only 340 other lives were lost in the relevant period. Four other vessels from Liverpool also met with accidents.

	Ships			Passengers and Crew		
	No	Lost	%	No	Lost	%
Chartered by this Board	127	Nil	Nil	45,382	Nil	Nil
From ports under emigration officers	702	6	.85	269,373	760	0.28
From ports not under emigration officers	121	3	2.47	8,180	Nil	Nil
Total	950	9	.94	322,935	760	0.23

By late 1854 roughly twice as many emigrants were leaving Liverpool as were leaving London.

Pilkington & Wilson received news from the captain of the *Arabian*, which was then at Melbourne and expected to leave on 20 December, that he was loading a cargo of wool. Nine hundred bales were already aboard at the time the captain wrote. Until the end of 1854 the transporting of Australian wool had been done almost entirely by London shipowners. For some time the White Star Line had been trying to gain a foothold in the trade and the message from the *Arabian* meant that at last it was succeeding.

On 13 January 1855 the Liverpool press reported that in the previous year some 214,627 emigrants had left the port, more than 4,000 a week, in 957 ships. Of those emigrants 152,936, mainly German or Irish, were heading for America, but 41,491 were on their way to Australia. The White Star Line had taken its share of the passenger trade, along with its chief rivals, the Black Ball and Eagle lines.

During the year 107 emigrant ships, ships that required government inspection before they could depart, each on average of 1,200 tons, sailed for Australian ports, carrying 40,123 persons looking for a new start in life. In the same period 87 Short Ships, with an average size of 513 tons, which required no inspection, also sailed with their loads of passengers. The figures included the vessels chartered by the government for the conveyance of free emigrants. Forty-three such vessels sailed from the Mersey with 17,096 emigrants, from all parts of the UK, who had been assembled at Birkenhead.

White Star chartered the *Australia* from C. Moore & Co in January 1855. She sailed from Liverpool for Melbourne under the command of Captain Mountain. Because of the fierce competition coming from the Black Ball and Eagle lines, White Star decided to charter the *Blue Jacket*[1] for the Australian run again. She left Liverpool, bound for Melbourne, in March 1855 and arrived in Australia 69 days later. Her best ever performance for the outward voyage was 67 days, and for the return trip she once managed to equal her outward-bound record.

Throughout 1855 competition between the White Star and Black Ball lines continued to be murderous. White Star, not wholly honestly, advertised that it had gone to considerable trouble to secure the services of captains who would put safety above all else, closely followed by the comfort of the passengers in their care. It was also quick to point out that its vessels were the largest, fastest and finest afloat, again stretching the truth a little. James Baines, of the Black Ball Line, meanwhile, was also advertising his fleet as being composed of the largest, fastest and finest ships afloat.

Even as this competition was going on, the lines were beginning to target different types of passenger. White Star was embarking on a policy that would remain, through successive owners, well into the next century, aiming its advertising at the more 'up market' end of the trade. It made a selling point of having a chaplain on each of its ships, and of the libraries each vessel carried for the convenience of its more cultured passengers. Baines countered by putting chess, draughts and backgammon sets aboard his ships for the amusement of his passengers, and there was a band aboard each vessel to help while away the long evenings. Another selling point the Black Ball Line was quite proud of was the cow carried by each ship. The Black Ball Line was also advertising baths for all classes of passengers, which leaves one wondering what conditions aboard these ships must have been like previously when an average voyage would take something like 10 weeks.

On 16 March 1855 the following list of prospective sailing dates for both the White Star and Black Ball Line fleets appeared in the Liverpool press:

White Star – for Melbourne

Ships	Captains	Tons reg.	Tons bur.	To sail
Golden Era	H. A. Brown	1,656	3,500	Mar. 20
White Star	J. R. Brown	2,440	5,000	Apr. 20
Arabian	N. Ballantyne	1,060	2,100	May 20
Emma	E. Underwood	1,150	2,300	June 20
Shalimar	A. Robertson	1,470	3,500	July 20
Red Jacket	M. M. Millward	2,460	4,300	Aug. 20
Fitzjames	M. J. Hamilton	1,350	3,000	Sep. 20
Mermaid	E. Devey	1,320	3,000	Oct. 20
Sultana	J. Taylor	1,350	3,000	Nov. 20
Annie Wilson	J. Langley	1,220	2,500	Dec. 20

Black Ball – for Melbourne

Vessels	Captains	Tonnage	Date
Marco Polo	Wild	1,625	April 5
Donald Mackay	Warner	2,500	May 5
Schomberg	Forbes	2,400	June 5
Champion of the Seas	Newlands	2,470	July 5
Indian Queen	M'Kirdy	1,050	Aug. 5
James Baines	M'Donnell	2,515	Sept. 5
Lightning	Enright	2,090	Oct. 5
Boomerang	Brown	1,824	Nov. 5
Oliver Lang	Manning	1,299	Dec.5
Montmorency	J. Kiddie	813	Mar. 25 (for Launceston)
Northumberland	Donaldson	593	Apr. 25 (for Launceston)
America	J. Gardyne	706	Apr. 10 (for Sydney)
Great Tasmania	E. Beauchamp	2,100	Apr. 1 (for Hobart)

White Star sailed from Liverpool on her first trip to Australia, under the White Star Line house flag on 20 April 1855. She had only light winds for the whole of the journey and her topsails were never lowered. Even without the benefit of favourable winds the *White Star* arrived at Melbourne only 79 days after leaving Liverpool.

Pilkington & Wilson bought the *Shepherdess* in 1855; she was a 1,226-ton wooden ship built for them at Sackville, New Brunswick. Command was given to Captain John Rodgers, who owned 8 shares in the ship.

Shalimar, under the command of Captain A. Robertson, returned to Liverpool at the end of her first voyage to the antipodes in June 1855. The ship, and her master, had performed exceptionally well under rather unfavourable conditions, especially on the outward run. She had reached Cape Northumberland, within a day's sailing of Hobson's Bay, in the remarkable time of just 67 days. On one day of the passage *Shalimar* had covered 420 nautical miles. Captain Robertson's passengers, who were all landed safely and in good health, presented him with a testimonial thanking him for his 'urbanity and attention' throughout the voyage. *Shalimar* arrived back at Liverpool only 6 months and 14 days after setting out; an outstanding feat considering that the ship had been detained for 45 days during the voyage.

In the summer of 1855 the *Tiptree* sailed for Australia, under the White Star flag, commanded by Captain Penreath. Clearly the vessel was not ideally suited to the antipodean trade and she was moved to other routes immediately after this first voyage, where she remained until 1860. As there were still more people wanting to go to Australia than White Star could accommodate in its own vessels it chartered the *Earl of Sefton*. She sailed for Australia in 1855, under the command of Captain John Noble.

Chapter 3

1856-1857

Intent on broadening his horizons, Thomas Henry Ismay, boarded the barque *Charles Jackson* on Thursday 3 January 1856. So that he would not have to get up too early the following morning, something he had a particular aversion to doing, and as the weather meant it was by no means certain that the ship would really sail then, he elected to spend the night on board. However, despite his predilection for lying in bed, young Ismay was already up and about as it grew light on the Friday morning. He noted that the weather was dull and that there was a slight mist on the Mersey. (There almost always is on any river, come the dawn!) The pilot came aboard at about 7.30am and the *Charles Jackson* eased away from the Albert Pier, being towed downriver by a steamer. The ship had all but a full complement of crew, being just one man short.

At about 10 o'clock, after taking last minute letters, the steamer was released and the barque was on her own. Five hours later they passed Great Ormes Head, and by 8 o'clock had sighted Holyhead. They would not see Britain again for some considerable time. Clearly not a natural sailor, Thomas Henry Ismay retired early that night and was tucked up by a quarter to nine, suffering from *mal de mer*. He took no further interest in the voyage for the next couple of days.

By 6 January he was on his feet again, and noted that during the night the ship had encountered strong winds and had lost her galley funnel, which might have proven very inconvenient. However, there was enough material aboard the ship to construct another and the damage was repaired quickly enough for Sunday dinner to be served on time. Ismay found that a Sunday at sea was very different from ones he was used to spending ashore. Except for working the ship, the crew were given the day off, and they made the most of it by reading, playing games and musical instruments or just relaxing.

Monday 7 January 1856 was Ismay's 19th birthday. It was a beautiful calm day and he spent most of it on deck, shooting seagulls. The crew, in the forecastle, had been given a bottle of brandy in order to celebrate the occasion. As the day wore on they could be heard singing, so the gift was clearly appreciated. In the evening Captain Rapp and Ismay amused themselves by singing such songs as *Home Sweet Home*. In Ismay's own appraisal of the concert he said, 'Of course, the performance would have elicited great applause from an audience endowed with taste. I do hope I may enjoy every anniversary as well.' Clearly, the young Ismay was not without a sense of humour, as we shall see again from time to time.

Two days later the *Charles Jackson* met the steamer *Sarah Sands*, on her way home from the Crimea with many military personnel aboard, bound for Liverpool. It amused Ismay to see that the steamer had used the greater part of her coal and, thus lightly laden, was pitching and rolling heavily, making life uncomfortable for all aboard. He, and the others aboard the *Charles Jackson*, also appreciated that the troopship would carry news of their progress back to their friends and families in England.

It would appear that Ismay was not the only man aboard the *Charles Jackson* with a ready wit. While he and the captain were at dinner on Friday 11 January the ship was struck by a particularly heavy wave, which upset the dishes containing their food and mixed it all together. Rapp commented that, 'it would have taken the celebrated Soyer to have given a name to the various ingredients so mingled together'. The ship was rolling and pitching so violently that Ismay had to hold on to his plate to stop it sliding away, to hold his glass to keep it from tipping its contents all over him, and to hold the table to avoid being either thrown on to or away from it. All this, while dodging about to avoid flying food and crockery catapulted into the air by the motion of the ship. As he said himself, 'A man that can get his victuals at sea on board a ship in a storm can get his living anywhere, he can have no fear of the future so far at least as eating is concerned.'

Four days later the *Charles Jackson* was in another gale and was forced to reduce sail. During the day young Ismay was amused to see the ship's pig get washed right along the deck, but was relieved that it was not washed overboard. Despite Ismay's humorous remarks about life on a sailing ship he does comment on the odd less wholesome aspect with lines such as, 'I have taken advantage of this fine day to get my clothes dried for the best of vessels are somewhat damp.'

On 24 January Captain Rapp was suffering from severe toothache which Ismay was able to alleviate to some extent by putting heated salt into a flannel stocking and persuading the captain to tie it around his jaw. If nothing else, the sight of the captain with a sock full of salt tied around his head would have cheered up the crew and made the skipper's inevitable lack of patience more bearable.

The vessel continued southwards for three days, and then land was sighted. Ismay described it thus:

'January 27, Sunday. At 10 a.m. passed the island of Bonavista on our right, its name implies an island of great beauty, but owing to the fog the outlines were scarcely visible, and so the world has lost the advantage of my opinion, whether its appearance gives the lie to its name or not. We have the awning spread over the quarter deck so as to keep the deck cooler.'

At about 6am on Tuesday 8 April 1856 the *Charles Jackson* arrived in Valparaiso and was towed by four whale boats, each with four Chilean oarsmen, the two miles to where it could drop anchor. Valparaiso Bay is not the safest port in the world because of the strong northerly gales that tend to sweep the anchorage. Captain Rapp therefore set two anchors at the bow and another at the stern. Ismay went ashore, to the theatre, and then to a hotel to spend the night. On the following day he went for a walk in the hills with Rapp, and then on to meet a local businessman named Nixon, to whom he had been introduced the previous day, and who had invited him to his father's house for dinner. The single thing that impressed him most about the senior Nixon's other guests, and indeed Nixon himself, was the amount they smoked, so much so that 'Baccy' commented on it.

Although he spent the greater part of his time among the more affluent residents of the South American port, Ismay also saw something of the less well off. He first noticed what appeared to be picturesque houses on the side of the hill opposite to where he was staying. On closer inspection these picturesque houses turned out to be the hovels of the poor. They were simple clay huts with outside hearths and no sanitation. Ismay's sheltered upbringing shows itself in his description of the residents of these huts: '...and dark wild looking, loathsome faces peep forth here and there'. He was also somewhat taken aback by the way minor offences were harshly dealt with by the authorities while major crimes went unpunished. There were a great number of stray dogs, which he described as 'infernal', scavenging around the city in a way that was offensive to the young Englishman's sensitivities.

On 19 May he wrote some graphic but hardly flattering observations on the local women. According to Ismay the Chilean women were reputed to be amongst the best formed in the world, between the ankles and chin, which leaves one wondering about their heads and feet. They were usually short in stature but, particularly the lower classes, were very erect when walking. He also noted that they had beautiful hair which they usually wore in two long braids. Their complexion was 'red and white greatly improved by the good human smiles', which they often wore. The women had an easy natural manner, which gave Ismay the impression that they were not given to affectation.

The women did have one habit that the young Ismay found distasteful, that of spitting, which the older ladies and poorer classes indulged in regularly. They also smoked excessively, although not quite so much as in years gone by, Thomas believed. The Chilean women were very fond of music, and Ismay was informed that there were more pianos in Valparaiso than in any town in England with the same population, although nearly all the pianos had to be imported. After paying freight, and duty, each piano represented a considerable investment. Unsurprisingly, some of the ladies played extremely well, and were rather more readily prepared to display their talents than a young English lady might have been.

On 1 June 1856 Ismay left Valparaiso aboard the steamer *Bogoto* bound for Caldera, which it reached on the 3rd. From there he took passage on the *Conrad*, but the account of him joining that vessel is best left to his own words:

'June 3rd, Tuesday. Had dinner on shore, wrote a letter home, then took it on board and bid my steamboat acquaintances goodbye, when on returning, it was quite dark, I made a spring for the *Conrad* and missed her, and down I went into the water some few feet. I rose and luckily caught hold of a piece of wood attached to the quay. I held on there and attempted to make myself heard, but without success for my throat was full of salt water. I then commenced splashing, and was eventually heard by a man on the pier, who cried out in Spanish saying there was a man in the water. They heard it on board of the ship, and passed me a rope, which I caught hold of and got on board. My hat had floated off, and was picked up sometime after. My watch stopped at 5 minutes to 7. My pocket book spoiled. Cigar case, etc. However, if in my descent I had knocked my head against the quay, I might have become senseless and have drowned, for no one heard my fall; once in a lifetime is rather too often to have the above, but I have had them too often.'

Ismay spent a little over a week with the *Conrad*, which remained in Caldera for the whole time. Then, on Friday 13 June 1856, he took the train to Copiapó, about 55 miles away, where he booked into the French Hotel for his stay. Ismay's visit to Copiapó was not an idle one. He had gone there specifically to look at the mining operations going on all around. His particular interest was in copper, but anything that showed a profit was of interest to Thomas Henry Ismay – on the train journey he managed to discover that the railroad paid its investors 15% per annum. Once he had seen as much as he wanted to he took another steamer to Cobija, where he was to rejoin the *Charles Jackson* for the return voyage to Liverpool, via Islay in Peru.

The journey home was relatively uneventful, but with brief spells of excitement, and young Ismay found the time to comment on the monotony of a long ocean voyage in his diary. His boredom, however, was alleviated as the *Charles Jackson* approached Cape Horn. On 22 July a strong squall struck the ship from directly astern and split the top mast and lower studding sails, and carried away the royal. So violent was the wind that Ismay had expected it to carry away the spars but the sails failed instead, much to his relief. He went on deck at about 1am, being unable to sleep, only to find that the sea was breaking right over the ship.

Thomas went below again and turned in. Just as he was dropping off to sleep he was shaken back to full wakefulness by a loud crash from the after cabin. He got up to see what was wrong, and found all lights out and that water was coming into the cabin. Then another large wave struck the ship and sent Ismay reeling across the darkened room. As he staggered, trying to regain his balance, he trod on a piece of glass and almost amputated the big toe of his right foot. When crew members reached the cabin with a light, Ismay was surprised to see that the floor was almost covered with his blood. Although the captain dressed the wound, it continued to bleed for some considerable time.

Over the next couple of days the weather worsened to the point where the captain told Ismay that he had never seen such seas before. Conditions remained much the same and the main deck was waist deep in water, with waves breaking right over the poop when the ship came within sight of the Horn on 7 August. On the next day Ismay, no longer quite so enamoured of a sailor's lot, wrote in his diary:

'True life on the ocean wave sounds very pleasant when in the tropics but when the cold sea comes over to an excess, then life on the ocean wave is all very fine especially off Cape Horn with such a night as last (which is by far the wildest we have experienced since leaving England), it is another thing.'

From 9–25 August the weather remained moderate but then the ship ran into another heavy gale in which she lost some more sails.

There were other problems with the voyage also. In September Ismay and a steward decided that they ought to do something about the rats aboard the ship. On the 2nd of the month he and the steward caught 15, six with their hands and the rest in a trap. On the nights of the 6th and 19th the rats got a little of their own back when exceptionally large ones walked over Ismay's face as he tried to sleep.

As the *Charles Jackson* neared Liverpool, all hands, including young Ismay, turned to painting the ship. The barque arrived back in Liverpool in the first half of October 1856, and with it T. H. Ismay, who was now ready to enter the hurly-burly of business.

During his absence, Ismay's uncle, Joseph Sealby, who was acting as trustee of his father's estate until the young Ismay came of age, had supposedly been looking after his interests in the two vessels he was part owner of, the *Mary Ismay* and the *Charles Brownell*. However, instead of looking after the supplying of the vessels himself, Sealby had delegated that responsibility to his son John. This delegation of responsibility gave Thomas Ismay just the opening he was looking for.

What Ismay thought of John Sealby's abilities in private is unknown, but he made it plain in commercial circles that he was not very impressed with John's fitness for the role of shipbroker. Ismay made a special trip to the *Charles Brownell* to give Captain Bexfield the benefit of that opinion, knowing full well it would soon reach the Sealbys' ears. He was absolutely right, and at the end of October he received a letter from John Sealby demanding an explanation of his outrageous behaviour in talking to the captain in this way. Ismay ignored the letter, compelling John Sealby to write again. This letter from the younger Sealby clearly showed that, while he might not be the greatest shipbroker around, he was certainly a very shrewd judge of character, especially T. H. Ismay's. In it he wrote that he considered Ismay's behaviour to be ungentlemanly, and added that he would resist any attempt by him to gain control of the *Charles Brownell*, which he had guessed, accurately, was what Ismay had in mind. John Sealby also sent a copy of the letter to his father, Joseph.

Ismay's reply to Sealby's letter is a model of precisely what should not have been said to defuse the situation. In it he accused John Sealby of being unfit to act as a shipbroker, and of being unable to judge if a captain's request for stores and replacements for his vessel was justifiable or not. There was no way on earth that John Sealby, or his father, could possibly swallow such an insult, and their predictable response was exactly what Ismay wanted. The deviousness of the whole operation leaves one wondering if somebody as young and inexperienced as Ismay (he was then still under 20) could have planned it alone, or if there was somebody else involved. If there was not, then Ismay would certainly become a force to be reckoned with in the business world of his day.

John Sealby's reply, a follow-up letter, and a letter from Joseph Sealby to the other owners of the *Charles Brownell* played right into Ismay's hands. In the first he invited Ismay to put his accusation of incompetence in writing so that the other owners might make their own decision. In the second letter John Sealby informed Ismay that the offer he had made, to purchase a controlling interest in the *Charles Brownell* and *Mary Ismay*, was wholly inadequate, and that it was his father's intention to sell both vessels, in which he too had a share, as quickly as possible. It was then Joseph Sealby's further intention to withdraw as trustee of Ismay's estate.

The letter to the other partners owning shares in the *Charles Brownell* and *Mary Ismay*, dated 25 November 1856, explained how the ships had been managed by Joseph Sealby and his son. He made it clear that, as the acting trustee of the late Thomas Ismay senior, the management of the *Charles Brownell* had always been his responsibility. However, he explained that as he was so overburdened with work he had been unable to look after the vessel as he would have liked and consequently his son had taken an active part in her management. This letter went on to say that the Sealbys expected nothing but unpleasantness from Ismay in the future, as he tried 'all in his power to get the vessel into his own hands'. Even after so much acrimony the elder Sealby still maintained his sense of fair play as far as the other owners were concerned, and requested their agreement on his intended course of action before he proceeded. It is plain to see that Joseph Sealby was in the unenviable position of being an honourable man having to deal with a dishonourable one. However, Ismay had won, and had managed to get rid of his trustees.

For the time being Ismay went back to work for Imrie Tomlinson, where, in the course of business, he met Philip Nelson. Nelson, who also came from Maryport, was a retired captain who still owned a ship, the *Anne Nelson*, named after his wife. (A model of the *Anne Nelson* is preserved in the Liverpool Maritime Museum.) Since his retirement Nelson had retained a keen interest in anything to do with shipping, and had tried his hand as a shipbroker and as a canvas merchant, trading as Nelson & Co. Not altogether surprisingly the acquaintanceship with Ismay soon grew into friendship; after all, here was a ship that Ismay just might be able to get his hands on.

By late 1857 Ismay and Nelson had decided to go into business as shipbrokers, something they both knew a little about. Owing to Ismay being below the age of majority, the articles of agreement, making the partnership official, could not be signed until after his birthday in January 1858. In the meantime the two set about preparing the ground by taking offices in Drury Buildings, 21 Water Street, Liverpool. Ismay's ambitions to become a major shipowner were beginning to be realised.

Possibly because there were a lot more people digging for it than in the preceding year, about 20% more gold was found in Australia in 1855 than in 1854. However, that the average find per person had remained much the same, did nothing to discourage would-be prospectors. Demand for places aboard vessels heading for the Australian gold diggings grew and the shipping lines had to charter more ships to meet it. Thus, early in 1856, the White Star Line advertised its latest hired vessel, the *Spray of the Ocean*, a 996-ton ship built in 1854 at Sunderland, chartered from Brice & Co of Liverpool, which would be leaving for Melbourne on 20 February, as a Royal Mail Packet.

Despite the confident manner in which White Star proclaimed its vessels as Royal Mail Packets, the days of sailing vessels transporting the mail were fast drawing to a close. By April 1856 the British Government was already planning to give the Australian mail contract to steamships, and the clipper owners were well aware of this. With a canny eye to the future the steamship owners had been preparing new routes, particularly suited to vessels that were not dependent on the whims of the weather. They were already planning a couple of little enterprises that would shorten the routes around the world: the Suez and Panama canals.

It had been established that the Suez Canal would shorten the run to Australia by over 3,000 miles. The Panama Canal would not only save 2,388 miles on the East to West from Britain to Australia but would also mean that vessels would not have to go around Cape Horn, or face the appalling weather that was often encountered there. It was argued that a steamer, averaging about 10kt, touching only at Diego Garcia, which as a Crown Dependency would make an ideal coaling station, and travelling straight across the Indian Ocean to Melbourne should be able to complete the voyage in 44 days. The route would not be practicable for sailing ships because the trade winds in the Indian Ocean blow from the east. The writing was on the wall.

Throughout 1856 the White Star Line chartered a relatively large number of ships; amongst them were the *Sir William Eyre*, *Miles Barton*, *Star of the East*, *Merry England* sometimes known as *Merrie England*, *Mindoro*, *Cyclone* and *Anglo Saxon*. However, not all of the vessels sailing between Liverpool and Australia for the White Star Line were chartered; a few were actually owned by the line. As we have already seen with the *Mystery*, details of vessels owned by the partners in this period are not always easy to pin down; for example the *Titan*. Nothing appears to be known about this vessel except that she was advertised as a 2,360-ton ship and that she sailed for Australia on 20 May 1856, under the command of Captain Seers. Another vessel it bought was the *Sardinian*, which had been actually built for the White Star Line.

At a time when the line seems have been desperately short of its own vessels to send to Australia it mysteriously transferred the *Emma* from the Australian run to Atlantic trade in 1856. Despite the obvious requirement for more and more ships to carry emigrants to the antipodes, the *Emma* remained on the Atlantic for a couple of years, until she was lost in June 1858.

According to the Emigrant Commissioners the average unassisted emigrant was a fairly healthy and hardy soul. Of the 14,077 unassisted emigrants who journeyed to Victoria in

1856 only 64 died on the way and 20 of those were children between one and 12 years old, and a further 15 were infants of less than one year (who did not really count anyway). The unassisted emigrants were those who had enough money to pay all of their own fare, and were therefore from the more affluent working and middle classes. These people would have lived reasonably well in their home countries and would have been relatively healthy when they set out.

The assisted emigrants were a different kettle of fish. Of the roughly 16,970 assisted emigrants who set out for Australia in 1856, 208 died *en route*, 106 of them children under ten, and a further 61 infants less than a year old. Although the figures now seem pretty horrific, they were viewed as quite acceptable at the time, and an improvement over the figures for 1855. The Commissioners put the improvement down to the regulations they had instigated, such as obliging every emigrant ship to carry a competent surgeon, and making sure that fresh bread was baked aboard at least once in every three days.

The Commissioners had also brought in regulations governing the lifeboats carried by emigrant ships, particularly requiring that at least one boat on each ship be fitted with a new type of apparatus for lowering, named after its inventor, Mr Clifford. Clifford had demonstrated his invention, in model form, to the Commissioners in London, and they had been so impressed that they adopted it straight away. The Admiralty was also impressed and quickly had Clifford's apparatus fitted to many warships. The apparatus was also taken up by the more responsible of the steamship owners.

When John Pilkington retired as a partner in the White Star Line on 31 December 1856, to take over another family enterprise, Pilkington Brothers, his place was taken by James Chambers, who had joined the company earlier that year. The company name was changed to H. T. Wilson & Chambers, of 21 Water Street, Liverpool, although it was still known as the White Star Line. Probably because of Pilkington's retirement from White Star, *Windsor Castle* was sold in 1857 to Captain C. Bruce, who became her new master. This ship had been used almost exclusively in trade with Valparaiso so the sale did not affect the Australian emigrant business.

By this time White Star was well established and owned a respectable fleet of first-class ships, although not as many as its main rival, James Baines' Black Ball Line. However, there was also a new player in the game, vying for the mail contract, in the shape of the Cunard Line, which had long held Royal Mail contracts for North America.

Samuel Cunard, founder of the line, was born in 1787 at Halifax, Nova Scotia. His family, who were Quakers, had originally come from Redditch in Worcestershire and had emigrated to Philadelphia in the 17th century. When the Americans declared their independence from the mother country the Cunard family had promptly upped sticks and patriotically moved to British North America (Canada). As he grew up, the young Cunard took an active interest in banking, lumber, whaling, fire insurance and the militia, becoming a colonel. By 1819 he had moved into shipping and had a British contract to carry mail, in sailing brigs, from St John's, Newfoundland, to Boston and Bermuda. Cunard was one of the earliest owners to realise that the future lay in steamships, and although his steamers were not the first to cross the Atlantic, they were the first to do so on a regular basis.

In 1838, when the British Government asked for tenders to carry mail across the Atlantic in steamships Samuel Cunard went to London to submit his bid. He offered to carry the mail in three steamships of 800 tons and 300hp to America and back twice a month for £55,000 a year. Although he did not yet have the three ships he was offering to use, he still got his contract and went back to Halifax to a tumultuous welcome from the shipbuilders there, who obviously expected the required vessels to be built by them. Cunard, a hard-headed business man, thought otherwise and ordered four ships from builders on the Clyde. They were to be paddle-steamers of about 1,150 tons and capable of about 9kt, the first to be called *Britannia*. The new ships were not to be the fastest or biggest vessels of their day – the *British Queen* was half as big again – but they were to be amongst the most reliable. The *Britannia* left Liverpool for the first time on 4 July 1840 and reached Halifax in 12 days, and Boston in another two.

Samuel Cunard was a cautious man who did not like to take risks. He was also a shrewd judge of character who was aware of what type of man became a ship's captain, as is evident in his orders to the captain of the *Britannia*:

'The *Britannia* is now put under your command for Halifax and Boston. It is understood that you have the direction of every thing and person aboard.

'Good steering is of great value.

'In navigation of our vessels we have great confidence in the ability of our captains, but in the matter of fog, the best officers become infatuated and often attempt to push through when prudence would indicate patience.'

Lloyd's agent in Quebec, Henry Fry, said in the 1890s that in 53 years Cunard had never lost the life of a passenger, and in the previous 44 years had never lost a letter, and no other company could say that. Fry was absolutely right and to the present day, with the exception of the wartime sinking of the *Lusitania*, Cunard has not lost a passenger to shipwreck. This then was the company that was muscling in on the Australian mail run.

On 19 February 1857 the Cunard screw-steamer *Etna* left Liverpool for Southampton. She was due to sail from the southern port on the 24th with the mail for Australia. For the foreseeable future the contract for the transportation of the mail to the antipodes, and just about everywhere else, would be held by the Cunard Line. Although losing the mail contract must have been a considerable blow, both financially and in terms of prestige, the White Star and Black Ball lines made the best of a bad job by advertising their fleets as 'ex-Royal Mail Packets'.

Another of the White Star Line's great competitors, Gibbs Bright, otherwise known as the Eagle Line, managed to hang on to its mail contract by the skin of its teeth, because it owned the auxiliary steam clippers *Great Britain* and *Royal Charter*. Vessels of the Eagle Line regularly sailed on the 15th day of the month, and *Great Britain* was no exception when she sailed for Australia on 15 February 1857. Fares for a first-class, saloon passage ranged from 65–80 guineas (£68.25–£84), and for the other classes from 16–30 guineas (£16.80–£31.50).

Continuing White Star's practice of chartering rather than buying ships for the Australian run, some 13 vessels were hired in 1857. These were the *Anne Royden*, *Salem*, *Algiers*, *Monarch of the Seas*, *Shaftsbury*, *John Barbour*, *British Lion*, *Anglo Saxon*, *Negotiator*, *Invincible*, *Chancellor*, *Merchant Prince* and *Miles Barton*. *Miles Barton* was later wrecked at Storring Bay, South Africa, on 8 February 1861. Luckily the vessel was insured for £7,000. In addition to the vessels listed above the *Samuel Locke* also sailed for Australia on 27 April 1857, under the command of Captain J. Sweetnam. Nothing appears to be known about this vessel except that she was advertised as an 800-ton ship, and for this voyage she was working for White Star.

Although White Star still seems to have been chartering just about anything that would float in order to meet the demand for berths on vessels bound for Australia, it found it appropriate to sell off a small part of its fleet, in the shape of the *Sardinian*.

In late summer of 1857 two more vessels under the White Star flag set out for Australia. On 20 August 1857 the *Guy Mannering*, a 1,700-ton ship, left Liverpool under the command of Captain Dollard. The following month the *Shakespear* sailed, under the command of Captain Norcross. Virtually nothing seems to be known about this vessel.

By 1857 about a quarter of all the sailing ships operating out of the United Kingdom had Liverpool owners. Even London only had about three-quarters the number of the ships that were registered in Liverpool and no other port even came close.

Many vessels from the merchant fleet based at Liverpool were chartered by the government to take fresh troops to India, to quell the Mutiny which began there in May 1857. James Baines' three most famous, and best, clippers, the *James Baines*, *Champion of the Seas* and *Lightning*, were requisitioned as troopships. Gibbs Bright's *Great Britain* was also pressed into service carrying the desperately needed regiments to India. Although some White Star vessels were also chartered, the pride of their fleet, the *Red Jacket* was not, but was allowed to continue plying back and forth between Liverpool and Australia, almost without competition.

As she was preparing for sea, on the morning of 20 November 1857, William Forward, a young man who would one day be a great shipowner himself, boarded the vessel ready to sail to Melbourne. As he came aboard he noticed that the crew were mustered on the forecastle, under the watchful gaze of the first mate, Mr Taylor. Almost immediately the order came to weigh anchor and get under way. Forward recalled that the crewmen manning the windlass to haul up the anchor sang the shanty:

In eighteen hundred and forty-seven
Paddy Murphy went to heaven
To work upon the railway.
A-working on the railway, the railway, the railway.
Oh! poor Paddy works upon the railway.

No sooner was the anchor raised and secured to the cathead than the steam tug *Retriever* began to tow *Red Jacket* down river toward the open sea. The ship's signal guns were fired four times to tell the world that she was carrying the Royal Mail, much to the delight of the large crowd that had gathered to watch the departure of this famous vessel. For this voyage *Red Jacket* was carrying twice her normal complement of seamen in the confident expectation of making a record run.

By the next morning *Red Jacket* was off Holyhead, still under tow, and making poor headway because of the stiff westerly breeze and heavy swell. Then the towline was cast off, and the clipper was on her own. Men swarmed into the rigging and within a very few minutes the sails were set and filling. *Red Jacket*, like a hound released from the leash, bounded forward.

As evening approached the wind increased, with squalls, and the captain ordered lifelines rigged fore and aft. The ship, running close to the wind, heeled over until her lee rail was skimming the surface of the sea, and occasionally waves were breaking over her bow. *Red Jacket* was doing precisely what she had been designed to do, and doing it well. When the log was checked it was found that the ship was cutting through the water at 18kt.

While the weather conditions might have suited the ship and her crew, they did not improve the lot of the emigrants and other travellers. The 50 saloon passengers and 600 steerage were kept below decks and out of the crew's way whenever such ideal fast-sailing weather occurred. However, whenever the weather was bright and sunny, and when the winds were light, the passengers made the most of it by spending a good part of the time on deck. Life aboard a first-class clipper like *Red Jacket* could hardly be described as boring. Something the passengers would find exciting happened most days, such as sails splitting, spars and rigging being carried away, and the occasional sightings of an albatross or cape pigeon. On this voyage *Red Jacket* reached Port Phillip Head at the entrance to Melbourne in the record time of just 64 days.

During 1857 about 61,000 individuals emigrated to Australia, compared to just under 45,000 in 1856 and 53,000 in 1855. The Emigration Commissioners were still worried about the child mortality rate among families taking assisted passage, and were working to ensure that all surgeons aboard emigrant ships were experienced men. To assist these surgeons they were also appointing matrons to the ships to look after the single women. For the benefit of anybody aboard ship who wanted to improve their education the Commissioners also put a religious teacher and a schoolmaster aboard to 'afford instruction' to all passengers who were interested. Originally the provision of the matrons and teachers was something of an experiment, but it was so successful that it soon became standard practice to have these personnel aboard government emigrant vessels. The times they were a-changing.

Chapter 4

1858-1862

In January 1858 the partnership between Philip Nelson and T. H. Ismay officially came into being. In setting up the business the young Ismay had managed to put up £2,000 of the capital required. For a while everything looked rosy, but it was not to last. Nelson was a very cautious and conservative individual, while Ismay, as we have already seen, was all for trying anything new, which inevitably caused a certain amount of friction. He was convinced that the day of the wooden ship was drawing to a close and that the future lay in vessels built of iron. He was only partly right; wooden ships were on their way out, but the future lay not in ships built of iron but of steel.

Soon after the partnership was formed, Ismay had his way when they commissioned the well known Clyde shipbuilder, Alexander Stephen, to build them an iron ship, the brigantine *Angelita*, of 129 tons. At about the same time as the *Angelita* was ordered Ismay met Miss Margaret Bruce, the eldest daughter of Luke Bruce, a shipowner, master mariner, and ship's surveyor, of 36 Dexter Street, Liverpool. Both ship and young lady would become Ismay's about a year later.

Meanwhile it was business as usual for the White Star Line. Throughout the year it chartered the *Senator*, *Northern Bride*, *Americana*, *Sirocco*, *Gertrude*, *Beejapore*, *Simonds*, *Invincible*, *General Windham*, *Shepherdess*, *Tasmania* and *Dirigo*. As well as chartering vessels, White Star bought the *Blue Jacket*², *Columbia*, *Prince of the Seas* and *Shalimar*.

The departure of Pilkington and arrival of Chambers does not seem to have affected the White Star Line's imaginative style of advertising unduly. Nor does it seem to have made any difference to the policy of chartering most of the ships for the Australian run, even though this was a particularly good time to buy ships from other owners because of a recession that had hit other areas of the industry.

Just into the second week of April 1858 news reached Liverpool of the incredible run from there to Melbourne that had been completed in a mere 68 days by the *Red Jacket*, even though she had been becalmed in the Channel for four days. For much of the outward journey, at least as far as the Cape of Good Hope, she had unfavourable or light winds and had taken 23 days to reach the Equator. On her arrival at Melbourne the Australian press were generous in their acclaim of Captain O'Halloran for making one of the fastest passages on record and were not slow to mention that there had been no deaths or sickness aboard *Red Jacket*. She set out for the return leg of the trip on 10 March.

Despite White Star's tendency to charter rather than buy ships, the White Star fleet was steadily growing and on 9 April 1858 the line advertised its latest sailing list:

Ship	Captain	Register tonnage	Tons bur.	To sail
Gertrude	Roberts	1,367	4,500	20 April
Sirocco	Thompson	1,344	4,200	27 April
Beejapore	Drenning	1,676	4,750	20 May
Red Jacket	O'Halloran	2,460	5,000	20 June
White Star	T. C. C. Kerr	2,360	5,000	20 July
Golden Era	H. A. Brown	1,556	4,200	
Mermaid	E. Devey	1,320	4,000	
Shalimar	J. R. Brown	1,432	4,000	

The *Gertrude*, advertised as a remarkably fast clipper, was to sail punctually at noon on 20 April, with mail, cargo and passengers. She had already made some very rapid passages, and had consequently been specially selected by the British Government for war service in the Black Sea, where she was employed for nearly two years. The magnificent three-decker *Sirocco*, 'the handsomest ship in port', which had made some of the fastest passages on record, was to sail a week later.

The vessels appearing in the advertisement were by no means the only ships sailing for the antipodes under the White Star flag. There were also the *Simonds* and the *Invincible*. Wilson & Chambers, as usual, advertised the *Invincible* a little over-enthusiastically, and while making the most of the exceptional time she had made on her last voyage to Australia and back, they completely forgot to mention that the voyage had been for James Baines. On that voyage the *Invincible* had completed the trip in 72 days, faster than any other vessel, steam or sail, that season. She was a remarkably consistent performer and had completed eight voyages to Australia or back in less than 76 days.

To counter this propaganda, Baines & Co now made a particular point of drawing the public's attention to the merits and records of its ships in advertisements, such as the 2,163-ton *Great Tasmania*, built by Donald Mackay, which had completed the run to Australia in 73 days. The *Lightning* had managed to make the trip from Liverpool to Melbourne in 68 and 69 days, and had accomplished a reciprocal voyage in an astonishing 63 days and the *James Baines* had reached Melbourne from Liverpool in just 63½ days.

As an illustration of just how far shipowners of the period were prepared to stretch the truth the above takes some beating. The *James Baines* had caught fire and burned out, while in port at Liverpool, almost a fortnight before the advertisement above appeared. Small details of that sort obviously were not enough to deter Baines from advertising the superior sailing qualities of what was nothing more than a charred hulk.

On 30 September 1858 an article appeared in *Trewman's Exeter Flying Post* extolling the excellence of White Star's clipper service to and from Australia.

'The celebrated Ex-Royal Mail clipper-ship *Shalimar*, Captain Brown, 1,456 tons register, 4,750 tons burthen, will be despatched from Liverpool to Melbourne as the packet of the 20th October, sailing punctually at Noon of that day. This noble vessel carried Her Majesty's Royal Mails, under contract, three successive voyages, during which she performed some of the most marvellous sailing feats on record; her first voyage was made from Liverpool to Australia (Cape Northumberland) in 67 days, from Melbourne to Liverpool in 75 days, and from Liverpool to Melbourne in 75 days. She has made four voyages round the world in two years and eight months and has sailed the extraordinary distance of 420 miles in one day, a feat never equalled by the fastest steamer afloat. Her saloons like those of the *Red Jacket*, *White Star* and other clippers of this line are handsomely furnished, and supplied with a Piano, Library, Linen and all necessaries; a Cow for saloon passengers.

'The second Cabin in the poop is an elegant and airy apartment; and the Between-Decks are lofty and thoroughly ventilated. Passengers must embark on the 19th without fail. For freight or passage apply to the owners, H. T. Wilson and Chambers, 21 Water-street, Liverpool; to J. B. Wilcocks, Agent, Plymouth; or to Mr W. Morris, Auctioneer, South Street, Exeter.'

During 1858, 100 vessels of an average 1,200 tons apiece left Liverpool for Australia with about 24,000 emigrants and passengers. Thirty of these ships were chartered by the government, while 56 more were private emigrant ships, plus assorted Short Ships, belonging to, or chartered by, the various lines engaged in the trade. A high percentage of these private emigrant ships were owned or managed by Wilson & Chambers, James Baines, or Gibbs Bright. Throughout 1858 Liverpool shipping generally had been in a poor state, mainly due to an economic depression that year. Things picked up a little in the last half of the year and the *White Star* sailed with 570 passengers aboard, while the *Red Jacket* managed 454, and the *Donald Mackay* 436.

Things were so bad that many owners decided to lay their ships up in their home ports rather than risk them being caught out on the other side of the world with no cargo or passengers to bring back. A. Gibbs & Co, who had regularly chartered some 120,000 tons of shipping to carry guano from the west coast of South America, called off that side of its operation, leaving the owners who had chartered the ships with many vessels laying idle, an opportunity that Wilson & Chambers, and T. H. Ismay, seem to have missed altogether.

While the emigration to Australia had fallen slightly, the bottom seemed to have dropped completely out of this trade with North America. Emigration to the New World had always been heavier than that to the antipodes, but the depression of 1858 had begun to change all that. The slump was felt so severely in the United States that many Liverpool-based passenger vessels were bringing as many, or more, would-be emigrants back as they had taken out. A large number of the returning emigrants were so destitute that several local appeals had to be made in order to raise enough money to get them back to the homes and families they had so recently left.

Of those private companies engaged in the Australian trade the White Star Line carried the most passengers that year with 6,724. The Black Ball Line carried almost as many with 6,388, the Mersey Line 3,006, Eagle Line 2,176 and J. M. Walthew at 512 brought up the rear. Not a single privately owned and operated vessel sailed from Liverpool with passengers for New Zealand, and there was not exactly overwhelming enthusiasm about going to Tasmania either.

As the figures illustrate, the White Star Line had moved to the top of the league table of Liverpool shipowners engaged in the Australian emigrant trade. While Wilson & Chambers were probably well pleased with this turn of events, James Baines was not. Never ones to let the grass grow under their feet, Baines and Gibbs Bright joined forces. Both companies gained from the amalgamation. Baines gained a first-class trading base in Australia while Bright Brothers & Co, the Australian branch of Gibbs Bright and the Eagle Line, instantly became part of the leading company on the Australian trade route. The merger was announced in the *Liverpool Mercury* on 17 December 1858.

The new line offered passage to Australia by auxiliary steamer for as little as £14 aboard the *Great Britain* and *Royal Charter*. Alternatively, a traveller could elect to take passage aboard one of the line's clippers, 'the largest, the finest, and fastest, merchant ships in the world', which sailed from Liverpool on the 5th and 15th of every month. The vessels on offer were the *Rowena, Marco Polo, British Trident, Eagle, Commodore Perry, Gipsy Bride, Lightning, Oliver Lang, Great Tasmania, Champion of the Seas, Ocean Chief, Donald Mackay, Indian Queen, Meteor, Montmorency,* and of course the auxiliary steamships *Royal Charter* and *Great Britain*. The auxiliary steamers were advertised as representing the only line to have been honoured by a visit from Her Majesty the Queen. They were also well known for their rapid passages and impressive accommodation, which was as good as that found aboard any ships in the world. And according to Baines and Gibbs Bright the commanders of their vessels were all experienced captains, noted for their kindness and attention to their passengers.

Undismayed, the White Star Line took up the challenge, and probably bought the *Tornado* in 1859, although it is possible that she was only chartered then and finally purchased in 1863. Anyway, she made her first voyage for the line in 1859 when she sailed to New Zealand, commanded by Captain Crighton. The line definitely bought the *Telegraph* in 1859, along with the *Phoenix*. During the year it also chartered the *Beechworth, Tudor, Scottish Chief, Miriam, Merchant Prince, Ida, Star of the East, Shooting Star, Argonaught, Herald of the Morning, Empire of Peace, Hilton, Greyhound* and the *James Cheston*.

Blue Jacket[2] sailed for Australia in February 1859, and on the trip proved to be not wholly suited to that trade. On returning from this voyage the vessel was transferred to the India run. The *Annie Wilson* was also put on the route to India, still under the command of Captain Langley, where she plied back and forth for about four years. The Indian trade offered some advantages to the White Star Line, which was experienced in transporting large numbers of second- and third-class passengers, along with regular cargoes. Governments and large businesses were prepared to subsidise the passage of cheap labour, and there was an abundant supply of that in India.

Early in the morning of All Fools' Day 1859 a series of events took place that graphically illustrates the professionalism and efficiency of the captains and crew of the ocean greyhounds of the time. At about 2am the Black Ball clipper *Indian Queen*, with 40 passengers and a cargo of wool and gold, crashed into an enormous iceberg about halfway between Australia and Cape Horn, and barely clear of Antarctica. The off-duty crew and passengers hurried on deck to find the ship's masts and rigging in tatters. The mainmast had gone along with the bowsprit and foremast; only the mizzen-mast remained standing. It did not take the passengers and crew long to realise that the port side lifeboat had been lowered. Captain Brewer and the mate along with 15 sailors had assumed that the ship was seriously damaged and promptly abandoned their sleeping shipmates to their fate.

As it turned out, the hull of the *Indian Queen* had withstood the impact with the berg and was still watertight. The passengers and remaining crew, the second mate, carpenter, boatswain, four seamen, two boys and the cooks, stewards, doctor and purser set about saving the ship by clearing the ice from the decks, cutting away the broken masts and rigging that festooned the side of the vessel, and getting some sail onto what masts and spars were still usable. Only then did they hear the cries for help from the captain and his crew in the small boat.

The people on the ship tried to throw ropes and lifebuoys to the lifeboat but they continually fell short and it soon became apparent that the lifeboat had lost its oars (there is nothing like a well-disciplined crew). Huge seas were breaking over the lifeboat and it was rapidly filling with water. Then the tiny boat was washed to windward of the *Indian Queen* and swept away.

Those remaining aboard the ship returned to trying to save their own lives. Slowly their efforts were rewarded and they pulled clear of the iceberg, only to be threatened by more bergs for the next six days, as they worked their way northwards. On 10 May, after being assisted first by the American whaling ship *La Fayette*, and then the French warship *Constantine*, the *Indian Queen* limped into Valparaiso, escorted by the British second-rater HMS *Ganges*. The ship was condemned but sold off and re-rigged, although she never sailed for the Black Ball Line again.

Thomas Henry Ismay married Miss Margaret Bruce on 7 April 1859, on the anniversary of his parents' marriage, at St Bride's Church, Percy Street, Liverpool. Ismay's choice of bride was inspired, probably the wisest decision he ever made. Throughout the rest of his life she would take an interest in everything he did, and whenever things went badly she was always there to help and encourage him.

Late October 1859 saw one of those days when nothing seemed to go right. The weather had been anything but clement for some little time previously but on the 26th one of the most ferocious gales on record struck north-west England. Liverpool was badly affected by the storm, and as the tide reached its highest so did the wind strength. From about 11.30am until 4pm navigation in the Mersey was hazardous if not impossible, and certainly imprudent. So bad were conditions that several steamers due to sail that afternoon were unable to take on passengers because the waves breaking over the landing stage meant that tenders dare not come alongside. The steamers *North American* and *City of Baltimore* were obliged to wait until the weather moderated on the following day.

Not so the Wilson & Chambers flagship *White Star*, which rather unadvisedly set out for Australia in the teeth of the gale. Not surprisingly the *White Star* did not get very far before the appalling weather forced her to turn back and seek the shelter of the Mersey, shelter that all too nearly proved illusory. Once back in the Mersey an attempt was made to moor the *White Star* but the wind began to drive her toward the Pluckington Sandbank, and certain destruction. Only the timely intervention of several powerful Mersey steam tugs saved the ship, and they managed, with difficulty, to manoeuvre her into a more sheltered position, where she was anchored. Despite the incredible stupidity of their captain in desperately trying to stick to an impossible schedule, something that White Star skippers were prone to doing, sometimes with disastrous results, Wilson & Chambers had been lucky.

James Baines and his relatively new partners Gibbs Bright were not blessed with the same fortune. The *Royal Charter* was battling her way homewards through the same gale that had so nearly destroyed the *White Star*. She was off the north-west coast of Wales when, at about 5am on the 26th, she was driven onto the rocky shores of Anglesey. Over 450 passengers and crew perished in the disaster. To this day the terrible storm is still referred to as the *Royal Charter* gale.

Nothing lasts for ever, and the foul weather moderated. White Star immediately returned to its practice of hiring in vessels to keep pace with the demand for places on vessels heading for Australia. The *Beejapore*, *David G. Fleming* and *White Jacket* were chartered in rapid succession.

According to the Emigration Commissioners 21,524 people emigrated to Australia in 1859. Of these, 8,630 had government-assisted passages, while the remaining 12,894 paid their own way. In the same year no fewer than 5,057 Australian emigrants became somewhat disenchanted with their new country and decided to return home.

In January 1860 the Liverpool–Melbourne trip took *Red Jacket* 84 days. By this point in her career she was also engaged in a little Australasian coastal work, and a voyage from Melbourne to Auckland took from 6–17 May. In 1868 she was still with White Star and her registered owners were now recorded as Wilson & Chambers of Liverpool. In 1871 she was involved in a collision in the Downs, off the coast of Kent, where she lost her jib-boom. In 1878 she collided with, and sank, the *Eliza Walker* but luckily no lives were lost. From here on the *Red Jacket's* career went downhill rapidly. In the 1880s she worked as a coal barge at the Cape Verde Islands and then spent her remaining years carrying timber across the Atlantic from Quebec.

During the 1840s and 50s, conditions aboard emigrant ships had been appalling. So as to be able to squeeze as many people in as possible, berths were crammed so closely together that passengers were obliged to climb over one another to go to bed. Between-decks ventilation was practically non-existent, as were washing facilities, and there was no privacy whatsoever. Food was only one short step away from being poisonous and was dispensed to the passengers from buckets, like pig swill, only pigs probably wouldn't have eaten it. All in all it required some pretty desperate circumstances at home to justify anybody taking passage under the conditions then prevailing.

Then parliament took action and passed the Passenger Act to improve the emigrants' lot. By the 1860s things had improved quite dramatically as a letter from an 1864 emigrant, Andrew Frazer, shows. Frazer had sailed for Australia aboard the Black Ball Line's *Bayswater*, and was impressed by the way the ship's captain, officers and doctor all treated the emigrants with courtesy and consideration. Although the passage, at 108 days, was not one of the fastest on record, it was one of the smoothest, and they enjoyed good weather all the way. The *Bayswater* had arrived in Keppel Bay on Monday 23 May. As that was as close as the captain dare take his vessel to the inhospitable shore of Rockhampton, the last 60 miles of the trip were taken by steamer. This steamship came out to meet them as soon as it became known that the *Bayswater* had arrived, and the passengers were finally landed at Rockhampton on the 26th.

The immigrants were all taken to a depot where they were given tea, sugar, bread and beef, at the expense of the Queensland Government. Frazer, having no work, or place to live, arranged to stay on at the depot until something could be found for him. Within a few days work had been got for him as a joiner, at 12 shillings (£0.60) a day. The ease with which he had found well-paid employment, compared with conditions in his home country, inspired Frazer to list the rates of pay a new immigrant could expect. Shoemakers earned from £3 to £3 15s (£3.75) a week, tailors made 10s (50p) a day, both with rations thrown in, and a labourer could expect from 18s (90p) to £1 5s (£1.25) a week, again with rations and lodgings for himself and his wife. It must have seemed like a dream come true to Frazer. Even single men with no skills at all would be found work, most probably as shepherds, where they could expect to earn £40–£50 a year, all found. All 78 of the young single men who made the trip out to Australia with Frazer, and who knew absolutely nothing about sheep, became shepherds, working anything up to 600 miles from Rockhampton.

In 1860, as usual, the line chartered ships on a wholesale basis. They were the *S. Curling, Britannia, Commodore Perry, Great Tasmania, Saldanha, C. W. White,*

Elizabeth Ann Bright, *Star of the East*, *Samaritan*, *Northern Bride* and the *S. Gildersleeve*. During the year it bought the *Ocean Home* (in a reversal of the normal practice of the time, in 1861 she sailed to Australia, under Captain Noble, for the Black Ball Line), and the *Electric*. *Phoenix*, which had probably been bought by Wilson & Chambers the preceding year, sailed for New Zealand on 10 October 1860 under the command of Captain Henry. She was a fairly successful vessel and made several other voyages to the antipodes between 1860 and when she was sold in 1863.

On 12 October 1860 the White Star Line advertised the sailing times and a list of its fleet. White Star vessels usually left Liverpool on the 20th of each month, and according to the advertisement the *Morning Light* would be sailing for Melbourne and Auckland in October under the command of Captain J. Gillies, and the *Red Jacket* would leave for Melbourne in November under Captain Reed. The vessels listed as supposedly belonging to the White Star Line were *Morning Light*, *Red Jacket*, *White Star*, *Sirocco*, *White Jacket*, *Shalimar*, *Prince of the Seas*, *Star of the East*, *Telegraph*, *Arabian* and *Blue Jacket*.

On 26 October *Red Jacket* arrived back in the Mersey from Australia. She was well overdue and had been causing some concern to the White Star line. Aboard were 25 first-class, 12 second-class and 103 third-class passengers and a large general cargo of Australian goods, as well as £156,000 worth of gold. Captain Reed had decided, for whatever reason, not to take the usual homeward route around Cape Horn but to sail via the Cape of Good Hope, which it took 58 days to reach. Overall, the one-way voyage had taken *Red Jacket* 97 days.

H. T. Wilson bought the *Blue Jacket*[1] and *Lord Raglan* in 1860; the first before the October advertisement and the second after it. The *Lord Raglan* had already seen considerable service, some of it as a trooper, and had more than one owner. Graves, for whom she had been built, had sold the vessel to Barcroft, Houghton & Carroll soon after receiving it from the builders. The ship had next passed to Carrol & Co of Cork, and it was from them that Wilson bought it, for use on the Liverpool–Melbourne route. Although the hiring of ships continued, Wilson & Chambers were buying more and more ships for the White Star Line.

In 1861, to supplement its own fleet, the line chartered the *Green Jacket*, *Commodore Perry*, *Star of India*, *Star of the East*, *Morning Light*, *Queen of the Mersey*, *Sovereign of the Seas*, *Empress of the Seas*, *Lillies* and the *Empire of Peace*. At least some of these chartered vessels had been listed in the October 1860 advertisement as then actually belonging to the White Star Line, which was clearly not quite a wholly truthful assessment of the situation.

The *Chariot of Fame* was bought by Wilson for the White Star Line in 1861, for use on the Liverpool–Melbourne route. The *Lord Raglan* was still on the same route under the command of Captain Roper. And the four-year-old *Electric* was still going strong in that year when she sailed to Australia under the command of Captain Underwood.

In another example of a clipper captain being too ready to abandon his ship, the Black Ball's *Conway* was dismasted in a storm in September 1861. Her master, believing that there was 8ft of water in the hold, decided to transfer his passengers to the *Summer Cloud*, which was standing by. Then, to prevent the *Conway* becoming a danger to other shipping he determined to scuttle her. However, the ship refused to sink and the next day she was found by the *Home*. When they checked, the crew of the *Home* found that, apart from the fact that she was dismasted, there was nothing wrong with the *Conway* and that there was now, despite the attempt to scuttle her, only 7ft of water in the hold. They promptly pumped the ship dry, jury rigged her, and got under way for Barbados, which they reached six weeks later.

The year 1862 did not begin at all well for the White Star Line when the *Prince of the Seas* caught fire and was burnt at Melbourne on 10 January. Undeterred, Wilson & Chambers, who still had a large slice of the Australian immigrant trade, set about chartering more ships to see them through the year. During 1862 they chartered the *Merchant Prince, Duke of Newcastle, Elizabeth Ann Bright, Morning Star, Mistress of the Seas, Great Australia, Royal Saxon, Silistria, Blanche Moore, Excellent, King of Algeria* and the *Rising Sun.* Some of these vessels were for use on the North Atlantic.

Early in 1862 gold was discovered in New Zealand, which prompted a mini gold rush from Australia. Curiously this discovery did not really affect the White Star Line, but a gold strike in British Columbia, made at about the same time, did. Pilkington & Wilson were quick to realise what the new strike on the other side of the Atlantic could mean and they transferred half a dozen of their ships from the Australian run.

It was not long before a notice appeared in the Liverpool press, pointing out the advantages of travelling to the new gold-fields with the White Star Line. While most lines were using small, second-rate vessels to convey would-be prospectors to the east coast of Canada, White Star was sending some of its fastest 'ex-Royal Mail' clippers directly to the shores of British Columbia. Although this would mean a very much longer sea voyage, it would eliminate the overland journey across Canada normally faced by immigrant prospectors. Because the trek across the vast expanse of the Canadian hinterland was so difficult and time-consuming it would be quicker to take the longer sea route. It also meant that the prospectors were paying the White Star Line for the entire journey rather than just the short haul across the North Atlantic. The first vessel advertised for the new route was the almost new 1,212-ton *Excellent*, followed by *Mermaid, Blue Jacket[1], Morning Star, Royal Saxon* and *Electric*, one of which was to sail on the 10th of each month, commencing in June 1862.

H. T. Wilson was still buying ships for the White Star Line as well as chartering them. In 1862 he bought the *Donna Maria, Queen of the North* and the *Glendevon*. But while the line seems to have been chartering and buying ships wherever possible, it still managed to find the *Telegraph* surplus to requirements, and sold her off to M. I. Wilson & Co.

On 22 January 1862 T. H. Ismay's first iron ship, the *Angelita*, encountered a ferocious storm off the south coast of Ireland as the little ship made her way towards Liverpool from Honduras with a cargo of mahogany. The weather forced the *Angelita* into Dunmanus Bay where Captain Peter Gardiner Dow hoped to land a sick crew member. Before the ailing seaman could be got ashore for medical attention he unfortunately expired, so Captain Dow anchored off Furze Island to ride out the storm. At about 4am the anchor cable snapped and the *Angelita* was swept onto the rocks off Horse Island. There was nothing the crew could do except abandon ship, so they took to the longboat; they all reached safety. The ship began to break up as it slipped off the rocks and sank in about six fathoms of water, with much of its cargo being washed ashore. Ismay had lost his first, but by no means last, ship.

The loss of the *Angelita* was the last straw as far as the partnership with Philip Nelson was concerned. The two men had already decided that they could not work together and should dissolve their association, which they did without further ado. It is already apparent that although people took an initial liking to T. H. Ismay, this affection did not seem to last.

After the break-up of the partnership with Nelson, Ismay set up on his own as T. H. Ismay & Co, and took offices at 10 Water Street, where he would remain until 1898 when he would move his headquarters to the specially designed building at 30 James Street, Liverpool. By then, of course, he would be world famous as the man who owned the White Star Line. In the meantime, Ismay was in business for himself, and quite successfully at that. By 1864 he had various ships, in some of which he owned shares, and some for which he was the agent, trading with South America.

In 1862 no fewer than 41,843 people emigrated to Australia and New Zealand — 8,189 on government-assisted passages. Despite the rise in numbers, helped by the New Zealand gold strike, the halcyon days of Australian emigration were drawing to a close.

On 12 December 1862 Margaret Ismay had a son. Christened Joseph Bruce, the new addition to the Ismay family would have at least as great an impact on the world of shipping in general, and on the White Star Line in particular, as his father.

Chapter 5
1863-1867

The *Mystery,* was a very aptly named vessel, and not the only mystery ship to have connections to the White Star Line. Next to nothing is known of this vessel between the time she was bought by the White Star Line in 1854 and when she sailed from Liverpool, bound for Australia on 5 January 1863. Equally mysteriously, very little is known of the vessel after she set out on this voyage. Although, as you would expect, there is little in the documentary record to show it, tiny snippets have come to light suggesting that Wilson & Chambers might have been engaged in what was by then no longer 'a respectable trade'. Slave trading had been outlawed by the British in 1807, although other countries, notably the United States, were slow to follow suit. There can be no doubt that the business still offered large profit margins in the 1850s and 60s, at a time when the White Star Line desperately required money to expand. The transportation of illegal, or forced, labour and the landing of such labour in countries where certain types of immigration were strictly prohibited was a practice that the line appears to have continued through several changes of management. This is clearly shown by the presence of Chinese immigrants aboard the *Titanic*, as witnessed by survivor Lawrence Beesley.

The ex-troopship *Lord Raglan*, presumably still under the command of Captain Roper, sailed for Melbourne on 20 February 1863. She was seen at 2°N, 22°W on 23 March. The vessel was never seen again, at least not to be positively identified. By September, having received no news of the ship, Wilson & Chambers were practically convinced that the *Lord Raglan* was lost. The following notice was posted in the Liverpool Underwriters' Rooms on 20 September 1863:

'The Captain of the ship *Imperatrice Eugenie*, arrived in London from Natal, reports seeing a large ship on fire, burnt to the water's edge on the 26th and 27th March, in lat.1°N, 26W. The Captain endeavoured to reach the burning vessel, and if possible to render assistance, but he was unable to do so owing to calms. The position of the burning wreck and that which the *Lord Raglan* would have occupied some two or three days after she was sighted are sufficiently near to suggest grave fears for the safety of the missing vessel.'

In May 1863 the Government Emigration Office issued an eight page pamphlet, the fifth in a series defining 'Mess Utensils, Small Stores, &c. for the use of the passengers on board Government Emigrant Ships'. The comprehensive little booklet, produced for Her Majesty's Stationery Office by George E. Eyre and William Spottiswoode, gives a fairly clear picture of what conditions aboard an emigrant ship of the period must have been like. The contents of the booklet are reproduced in the Appendix.

Trade with Australia was still relatively good in 1863 and White Star was still finding ships for that route wherever it could. During the year it chartered the *Southern Empire*,

Star of India, *Vanguard*, *Queen of the South* and *Morning Light*, which was at least partly owned by the Black Ball Line. Despite this, the *Morning Light* would remain in White Star service until February 1866, making regular voyages between Liverpool and Melbourne.

In May 1863 the *Albert Williams*, a 505-ton barque, was launched by J. Laing & Co of Sunderland, for Wilson & Chambers. Unlike the other small vessels purchased by the partners around this time, the *Albert Williams* was a steamship. Although obviously unsuitable for the task – small steamships at that time were incapable of carrying enough coal to undertake long voyages – she was advertised as a passenger ship on the New Zealand run, and leaving London on 5 August 1863. Under the command of Captains Brown and Walker the *Albert Williams* served on the London antipodean route in 1863 and 1864 before being put to trading with South America. In later life she was re-rigged as a barquentine, and renamed the *Else*. She was finally wrecked in 1900 on her way to South Africa.

Even though the *Albert Williams* was not exactly a resounding success, she did convince the partners that there was a future in steamships. Early in 1863 Wilson & Chambers decided to add much larger steamers to their already existing fleet of clippers. Steamships at that time were still in their infancy and the small engines they carried were merely an auxiliary power supply, should the wind fail them. They were really still sailing clippers but with a small motor for emergency use.

Royal Standard, the first large steamer ordered by the White Star Line, came into this category. The vessel would be 225ft long and 40ft wide. The new ship would measure 2,033 gross register tons (1,598 tons net), have two decks, five holds and three masts equipped with a full set of sails. Primarily intended as an emigrant ship the vessel had accommodation for 800 passengers in steerage but only 40 in first class. Down in the bowels of the ship there was a two-cylinder steam engine capable of producing around 165hp.

Built by Palmer Brothers & Co of Jarrow at their Tyneside yard, the new ship was launched in August 1863. It was to take the builders a mere six weeks more completely to fit the vessel out ready to enter service. Despite the speed at which the vessel was completed she was described in the press as one of the best looking and most completely equipped steamers afloat. Her saloons were spacious and well furnished, and little luxuries such as a piano and a library were provided. All the necessities for safe and comfortable ocean travel, as they were understood then, were included in the fitting out of the ship.

At the end of those six weeks the *Royal Standard* sailed from Jarrow for Liverpool. The trip down the east coast of England, through the Strait of Dover and back up the west coast to the home port of the White Star Line was fast but otherwise uneventful. Even on that short journey the vessel had demonstrated that she was capable of holding her own against any competition she might encounter.

On 23 November the *Royal Standard* left Liverpool on her maiden voyage, bound for Melbourne, under the command of Captain E. J. Allen. The White Star Company was never the luckiest of shipping lines, particularly where maiden voyages were concerned, as will become apparent.

In a curious parallel with the *Mary Celeste*, Captain Allen, a former master of the *Shalimar*, died during the voyage to Australia. For the return journey Captain G. H. Dorvell would take command of the *Royal Standard*. The vessel sailed from Melbourne on 21 March 1864, with more than half a ton of gold aboard. For a fortnight all went well and the ship made good time. So good, in fact, that Captain Dorvell was confident they would complete the passage in 65 days.

Then their luck changed for the worse. On 4 April at 11am, when the ship was at latitude 54° 50' South, longitude 145° 27' West, running under sail, she ran into thick fog. Almost immediately the lookout reported, 'Broken water ahead'. A huge iceberg appeared out of the fog, just a little way ahead of the ship and slightly to starboard. The helm was instantly put hard a-starboard and all hands were called to help trim the sails and swing the bow away from the iceberg. They almost managed to steer clear of the mountain of ice that threatened them. The ship swung to port until it was running parallel with the face of the berg but the wind steadily pushed her towards the 600ft-high monster. The starboard side of the ship crashed into the berg with such violence that she bounced off, rolling heavily. As the *Royal Standard* rolled, her yards smashed into the berg, bringing a mass of ice down on her decks before the spars broke.

The main and mizzen topmasts snapped, bringing yards, sails and rigging down on the decks, destroying rigging lower down and crippling the ship even more. With most of the sails on the aft masts either down or torn to shreds the stern of the vessel moved clear of the berg, bringing the forward yards and rigging into contact with it. The upper foremast did not last long before it, and the sails it carried, were torn away. However, there were still some sails on what remained of the snapped masts and the ship was still able to make headway.

Royal Standard scraped along the berg, crushing the starboard lifeboat and its davits. Then the ship's stern again smashed into the iceberg, causing damage to her starboard quarter, and destroying the captain's cabin. The impact seriously damaged the ship's chronometer and other instruments, lifted a poop deck beam by 12in and split one upper plate amidships.

Everybody aboard thought that their end had come, but they did not give up. They cut away the fallen rigging and debris from the broken masts, and regained a small measure of control. It was enough, and eventually the ship managed to pull clear of the iceberg. Captain Dorvell immediately ordered that all compartments should be sounded to ascertain how quickly the ship was sinking. He was somewhat surprised to learn that the ship was not making any water whatever. Steam was raised, the propeller was lowered, and the engine was started in less than three-quarters of an hour.

Later, Captain Dorvell described the iceberg as, 'being enveloped in dense fog and upwards of 600ft high. In the immediate vicinity and surrounding the vessel were several others of similar magnitude.' The *Royal Standard* limped away, using her steam engine, towards Rio de Janeiro, where she arrived on 9 May for three days of emergency repairs and to restock her bunkers with 350 tons of coal.

If *Royal Standard* had been in contact with the berg for almost 30 minutes, as was reported, she had escaped lightly. Although her masts and rigging were in tatters, the hull was still sound. She left Rio on the 12th, but with so short a repair time she must have completed the homeward voyage under jury rig, relying to a great extent on the pathetically inadequate 165hp steam engine. *Royal Standard* arrived at Liverpool on 19 June, five and a half weeks after leaving Rio.

Captain Dorvell, while reporting events on 4 April, omitted to explain how or why, in full daylight at 11 o'clock in the morning, his lookout (only one?) failed to see a dense bank of fog directly ahead of the ship until it was too late to avoid the iceberg it contained, which was only one of many in the area. Nor did the captain, clearly an extraordinarily lucky man, explain his decision to sail across the Atlantic in a ship that was anything but fully seaworthy, which can only be described as reckless, a quality that White Star masters were to become notable for.

In 1862 a new Companies Act paved the way for the formation of limited liability joint stock companies in Britain. In a limited liability company capital is raised by selling shares to the general public. The beauty of the system is that, should the venture fail, then investors only stand to lose the value of the shares they hold. In the earlier share system investors owned a percentage of a company, as they would under the new arrangement, but should the company fail then they would be liable for that percentage of the debts incurred. Before the new act investors had taken tremendous risks in accepting liability for the enormous debts a shipping line could generate if it failed. The removal of that risk meant, of course, that many more investors could be expected. Even those who had only a small amount to invest could afford to take the gamble.

Because it cost so much more to build and run steamships, and because of the increasing competition from London-based shipping companies, a complete restructuring of the business empires that were the Liverpool shipping lines seemed to be in order. With an injection of new capital as an incentive, early in 1864 Wilson & Chambers tried to merge their company with the Eagle and Black Ball lines. The new combine would form a single entity to be known as the Australian and Eastern Navigation Company Limited and would operate steamships on its then preferred Liverpool–Australia route.

It should come as no surprise, however, to learn that when H. T. Wilson, James Chambers, James Baines and Gibbs Bright got together to cook up a business deal then the outcome was anything but 'above board'. First, a publicity campaign was started (we already know how realistic their advertisements tended to be), posters were displayed, circulars were distributed, and the newspapers played their part. Within days the gullible public had swallowed the bait, and there was a huge demand for shares.

As was only to be expected (it was certainly expected by the shipowners, as we shall see) the demand for shares began to push their price up. People began to speculate in shares that they had not even received by selling them at a higher price than they had supposedly paid. Had the new company been legitimately set up and run then this perfectly normal practice by today's standards would have presented no problems; everyone would have finished up with whatever they had bought and paid for. The problem lay in that this was not a company that had been properly set up, and the shipowners who had formed it hadn't the slightest intention of running it honestly.

Baines, Wilson, Chambers and Gibbs Bright had arranged things so that hardly any shares at all would be made available to the public, but that most would remain in the hands of the would-be partners. The scarcity of shares, they had accurately reasoned, would push the price up, making their own holdings that much more valuable, and making them all a good deal richer.

Their advertising campaign had been too successful and, hoist by their own petard, the whole plot was made public when the unavailability of shares became apparent. The affair blew up into such a scandal that the Stock Exchange Committee was forced to take action. They quickly discovered that more than 38,000 of the supposed issue of 40,000 shares in the new company, which should have been available to the public, had been bought by the directors of the line and their partners. The committee refused to appoint a settling day for transactions in the shares of the company, which meant that it could not exist. Thanks to the timely action of the Stock Exchange the whole swindle had been exposed and halted. The affair did nothing to enhance the reputations of those involved and could fairly be described as the beginning of the end, putting as it did an end to their dream of placing a fleet of steamers on the Liverpool–Australia run.

Back in 1807 the British Government had agreed to outlaw the slave trade, and within a few years British warships were to be found policing the slave routes from Africa to North America and elsewhere. Other countries in Europe were persuaded to join the ban on slave trading, sometimes diplomatically, sometimes otherwise. However, there was a great deal of money to be made transporting slaves from West Africa to the United States, where slavery was not abolished until the end of the Civil War in 1865, so unscrupulous shipowners and captains ran the risk of falling foul of the Royal Navy by continuing to transport their slaves. Others soon turned to a related and in many ways equally unpleasant trade.

Employers in areas where slavery was now banned soon noticed the immense, and relatively untapped, sources of labour in India, China and the Far East. 'Coolies' were labourers, usually unskilled, from underdeveloped countries, who accept assisted passages to another country where they could find work, and hopefully a better standard of living. In return for the assisted passage the 'coolie' labourer was legally bound for a period of years to a single employer. Because a 'coolie' had no right to withdraw his labour, or to seek other employment, he was completely at the mercy of whomever he worked for. For the period he was contracted to work to repay his fare he was effectively a slave, with little in the way of rights.

In 1837 the first 'Coolie' Emigration Act was passed, allowing free emigration from India to the Caribbean, in an effort to control the conditions in which the 'coolies' were transported. The act required that only first-class ships were used, and quite stringent obligations had to be met. Understandably, allowing that there were still slave ships carrying Africans across the Atlantic at the time, the legitimate (if reprehensible) 'coolie' trade was a little erratic in the early years, but with the end of open slavery in America it began to pick up quite noticeably. As early as 1863 certain Liverpool shipowners were transporting up to 4,000 Indian 'coolies' a year, at between £13 and £14 a head. (Who needed the slave trade?).

As we know, White Star was not only engaged in transporting emigrants to the antipodes but was quite happily carrying cargo and people all over the place, including from the Indian sub-continent and China.

Thomas Henry Ismay became a director of the hitherto successful National Line of Steamships in 1864. The line had been founded the previous year by a group of Liverpool business men with the intention of carrying cargo and steerage passengers to the Southern States of America. With that intention in mind, the line's ships were all given the names of Southern states. This, of course, became a little embarrassing when the Confederates lost the Civil War, and the ships' names had to be tactfully changed so that they could trade with the Union.

The war between the states of North America had already had a serious knock-on effect in the north of England. The supply of raw cotton from what were briefly the Confederate States dried up, throwing the cotton workers out of work. 'It's an ill wind that blows nobody any good' and the hardship suffered by the Lancashire cotton mill workers started them thinking about seeking a better life elsewhere. British Columbia, Vancouver Island, New Brunswick and Canada made it clear that they did not want immigrants who were not accustomed to the rigours of an outdoor life, which ruled out the mill workers. Luckily for all concerned, Australia, formerly in the habit of accepting the dregs of humanity in the shape of transported convicts, was not so fussy. Queensland and South Australia offered to take the unemployed mill workers, as did New Zealand and Victoria, who put up £10,000 and £5,000 respectively to assist with their passage. After all, now that the gold rush was over, they needed to offer some incentive to people to induce them to travel halfway around the world in search of a better life.

T. H. Ismay bought the *Pampero*, a 558-ton iron barque launched in January 1864 by Royden & Co of Liverpool, on completion. She was used throughout her 10-year life, half of it with the White Star Line, on the route between Liverpool and Callao, on the coast of Peru. First commanded by Captain Lesley, she was later skippered by Captains Waller and Metcalfe. Ismay's empire was steadily growing, although, at this stage in its development, it was still no threat to White Star.

In 1864 some Liverpool businessmen, including Ismay, got together and founded a training ship for the sons of seamen and other boys of good character, the *Indefatigable*. Many of the boys who trained aboard the ship, stationed in the Mersey, would go on to serve in the merchant navy, which of course ensured a steady supply of skilled seamen for the shipowners. Characteristically of the time, there was a set fee of £30 per year for training aboard the *Indefatigable*, but this was invariably waived if parents could not afford it, and only as much as could be spared was collected instead. T. H. Ismay took a great interest in the training ship and the organisation behind it. In time he became treasurer, and then in 1878 he was made chairman of the board of directors, which he remained until his death in 1899.

In 1864 the White Star Line began to sell off some of its fleet in an effort to cover some of the enormous debts the company had run up by expanding too rapidly. The 12-year-old *Colonist* was sold to R. Wilson & Company of Liverpool. The 7-year-old *Electric* was also sold, to Alfred Cleve & Co of Sydney and Dunedin at round about this time. *Electric* was condemned at Bluff Harbour, New Zealand, in 1864 but seems to have been repaired and then sold.

Even though it was selling ships White Star was still chartering others. In April 1864 the line chartered two: the *Industry* and the *Envoy*. By this time the system whereby emigrants could obtain a free passage to Australia was all but a thing of the past. Although some passages were assisted by having at least part of the fare paid from public funds, emigrants were expected to make a contribution towards their own futures. Inevitably this added expense had its effect on the numbers of those willing to take the chance on a new life. Only 40,942 people emigrated to Australia, Tasmania and New Zealand that year – 12,112 fewer than in the previous 12 months. Slightly less than 1% of those who set out in high hopes of a better future failed to arrive, having died on the way for one reason or another.

In the meantime T. H. Ismay was fast becoming a wealthy man and in 1865 he and his family moved to Beech Lawn House, Waterloo, a large Georgian house overlooking the Mersey. At Beech Lawn, Thomas indulged his interest in outlandish gardening by growing peaches, grapes and other tropical fruits under glass. He also built what he called his 'Grotto', which was a water garden made from large red rocks, faced with mirrors, with water running over them. (To their everlasting credit the Luftwaffe made a determined attempt to eradicate this monstrosity during the Liverpool blitz in 1940/41, but without complete success.) In the great days of the White Star Line, as its ships passed the house they would sound their whistles in salute. Nobody could accuse Thomas Henry Ismay of false modesty.

Even as the storm clouds gathered around the White Star Line, there were moments when fortune smiled on it, such as when *Chariot of Fame* rescued six men from the sea in

1865, one of them a Thomas Baines, who might well have been related to the Liverpool shipowner James Baines. At about 4pm on Sunday 24 April the *Chariot of Fame* came upon a ship's topgallant mast that had only recently gone into the water. The *Chariot of Fame* sailed on to the NNW for about an hour before the helmsman spotted what looked like a small boat about two miles off the port beam. Captain Clarke came on deck and had a look at this 'small boat' through his telescope, only to discover that it was a raft with several people aboard. The people on the raft were frantically trying to attract the *Chariot of Fame's* attention by waving. Captain Clarke quickly realised that the waving was a distress signal. When the ship was about half a mile from the raft a boat was lowered, under the command of the chief officer, to go to the rescue. The raft turned out to be part of a ship's poop deck, and there were six men on it holding on to a piece of rope attached to a couple of eyebolts. The shipwrecked men were in a pitiable condition, almost dead from hunger and thirst, and in constant danger of being washed from their inadequate sanctuary by the waves that continuously broke over it. They were taken on board *Chariot of Fame's* boat as rapidly as possible and taken back to the ship.

Baines soon recovered enough to tell his rescuers how the men came to be floating about on nothing more than a section of the *Sam Dunning's* poop deck. He said that the *Sam Dunning* had left Rangoon on 18 March and that the ship had a slight list to port. When they reached the Equator they ran into bad weather, which steadily got worse until, by 18 April, they were in a full gale with heavy seas, which increased in strength. By 10pm on the 18th the gale had grown into a full hurricane. The holds of the ship began to fill with water and the captain ordered the pumps started, but they did not work and wouldn't lift the water.

Throughout the night the wind increased in strength and the vessel settled ever lower, and the list to port increased. At about 8.30am on the 19th the crew set the mainsail to help bring the ship about but by that time things had deteriorated to the point that she would no longer answer her helm.

Captain Whitehouse had no real idea of what might be done to save his ship. The crew advised him that he should cut away the masts in the hope that, with their weight gone, the ship might right herself. The captain made no comment, even though it was now evident to all on board that the waterlogged ship was becoming more and more sluggish. Three of the crew went below to find out just how bad things were. When they returned they reported that the cargo had shifted over to the port side and water was coming into the ship from everywhere. In their opinion, unless the masts were cut down, then the ship would not last another half hour.

The mate asked the captain for permission to cut away the masts but the skipper refused, saying that the ship 'will last till daylight'. The mate was of a different opinion and ordered the crew to get on with cutting down the masts. Captain Whitehouse promptly countermanded the order, and the crew, long conditioned to obeying orders without question, followed the captain's orders and waited for another 15 minutes before he relented. By then it was too late. The crew cut down the mizzen mast but even as it fell, the ship sank underneath them.

Baines had been on the weather side of the poop-house, close to the captain, when the ship sank. He got over the side and caught hold of the mainbrace, while the sea washed over him and the ship's decks. He was finally forced to release his hold on the mainbrace when the ship started to drag him under, and he surfaced close to a piece of wreckage about 6ft long. He clung to the wreckage for about five minutes while he looked to see if there was anybody else still alive. Then he spotted the section of poop deck with six or seven men on it, whom he promptly joined.

Probably much to the delight of Messrs Wilson & Chambers the Black Ball Line was having a run of bad luck (if that is what it was). Their aptly named *Fiery Star* had caught fire while making its way from New Zealand to Liverpool. The captain, all but one of the passengers, and most of the crew abandoned the stricken vessel and made for the Chatham Islands in the small boats, but the first mate, Mr Sargeant, and 16 of the crew stayed aboard in an attempt to save the ship. They struggled for 21 days before the ship partly drifted, and partly sailed, back to New Zealand. About 60 miles off the New Zealand coast the ship was sighted by the *Dauntless*, which rescued the crew and took them to Auckland. HMS *Brisk* went in search of the captain, passengers and crew who had abandoned the *Fiery Star* but no trace of them was ever found.

Then came the *Hannah Moore*. The *Hannah Moore* was on her way home from the Chincha Islands in Peru, with a cargo of guano, when she ran into a storm and took shelter in the lee of Lundy Island in the Bristol Channel. While the ship lay at anchor the wind changed direction until it was blowing her toward the island. The *Hannah Moore* tried to run out to sea but the wind was so powerful that it shredded her sails as fast as they were set. Then it was discovered that she was dragging her anchors and drifting towards the island's cliffs.

The strain proved too much for an anchor cable, which snapped, and the ship swung broadside on to the seas. Almost immediately the sea swept away the boats, bulwarks and everything else that was above deck. A desperate rescue attempt was made by the islanders, using a punt, but it was no use. Eventually the islanders managed to rescue six crewmen from the stricken vessel, but not before she had been pounded to pieces on a rocky outcrop known as Rat Island.

Then, as far as the White Star Line's main rivals were concerned, came the final blow. James Baines and his associates were heavily involved in Barned's Bank, which in 1865 announced a project to convert the private bank into a joint stock company. You might have expected Baines to have learned his lesson about limited liability companies, but no. The bank published a very favourable statement of its condition and prospects, taking no account of the fact that its major source of income was the Australian emigrant trade, which was in sharp decline. Only eight months later the bank failed, with liabilities of almost £4,000,000. When the bank collapsed it effectively took James Baines & Co with it, leaving Baines with debts of more than £500,000. The liquidators were called in and two-thirds of the line's ships were sold off to meet the debts. Somehow, in much reduced circumstances, the line managed to survive.

John Morris, Baines' wealthy brother-in-law, poured money into the company to help keep it afloat. Other shipowners, who had bought the ships Baines had been obliged to sell, chartered them back to him. Overheads were reduced by cutting staff and moving to much less expensive offices. One can imagine the partners in the White Star Line rubbing their hands with glee at what had befallen the Black Ball Line, little knowing that much the same fate lay in store for them within the year.

By late 1865 H. T. Wilson and John Cunningham were the main shareholders in the White Star Line, although, on paper at least, James Chambers was still the senior partner with Wilson, and it was still Wilson & Chambers in name. However, Cunningham had been taking an active part in the company for some time, and during that time he and Wilson had borrowed a lot of money from the banks.

Above: Penny Lane, 1912. The Beatles connection! *Robert McDougall collection*

Left: A 1911 White Star Line publication, advertising the company's Liverpool services. *Robert McDougall collection*

Above left: Portrait of Thomas Henry Ismay. *Robert McDougall collection*

Above right: Thomas Henry Ismay. *Robert McDougall collection*

Below: Thomas Ismay and sons aboard *Adriatic*, 1888.*Robert McDougall collection*

Above left: Joseph Bruce Ismay. *Robert McDougall collection*

Above right: An unknown White Star Line official at the 30 James Street offices. *Robert McDougall collection*

Below left: J. Bruce Ismay (right), Managing Director of White Star Line, in conversation with Alexander Carlisle (left), Chief Designer, Harland & Wolff, and Captain E. J. Smith, Commodore of the White Star Line. *Robert McDougall collection*

Below right: Captain E. J. Smith explains the workings of a ship's engine room telegraph to a young passenger. *Robert McDougall collection*

R.M.S. Teutonic
Length, 565 ft.
Breadth, 51 ft.
Tonnage, 9,984

Above: Teutonic at sea. *Robert McDougall collection*

Below: Majestic¹ at Liverpool prior to her 1911 rebuild. Note the seaman in the foreground wearing the White Star uniform jersey. *Robert McDougall collection*

Above: A picture postcard showing *Oceanic*[2] leaving New York.
Robert McDougall collection

Below: A postcard of *Persic*. *Robert McDougall collection*

Top: Oceanic¹. Real Photographs

Above: Britannic¹. Ian Allan Library

Below: Germanic — one of the longest-lived ships ever built.
Robert McDougall collection

Top: Ceramic. Real Photographs

Above: Teutonic at a Liverpool landing stage.
Robert McDougall collection

Right: An advertisement for White Star's
weekly Liverpool to New York run.
Robert McDougall collection

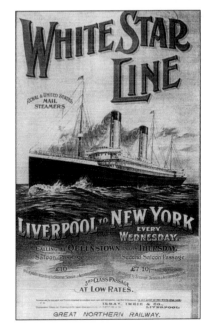

Above: Celtic² at sea. Robert McDougall collection

Below: Celtic² arriving back in the River Mersey from New York, with Magnetic at her port bow. Robert McDougall collection

Above: The River Mersey ferry, the paddle-steamer *Birkenhead*, later to become the White Star tender *Gallic. Robert McDougall collection*

Below: Republic² and the tender *Gallic* (front) moored at Prince's Landing Stage, Liverpool circa 1907. Another tender, *Magnetic*, is passing to the left of the picture. *Robert McDougall collection*

Above left: The Palm Court and Restaurant of *Majestic*[1]. *Robert McDougall collection*

Left: Oceanic[2]. *Robert McDougall collection*

Below left: Afric. Robert McDougall collection

Above: Canopic. Robert McDougall collection

Below: Cretic. Robert McDougall collection

LANDING STAGE, FROM RIVER, LIVERPOOL.

Above: The tender *Gallic* hard by the landing stage at Liverpool.
Robert McDougall collection

Below: The tender *Magnetic* leaving a Liverpool landing stage to embark passengers on to an awaiting White Star liner. *Robert McDougall collection*

ender leaving Landing Stage, Liverpool.

Above: White Star liners crowd Liverpool's Canada Dock in the early 20th century. (Top left *Celtic²*; bottom left *Ceramic*; top right *Republic²*; bottom right *Majestic¹*.) *Robert McDougall collection*

Below: An early 20th century photograph of *Baltic²* in the Mersey with *Magnetic* alongside. *Robert McDougall collection*

Above: A view of Cherbourg in the early 1900s, showing the harbour and the breakwater. *Robert McDougall collection*

Below: The South Western Hotel in the early 1900s, where many White Star first class passengers embarking from Southampton stayed overnight. *Robert McDougall collection*

Above right: White Star Line's James Street, Liverpool offices, circa 1900.

Centre right: A group photograph of White Star Line staff, including Deputy Chairman Harold Sanderson (4th from the right, standing). *Robert McDougall collection*

Below right: A Liverpool landing stage early in the 20th century, showing the Ismay brothers, James, Bower and Joseph Bruce. *Robert McDougall collection*

Above: A Liverpool landing stage, showing horse-drawn vehicles bringing up cargo/supplies to the dockside.
Robert McDougall collection

Below: Baltic² moored up at a crowded Liverpool landing stage.
Robert McDougall collection

By 1865 Wilson and Cunningham owed the Royal Bank of Liverpool the then huge sum of £179,704, and other banks another £190,000. It was this reckless borrowing that had allowed the line to buy so many ships during 1863 and 1864, and it was to prove their undoing. Despite there not being more than an outside chance, at best, that the partners might repay the loan, the Royal Bank of Liverpool agreed to carry the line for a further six years, at considerable risk to itself.

In an attempt to maximise profits the *Glendevon* was transferred from the Australian to the Indian run in early 1866, and the *Santon* and *Cecelia* were sold off. The *Fitzjames* left Liverpool for Melbourne, carrying emigrants, on 20 January 1866. A few days out she sprang a leak and had to put in to Lisbon for repairs. While at Lisbon *Fitzjames* was condemned as unseaworthy and the remainder of the voyage was cancelled. The financial problems facing the White Star Line are all too apparent in their readiness to send a vessel full of emigrants to sea when it was so clearly in need of a considerable amount of repair.

Speed had always been an objective of the lines running would-be prospectors out to Australia, so that they might arrive before the diggings were worked out. Henry Wilson, in his determination to win passengers from other lines, had always advertised his vessels as 'under penalty' to complete the outward passage in 68 days. This penalty clause had long been a source of consternation to Chambers, but he was unable to persuade Wilson to change his tactics. On 26 April 1866 James Chambers decided that he had had enough of Henry Wilson and the White Star Line and finally stepped aside to allow Cunningham to take his place.

When it came to predicting the future, at least where business was concerned, Chambers outshone his former partners Wilson and Cunningham. On the same day that he stood down as a partner in the White Star Line he had received notice that he had been accepted as a director of the Lancaster Shipowners' Company, whose vessels had been sailing under the White Star flag since the company was founded in 1864. Chambers had obviously seen the writing on the wall because no sooner had he divorced himself from White Star than he set himself up under his own name again in an office in Coopers Row, Liverpool.

Despite mounting financial problems Henry Wilson bought the *Western Empire*, and the 970-ton *Whittington* in 1866, but time was fast running out for the White Star Line, at least in its present incarnation. One of the line's most famous vessels, *Blue Jacket[1]* sailed on 20 May 1866, from London to Melbourne. It was her last advertised sailing for the White Star Line.

As the White Star Line's prospects became ever more bleak, those of Thomas Henry Ismay did the opposite. He had now reached the position where he was able to charter his own vessels to White Star, such as the *Fletcheroo* and the *Explorer*. While Wilson and Cunningham were wrestling with the financial problems, which would inevitably prove fatal to their company, T. H. Ismay was steadily growing ever more powerful. In 1867 he managed to buy the *Arriero* and another four vessels, the *Arrowe*, *Delmira*, *Don Guillermo* and the *Castlehow*. In the same year Ismay's soon to be partner, William Imrie, bought the 730-ton *Esmeralda*.

In 1867 the Royal Bank of Liverpool failed, and because of the large amount of money owed to it by Wilson and Cunningham, about £527,000, the White Star Line failed with it. After successfully trading for more than 20 years, the line had foundered because the partners had tried too hard to expand by buying ships that they couldn't afford to pay for, a failing that would bedevil the company in the future. However, not quite everything was lost. After the fleet had been sold to cover the debts the company name remained.

The *Oliver Cromwell, Donna Maria, Western Empire, Red Jacket, Arabian, Chariot of Fame, Royal Standard, Glendevon, Mermaid, W. H. Haselden, Ulcoats* and *Tornado* were all sold in 1867 to help offset some of the company's enormous debts. As if having to sell off the fleet was not bad enough, two of the White Star Line's vessels were lost in rapid succession in 1867. The *Blanche Moore* was lost on the coast of Ireland on 26 May; the *Annie Wilson*, while still on a run to New Zealand and back was abandoned in June. The *Shalimar* and *Albert Williams* were taken over by the Royal Bank of Liverpool.

The White Star Line, in its first incarnation, was finished, but its greatest days still lay ahead.

Henry Threlfall Wilson was a broken man, in the closing days of 1867, when he sold the goodwill, name and the famous flag of the White Star Line to that familiar shipowner from Maryport in Cumberland, Thomas Henry Ismay, for £1,000. Almost immediately White Star was back in business, this time with iron ships on the Liverpool–Australia route, probably much to the chagrin of James Baines and his somewhat reduced Black Ball Line, who would find T. H. Ismay a far more formidable opponent than Wilson had ever been. Henry Wilson retired, in reduced circumstances, to Surbiton, Surrey. He died of stomach cancer on 1 November 1869, aged 44. John Pilkington outlived Henry Wilson by about 20 years and died in 1890 at his home, 41 Shrewsbury Road, Birkenhead. He is buried in Wallasey churchyard. An era had ended.

Chapter 6
1868-1871

On Friday 10 April 1868, exactly 44 years to the day before its most famous vessel would set out on her maiden voyage, the White Star Line advertised once more in the Liverpool press. According to the notice the *Duke of Edinburgh* would sail for Melbourne from Liverpool on 20 April, and the *Woosung* would sail for Melbourne exactly a month later, on 20 May. What records exist appear to show that the *Explorer* was also sailing on the Australia run from 1868–70, under the command of Captain Trumble. Not untypically, the record has to be wrong unless the good Captain Trumble had mastered the art of being in two places at once. The record also shows that for this period, 1867–72, he was commanding the *Castlehow* as she plied back and forth on the China trade. Accurate information on the White Star Line is about as common as hen's teeth, a situation not helped by the destruction, or disposal, of archive material in the 1930s and later.

Ismay had therefore lost no time in re-establishing the White Star Line's monthly service on the Liverpool–Australia route, even if it did mean that, like Henry Wilson, he would have to charter the vessels to do it. Those chartered during 1868 were the *Duke of Edinburgh* in April, the *Woosung* in May, the *British Statesman* in June, the *Bucton Castle* in July, the *Globe* in August, the *Nereus* in October and the *Borrowdale* in November. Whether this last vessel sailed in November or December is still to be determined, but either way there does seem to be at least one month when no White Star ship left Liverpool for the antipodes.

To begin with at least, the resurrected line under T. H. Ismay appears to have been run in a more businesslike fashion altogether than in its earlier form. *Fletcheroo* was transferred in 1869 to the American trade under the command of Captain Waller. While it is apparent that Ismay was desperately short of ships to maintain his schedules, he still found it expedient to sell the *Arrowe* while she was at Valparaiso. The 730-ton ship was only three years old at the time.

T. H. Ismay continued his policy of chartering ships for the Australian run into 1869, although he did also buy ships whenever he could raise the necessary capital. He took an active interest in the Indian trade as well, which, as we know, would have involved the line in the highly profitable transportation of 'coolie' labour.

Ships, then as now, were expensive items to buy and maintain. Financing his burgeoning fleet would have been a continual nightmare to Ismay and there can be little doubt that he would have used any and every means at his disposal to increase profits, and therefore increase the number of people prepared to invest in his enterprise. What were then known as the African and China trades had long been recognised as a very profitable, if a little risky, business. I suspect that at least some of the vessels, about the comings and goings of which little is known, were engaged in this trade, and perhaps some other dubious enterprises.

Amongst the chartered vessels during the first half of 1869 were the *Weathersfield* and *British Prince* in February, *Dallam Towers* in March, *Bucton Castle* in April, *Remington* in April and the *Hecuba* in May. By June 1869 Ismay was advertising four more ships preparing to sail for Australia and New Zealand: *Pride of the Thames*, *Hoghton Towers*, *Victoria Tower* and *Warwickshire*. The *Pride of the Thames*, which sailed in June, and the *Warwickshire*, which had already sailed in April, were both chartered but the *Hoghton Towers* and the *Victoria Tower*, which both sailed in June, were owned by T. H. Ismay.

Echoes of the old White Star Line were still to be heard when the *Blue Jacket¹*, now principally owned by H. T. Wilson & Co of Liverpool, although her original owners, including James Chambers, still had a share in her, caught fire and was abandoned off the Falkland Islands in 1869. The *Blue Jacket¹* had sailed from Lyttelton, New Zealand, heading for London, on 1 February. As well as the general cargo of cotton, wool, flax, skins and tallow, she had £63,390 worth of gold aboard. On 9 March, while the ship was off the Falkland Islands, fire broke out among the cotton. The combustible nature of the cargo did nothing to help the situation and within a few hours the vessel was an inferno, and the crew and passengers were forced to abandon her at 50°S, 47°W.

The captain, with his first officer, seven of the crew members and all 21 of the passengers got into one of the boats. Unfortunately, the boat they had chosen leaked like a sieve, and to make matters worse the weather turned against them as well. Nevertheless, the captain's boat was the most fortunate of the three to escape the burning *Blue Jacket* because they were picked up by the German barque *Pyramont*. Two of the passengers and a crew member were in such bad condition when the German vessel took them aboard that they died two days later. Because of the extra mouths to feed, conditions aboard the little German ship could best be described as desperate. It was only because they managed to replenish their supplies from other vessels, met on the way, that they managed to reach Queenstown without anyone actually starving to death.

The third mate and seven seamen from the *Blue Jacket* were picked up from another of the boats by the barque *Antonio Vincent*, out of Swansea. These eight rescued sailors were all that remained alive in a boat otherwise filled with corpses, which the survivors were too weak to throw overboard. The *Antonio Vincent* took the survivors to the Falklands, along with £12,000 worth of gold that they had managed to rescue! (Over £50,000 worth of gold, at 1869 values, still remains with the wreck of the *Blue Jacket*.) The eight who were taken to the Falklands were later brought home aboard HMS *Megaera*. In a curious epilogue to the story of the loss of the *Blue Jacket*, her charred figurehead, in the shape of an old-time sailor, was washed up at Fremantle, three years after the ship was lost.

Some time during 1869 T. H. Ismay was invited to dine with Gustavus C. Schwabe, a prominent merchant. Over a game of billiards after dinner, Schwabe told him that his nephew Gustav Wolff had entered into partnership with Edward Harland in a shipbuilding enterprise at Belfast and that they had already built some radical ships for the Bibby Line. Schwabe had invested as much as was possible in Harland & Wolff and there were no more shares available, but he wanted to invest more money in shipping. He suggested to Ismay that there was room for a new company operating steamships on the North Atlantic. Schwabe also said that he believed Ismay was the man to start such a company. If Ismay was prepared to have all his new steamships built by Harland & Wolff, the financier declared that he would back the line to the limit and get other Liverpool businessmen to do the same. Ismay agreed, provided that Harland & Wolff undertook not to build ships for his competitors. Under this agreement the Belfast shipyard was to build every one of White Star's ships, with the single exception of the *Laurentic*[2], on a cost plus profit basis.

In the meantime Ismay still had a shipping line to run, and he was still short of ships. Amongst those he chartered to make up the shortfall were the *Hawarden Castle* and the *Vancouver*, which sailed on the same day in August.

The year 1869 was an eventful one for Thomas Ismay for other reasons, not all of them necessarily to his liking. His mother, who was staying at Lea in Kent, died at the age of 63. Mrs Ismay failed to leave a will so her property and estate, including the two houses in Maryport, passed to her eldest son, Thomas. The demise of his mother could hardly have come at a better time for Ismay, who needed every penny he could lay his hands on then. Displaying his usual familial consideration, Thomas promptly sold the Whillan's Yard house to his brother John, for £50. Not long afterwards he also sold Ropery House. Still, life, and business, goes on despite family bereavements, and Ismay had his monthly Australian runs to keep up.

On 6 September 1869 the Oceanic Steam Navigation Company was formed with £400,000 capital in £1,000 shares, of which Ismay subscribed a large proportion. The first list of shareholders included the names T. H. Ismay, E. J. Harland and Gustav W. Wolff, these last two with a vested interest in iron ships. The company was intended, right from day one, to operate steam passenger ships on the North Atlantic. Immediately after it was founded the Oceanic Steam Navigation Company ordered four new ships from Harland & Wolff, the first to be the *Oceanic*[1] followed by the *Atlantic*. The original order was soon increased to six new ships. This was the beginning of a relationship between the two companies that would endure for more than half a century.

The agreement whereby the shipping line would not buy ships from any other builder, and whereby the builders would not construct ships for the line's competitors, effectively shackled the two companies together. Neither one could operate successfully without the other; they were, to all intents and purposes, one. There was one major advantage to the arrangement inasmuch as the shipbuilders, without fear of showing a loss, could build the very finest ships, which is exactly what they did. The White Star Line stuck to the agreement as far as new ships were concerned, although it would on occasion buy in existing ships from other owners, but Harland & Wolff, under the control of William James Pirrie, was to stretch the terms of the agreement somewhat in the years to come.

Even though his plans to concentrate the White Star Line's main efforts on the North Atlantic routes were going ahead, Ismay did not neglect his Australian commitments. To fill at least some of the gaps in his schedule he bought the *Castlehead*, which sailed for Sydney in August, and the *Comandre*, which sailed in October, and he chartered the *Vandieman*, which sailed in October, and the *Seatoller*, which sailed the same month. October 1869 seems to have been a particularly busy month for Ismay's line with no fewer than three ships either belonging to, or chartered by, him leaving the Mersey for Australia. In the same month the *Casma*, a barque, sailed for New Zealand. November was another busy month with the *Compadre*, owned by Ismay & Co, sailing along with the chartered *Bayard*.

Late in 1869 we again come up against the White Star Line's unusual style, by today's standards, of advertising. The *British Admiral* was advertised as sailing to Australia in November 1869. Nothing seems to be known about this vessel although there was a ship of that name, but it was owned by Fermies and not launched until 1873. The advertised vessel was possibly replaced for the voyage by the *Bayard*.

Ismay seems to have been promoting a number of vessels that did not actually exist at about this time, for his own reasons. Along with the *British Admiral* we find the *Carma*. Nothing appears to be known about this vessel except that she was advertised as being of 650 tons and sailing for Australia in November, under the command of Captain McCulloch. She was most probably really the *Casma*, which had sailed under the same captain a month earlier, but as she was almost certainly still on her outward passage at the time of the advertised sailing this is by no means certain.

Probably much to the relief of those who had booked passage aboard them, not all of the vessels advertised by the White Star Line were phantoms. The *Montrose*, a chartered vessel, sailed for Australia in December. The *Ismay*, probably owned and renamed by T. H. Ismay, also sailed in December, but for New Zealand.

With the new year of 1870 would come a major change for the White Star Line. As the year began T. H. Ismay's dominant business was still the trade with the antipodes, and the line was still chartering ships for that purpose. They were the *Estrella*, *Pembroke Castle*, *Hausquina* and *Rajah*, which all sailed in January.

When William Imrie of Imrie Tomlinson died in 1870 his son William Imrie (Jnr) transferred the whole of his business to T. H. Ismay & Company. Ismay and Imrie, it will be recalled, had met as apprentices while working for Imrie Tomlinson and had remained firm friends ever since. The company name was changed from T. H. Ismay & Company to Ismay, Imrie & Co. Ismay was to run the new steamers under the White Star flag, and Imrie the sailing vessels as the North Western Shipping Company, but despite the different names the two lines would remain, in many respects, the same company. As if the difference between sailing and steamships was not already obvious enough, all new White Star steamers would have a gold band around the hull, immediately below the white painted superstructure, while this decorative feature was consciously omitted from North Western's clippers.

While they waited for the first of the new steamers to come from Harland & Wolff, which would not arrive until the next year, Ismay and Imrie continued to run their mainly chartered fleet to the antipodes and back. The *British Navy* and the *Cairnsmore* were both chartered ships that sailed in February 1870. The *Santon* and the *Kirkwood* were chartered vessels that sailed in March. The *Delhi*, *Merwanjee Framjee* and *Ravenscrag* all sailed under the White Star flag in April. May seems to have been a fairly quiet month but in June the line chartered the *Cape Clear* and *Dallam Towers*. In July it was the turn of the *Grace Gibson* and *Hannibal*, and the *Cardigan Castle* and the *Santiago* were both chartered for trips to Australia in August. Amid all of this chartering of vessels Ismay Imrie found it necessary to transfer the *Explorer* from the Australian run onto the South American trade.

Still Ismay awaited the arrival of the first of his new steamers. However, there was a good reason for the slight delay in beginning the new North Atlantic service. Edward Harland had had a revolutionary new idea about ship design. Instead of building a hull, putting on the top deck and then building passenger accommodation on that deck he proposed that the hull sides should continue up to form the sides of the passenger accommodation, thus avoiding the necessity for deckhouses. The new steamers for Oceanic Steam Navigation would be built on this principle and would represent the shape of things to come.

In the meantime the rash of charterings continued. The *Ardgowan* and *Jason* were hired for trips to the antipodes in September. The *Cornwallis* sailed for Sydney in November, along with the *Malleny* and the *Harvest Home*. On 26 November 1870 the second of T. H. Ismay's new steamships was launched. Built to White Star orders, the new *Atlantic* was sister ship to the *Oceanic* and had all of the same refinements in her layout, fittings and passenger accommodation. Still Ismay waited, and still the partners chartered ships for the antipodean trade. The *British Peer* and *British Sovereign* were both chartered by the White Star Line for voyages to Australia in December 1870.

While still awaiting delivery of the first of his new line of large steamers Ismay drafted the rules and regulations for them:

'WHITE STAR LINE-OCEANIC STEAM NAVIGATION COMPANY, LTD.

REGULATIONS for the Safe and Efficient Navigation of the Company's Steamships.

GENERAL RULES.

1. *Instructions to be attended to*. The Company's commanders and officers are particularly enjoined to make themselves not only acquainted, but familiar with the following rules and regulations.

2. *Responsibility of Commanders*. The commanders must distinctly understand that the issue of the following instructions does not in any way, relieve them from entire responsibility for the safe and efficient navigation of their respective vessels; and they are also enjoined to remember that, whilst they are expected to use every diligence to secure a speedy voyage, they must run no risk which might by any possibility result in accident to their ships. It is to be hoped that they will ever bear in mind that the safety of lives and property entrusted to their care is the ruling principle that should govern them in the navigation of their ships and no supposed gain in expedition, or saving of time on the voyage, is to be purchased at the risk of accident. The Company desires to establish and maintain for its vessels a reputation for safety, and only looks for such speed on various voyages as is consistent with safe and prudent navigation.

3. *Authority of Commanders*. The officers, engineers, and all others borne upon the ship's books, are subject to the control and orders of the commander, and all on board, of every rank, must be careful to respect his authority. Leave of absence in all cases, is only to be granted by the commander or commanding officer for the time being, and the return to duty must be reported in a like manner it being understood that in no case, when the ship is in a foreign port, are the chief and second officers to be absent from the ship at the same time, and that a junior officer is always to be on board.

4. *Respect due to officers*. Every superior officer is to exact, upon all occasions, from those under him, unequivocal and respectful compliance with his orders, and it is expected of all that they will not neglect the usual exterior mark of respect, either when they address or are addressed by a superior officer.

5. *Watches*. The watches must be equally divided, and the ship is never to be left without an officer in charge of the deck, either at sea or in harbour; and no officer is, on any occasion, to leave the deck during his watch, nor until he is relieved of his duty; and officers are expected, when performing the duties of the ship, or when at their different stations, to preserve silence among the men, and to see that orders from the bridge or upper deck are executed with promptitude, and without confusion or noise. At sea, when the officer of the watch believes his ship to be running into danger, it is his duty to act, at once, upon his own responsibility: at the same time, he must pass the word to call the commander. The first and second officers should never give up charge of the bridge during

their watch excepting in clear weather and open sea, while they may be relieved for their meals by the third and fourth officers, but at no other time, unless with the express permission of the commander.

6. *Watch in dock, Liverpool.* In dock, at Liverpool, an officer is always to be on deck with the quartermaster as a day watch, until relieved by the night officer, one quartermaster and one watchman.

7. *Watch in dock, abroad.* In port abroad, an officer of the ship is always to be on the upper or spar deck, in charge, together with the two quartermasters in the day-time. At night the watch is to be kept by an officer and two quartermasters.

8. *Anchor watch.* In harbour, when the ship is at anchor, the watch, night and day, is to consist of a junior officer, two quartermasters and four seamen.

9. *Junior officers.* The junior officers must exert themselves to afford every assistance in the navigation of the ship, by perfecting themselves in the practice of solar and stellar observations, both for the correction of the compasses and ascertaining the position of the ship.

10. *Junior officers.* In ships carrying third and fourth officers, those officers are not to have charge of a watch at sea except at the discretion of the commander.

11. *Log and observations for position of ship.* The log to be regularly hove, and the ship's position to be ascertained each day by solar observation when obtainable. The chief officer is required to work out the ship's position as soon after noon as practicable, and then to take it to the commander in the chart-room, where he will see the place of the ship pricked on the chart, so as always to keep himself posted as to steamer's position and course.

12. *Compasses.* The compasses should be carefully watched, and any difference that may be observed between local deviation and that shown by the table of corrections to be noted in the compass-book kept for the purpose.

13. *Night order book.* The commander to enter in the night order book the course to be steered, and all other necessary instructions.

14. *Nearing the land and heaving the lead.* A wide berth to be given to all headlands, islands, shoals, and the coast generally; and the commanders are particularly enjoined, on all occasions when nearing the land or in places of intricate navigation, to take frequent cross-bearings of any well-marked objects that may be visible and suitable for verifying the position of the ship. Should the weather be unsuitable for cross-bearings the engines should be eased, and, if necessary, stopped occasionally, and casts of the deep sea lead taken. The steam-whistle to be sounded during the prevalence of fogs, and the fact recorded in the log book.

15. *Boats, fire-hose, pumps, etc.* A crew to be appointed to each boat, which, with the tackling, is required to be kept in good order and ready for immediate service. The ship's company to be exercised at their stations occasionally, in working the pumps, fire-hose, and handing along buckets, etc., so that the crew may be kept in proper training and the stores in efficient order, in case of fire or other accident.

16. *Lights.* The side and mast-head lights to be particularly attended to and always ready, and when in use to be placed according to Government regulations. All lights, except such as the captain or executive officer shall suffer (or the law requires), are to be put out every

evening at 10 o'clock in forecastle and steerage, at 11 o'clock in the saloon, at 11.15 p.m. in the smoke rooms, and at 11.30 o'clock in the sleeping berths or state rooms.

17. *Fires*. No fire to be allowed in the galleys after 10 o'clock p.m., unless with the express permission of the commander.

18. *Sounding the wells, etc.* The holds and fresh water tanks to be sounded twice a day by the carpenter, who is also required to turn the cocks in the water-tight bulkheads every 24 hours; pump gear to be examined, and everything kept in order for immediate use. A sounding book must be kept by the carpenter, and each examination recorded. The chief officer to inspect the book daily and initial it.

19. *Inspection of ship by commander*. The commander is expected to make a thorough inspection of the ship, at least once in every 24 hours, accompanied by the purser and surgeon. 11 a.m. would probably be found the most convenient hour for this duty. In the engine room inspection, the commander should be attended by the chief engineer only.

20. *Spirit-room*. The spirit-room is, under no circumstances, to be opened except during the day, and then only in the presence of the purser. No light is to be taken into the spirit-room on any pretext whatever. The key of the spirit-room to be kept by the purser.

21. *Smoking*. Smoking by the officers when on duty is strictly prohibited, and is allowed only in their own cabins or on the main deck, but on no account in any of the companion ways. Smoking by seamen, firemen, stewards, and others, allowed only on the main deck, forward of the main mast, when off duty.

22. *Parcels, etc., not to be carried by ship's company*. No parcels or goods of any description are to be carried by the ship's company for any person whatsoever.

23. *Smuggling*. The ship is to be searched for contraband goods before entering any port, and the result entered in the official log book. The chief of each department to conduct the search, accompanied by the purser. Any person detected in smuggling will be dismissed the service, any fines incurred being deducted from the wages due to the offender; and the heads of the different departments will be held responsible for those people immediately under their orders.

24. *Signal lights*. Rockets and blue or green lights, especially company's private signals, to be always kept at hand, ready for night signals, but on no account to be stowed in the powder magazine.

25. *Flags*. In port, from 21st day of March to 21st day of September, the ensign and company's signal to be hoisted at 8.30 a.m., and from 22nd day of September to 20th day of March, at 9 a.m., and hauled down at sunset. In stormy weather, small flags must be substituted.

26. *Punishment*. No man to be confined or punished in any way, when the commander is on board, without his order, and the punishment must be registered in the official log book. In the absence of the captain, the offender is to be confined, if it be necessary, but at no time in port, without acquainting the peace authorities of the port; if at a wharf, or in dock, the police are to be called promptly.

27. *Uniform*. The uniform prescribed by the company is to be worn on board, at all times, by the officers (the engineer on watch excepted). The crew (consisting of the seamen, firemen, and stewards), excepting firemen on duty, must always wear it on Sundays, at sea

or in port; also on the days of sailing from or arriving in port, each one of the crew being compelled to provide himself with a uniform.

28. *Divine Service*. Divine Service is to be performed on board every Sunday, weather permitting.

29. *Report on officers*. The commanders are required to give a faithful and conscientious report of the conduct, qualifications and sobriety of officers, engineers, and petty officers, individually at the end of each voyage.

30. *Rules of the road*. The commanders and officers of the several ships are strictly enjoined to make themselves perfectly familiar with the rules of the road, as issued by the Board of Trade, a copy being attached hereto for general reference.

31. *Change of commanders*. When any change of commander takes place, the officer relieved must hand to his successor this Book of Instructions, the copy of mail contract (if any), and all other ship's papers, especially those relating to the compasses and chronometers.

32. *Log-Book*. The log-book is to be kept by the chief officer, who is required to write it up daily from the log-slate, and submit it for the commander's inspection and signature.

33. *Log-slate; directions for keeping it*. The log-slate to be carefully written up, by the officer in charge of the deck, every watch, at sea or in port, and the particulars noted below punctually attended to:

(i) Courses (in degrees) by standard compass.

(ii) Courses (in degrees) true.

(iii) Speed of ship by log.

(iv) Direction and force of wind.

(v) Barometer and thermometer.

(vi) Revolutions of engines.

(vii) Number of inches of water in the wells

(viii) Remarks upon the weather, and other particulars; such as, what sail set and when taken in, if any and what signals are made, vessels met or spoken, especially those belonging to the company.

(ix) The true bearings and distance of any land or lights in sight, particularly cross-bearings.

(x) When and what soundings are obtained.

(xi) Lunar or stellar observations, azimuths, or amplitudes.

(xii) Time of arrival and departure from any place, with the ship's draught of water.

(xiii) Time when passengers (and mails, if any) are landed and embarked.

(xiv) Any births or deaths that may occur on board, and in the latter case time of burial.

(xv) When and for what purpose boats leave the ship and return.

(xvi) When the anchor is let go at any port or place, the depth of water, the number of fathoms of cable veered to, and cross bearings taken to determine the exact position of the ship.

(xvii) How the hands of watches are employed during the day.

(xviii) The exact quantity of coal and water received at the respective ports, and the expenditure each day.

(xix) Any case of collision or touching the ground, or other accident, to be carefully noted, giving the name of the officer of the watch, and the names and stations of the men on the look out.

(xx) Any case of misconduct among the crew (required by the Merchant Seamen's Act), particularly in reference to forfeiture of wages.

(xxi) When the ship's company are exercised at their stations.

(xxii) When Divine Service is performed, or why omitted.

(xxiii) The names of all persons on the sick list to be entered each day at noon.

(xxiv) The ship's reckoning, up to noon each day, both by observation and account, complete.

34. *Log-book*. The log, when completed by the chief officer, is to have its correctness certified by the officer of each watch, and to be placed before the commander daily for his inspection and signature.

35. *Log-book*. A leaf must never be removed or closed up in the log-book, nor an erasure made under any circumstances, but all errors are to be cancelled by ruling a line through them, with the initials attached.

36. *Log-book*. At the end of the voyage the log-book must be signed by the commander and chief officer, and then delivered over to the managers of the company.

37. *Engineer's log-book to be examined by the commander*. The commander is required each day to examine and sign the engineer's log-book, and shall be responsible for any omission that may occur in the same. The commander is likewise enjoined to pay special attention to the daily consumption and remaining stock of coal.

38. *Tracks*. It is not desirable to specify in these instructions any particular route to take between Liverpool and New York, as commanders must, in a great measure, be left to their own judgment in the matter, and be guided by circumstances; but the following may be taken as a guide, as emanating from officers of great experience in the Atlantic trade:

"We consider the best and safest track to take in crossing the Banks of Newfoundland, say, from the middle of March to the middle of December, is to strike the Flemish Cap, and then shape a course to take the ship about 35 miles south of Virgin Rocks. The remaining three months we think it prudent to take the southern passage, as the field-ice is then forming on the edge of the banks."

Note: During the month of November and half of December, the passage via Cape Race may be taken with safety, there being little fog there at the time.

Sable Island. This island should always be passed to the westward, as strong currents, fogs, and great local attraction are known to exist in the channel, between the island and the main, rendering the navigation extremely hazardous.

Skerries. The commanders are required invariably to pass to the northward, or outside this group of rocks, the channel inside being considered too narrow and dangerous to admit of large steamers being navigated through in perfect safety.

Course down channel. In leaving Liverpool, after passing the Skerries, it is usual in all steamship lines to steer for the Stack; with the Stack abeam and close aboard, shape a course for the Saltees Lightship; this will take a steamer about four miles south of the fair way of steam-ships, and ships, with a fair wind, bound to Liverpool.

39. *Special reports*. Commanders are required to furnish the managers with a special report, in writing, of any unusual occurrence which may have taken place on board, or in connection with their ships – such as accidents to life or limb, misconduct or mismanagement on the part of, or any serious complaint against, any of the company's servants, or anything requiring an entry in the official log of the vessel.

40. This book is to be returned to the company's office in the event of the holder leaving the service.'

On taking command of a White Star ship the captain also received a copy of a letter clearly saying that no risks to the ship or persons were to be taken under any conditions. Speed of passage was to be sacrificed rather than the slightest risk taken with the ship. Record breaking runs were not to be attempted at any time. The owners were well aware of the prestige that attached to a fast Atlantic crossing, and of a captain's natural tendency to show off the capabilities of his vessel, but they emphatically forbade any course of action which involved the slightest risk. The master should be on deck in anything less than perfect conditions, and when his vessel was within 60 miles of land, when the sounding lead should be used constantly. The same use of the lead was recommended whenever a vessel was approaching a headland or shallows, but these should be avoided wherever possible.

Rigid discipline was to be observed at all times, and unnecessary fraternisation between the ship's officers and passengers avoided as far as possible. The lookout should be watched, and required to report in a loud voice after each bell was sounded, simply to make sure that they were awake. Needless to say, drinking by the captain or his officers was strictly frowned upon.

The instructions continued with the advice that coals, stores and provisions and all other of the ship's equipment should be checked on a daily basis, preferably at the same time each day. As the captain was only one man, this daily checking would have to be carried out by the ship's officers. His report to the owners on the efficiency of those officers would determine their prospects of promotion within the company.

While they waited for the arrival of the new *Oceanic[1]* the partners still had their Australian trade to consider and continued chartering ships. In January 1871 they chartered the *Otago*, which sailed for Otago and Wellington, and the *British Princess*, which sailed for Melbourne. The *Khandeish*, another chartered vessel, sailed for Australia in February.

On 27 August 1870 the first of T. H. Ismay's new steamships was launched at Harland & Wolff's Belfast yard. As the first ship to belong to the new Oceanic Steam Navigation Company she was given the company name *Oceanic[1]*. The revolutionary new ship was the first vessel in the world to provide modern, comfortable cabins for her passengers when she finally entered service.

Oceanic[1] made her way into the Mersey in February 1871, and began preparing for her maiden voyage, scheduled to begin on 2 March. The first of her class, she was soon to be followed by another three ships, the *Atlantic, Baltic[1]* and *Republic[1]*, then another two ships constructed along very similar lines but slightly larger would join the company in the shape of the *Adriatic[1]* and *Celtic[1]*.

As mentioned earlier, the new ships would not have individual deckhouses, as every passenger vessel before then had, but all the deckhouses would be joined together and extended out to the sides of the hull. What would have been open decks adjoining passenger accommodation on earlier ships were roofed over with relatively lightweight iron sheeting, forming what is now known as a promenade deck. Instead of the traditional solid bulwark with scuppers there were open railings, so that any wave that should break over the decks could run off easily. All in all, this new class of vessel would be the first to have a superstructure that would instantly identify it to a modern eye as an ocean liner.

Early in 1871 a stroke of ill fortune befell Thomas Henry Ismay and his family: his 11-year-old eldest daughter succumbed to scarlet fever. At the time she was staying with her grandfather, Luke Bruce, at 126 Faulkner Street, Liverpool. From the fact that Ismay clan members seem to have died anywhere but in the family home it is reasonable to assume that as relations they were not all that close. It is also a curious fact that whenever anything good happened to the White Star Line, like taking delivery of the first of the new liners, something unpleasant also occurred to offset it.

The public had grown used to the idea that White Star operated sailing ships on the Liverpool–Australia run, which indeed had been the case under previous management, and had even been the case under the present owners. Their whole concept of the White Star Line must have been altered by the advertisements that appeared to introduce the new ships.

The new liners would depart Liverpool on Thursdays, stop off at Queenstown on Fridays, and then carry on to New York. The first such sailing was to be that of the new 4,500-ton *Oceanic*, on Thursday 2 March 1871. Saloon, or first-class, tickets for a one way passage cost 18 guineas (£18.90) or 16 guineas (£16.80) while return tickets could be purchased for 27 guineas (£28.35).

At 420ft long and 40ft in beam the *Oceanic* demonstrated another design feature that remains with ocean liners to the present day: the ship was about 10 times as long as she was wide. This long slim hull arrangement meant that a ship could attain a relatively high speed at minimal cost in fuel. Powered by two four-cylinder compound steam engines by Maudsley, Sons and Field of London, developing 1,990hp, the 3,707-ton vessel could maintain a speed of 14kt on her single propeller by consuming about 65 tons of coal per day. Steam was fed to the engines from 12 boilers, each with two furnaces, at 65lb/sq in. The engines were of the double expansion type, having two 41in diameter high pressure cylinders and two 78in low pressure ones, and a stroke of 5ft.

In the days of sail, the best passenger accommodation had always been considered to be at the stern of a ship. With the new *Oceanic* all that was to change; from now onwards the best cabins were situated amidships where the pitch and roll of the vessel was least noticeable, and those cabins were far larger than those aboard any previous vessel. In the nature of a bonus, the newly developed steam engines were placed towards the stern of a ship, so the vibration from those engines would be far less of an irritation; unless of course you were a third-class passenger whose accommodation was also in the rear part of the ship.

The new ships also made use of another novelty, electricity. Push buttons in first-class cabins would summon a steward or stewardess, without the need for cabin passengers to send a servant or valet to find them, or worse still, have to seek out a member of the ship's domestic crew themselves. The first-class dining room was another innovation. At 40ft by 80ft the dining saloon could seat all of the possible 166 first-class passengers at a single sitting, and each of them in an individual chair instead of the long benches to be found in other ships. There was even a smoking room where first-class male passengers could enjoy their after-dinner cigars without the necessity as hitherto of going on deck and facing the elements.

Instead of the usual jug of water and bowl provided for washing, the *Oceanic* had running water to many of her cabins. The cabins themselves were lighter and airier than on vessels belonging to other lines because White Star, and Harland & Wolff, had fitted the new ship with portholes that were twice the usual size (an innovation that was to demonstrate its drawbacks, rather forcibly, in 1873 on the *Atlantic*).

Oceanic also had accommodation for 1,000 steerage (third-class) passengers. Not for them the opulence of first class, instead they were crammed into the bow and stern of the ship. Single male steerage passengers were berthed forward while married couples, families and unmarried females were accommodated in the after part of the vessel, strict segregation of unmarried male and female passengers being the order of the day. It was not only the unmarried male and female third-class passengers who were to be kept well away from one another; steel bulkheads separated first-class areas of the ship from those occupied by the less wealthy.

On 2 March 1871 the *Oceanic* sailed from Liverpool on her maiden voyage. There was a considerable amount of competition for transatlantic passengers and lines like Cunard, Inman, and Guion were well established. The revolutionary appearance of the *Oceanic* probably did little to reassure or attract people, so when she slipped out of Liverpool there was a scant 64 passengers aboard and 1,102 empty berths. As if that beginning was not inauspicious enough, the White Star's maiden voyage curse made itself felt. Soon after the vessel left harbour, crankshaft bearings began to overheat and she was forced to put in to Holyhead on the Welsh coast before returning to Liverpool for permanent repair.

The advent of the new large steamers in 1871 brought an old problem to a head. Liverpool had long been a very busy port, with many ships jockeying for berths. Because of their intention to run a regular weekly service, Ismay and Imrie believed that it was high time that the Docks and Quays Committee set aside pier space for them. After some discussion the committee initially offered White Star space on the south side of the Morpeth Dock, but Ismay wanted something better. Eighteen months after the committee's initial offer Ismay got his way in the form of a permanent berth for White Star steamers in the West Waterloo Dock, of some 2,772sq yd.

Having failed to move with the times, White Star's long time rival and most consistent competitor, James Baines' Black Ball Line, was forced to close down in early April 1871. However, despite its many trials and tribulations, the Black Ball Line had outlasted the first incarnation of its more famous rivals.

The Australian route was still Ismay Imrie's mainstay, and the *Aminta* sailed from Liverpool for Melbourne on 20 May 1871. Unusually for a vessel on the Australian route the *Aminta* was owned by Thomas Ismay.

Atlantic was the second of the four vessels ordered from Harland & Wolff soon after T. H. Ismay bought the White Star flag. She was taken over by the line, from the builders, on 3 June 1871. *Atlantic* sailed from Liverpool on her maiden voyage a mere three days later. She was an immediate success. The third of the new liners was not slow in arriving from the builders, and she sailed on her maiden voyage in September 1871. Originally planned as the *Pacific*, *Baltic's* name was changed when it was recalled that a Collins Line vessel named *Pacific* disappeared in 1856.

Even though the line's involvement in the North Atlantic passenger trade seemed to be going extremely well, the company was not without its problems. For instance, the *Sam Cearns*, was lost on Tierra del Fuego or the Falkland Islands on 26 June 1871. Ever since the days of Nelson, Ismay & Co, T. H. Ismay had indeed been running sailing ships to

South America. With the advent of the new steamships he was now wondering if it might not be time to begin a changeover to steam on that route as well. With that in mind he dispatched an agent, Henry Griffin, to South America to find out if there was an opening for steamships trading with countries there. Griffin was back within the year to report that there was indeed. As a result of Griffin's favourable report Ismay Imrie bought two steamships from J. M. Wood for use in the South Atlantic trade: the 2,652-ton *Asiatic* and the 2,650-ton *Tropic[1]*.

As well designed as the new liners might be, they were, for all that, a new breed of ship. Masters and crews would take time to learn how to use them, and in that time anything could happen. The *Baltic* collided with the French brig *Confiance* which was at anchor close to Sandy Hook at the entrance to New York harbour on 7 October 1871. The French vessel's foremast was broken off and a lifeboat was smashed in the collision as well as some structural damage to her hull. Water poured into the *Confiance* and she had to be towed into harbour for repairs (in the Atlantic Dock).

The inexperience of captains and crews of the new large steamers soon made itself felt again. As *Atlantic* was making her way up the River Mersey, on her return from New York under the command of Captain Digby Murray on 23 November 1871, she collided with the *Alexandria*. The *Alexandria* was also returning to port, from the very city she had been named after. Both vessels suffered some slight damage but were able to continue to their respective berths and tie up without further incident. No matter how fast seamen learned the eccentricities of the new ships, they would, for many years to come, always be at least one step behind. From this point in time steamships would grow in size and complexity at an incredible rate.

Atlantic's next voyage was a little fraught as well. She left the Mersey on 30 November 1871 bound for New York via Queenstown. Half an hour after she departed, the Inman liner *City of Paris* also left Liverpool. For whatever reason the *Atlantic* had been instructed to keep the speed down as far as the Irish port and not to use her sails, with the result that at about 5pm she was overhauled by the *City of Paris*. No sooner had the Inman vessel overtaken the White Star vessel than she suddenly turned to port, cutting across the bows of the White Star ship, a mere 50yd to 60yd away. As both ships were travelling at somewhere between 10kt and 12kt this was much too close for comfort, and the *City of Paris* was almost run down. Luckily the two ships managed to miss one another but it does serve to illustrate the childish sense of one-upmanship and disregard for danger that existed between captains, even if it was frowned upon by the owners.

This concern felt by owners is illustrated in an excerpt from a letter from T. H. Ismay to Inmans dated 8 December 1871, 'We have enjoined the masters and officers under our charge, to act on all occasions even in excess of mere prudence to avoid the possibility of danger.' As we shall see, captains not only disregarded this enjoinder but seem to have regarded it as a personal insult to their abilities. To be fair, there does not appear to be any record of a skipper being reprimanded for making a particularly fast passage, provided that nothing untoward occurred during it. In fact, scheduled departure and arrival times left a captain with little option but to proceed at full speed regardless of conditions.

While on her way from Liverpool to New York on Boxing Day 1871, *Oceanic* ran into a tremendous storm. Labouring through the heavy seas she lost three of her four propeller blades and had to stop her engine. Without steerage way the vessel was at the mercy of the sea so an attempt was made to set sail, but the wind was so strong that as fast as the sails were set it tore them to shreds. Eventually the weather moderated and *Oceanic* was able to limp upon her way toward New York but the excitement of the voyage was far from over.

On 8 January 1872, while still creeping towards America and safety, a brig was sighted. The *Mountain Eagle* was clearly in serious trouble, with her decks under water and the seas washing over her. To emphasise her predicament the American vessel was flying her national flag upside down, a universal signal of distress. *Oceanic* lowered a lifeboat and took the crew of the *Mountain Eagle* off the sinking brig, where they had been up to their waists in water and without food or sleep for 24 hours. The fortunate American seamen were safely landed in their home country when the somewhat overdue *Oceanic* finally arrived at her destination.

Chapter 7

1872-1879

With the coming of the new liners, Ismay Imrie felt able to dispose of one or two of its older sailing vessels. The 12-year-old *Castlehow* was one of the first to go, and *Arriero* was another; the *Delmira* and *Pampero* soon followed.

Republic¹, the third of Ismay's new breed, sailed on her maiden voyage early in 1872. On the bridge was the now familiar figure of Captain Digby Murray, who had taken each of the new class on its first run across the Atlantic and who was not wholly convinced by either the design or quality of construction of the new ships; nor was he delighted with his crew. He made his dissatisfaction evident in his report to the company on the *Republic's* maiden voyage:

'REPORT OF CAPTAIN OF STEAMSHIP *REPUBLIC*

Steamship *Republic* at sea,

February 3rd, 1872.

Gentlemen,

Since leaving Liverpool we have had nothing but bad weather. In my letter to you from Queenstown, I told you of the detention from leakage in upper between-decks, forward of saloon; I am sorry to say it still continues, and we have many other difficulties to contend with; the saloon and state-rooms have been flooded through the new ventilation; the windows of wheel-house have been dashed in by a sea, and compass unshipped and broken, thermometers broken, etc.; the stanchions of the bridge and bridge compass carried away, gangway abreast of saloon unshipped and carried aft, chocks of two boats washed away, and keel of No. 4 boat started; wooden cover of forward ventilator washed overboard, a great deal of water washing down companion-way into women's quarters aft; said hatch companion is a nuisance, and if the ship is to continue to use it a proper cover should be furnished, though that will never make it tight. Work has so multiplied on our hands since leaving, that we have not been able to do all that is even absolutely necessary. We had great difficulty in getting our yards down, lift blocks being too small in the mortise; we had to give up the attempt the first night. Main-hatch tarpaulins are too small; and I think the officers had better join the next ship a little sooner, so as to attend to their own details of work; the officers and men are getting worn out; Mr. Steele and the boatswain are both laid up. I think the ship is too deep for the time of year. I should much like to see a fixed rule as to the loading draught of the ships from either November or December to April, and from that month for the rest of the year; loading, also, to the last minute in the river, and then survey, stops the officers and crew from getting the ship into proper sea-going order. [Captain Murray would have his wish granted a year later when Samuel

Plimsoll's system of marking safe load-lines on ships became law.] I have not been able to swing my quarter-boats in yet, and we have had all hands on deck the best portion of the time since we left. Mr. Williams hardly leaves the deck, and I was compelled to order him below this morning, fearing I should have him knocked up. Mr. Whittle had a very narrow escape this morning while securing the forward ventilator; I thought at one time he was gone. The ship dips her stern in pretty frequently and very heavily; at the same time has so much weight in her fore end that it gives her no chance to rise, and, though I have the will, I am quite unable to drive her. Boats chocks had better be a hollow iron frame, so as to show but little resistance to sea. Seamen's forecastle should be thoroughly cemented off from cargo, as it is simply impossible to keep scuppers in water-ways from choking. I have represented this every voyage.

'The iron bulkhead forward of saloon has been cut right through to the deck, and then a piece of angle iron bolted to the deck for a door-sill, instead of leaving part of bulkhead to form it; and water consequently runs under it into saloon.

'Passengers complain of difficulty of seating themselves at table; settee should have an extension stool, and be the width of the stool apart.

'The turtle back has completely caved in; the beams from the hatch forward all gone, most of them, in two or three places; the riveting has gone more or less. To give the present turtle backs sufficient strength, I think a pitch pine stringer, about 3 feet wide, should be introduced on each side, fitted to admit the beams and lie close to the deck, and then thoroughly stanchioned, as also a good iron thwart-ship stringer on the plate forward from anchor to anchor. We have cut up all boats and awning spars, and have a complete forest of shores under it. The new ventilators, as before mentioned, are a perfect failure, drowning the passengers out, nor can we make them tight.

'February 7th.

It is still blowing a heavy gale; but, the ship having lightened, there is no longer any difficulty in driving her. Mr Fair and I have carefully gone over the bunker plates together, and we can come to no other conclusion than that 900 tons was the extreme quantity of coal we had, leaving 885 tons, calculating 45 cubic feet to the ton. Mr Fair seems to be a very first-class man. Everything is very satisfactory in the engine room.

'Ventilator covers forward want altering; there should either be a top to screw on or a deep tight fitting plug to drive in. I fear a great deal of water has gone down them. We have had several times to ease to dead slow, and even then men have worked at them at the risk of their lives. I have been fearful of the effect on the bleaching powder, as much water has undoubtedly gone down.

'February 8th.

We encountered a terrific gale in about lat. 47° and long. 42° W., our decks were swept, all boats but two entirely destroyed, one of the two left opened right out, the engine-room skylight smashed and driven down on top of the cylinders; this skylight had never been properly bolted or secured. Mr. Williams the second officer, whose pluck and endurance has been beyond all praise, was securing a sail over fidley (great quantities of water having gone down and put out the lee fires), was caught by No. 4 boat as it was dashed a perfect wreck inboard, one of the davits unshipping and coming with it, and crushed against the railing round the funnel; his left thigh broke a little above the knee; his left ankle was dislocated; we fear some of the ribs broke. We trust the accident may not prove fatal, but time only will tell us; he shows amazing pluck, and is at present doing well; if he does not recover, he will be a very great loss to the company, for men like him are very few and far between. No canvas was set during the gale; it was ordered at one time but the utter worthlessness of the crew, skulking and stowing away, crying like children, made it difficult to do anything; it was as well it was not set, as it would only have blown away. A sea struck the mizzen boom, and broke it clean in two; imagine where a sail would have been! We steamed against the gale about twenty revolutions, making from one-and-a-half to two knots. I tried her slower, but could not keep her up to the sea; having previously burnt 400 tons of coal, the ship herself behaved well, shipped no heavy water forward, and consequently did not increase damage to turtle back; the rails on promenade deck have been mostly swept away, telegraphs broken and thrown down, top of standard binnacle washed overboard, forward gangway ditto, large ventilator, three davits, ditto, doors and windows, shutters and all, smashed in bodily.

'The ships, with their present doors, are not seaworthy, and if they are not altered we shall yet lose a ship by them; had we been running instead of hove to, I doubt if we could have prevented the fires from being put out. Our carpenters are precious little account in bad weather, and a very slow lot at any time; our crew often a lot of curs; to have got a sail up, or cut away for use, I should have had to ask assistance from the passengers; to have got one from below, would have been impossible. I feel rather discouraged in again applying for stronger doors; and if I have expressed myself strongly, I feel very strongly on the subject; there ought also to be proper protection to fidley, gratings, iron shutters, and I think also a proper cover to engine-room skylight, with three ring-bolts on each side of deck to pass overhaul lashings to. I fear Mr. Harland will say this is an exceptional gale; these ships, during their career, will run long enough, I hope, to encounter many exceptional gales.

'I am not satisfied with the manner in which boats are secured, but will go into it with Captain Spear and yourselves on my return; they are now over-secured; a sea strikes them, and they are torn asunder; the only boat we have saved was insecurely lashed, and that, strange to say, proved her salvation; there was something to give. I shall enclose a catalogue of damage on arrival, so will not say any more about it at present. We were unable to cook for two days, indeed not properly for two-and-a-half. No communication with the icehouse, and for a considerable time with the storeroom; the after door being broken in, water came down the hatches in large quantities, and we could not get to them; the quadrant was half the time entirely under water, the ship dipping occasionally to the wheel-house. It is useless my saying more till my return. I should like, however, to see all windows built up; charts, books, and clothes are wet all the time; windows are not fit for the trade. Pray condemn bad weather ventilators; passengers will stand a little closeness, but not wet; and it has fairly ruined carpets, paint, cushions, etc., etc. Smoking room ventilators are worse still. The crew (excepting only the seamen), officers, engineers, and stewards, firemen and coal trimmers, have behaved splendidly. When the lee fires were put out, the watch below turned out without being ordered, kept below, and worked like men. We have much to be thankful for in the performance of both the engines and the men.

'I had one seaman (so-called) rope's-ended for stowing away in the coal bunkers for the fourth time; it had become really a serious question; we could only get four men of the starboard watch the other night; I therefore consulted with the officers and chief engineer, and we have decided that the safety of the ship requires decisive measures, and that after this we will strip and flog every man stowing away while on watch; the crew were mustered and notified, and an entry made to that effect in the official log. We are making some water in No. 5 hold; I do not think it can be serious, but I shall carefully watch it. I think it would be a great advantage if three-cornered, i.e. jib-headed trysails, of storm canvas, were fitted to the mizzen and jigger-masts of these ships during the winter; there would then be but little difficulty in getting after canvas on the ship, which enable engines to be slowed more than on this occasion. I have found practicable the cut-away forefoot, allowing the bow to be easily knocked to the leeward by a sea.

'The *Atlantic* is so soon after us, that I question if it would not be better for this ship to return without passengers; but I shall consult Mr. Sparks, and the result you will hear by him long before you receive this.

'Anchored off the bar at 3 p.m. this day, Wednesday 14th.

'Some of the coal on board, Mr. Fair complains bitterly of; full of sand and dirt; the passengers appear to be satisfied with the voyage; and though I do not generally lay much stress on their letters, owing to the very exceptional weather, I have requested the Purser to forward a copy to the office.

'I know of nothing further to add at present; we shall not arrive at quarantine till midnight, and cannot dock till 1 p.m. on Thursday.

I remain, etc.

(Signed)

Digby Murray.'

The first letter was almost immediately followed by another.

'Messrs. Ismay, Imrie & Co.

New York, Wednesday, February 14th, 1872.

I have omitted, I see, urging the necessity of a communication with engine-room; perfectly independent of telegraph, there should be bells or gongs from forward wheel-house; during a great portion of the gale, we had no communication with the engine-room, and when, through the wind moderating more rapidly than the sea, it became necessary to still further moderate the speed of the engines, the only way we could communicate was by shouting down the fidley to tell firemen. It made Mr. Fair, too, very uneasy, as he could not tell what was happening on deck, or at what speed he was required to drive; indeed he expressed an unhappy uncertainty as to whether we might not all have been overboard.

'I regret to have to add, that while docking the *Republic*, although nearly half-an-hour after high water, the ship's bow, when close to the pier, was caught by a strong eddy from the south, i.e. flood; she was instantly reversed full speed, but struck the wooden piles at the end of the pier; the ship had very little way on at the time, and the pier suffered hardly any damage, but owing to the severity of the frost the iron had become so brittle that two bow plates have gone in the wake of the rivets. I cannot blame myself, as I do not think the accident was attributable to any lack of judgement on my own part; but as Mr. Sparks was fortunately on board at the time I trust he will frankly give you his impression as to the accident.'

Another of the *Oceanic* Class ships, so highly thought of by the commodore of the line, the *Adriatic*, was launched on 17 October 1871. Although more spacious than *Oceanic*, *Adriatic* only had a capacity of 1,150 passengers, 1,000 of them in steerage.

Despite being fitted with electric bells to summon stewards the vessel was originally lit by gas, which was produced aboard from non-explosive oil, but the system gave so much trouble, explosive gas leaking anywhere and everywhere, that it was abandoned and more traditional lighting adopted. In common with her sisters, she too had running water to her first-class cabins (much of it coming from the ventilators it would appear, if she performed like her sister). She sailed on her maiden voyage on 11 March 1872. The ship set a new east to west Atlantic record at 14.52kt in June 1872.

White Star's New York agent, Mr Sparks, had received a number of complaints from steerage passengers about conditions aboard the ships. He wrote to Ismay who hit on the idea of sending out a mystery passenger, an agent of Ismay's who was unknown to the officers and crew of the vessel in question. On 25 September 1872 Ismay sent a letter to Sparks on the subject of complaints by steerage passengers. In the letter he agreed that, even though they had already done much towards the comfort of steerage passengers, there was still room for improvement, 'without incurring additional expense'. In order to obtain reliable information regarding the comfort of third-class accommodation under actual seagoing conditions Ismay had decided to send Captain Hinds, who was unknown to the crews of the new steamers, across the Atlantic, posing as a steerage passenger. From Hinds' unbiased report Ismay hoped to be able to ascertain what improvements were advisable. In order to be sure that the identity of the mystery passenger should remain a secret from the crew of the vessel he sailed on, even the office staff in Liverpool were kept in ignorance of the trip. Hinds had not visited New York before so Ismay instructed Sparks to advance him a little money, up to £20, advise him on the best place to stay, and arrange his passage back to England.

Captain Hinds duly made his report on conditions in steerage, which led to Ismay Imrie changing the layout of third-class accommodation on its ships. Until that time third-class passengers aboard steamers had traditionally been accommodated aft, where they had to put up with noise and vibration caused by the engines and propellers; under Ismay's direction the line began moving steerage quarters forward and up, away from the machinery. Married couples began to be provided with their own accommodation, instead of sharing dormitories for 20 to 30 people. White Star also abolished the practice of third-class passengers providing their own beds, bedding and eating utensils. Of course, the improved conditions brought more passengers to the line, forcing the other lines to follow suit in order to hold on to their share of the market.

The new steamers, with their single-screw propulsion, were taking much longer for officers and crews to learn how to handle than might reasonably have been expected. Supposedly as a result of this inexperience, *Atlantic* collided with the *Wisconsin* while in the Crosby Channel on the River Mersey, on 15 October 1872. The *Wisconsin*, luckily, was only slightly damaged in the incident.

Inexperience could not be blamed on 18 October when the newly completed *Celtic¹*, having just been handed over to her new owners by Harland & Wolff, ran aground as she was steaming down Belfast Lough. In these familiar waters carelessness or incompetence were more likely causes. Despite the best efforts of the crew, the vessel obstinately remained where she was until the next tide, when she floated off and continued on her way to Liverpool.

The *Celtic* made her maiden voyage for the White Star Line a little later in October. She was an almost exact duplicate of her sister ship *Adriatic*. This practice of building more than one vessel from what were effectively the same set of plans was a very effective means of cutting construction cost, as one design covered a number of ships. It also meant that certain of the line's vessels were practically indistinguishable one from another, a happenstance that would come in quite useful in the future.

In December 1872, during a westbound Atlantic crossing. *Adriatic* ran into a particularly severe storm. Labouring through tremendous seas, she broke two of the four blades off her single 22½ft propeller. As Captain Hamilton Perry nursed his crippled vessel towards New York he came across the sailing ship *Allan*, which had been severely damaged by the storm and was sinking. Despite her somewhat reduced performance *Adriatic* managed to save 20 crew members from the sailing vessel before proceeding on her way. She arrived after a 15-day crossing at Sandy Hook on 22 December with her 47 first-class and 141 steerage passengers safe, along with the 20 seamen taken from the *Allan*.

As will perhaps have been noticed, while Harland & Wolff might have built the best ships in the world, the yard had yet to master the art of building serviceable propellers. In the two months up to Christmas 1872 no less than seven propeller blades had been broken on White Star ships, the *Oceanic, Atlantic* and *Baltic*. The almost continual disablement of its vessels was causing a little concern. Ismay Imrie wrote to Harland & Wolff asking for suggestions as to how the defect could be best rectified.

The letter was at some pains to point out that the continual breakages were not only costing White Star a great deal of money but were also beginning adversely to affect the prestige of the line. They also requested answers to four basic questions and, if possible, suggestions as to how the problem could be avoided in the future. Were the propeller breakages caused by faulty construction, or were they the result of the screws striking something such as timber or wreckage? Could the builders justify the continued use of cast steel for the propeller blades instead of cast iron? (Steel at the time was of uncertain quality while cast iron was a tried and tested material.) Were blades bolted to the propeller boss as strong as if the whole assembly had been cast in one piece? Might it not be a better idea, despite the very much higher initial cost, to use gunmetal blades as the Royal Navy did, as these did not seem to keep falling to pieces? It seems that Harland & Wolff had no answers to the questions as the breakages continued until the introduction of twin-screw vessels over a decade later.

Perhaps it should be mentioned here that Harland & Wolff's propellers at this time did not always break as soon as they were subjected to any load. During an 1873 west to east Atlantic crossing *Baltic* set a new record by averaging better than 15kt. However, delays caused by propeller problems were not the most serious difficulties that could be faced by people travelling by sea.

On All Fools' Day 1873 the White Star Company, for the second time, became the holders of a dubious record, for the worst shipping disaster in history. In a remarkable parallel with the *Titanic* 41 years later, *Atlantic* was designed to carry up to 1,166 passengers but only carried 10 lifeboats with a total capacity of 600 people – and even this exceeded the then Board of Trade regulations by 50%. In another parallel with *Titanic* the shortage of lifeboat accommodation would make absolutely no difference to the numbers saved or lost in the event of the vessel foundering.

Twelve days before, on Thursday 20 March, *Atlantic* left Liverpool on her 19th and last voyage with about 967 tons of mixed Welsh and Lancashire coal in her bunkers. Under normal conditions the vessel used about 58 tons of coal a day so she had enough aboard for slightly more than 15 days' steaming. On her previous 18 voyages the longest time she had taken for a crossing had been 13 days 10 hours, and her best time was 10 days 3 hours, so there should have been no problems over the quantity of coal aboard. Bestriding the bridge was Captain James Agnew Williams, aged 33.

Atlantic stopped at Queenstown to pick up a few more passengers and then set out to cross the North Atlantic. Aboard the vessel officially were just 32 first-class and 767 steerage passengers, plus 143 crew members. There were also 14 stowaways aboard unofficially, making 956 in all. Of the people aboard there were probably more than 100 and possibly as many as 200 children. We do know that there were 88 children and infants on board when the ship left Liverpool.

As the ship sailed steadily westward at about 12½kt, the weather deteriorated. By Tuesday the 25th a full south-westerly gale was battering the liner, slowing her to about 8kt. By the following day the storm had worsened considerably, the waves demolishing Lifeboat Number 4, damaging Number 10 and smashing a wheelhouse window. Then the steering gear was damaged and the emergency hand gear had to be used until repairs could be made. This slowed the vessel even further until she was making no more than 5kt.

At noon on Monday 31 March, after 11 days at sea *Atlantic* was still 460 miles east of Sandy Hook, the entrance to New York harbour. For some reason, as yet unexplained, the *Atlantic's* stokers are reported to have been a little over-enthusiastic and had allegedly been shovelling 12 more tons of coal a day into the furnaces than was actually required. This over-enthusiasm on the part of the firemen is of course totally unbelievable, and suggests that in reality the vessel had cleared port with less fuel in her bunkers than safety demanded. It was at this point in the voyage that Chief Engineer Foxley reported that only 128 tons of coal remained in the bunkers, just enough to get them to within 80 miles of Sandy Hook. Captain Williams altered course for Halifax, Nova Scotia, some 170 miles away. At the Canadian port the ship could obtain additional coal and provisions to assure a safe if somewhat overdue arrival in New York.

Taking full advantage of the smoother passage afforded by the ship running before the wind, the over-enthusiastic firemen decided to clean the fires. Although this was a normal maintenance job, the stokehold men neglected to inform the bridge of what they were doing. The cleaned-out furnaces produced more heat and as a result the ship gained a little speed. Normally this would not have mattered to any great extent. The officers of the watch would ordinarily notice the increase in speed when they next took a sight and worked out the vessel's position. This time, incredibly, they did not notice.

At close to midnight, shortly before retiring, Captain Williams ordered Second Officer Henry Ismay Metcalf to keep a sharp lookout for ice. At the same time the captain ordered the officer to keep a special watch for the Sambro Light. If the light, which was situated on an island to the south of the harbour entrance, was sighted or visibility deteriorated, Williams was to be called immediately. It was supposedly Captain Williams' intention, upon sighting the light, to heave to and wait for full daylight before going any closer to the rocky shore. The captain ordered that he was to be wakened at 3am at the latest and asked that his steward bring him a hot cocoa at 2.40am Unfortunately the steward, instead of taking the cocoa directly to the captain, first visited the bridge. While he was there Metcalf remembered that Williams had asked to be awakened at 3am. Believing that the steward was 20 minutes early the second officer said, 'Never mind calling him. I will call him myself in a moment.'

As usual in these cases there is evidence to suggest that it was not the second officer at all who stopped the steward rousing the captain but the fourth officer, John Brown, who happened to be amongst those who survived what was about to happen while the second officer did not. As the failure to rouse Captain Williams, as he had ordered, was to have such dire consequences then perhaps it is understandable that Mr Brown was not all that keen on admitting that he might have been responsible.

At 3 o'clock that morning there was nothing in sight even though visibility was good and the lookouts should have been able to see the Sambro Light. At 3.12, contrary to regulations, Metcalf left the bridge unattended and went to call the captain, or so the story goes. Even as the second officer shook the captain awake, Joseph Carroll, a forward lookout, cried 'Breakers ahead!' Metcalf rushed from the chartroom to the bridge and pulled the telegraph handle to full astern. The helmsman, Quartermaster Robert Thomas, put the wheel hard a-starboard. It was all to no avail. Before the engines could be reversed the vessel struck Marr's Rock, about 50yd from Meagher's Island, Nova Scotia, and heeled over to port. The *Atlantic* was 12 to 13 miles west of where the officers thought she was.

In seconds, five great holes were torn in her iron plating and the vessel settled more firmly onto the rocks. The only warning that anything was amiss the passengers received was the noise and shock of the ship grinding on the rock. Within seconds all was pandemonium as panic set in amongst the passengers. Heavy seas pushed the ship's stern round until the port side was exposed to the full fury of the elements. One by one the port side lifeboats were smashed to splinters or washed away by the waves. On the starboard side things were a little better as the officers and crew struggled to lower the boats from that side. Boat 3 left the ship with no plug in the drainage hole below the waterline. Boat 7 was swept away and lost. By this time the vessel was listing so badly that it had become impossible to lower the starboard boats. As the list increased, dozens of people were swept off the deck by the merciless waves. Captain Williams tried to get the second officer to abandon his attempt to leave the stricken ship in Boat 5 but, before the officer could comply, Boat 5 with Metcalf and between 30 and 40 others aboard, rolled over and was crushed under the ship's hull as the list increased to 50 degrees.

Water poured into the hull through every opening, drowning those who were still below decks. The survivors were obliged to climb the rigging to escape the raging seas. Then, with a huge roar the boilers exploded.

At 6.30am the first local fishing boats arrived on the scene to pick up survivors from the wreck and from the rocks which the ship had struck. Once ashore Third Officer Brady commandeered a boat and returned to the wreck in an attempt to save some of the people who were still clinging to the rigging. These included Captain Williams, whose hair had begun to turn white overnight.

Steadily Brady and the fishermen rescued those who remained on the wreck and all but two were safely away from the ship by 8.45am. The two people who remained were rescued by a volunteer crew in a boat commanded by a 36-year-old cleric, Rev William J. Ancient. One of these last two was the only child to survive the disaster. Of the unknown number of women who had taken passage on the vessel, not a single one survived. In the worst merchant shipwreck up to that time 565 men, women and children had perished.

In the Inquiry into the causes of the disaster beginning on 5 April at Halifax, E. M. MacDonald, Collector of Customs, heard four days of testimony from 22 witnesses. At the end of that Inquiry he was in no doubt about the cause of the accident.

Captain Williams' defence, that his decision to alter course for Halifax was 'prudent and justifiable' was accepted; as was his statement that he was asleep, fully clothed, about 30ft abaft the bridge in the chartroom, within easy call of the bridge. Captain Williams also pointed out that he had left instructions he was to be wakened before 3am and that he had every confidence in his second officer. As far as it went Williams' defence was upheld by the Inquiry.

However, in his report MacDonald said that the only possible reasons for the error in estimating the ship's speed were incompetency or carelessness. The Halifax Customs Officer also thought that it had been extremely reckless of Captain Williams to order his vessel to be run at full speed towards land for three hours, without taking any precautions whatsoever to check its position. The greatest mistake, MacDonald believed, was that the sounding lead was never used, even though the ship was in relatively shallow water for eight hours before she struck the rocks. That alone was enough to show Captain Williams' neglect of duty; there could be no excuse. However, in the captain's favour, MacDonald did say that the ship had been insufficiently provisioned with coal by the owners, and that the fourth officer had 'improperly' prevented the steward from waking Captain Williams at 2.40am. In a display of charity rarely seen at such Inquiries MacDonald said that, although revocation of Williams' master's certificate was justified, he would show leniency. In view of the captain's heroic behaviour subsequent to the collision, the certificate would merely be suspended for two years.

Even before the Inquiry decided that the *Atlantic* had left Liverpool with insufficient coal safely to attempt an Atlantic crossing, gossip to that effect was already rife. In an effort to scotch the rumours before they took hold, Thomas Ismay wrote to *The Times* on 3 April, denying the coal shortage.

When the Inquiry findings were made public they not only embarrassed Ismay but did nothing for his company's reputation. The management of the White Star Line was so incensed by the findings of the Halifax Inquiry that they campaigned for another, to be held in Liverpool. Eventually the Board of Trade agreed and a British Inquiry was held, which made its findings public on 11 June. They agreed with the Halifax findings.

The loss of the *Atlantic*, and the findings of both Inquiries, dealt Ismay Imrie a serious blow. To make up some of the money lost in the disaster they were obliged to sell both of the steamers they then had on the South American run, the *Asiatic* and the *Tropic*, for £50,000 and £52,500 respectively, reverting to an all sailing vessel service across the South Atlantic. The all steamship service from Liverpool to New York continued to be operated exclusively by the best known part of the Ismay Imrie company, the Oceanic Steam Navigation Company, or White Star Line.

Recovering from the financial setback of the *Atlantic's* loss, and the damage to the line's reputation, was no easy task, but T. H. Ismay was nothing if not resolute and resourceful. He was also secretive. All the while keeping the status of his own business in the dark, he carefully noted the progress of his two main rivals, the Inman and Cunard lines. The two books, one for each line, that he compiled are still in existence. With the information he gathered he was able to stay ahead of the game and White Star managed to show a profit, even when the others did not.

To help make up a little of the loss the four-year-old *Hoghton Towers* was transferred onto the Liverpool–India route, where she could be expected to return a relatively quick profit. It is fairly clear that whenever White Star was in desperate need of a little extra cash it almost invariably turned to the Indian trade to provide it.

The White Star Line found, in 1873, that it needed a small vessel to ferry passengers from the quayside out to larger liners lying in the deeper waters of the River Mersey. To answer this basic need Speakman of Runcorn built the little tender *Traffic*. The tiny vessel would serve the line faithfully for the next 23 years before being sold off in 1896.

Traffic was not the only vessel the line acquired in 1873. White Star also purchased the 2,652-ton *Gaelic*, which was bought on the stocks from the owners of the Bibby Line, for whom the vessel had been built. *Gaelic* turned out to be one of the line's more fortunate vessels and she served White Star for a decade without serious mishap. She had been with the company for less than a year when she first demonstrated her worth in adversity.

After leaving Liverpool on 15 January 1874 *Celtic* ran into some floating wreckage and broke off all four of her propeller blades. She was towed into Queenstown by the *Gaelic* and her passengers left the ship. The passengers resumed their interrupted passage eight days later when *Baltic* picked them up on her way to New York. In the meantime *Gaelic* towed the helpless *Celtic* to the Alfred Dock at Birkenhead so that her propeller could be repaired or replaced.

A new 5,004-ton vessel, designed by Edward J. Harland, was launched at Belfast on 3 February 1874. The ship was originally to be called *Hellenic* but the name was changed to *Britannic¹* before she was handed over to the White Star Line. As we have seen, it was not uncommon for White Star to change a vessel's name between construction beginning and when she was launched.

The new *Britannic* sailed on her maiden voyage in June. The ship was originally fitted with an adjustable propeller shaft that could be raised and lowered to alter the angle of the propeller and improve thrust; a complication suggested and designed by Edward Harland. The adjustable shaft turned out to be not such a clever idea after all and after crossing the Atlantic nine times the ship returned to Belfast to have the Heath Robinson contraption removed and a more normal propeller shaft installed. With the ordinary propulsion system fitted, the *Britannic* quickly set new records for both east- and westbound Atlantic crossings, reducing the time spent on passage to less than seven and a half days.

Ismay Imrie were still selling off some of their older and smaller sailing ships and in 1874 came time for the *Ismay* to be disposed of.

The first vessel to transport live cattle in commercial quantities across the Atlantic arrived at Liverpool in July; she was the *Europe*, owned by H. N. Hughes and Nephew. Three of the 373 head of cattle put aboard the vessel had died during the voyage (not a bad performance allowing for the vagaries of the weather on the North Atlantic). The following year the *San Marcos* repeated the voyage with 276 head of cattle aboard, for the firm of George Roddick. The trade in live cattle grew quickly and 18 years later nearly half a million animals were landed at Liverpool from almost 50 ships, operated by almost 50 shipping companies, White Star among them, but we will come back to that in a moment.

White Star bought the *Belgic¹* in 1874. The new ship had been built as the *Gaelic* but as the line already had a vessel of that name an alternative had to be found. As she was leaving the Victoria Docks in London on 24 November she ran into two barges. One of the barges was unladen but the other was carrying the rudder of an ironclad warship; they both sank. *Belgic* was undamaged and, in what was to become classic White Star fashion, proceeded on her way as if nothing had occurred.

While coming in to Liverpool on 8 March 1875 the *Adriatic¹* rammed and sank the schooner *Columbus*. *Adriatic* had passed the Crosby lightship and was effectively under the command of the Mersey pilot but undoubtedly Captain Perry was on the bridge. Captain Perry was to become quite efficient when it came to ramming other ships, but only because he practised regularly, as we shall see. It was a clear night and *Adriatic* was steaming slowly upstream when the forecastle lookout reported a sail ahead. Even though her helm was put hard a-starboard and the engine stopped, *Adriatic* crashed into the starboard quarter of the smaller vessel.

Obviously considering that he had taken enough chances for one day, Captain Perry, instead of immediately going to the assistance of his victim, proceeded to fire rockets and burn blue lights. Two other steamers, their skippers probably realising that something was amiss, came within hailing distance, so Captain Perry asked them to see if the *Columbus* needed assistance. Rather than hang about at the scene Captain Perry then got the undamaged *Adriatic* under way and was soon tied up safely in harbour.

One of the steamers hailed by Perry, the *Enterprise*, had found the *Columbus*, or rather all that remained of her above water. *Enterprise* rescued the crew, captain, and his wife, from the masts and rigging of the schooner, the only casualty of the collision being the schooner captain's child, who clearly was not athletic enough to swarm up the rigging as the vessel sank underneath them. Had Captain Perry gone to the assistance of the *Columbus* straight after the accident then it is highly possible that the child might have been rescued from the deck of the small vessel before it sank.

Adriatic left Liverpool on 30 December 1875, heading for Queenstown and New York. Captain Perry had been replaced as commander of the liner by Captain Jennings but the new skipper does not seem to have brought any more luck with him. Less than a full day out, at about 2.20am on 31 December, a green light was sighted off the starboard bow. As the vessel ahead of the liner changed course the green light vanished and was replaced by a red one. Then the mystery ship altered course again and the colour of the light turned back to green. Realising that the vessel ahead of them was undecided as to how to proceed *Adriatic*'s first officer slowed the ship's engines, then stopped them, and then realising that the other vessel was coming too close for comfort ordered full astern. He then called Captain Jennings to the bridge. Even as Jennings reached the bridge the stranger's lights changed colour again, to red, and steadied, indicating that she was going to attempt to cross *Adriatic*'s bows, or so the witnesses aboard the liner thought.

Even though *Adriatic*'s engines were now going full astern the unknown vessel continued to come closer until she collided with the liner. According to Captain Jennings the stranger had succeeded in hooking its port jib guy in *Adriatic*'s port anchor stock. A mass of rigging and other paraphernalia landed on *Adriatic*'s foredeck, shaken free in the collision. The mystery vessel had still shown no other lights, except her port and starboard riding lights, and she made no attempt to signal the *Adriatic* either before, during or after the encounter. As the two vessels separated the stranger vanished into the darkness. Instead of taking a leaf out of Captain Perry's book Captain Jennings at least had two lifeboats lowered. He then cruised about the area, looking for the mystery ship to see if assistance was required. He found nothing and after three-quarters of an hour he collected his two boats and resumed his voyage.

Adriatic's victim has never been positively identified – but how could it have been when there were no survivors from the victim and nobody aboard the *Adriatic* was about to admit anything? However, the *Harvest Queen*, a sailing packet owned by C. H. Marshall & Co was approaching Liverpool from San Francisco. She had called at Queenstown and had only left there on the evening of 30 December. Sailing on a reciprocal course to that of *Adriatic* her speed would have put her in the right (or rather the 'wrong') place at the relevant time. The *Harvest Queen* was never seen again, although wreckage that came ashore on a Wexford beach was positively identified, by a representative of her agents, as coming from her.

Captain Jennings later said that the hull of his vessel had never come into contact with that of the mystery ship, but his assertion seems unlikely in the light of other evidence. A seaman who had previously served aboard the *Harvest Queen* as a mate, identified two jibsheet blocks recovered from *Adriatic's* foredeck as ones that had been made aboard the packet under his supervision. Crew members from *Adriatic* were also sure that a collision had taken place. They also recalled hearing the cries of drowning men after the liner had stopped to search the area. Members of the liner's crew also believed that the search made by the two lifeboats was wholly inadequate.

C. H. Marshall & Co brought a £35,000 writ against the White Star Line and when *Adriatic* next entered New York harbour, on 13 February 1876, the ship was prevented by the authorities from leaving until a bond of double the amount of compensation sought was posted. White Star posted the bond and the ship left New York to continue on its disaster-strewn way. Eventually Marshall & Co was awarded its compensation.

Germanic, built at a cost of £200,000, entered service in 1875. Despite one or two quite spectacular mishaps *Germanic* was to become White Star's longest lived liner, lasting for no less than three-quarters of a century. With the *Britannic*, she was considerably larger than the other vessels in the White Star fleet. Being larger vessels than the others in the fleet meant that both *Britannic* and *Germanic* had larger engines, although of the same type, than those fitted to the earlier class of ship though they worked at a steam pressure of 75lb/sq in, as had the earlier ones. The engines, which were built by Maudsley, Field & Co, were supplied with steam from eight boilers, which burned 110 tons of coal a day in their 32 furnaces.

In February 1876 the *Germanic* set a new record for an eastbound crossing of the North Atlantic when she completed the trip in 7 days, 15 hours and 17 minutes, at an average speed of 15.79kt. The White Star liner set a new record for a westbound North Atlantic crossing 14 months later, in April 1877, when she completed the voyage in 7 days, 11 hours and 37 minutes, at an average speed of 15.76kt.

It is a curious fact that Victorian businessmen, though absolutely ruthless in their commercial dealings, suffered from a powerful social conscience. It has been suggested that this apparent concern for those less well off was nothing more than an attempt to purchase themselves a place in heaven, when their time came. This might well be the case, but there can be no doubt that they did a tremendous amount of good with their fortunes, even if their motives might have been questionable.

In 1876 T. H. Ismay started a fund to help the old people of his home town, Maryport. He subscribed £20 for blankets, and £5 for coal to be distributed to the aged and needy each Christmas. In 1877 he increased the fund by a further £25, which was to be handed out at the rate of one shilling's worth of groceries per person per week. The Maryport fund still exists to this day, although one cannot help wondering if the local pensioners are all that impressed with their five pence worth of comestibles a week!

In 1877 Ismay bought the 390-acre Dawpool estate in Cheshire. The estate had taken its name from a hamlet at the mouth of the Dee, which had once been a port but because of the silting up of the river it had fallen into disuse. The house had originally been built in 1865 by James Hegan, but after he died his daughters first let the estate, and then decided to sell it. The house and estate were too far from the Liverpool offices to allow Ismay to use it as his main home but, being only 12 miles by ferry from Liverpool, it was ideal for weekends and holidays. The principal family home remained at Beech Lawn. The farm on the estate was let to a tenant farmer.

Harland & Wolff's problem with building a better propeller was still ongoing when *Oceanic*, now on long-term charter with the Occidental & Oriental Company along with the *Gaelic* and *Belgic*, sailing back and forth on the Pacific Ocean between China, Japan and North America, lost hers completely on 25 July 1877 while sailing from Yokohama to Hong Kong. She completed the journey using her sails alone. Gremlins again managed to get at *Oceanic's* machinery as she prepared, on 19 September, to sail from San Francisco with mail for China and Japan. The 'accident to her machinery' kept her in San Francisco for another 10 days.

The *Don Guillermo* was sold to Paulsen & Co of Elsfleth in Germany in 1877. Other ships were leaving the company by other means! The *Wennington* was sighted in the Bali Straits on 30 January 1878 but was never seen again. *Wennington* had been built for the White Star Line in 1865, and had been employed on the Australian trade, and later in trade with the Orient.

By 1878 competition between the shipping companies on the North Atlantic had become so fierce that John Burns, who was then the head of the Cunard Line, tried to remove some of it by suggesting to T. H. Ismay that Cunard and White Star should merge; Ismay refused. More than half a century later John Burns would have his way. Far from trying to cut down on the amount of competition around in 1878, Imrie and Ismay helped the Turner family start a new shipping line, the Asiatic Steam Navigation Company. The new line would principally engage in coastal trade between the ports of Ceylon and India. Small steamers, with Indian names, would be used to carry general cargoes and passengers. The company's offices were in Liverpool to begin with but after the Great War they moved their headquarters to London. Years later, in 1907, J. Bruce Ismay became chairman of the Asiatic Steam Navigation Line, and remained so until his retirement in 1934.

Sailing from Liverpool late on 18 July 1878, bound for Queenstown and New York, the *Adriatic* ran into dense fog. Speed was reduced to dead slow. At about 4.30 the following morning, about 18 miles west of Holyhead, *Adriatic* collided with the *Hengist*, which was being towed by a tug to Liverpool. *Hengist's* mainbrace was carried away and her starboard quarter was damaged but she was in no danger of sinking and she completed the journey to Liverpool.

Rather than take any more risks the *Adriatic* was stopped and anchored in St George's Channel, waiting for the fog to clear. Lookouts were posted as the ship waited throughout the morning for the weather to improve. Suddenly, out of the fog loomed the Dublin-bound brig *G. A. Pike* from London. Before any action could be taken by either vessel the brig ran full tilt into *Adriatic* and sank at once. For once, the crew of the White Star vessel behaved as we would all like to believe British sailors behave. *Adriatic's* boats were quickly lowered and went to the assistance of the *G. A. Pike's* crew but again luck was against them. Of the six crew members who had been aboard the brig, only one was plucked alive from the sea.

As 1879 drew to a close even the weather seems to have turned against the White Star Line. A couple of days before Christmas while *Republic* was steaming towards New York from Liverpool and Queenstown she ran into a fierce gale and huge seas. A gigantic wave broke over her port quarter, tearing up wooden decks, smashing a lifeboat and severely damaging the funnel. With the funnel damaged, the furnaces would not draw properly and steam pressure for the engines would soon be lost. Without the engines to keep the ship's head into the waves, in such a storm, it would almost certainly be lost. The ship's engineers worked heroically. Using oars taken from lifeboats as splints and canvas as bandages they patched the funnel well enough for steam pressure to be maintained. As soon as the weather improved, the engineers replaced their innovative patchwork with sheet iron and *Republic* went on her way.

Chapter 8
1880-1888

B y 1880 White Star was one of the most successful lines operating on the North Atlantic and elsewhere. Its reputation for the highest quality accommodation and comfort afloat was second to none. T. H. Ismay had risen to eminence with his shipping line and he was also a director of the London and North Western Railway, the Royal Insurance Company, and on the board of governors of the Seaman's Orphanage, and the training ship *Indefatigable*.

As you would expect, Ismay and his wife were pillars of the local community. As befitted a successful Victorian family, the Ismays entertained on a lavish scale, sometimes having as many as 20 house guests at Beech Lawn, when they were in Liverpool. However, they now considered the Dawpool house to be rather less than they required. Their answer was simple, they would have it demolished and a new one built in its place. With this in mind they went to Shrewsbury in early January 1881 to look at a house built by Norman Shaw. Shaw had already made a name for himself as an architect and would soon become famous as the designer of New Scotland Yard in London. The Ismays were suitably impressed by Shaw's work and he was engaged to build the new Dawpool home.

Once again, as in the Grotto at Beech Lawn, Ismay's passion for red stone asserted itself and, as there was an adequate supply locally, this is what the new house was built of. On 29 July 1882 the foundation stone for the new house was laid by Thomas and his wife. It would take two and a half years to complete and was ready in December 1884. The Ismays spent their first night under its roof on 4 December.

The new house was enormous, even by the standards of the wealthy of the day, the south front being more than 250ft long. Ismay spent the then colossal sum of £53,000 on it. It seems that even Norman Shaw had his off days, and the new Dawpool house was clearly the result of one of them. No doubt the influence of T. H. Ismay did nothing to soften the aspect of the new structure. The over-ornate red stone monstrosity could at best be described as an eyesore. When Mrs Ismay died in 1907 each of her three sons was offered the house in turn. They all declined, showing that they, at least, had some taste. As none of the immediate family was prepared to live in Thomas's creation the house was put up for sale. The selling agents considered the house to be a 'fetter' on the land rather than an asset. In other words, the value of the land would increase if somebody blew up the house. Thomas Henry Ismay might have been a first-class shipowner and broker but he was an abysmal house designer.

At about the same time as Ismay was building his blot on the Cheshire landscape his partner William Imrie was also moving upmarket. He bought himself the Homestead, a large stone-built Victorian mansion, with an enormous conservatory, in Mossley Hill Road, Liverpool. Imrie clearly had better taste when it came to houses than his partner.

T. H. Ismay's eldest son, Joseph Bruce, completed his schooling in 1880 and on 13 September he began his apprenticeship with Ismay Imrie. J. Bruce Ismay had been educated at New Brighton, Elstree and Harrow, before being sent at the tender age of 16 to a private tutor at Dinard in France. His time as a student had not been happy because he was extremely shy and more than usually sensitive. To cover up this perceived failing he adopted an abrupt attitude that tended to make people dislike dealing with him, until they got to know him well enough to see through the façade, when most of them stopped dealing with him altogether! Although he thought the world of his parents, the feeling was not reciprocated by his father.

While he was still at school the young Joseph, during the long summer holiday, had occasionally accompanied his father to the office. At those times he had habitually hung his coat and hat alongside his father's in his father's office. On his first day as an employee of Ismay Imrie he did the same thing before receiving his instructions for the day from his father. No sooner had he left the room than Thomas Ismay called for a clerk and said to him, 'Please inform the new office boy that he is not to leave his hat and coat lying about in my office.' Joseph was so hurt by this public embarrassment in front of the office staff that he seldom wore a coat to work again.

On another occasion, Joseph Ismay arrived home before his father. It was a fine evening, so he decided to go horseback riding. Rather stupidly perhaps, he took his father's favourite horse for a gallop on the sands. Predictably, the horse fell, broke its leg and had to be shot. Thomas Ismay was furious with his son for taking the animal without his permission, which is perhaps understandable, and gave him such a dressing down that Joseph never rode again, which is rather more than was required. It is little wonder that Joseph Bruce Ismay began to take every opportunity to distance himself from his father.

During this time minor problems still beset the line even though its masters now had almost 10 years' experience with the large liners. As *Baltic*[1] steamed down river from Liverpool on 17 August 1880, she was in collision with a steamer from Dublin, the *Longford*. Both ships were badly damaged and the *Longford* had to be beached and filled with water. *Baltic* was taken into dock, where most of her cargo was removed so that repairs to her hull could be carried out. She was soon back in service, but on 20 September, just over a month later, after waiting for four hours at Sandy Hook because of fog, *Baltic* made her way towards her normal berth in New York harbour. On the way she rammed the schooner *Sarah Burns* and tore a hole in her side. It would appear that the *Sarah Burns* remained afloat and was able to reach a repair facility, no thanks to the *Baltic*.

Collision was, it seems, an all too common occurrence. *Germanic*, after being held up for a day because of thick fog, left New York on 7 November. On her way out she ran into the full rigged Dutch cargo ship *Samarang*, tearing a large hole in the side of the 1,076-ton vessel. Luckily the incident occurred in relatively shallow water because the *Samarang* promptly sank until only her deck, masts and rigging remained above water. Unusually for a White Star vessel, *Germanic* stopped and picked up the crew of her victim.

It was not all doom and gloom for the line, though. New vessels were still being built by Harland & Wolff. The *Arabic*[1] entered service with the line in 1881, along with the *Coptic*.

Some of White Star's commanders appear to have been a little more accident prone than others, Captain Hamilton Perry being a fair example of the former. Soon after leaving Liverpool, heading for New York on 31 March 1881, *Britannic*[1], under the command of Captain Perry, collided with the schooner *Julia*, out of Dublin. The schooner quickly sank but her crew were all picked up. Luckily the *Britannic* was undamaged and able to proceed on her way to the New World.

The *Britannic* departed New York bound for Queenstown and Liverpool on 25 June. Bestriding the bridge was the now familiar Captain Hamilton Perry. After a brief stopover at Queenstown she set off on the last leg of the journey, only to encounter heavy fog. At about 7.30 on the morning of 4 July 1881, Captain Perry heard what he thought was the fog signal from the Tuskar Light, and accordingly altered course toward Holyhead (or so he believed). The ship was somewhere off Kilmore, County Wexford, Ireland.

The fog signal from the Tuskar Light was a gun, fired every 5 minutes. In fact the signal Captain Perry had heard was that of Hoots, which was a gun fired every 10 minutes. Quite how Captain Perry could have been mistaken in determining which signal he heard when they were so unlike one another must be food for thought. Hopelessly off course, *Britannic* soon found herself in serious trouble. Only about five minutes after the course change shallow water was sounded. Captain Perry immediately ordered the engine astern but it was already too late and the ship went hard aground.

Nobody had been hurt in the grounding and at first there seemed to be no damage to the ship, although there was no immediate prospect of being able to continue the voyage. Later in the morning ship's boats were swung out and lowered, mail and passengers were loaded into the boats and taken ashore at Wexford, whence they could be transported to Dublin and on to Liverpool. Then Captain Perry set about trying to refloat his ship. Cargo was jettisoned to lighten the *Britannic* in the hope that she would float off with the next high tide, but with the rising tide came a more immediate problem. During the afternoon the Number 2 hold began to fill with seawater and the ship developed a 12 degree list to port. Luckily (or unluckily!) the *Britannic* was still hard aground and therefore not in danger of sinking in the foreseeable future.

The Liverpool Salvage Association soon had men on the scene and they set to work, pumping the water out of the ship and patching her up. Over the next day or so a further 1,500 tons of cargo were removed from the holds and taken to Waterford. On 6 July, sufficiently lightened, *Britannic* righted herself. Two days later, soon after midday the ship lifted off the bottom and was once again afloat, but she was in no condition to proceed under her own power.

At about 8.30am on 9 July, when just off the Barrels and being towed towards Liverpool, *Britannic* sprang another leak. Within an hour her engine room was flooded and there was a very real possibility that the vessel might sink. With no time to waste the *Britannic* was towed to South Bay, where she could be beached on a smooth, sandy bottom. Before extra pumps could reach the stranded liner from Liverpool, she had flooded up to the saloon deck.

By 12 July the water had again been pumped out of the ship and she was afloat. At about two o'clock in the afternoon, with her hull patched again, she left the Irish coast for Liverpool, and a hasty drying out. *Britannic* reached her home port on 14 July, 19 eventful days after leaving the safety of New York. Examination of the ship's hull showed her injuries to be relatively minor. Although she had been holed, there was no sign that the vessel had been strained and her plating was still tight. Repairs were carried out, and as far as practicable the interior of the vessel was dried out, and she was able to depart for New York on 18 July as advertised.

The White Star Line was doing so well by 1881 that the shareholders suggested that Thomas Ismay and William Imrie should take a larger percentage of the profits. Neither of them would agree so the shareholders came up with the idea that Thomas should have his portrait painted and be presented with a fine silver gilt dinner service.

On 8 September the North Docks, Liverpool, were opened by the Prince and Princess of Wales. During the ceremonies Thomas and Mrs Ismay were presented to the royal couple. The whole occasion was described by Mrs Ismay as 'a beautiful day'. Towards the end of 1881 Ismay's favourite son, James, changed schools from Elstree to Harrow. A couple of years later, instead of sending him to Europe, out of the way like his brother, James was sent to university in Oxford.

By 1882 both the Atlantic and Pacific services offered by Ismay Imrie were doing well. The fleet of sailing ships had been voyaging to Australia and back ever since 1867, and from 1870 it had done so under the direction of William Imrie, while Thomas Ismay directed the steamers on the North Atlantic. It was now time, Ismay Imrie decided, to put steamers on to the antipodean run.

As it happened, the Shaw Savill and Albion lines had recently amalgamated, and because they had so much experience in the New Zealand trade Thomas Ismay believed that they would make ideal managers for Ismay Imrie vessels engaged in that trade. An agreement was soon reached whereby the White Star Line would supply vessels and their crews while Shaw Savill and Albion would arrange passengers, cargoes and schedules. The arrangements between Shaw Savill and White Star, which were agreed in 1883, would remain in effect for more than 60 years.

With the new services in mind two new ships were ordered from Harland & Wolff, the *Ionic¹* and the *Doric¹*. Both the *Ionic* and the *Doric* were specially built for the antipodean trade and were developments of the earlier *Oceanic* Class ships. They were of the layout favoured by Harland & Wolff whereby there were no deckhouses as such but the superstructure, which contained most of the public rooms, extended right out to the full width of the hull, just as in more modern liners.

These two vessels were special because they were the first ships built by the Belfast shipbuilders from steel instead of iron. They were each capable of transporting about 70 first-class passengers. In one of his first appearances in The History of the White Star Line, J. Bruce Ismay joined the *Ionic* at Belfast on 26 March 1883, as she was being handed over by the builders, and made the trip from there to London aboard her, arriving on 1 April.

The service between England and New Zealand was to operate from London rather than Liverpool. While the *Ionic* was in London before her maiden voyage the Prince of Wales expressed a desire to see over her, so arrangements were made. On 23 April T. H. Ismay travelled down to the capital on an early train to receive the Prince aboard the ship. The event went off smoothly and the Prince was suitably impressed, so with this new feather in his cap Ismay boarded the midnight train and returned to Liverpool, a four-hour journey in those far-off days.

While effectively under charter to the New Zealand Shipping Company in 1883, *Ionic* set a new record for the London–Wellington run. The New Zealand Line had close ties with the Ismay Imrie group but it operated as an independent line under Shaw Savill management, although there was regular co-operation between them.

May 1883 was not an especially good month for Thomas Ismay. On Friday the 4th he again made the journey to London, this time for a private viewing of the portrait that had been commissioned of him. He was not impressed, thinking that the picture did not do him justice, and he did not like its expression.

On 13 May *Britannic* stopped at Queenstown to drop off mail and passengers before continuing her eastbound voyage to Liverpool. During the last leg of that journey, which would have taken her about 24 hours, a rumour was spread in New York that she had been destroyed by dynamite, which had been placed aboard at Queenstown. This rumour gained enough credence to be reported in several New York papers although it had no basis in fact. There is a theory that the rumour may have been inspired by the presence aboard *Britannic* of the American multimillionaire William H. Vanderbilt, who sent a cable from Queenstown advising his family of his safe arrival, which might have been misunderstood.

Doric was completed and ready for delivery to the White Star Line early in July 1883, so on the 6th T. H. Ismay journeyed to Holyhead to join the vessel for the trip round to London. He was not alone but was accompanied by a large party of guests, including the Duke of Sutherland and the Bishop of Newcastle.

When the *Ionic* and *Doric* were commissioned they were chartered by the New Zealand Shipping Company as a stopgap measure until their own ships were ready. This suited all concerned because neither White Star nor Shaw Savill & Albion was quite ready to begin the regular monthly service to New Zealand and Australia. Shaw Savill & Albion was waiting until its *Arawa* and *Tainui* were ready to join forces with White Star's *Ionic, Doric, Arabic* and *Coptic* before they began.

While on a yachting holiday in August 1883 with his wife and two sons Ismay decided to call in at Belfast to see his old friends, Edward Harland and Gustav Wolff. Harland met the family and took them to Ormiston to visit his wife. After tea the Ismays took their leave of the Harlands, and called on Wolff, who happened to be out shooting. On hearing of their arrival Gustav Wolff abandoned his attempts to exterminate the local game bird population, returned to his house and presented the Ismays with 'some grouse'. On the following morning, 1 September, Wolff joined the Ismays for breakfast aboard their yacht *Vanadis*. From the informality of the visit it is clear that the relationship between the Liverpool shipowner and his family and the Belfast shipbuilders was rather closer than a purely business association. This close relationship between the owners of the two companies would continue for many years, through generations and changes of management.

Celtic, due to arrive in Liverpool on Christmas Eve 1883, was a little late arriving, and beginning to cause some concern. It was not until six days later that word reached the management of the White Star Line that there was nothing to worry about, and that the ship had merely broken a propeller shaft, and was disabled. She was taken in tow by *Britannic*, which was returning from America, and assisted back to Liverpool for repair. *Britannic* towed the crippled *Celtic* into the Mersey on 15 January 1884, much to the relief of T. H. Ismay.

It was again time for T. H. Ismay to begin selling off some of his older vessels and so the *Gaelic¹* and *Belgic¹*, so prone to propeller damage, were disposed of to new Spanish owners.

On 16 January 1884 word reached Liverpool that *Germanic*, which had taken *Celtic's* place on the Atlantic route, had also broken a propeller and was returning to her home port under sail. Although the shedding of propellers and blades was common with White Star ships built by Harland & Wolff, even Mrs Margaret Ismay thought it curious that both vessels should be disabled in the same way in such a short space of time. *Germanic* reached Waterford on 24 January and was towed into the Mersey by steam tugs two days later.

During 1884 Thomas Ismay served on Lord Ravensworth's Admiralty Committee, to enquire into whether the dockyard or contract system was the more satisfactory when it came to repair and construction of naval vessels. In the dockyard system work on naval vessels was carried out by naval personnel using Navy bases. Under the contract system work was done by civilian contractors. Contacts made while serving on this committee must have come in handy two or three years later when Ismay came up with an idea for a type of vessel that he managed to convince the government would be useful to both the Navy and himself.

Despite the fact that he had initially opposed the venture, to the extent of travelling to London to attend a protest meeting three years earlier, Thomas Ismay, with his wife and Joseph Bruce, turned out to celebrate the opening of the Wirral Railway, on 16 October 1884. His change of heart might have been influenced by the fact that William Ewart Gladstone was officiating at the opening ceremony. Ismay would have been well aware that it did a businessman no harm to have friends and acquaintances in high places.

Soon after he attended the ceremony to celebrate the opening of the new railway, J. Bruce Ismay sailed for New Zealand aboard the *Doric¹*. The young Ismay had slightly less than a year to go to complete his apprenticeship and his father thought that it was time that he saw a little bit of the world for himself. It should also be remembered that father and son did not exactly see eye to eye, and the trip would keep J. Bruce away from home for about 11 months.

With the new year of 1885 came a couple of new ships for the White Star Line: a second *Belgic* and a second *Gaelic*. Neither of the new ships was intended for the North Atlantic passenger trade, but for the Australia and New Zealand routes.

Although Ismay had turned down Cunard's suggested merger in 1878, he remained in touch with John Burns, the head of that company. In January 1885 the two men met and discussed the steady decline in the volume of traffic crossing the North Atlantic, which was making the competition even more ferocious than before. On 3 February Ismay wrote a strongly worded, although friendly, letter to Burns pointing out that despite the fall in the numbers of passengers wanting to go to New York a large number of extra ships had been built to carry them. Ismay also pointed out that the company responsible for building the extra tonnage for the New York trade was none other than Cunard.

Ismay did have some justification for his remarks as Cunard had almost doubled its tonnage on the Atlantic in the previous five years. Cunard's own published figures show that in 1880 they had 61,379 tons of shipping earning £2 12s 6d (£2.63) per ton, but in 1883 the tonnage had risen to 82,945 while profit had fallen to £1 2s (£1.10) per ton. Ismay suggested that Cunard adopt a more 'live and let live' approach, and stop building more and more ships. It had been 11 years since White Star had put any new ships on the Atlantic route, but Ismay threatened to take up the challenge by building bigger, more powerful ships if Cunard failed to take up his suggestions, and thus aggravate the situation even further.

In the same letter Ismay also complained about Cunard's advertised change of sailing days for their Royal Mail Steamers, to Saturdays, which would clash with the sailing of White Star's own mail ships. The scheduled changes would, Ismay believed, only serve to increase the already cut-throat rivalry between the mail carrying companies, Cunard, Inmans and White Star.

Burns did not agree. He wrote back to Ismay saying that he did not foresee any difficulty in obtaining adequate remuneration for the policy adopted by Cunard. In his view the experience of the past had no bearing on the future, and in any event the company was obliged to use its capital in the manner most advantageous to its shareholders. Cunard policy would be to put as many ships on the New York run as possible thereby ensuring a quick turnaround which would automatically attract more passengers and mail. Burns also reminded Ismay, good naturedly, that when the occasion suited him, White Star schedules had been changed to clash with sailing times of Cunard vessels. Burns failed to respond to the White Star threat to build more ships except to say that it was none of his concern and would have no effect whatsoever on Cunard policy.

Ismay must have known why Cunard was putting more and more ships on to the New York run. It was to demonstrate to the Post Office that Cunard's was the fleet best able to transport the Royal Mail, and had very little to do with passengers. Cunard was after a government subsidy, and while it might not be able to eliminate the competition from the powerful White Star Line, it could hope to get rid of Inmans.

April 1885 was a quite exceptional period for gales in the North Atlantic. For the first time in its history a White Star Line ship was forced to return to port because of bad weather. On 5 April the *Germanic*, on her way to New York after calling at Queenstown, with about 850 passengers on board ran into a massive storm. When the vessel was about 500 miles west of Fastnet she was struck by the first, and smaller, of two tidal waves. This wave swept her boats away, smashed skylights and destroyed her pilot house. Then the second wave struck the ship. It broke into the reading room and through the bulkhead to flood the saloon and staterooms. The damage was so severe that *Germanic's* captain prudently decided to return to Liverpool for repairs before continuing the crossing.

In 1885 there was another royal occasion when the Prince and Princess of Wales visited Harland & Wolff in Belfast. Gustav Wolff gave a ball in their honour, and of course invited Mr and Mrs Ismay. When they arrived they were met by William Pirrie, who had joined Harland & Wolff as their first apprentice in 1862 and had proved so valuable to the company that he was made a partner in 1874.

By the middle of the 1880s competition on the North Atlantic had reached the point where many of the shipping lines operating there were suffering severe financial hardship. However, White Star's passengers seem to have remained loyal to the company and while other lines were unable to pay their shareholders a dividend, Ismay's line continued to do so. In gratitude to the management of the line the shareholders arranged a gala dinner in their honour, at which they could present the dinner service and painting commissioned four years earlier. As if in defiance of the ill luck that had dogged the ship, 100 guests, about 70 of them shareholders, would attend the function aboard the *Adriatic*, which lay anchored in the Mersey, on 16 September 1885.

Dinner was served at 5pm and afterwards Ismay was presented with the silver gilt dinner service, designed and made by Hunt and Roskell, which had taken three years to produce and was valued at more than £4,000, and the portrait of himself painted by Sir John Everett Millais, valued at another £1,000. William Imrie was presented with two paintings of his own choosing, one was 'Melittion' by Sir Frederic Leighton RA, and the other was 'The Feast of Pomona' by Lawrence Alma-Tadema RA.

Just four days after the shareholders in the Oceanic Steam Navigation Company expressed their grateful thanks to Ismay and Imrie for maintaining profits at a difficult time, those times got a little harder. While under charter to the Inman Line, on 20 September, the *Republic* ran into the Cunard steamer *Aurania* while leaving New York harbour. The accident was put down to pilots on both vessels being unsure of what the other was doing. In the collision *Republic's* bow was split open from top to bottom, with a hole 4ft wide at its upper extremity tapering down to 1ft at the bottom. She required dry-docking for repairs. *Aurania* fared rather better with only a large V-shaped dent in her port quarter to show for the encounter. She was able to continue her voyage.

Joseph Bruce Ismay returned to Liverpool just before Christmas 1885. He was met by his father, who despite the fact that they were not wholly compatible, seems to have been glad to see him. His mother on the other hand was genuinely pleased to have her son home for the festive season and guests were invited to the Ismay's monstrous rural edifice, Dawpool, to share the holiday; there were 19 in all. J. Bruce would not remain in his father's house for long and soon afterwards he was packed off to New York to gain some experience in the company's offices there, with the object of one day becoming the agent.

The battle between the shipping companies over who should have the contract to carry the mail was still raging when, on 22 December, an agreement was reached between the Cunard, White Star and Inman companies whereby Inmans and White Star both agreed to pay Cunard a third of their mail earnings. By this time Cunard was carrying well over half the mail on its twice weekly service. This agreement would only last a year, until a new contract was negotiated with the Post Office by which only Cunard and White Star would carry the Royal Mail, and share the subsidy 50/50. Because Cunard would still be carrying quite a lot more mail, White Star agreed to pay over 20% of its subsidy 'in consideration of the superiority of the Cunard service'. You can just imagine Thomas Henry frothing at the mouth over that insult.

By 1886 T. H. Ismay had become a significant figure in Liverpool society and on 5 January the Prince of Siam called on him at Dawpool House. He was also asked to 'entertain the Queen on board the ferry boat *Claughton* for tea and accompany her on the river' when she visited Liverpool later in the year, which he did.

The White Star fleet was getting a bit long in the tooth by 1887 and Ismay decided it was high time the line built some new ships. However, he was not about to spend any more of his, or his shareholders', money than he could possibly avoid. Some years before he had offered to put the White Star fleet at the disposal of the Admiralty, with whom he had close ties that were soon to become even closer, but that had been when war with Russia had seemed a possibility. Now he came up with a new scheme to gain financial backing from the government in order to build new ships for the line. He suggested to the Admiralty that new ships should be built under their supervision, ships that could be easily turned into armed merchant cruisers in the event of war. The government agreed and White Star immediately turned to Edward Harland to design two such vessels. When the Admiralty saw the plans they thought they were the best ever presented, and in March 1887 the first keel, *Teutonic*, was laid, closely followed by that of *Majestic*.

The new liners were another breakthrough in technology for Edward Harland. They were the first modern liners; fitted with twin screws they could rely on being able to complete a voyage under steam alone, and although they had three masts they were not fitted with yards and sails. The ships were also of a considerable size at about 10,000 tons apiece and were to be capable of 20kt.

In May 1887 J. Bruce Ismay became the White Star agent in New York. At that time he was the youngest agent to represent a major shipping company anywhere. It is a curious fact, which we have come across before, that whenever J. Bruce received a promotion, or anything else good happened to him, the White Star Line suffered some sort of catastrophe. This time it was a collision between two of the company's liners.

As a general rule Captain Hamilton Perry specialised in ramming and sinking ships that had no direct connection to his employers, the White Star Line, but in May 1887 he made a notable exception to this general rule. (Perry was captain of *Britannic* for the majority if not all of her misadventures, as well as having a hand in those of *Adriatic*.)

On 11 May 1887 *Celtic* departed Liverpool, bound for New York; she had 104 first-class and 765 steerage passengers aboard. Commanding *Celtic* was Captain Peter J. Irvine. A week later, on 18 May 1887, *Britannic*, under the command of Captain Hamilton Perry, left New York bound for Liverpool, with 176 first-class and 300 steerage passengers. Their tracks would cross on the 19th.

As described by Captain Perry, *Britannic* was steaming through fog on the afternoon of 19 May. The fog was patchy, sometimes very thick and at other times lifting. From about 4 o'clock, though, it settled down very heavily and there was no wind to disperse it. Captain Perry was steaming at a speed he considered reasonable given the prevailing weather conditions, 14½kt, or full ahead, when at about 5.15 a whistle was heard. *Britannic* changed course two points (22.5°) to starboard and Captain Perry ordered the whistle sounded at one minute intervals.

Meanwhile, *Celtic* had been steaming on a roughly reciprocal course to *Britannic* at a speed Captain Irvine considered appropriate for the prevailing conditions, 13½kt, or full ahead. Up on his bridge Captain Irvine heard a ship's whistle about three points off his starboard bow, but ignored it. About five minutes later he heard the whistle again and ordered a course change of a point and a half (almost 17°) to starboard and the engine revolutions reduced.

As *Celtic* swung onto her new heading Irvine ordered two short blasts on the whistle (a conventional signal meaning 'I am going to starboard'). A couple of minutes later he ordered the engines to dead slow. The scene was set. In an era renowned for robust captaincy Captain Irvine was clearly nothing like as robust as Captain Perry. However, a new fourth officer had joined the *Celtic* in 1887, at the start of his service with the White Star Line. He would turn out to be one of the most robust skippers of them all, E. J. Smith.

The *New York Herald* described events:

'A white fog had snowed down upon the ocean and both vessels kept up the monotonous chant of the steam whistles. The officers of the *Britannic* heard the whistles of the *Celtic*, and soon the two big steamships were engaged in an awful game of blindman's buff. Crowds of *Britannic's* passengers ran from side to side as the sound of the *Celtic's* hoarse warning came weirdly, now from one direction and now from another through the damp, thick vapour. Both vessels slackened speed as they approached nearer and nearer.

'Suddenly a huge shadow loomed up. There was a general cry of delight as the majestic *Celtic* swept grandly into sight. It was followed by shrieks of terror. The sharp, giant prow of the oncoming steamship was headed straight for the *Britannic*. The *Celtic* reversed her engines. It was too late.

'As the two vessels struck there was a terrific roar, and the sea was churned into foam by the shock. The prow of the *Celtic* struck the port side of the *Britannic* abaft the mizzenmast, tearing a gap four feet wide in her side at the water line.

'It was a glancing blow. Plunging ahead with her helm hard a port, the torn prow of the *Celtic* swept back along her ponderous rival groaning and tearing away the massive iron bulwarks of the main deck like so much brown paper.'

The damage to both vessels was considerable. However, in one respect at least, *Britannic* had been lucky. Had *Celtic's* bow struck her a couple of feet further forward then her engine room would have been opened to the sea and she would almost certainly have foundered. Instead the damage was just aft of the bulkhead at the rear end of the engine room, and Number 4 hold was flooded. The hole in her side extended to about 4ft below the water line. Three of her lifeboats had been smashed and deckhouses had been damaged. Four of *Britannic's* steerage passengers had been killed in the collision and a further nine were severely injured.

At first there was a very real possibility that *Britannic* might sink, so it was thought advisable to transfer her passengers to the slightly less battered *Celtic*. In short order half a dozen boatloads were rowed to the other vessel. Meanwhile *Britannic's* carpenters were more than equalling the efforts of those aboard *Celtic*, after all they were more used to this sort of emergency repair work, serving as they did with Captain Perry. By midnight they had managed to patch the hole in the ship's side sufficiently to halt the incoming water but the vessel had settled about 5ft deeper than usual in the water and had developed a pronounced list to starboard. *Celtic* had fared better in the collision, but not by much. Her bow below deck level had been completely torn away and only outstanding work by her carpenters in shoring up the forward bulkheads kept her afloat.

Soon after midnight both vessels were able to get under way. As they steamed slowly towards New York guns were fired, at one-minute intervals, and all lights were turned on so that each could be sure the other was still afloat. During the night *Britannic* buried her dead; sewn into canvas sacks they were quietly consigned to the deep. *Britannic* and *Celtic* arrived off New York at about 1am on 24 May. Still shrouded in fog, both ships declined to attempt entering the harbour and dropped anchor outside. Two and a half miles from harbour *Britannic* was met by the *J. G. Merritt*, a steamer owned by the Merritt Wrecking Company, which added her pumps to those of the White Star vessel. The mail from both ships was removed by the tug *Fletcher*.

Celtic was towed into harbour and berthed at the White Star pier, at the foot of West Tenth Street. *Britannic* was also towed in, but to a Brooklyn dry-dock for repairs to her battered hull. The repairs, surprisingly, took the Brooklyn yard less than three weeks, and on 15 June *Britannic* left New York to complete her voyage.

As is usual after a collision involving loss of life an Inquiry was convened to determine who, if anyone, was to blame for the incident. Held at the New York office of the British Consul under Vice-Consul William R. Hoare, the Inquiry began on 7 June 1887. Assisting Vice-Consul Hoare were three Atlantic steamer captains. Evidence was heard from the masters and crew of both vessels and on 9 June the Inquiry declared both captains guilty of failing to observe regulations for the prevention of collisions at sea, Perry for steaming at too high a speed under the conditions prevailing and for failing to sound his whistle at not more than two minute intervals when in fog, and Irvine for steaming at speeds greater than could be considered prudent. A copy of the Inquiry's findings was lodged with the Board of Trade.

On 4 June 1887 Ismay wrote to the Mayor of Liverpool announcing his intention, in commemoration of Queen Victoria's 50 years on the throne, and his own 50th birthday, of establishing a seamen's pension fund open to all who had served in the mercantile marine for at least 25 years, and were no longer able to serve, and who had attained the age of 50. By putting up £20,000 of his own money Ismay could supply a number of £20 per annum pensions. The whole scheme was to be administered by the Mercantile Marine Service

Association.

In an age notable for rich men's philanthropy T. H. Ismay most certainly was not backward in doing his bit to help the needy. Mrs Ismay wrote of him, 'Mr Ismay is regarded as a friend in thousands of homes, where his name is associated with the comfort, happiness and prosperity of those who have found pleasure in his service.'

Because of the interest T. H. Ismay and William Imrie held in the Asiatic Steam Navigation Company, Ismay and his wife, Margaret, decided to take a trip to India, partly to see how the line was getting on, and partly as a holiday. On 26 October they left Dawpool accompanied by Gustav Wolff, and set out on the five month trip. As the junket was at least partly a holiday they travelled by train across Europe, taking in the sights of France, Switzerland and Italy where they joined the SS *Nizam*, bound for Alexandria. Once in Egypt they visited the Pyramids, the Nile, Cairo and everywhere else they could think of. Having exhausted the sights of Egypt they boarded the SS *Peshawar* and headed for Bombay.

Once in India the group proceeded to see as many of the sights on offer in the sub-continent as possible, by elephant, train, steam launch, horse, carriage and pony. On one occasion they were supposedly travelling by night sleeper from Lucknow to Allahabad when Wolff had a slight disagreement with the stationmaster at Cawnpore over the price of the fare. The argument was definitely won by the stationmaster who quietly had Wolff's carriage uncoupled from the train. When the party awoke the following morning Mr and Mrs Ismay were in Allahabad, while Gustav Wolff was still in a siding at Cawnpore.

On 28 March 1888 the Ismays arrived home from their trip to the east to learn that, while they had been away, J. Bruce had met, and become unofficially engaged to, Miss Florence Schieffelin of New York.

As far as Thomas and Margaret were concerned, the engagement of their eldest son could only bring a change for the better. Since his arrival in New York, being beyond the immediate reach of his father's discipline, the young J. Bruce had become something of a tearaway. He had teamed up with a few other rich young men of his own age, among them Harold Sanderson who would loom large in the fortunes of the White Star Line, and set about enjoying the pleasures on offer. Thomas and Margaret had been quite worried about the direction J. Bruce's life seemed to be taking, and were trying to decide what to do about him when he suddenly gave up his wild ways in favour of devoting his time to Miss Schieffelin.

Florence Schieffelin was no mean catch for the young Englishman. She was the eldest daughter of Mr and Mrs George Schieffelin, who were members of one of the oldest and most respected families in New York. When she and J. Bruce first met, Florence was not over impressed with him, but young Ismay bided his time, taking every opportunity to meet the young lady again. On Thanksgiving Day 1887 Mrs Hude Beekman, Florence's aunt, threw a party at the Tuxedo Club, in New Jersey, to which both Florence and J. Bruce were invited. During the course of the party Ismay managed to talk Florence into accompanying him on a walk by the lake. By the time they returned to the party he had persuaded her to marry him.

Mr Schieffelin was not pleased by the prospect of his daughter marrying an Englishman, and said so. He did not relish the idea of Florence going to live in England, so he insisted that the couple wait for a year, to be absolutely sure of their feelings. Thomas and Margaret Ismay responded in exactly the same manner when they first heard of the unofficial engagement. By April 1888 it had become apparent to Mr and Mrs Schieffelin that their daughter and Joseph Bruce were still intent on getting married, so they gave their consent with one proviso, that they would always live in America.

Demonstrating conclusively that he really was a chip off the old block, Ismay agreed at once, and the engagement was formally announced in the New York papers on 12 April. They were married on 4 December 1888, at the Church of the Heavenly Rest, New York. Thomas and Margaret Ismay were unable to attend the wedding of their eldest son, however, supposedly because of Thomas's commitments as a member of Lord Hartington's Royal Commission on the administration of the Army and Navy.

Because of the ever growing demand for fresh meat, and the consequent need for vessels capable of transporting live animals across the Atlantic, the White Star Line had commissioned six such vessels. *Cufic[1]*, the first of these White Star livestock carriers, was launched at Belfast on 10 October 1888.

Despite his promise to Mr and Mrs Schieffelin always to live in America, J. Bruce and Florence arrived in Liverpool, aboard the *Adriatic*, on 22 December 1888, where they were met aboard by T. H. Ismay. The happy couple were taken to Dawpool where they were made welcome by the rest of the family. Florence's reaction to the house was entirely predictable; she hated it. She found it cold as there was no central heating and Thomas Ismay would not allow fires to be lit in the bedrooms until teatime. Also Florence found the house to have too few bathrooms, baths being taken in the bedroom.

The Ismays, however, were delighted with their new family member. Her typical American lack of formality in a Victorian society that held formality above all else, especially where young women were concerned, made Florence a real favourite with the younger female Ismays.

Although a great philanthropist, in his private life Thomas could at times be parsimonious and exacting with his servants. Every morning Thomas Henry left the house for work at 8 o'clock. He usually walked to the station, where he caught the train to James Street. If he happened to see a fallen leaf on the drive as he walked down it, he would place a stone on top of the offending fragment of foliage. If the leaf was still there when he got home that evening he would summon all 10 gardeners and demand to know what they had been doing all day.

Chapter 9
1889-1899

The year 1889 began tolerably well for the White Star Line with the launch, on 1 January, of the second of their livestock carriers, the *Runic¹*. The ship would enter service with the line the following year. However, things never seemed to run smoothly for long. Less than four weeks later, the *Republic¹*, under the command of Captain Edward John Smith, ran aground off Sandy Hook when she arrived from Liverpool on 27 January. After five hours the ship was refloated and managed to navigate safely to the White Star pier in New York harbour and offload her passengers. Shortly afterwards a furnace flue in the forward, lower boiler fractured. Three men were killed and another seven were seriously injured. Not a man to over-dramatise events Captain Smith dismissed the incident, describing the damage to his ship as slight and saying that it could be repaired in a few hours. He was able to add, in a lighter vein, that the injured crewmen had been able to walk from the ship to a waiting ambulance.

On 20 February J. Bruce Ismay and his wife returned to New York, aboard the *Germanic*. Once there J. Bruce demonstrated his intention not to remain for too long by renting a house, 444 Madison Avenue, rather that buying one outright. In July of the following year they were back in England, where events took a turn that would make Joseph Bruce Ismay's return to the United Kingdom permanent.

Sometime in 1889 Thomas Henry Ismay was, rather ironically as things were to turn out, appointed chairman of the Board of Trade Lifesaving Appliances Committee. Five years later that same committee would lay down regulations covering the number of lifeboats a new passenger vessel must have, based on the tonnage of the ship. Those regulations, which did not envisage a vessel of more than 10,000 tons, would remain in effect for almost 20 years and were long believed to be at least partly responsible for the terrific loss of life in the *Titanic* disaster of 1912.

Mr and Mrs T. H. Ismay were in Belfast on 21 May 1889, inspecting the new *Teutonic*, when the Prince of Wales visited Harland & Wolff to open a new dock. After the dockside ceremony the Prince, with Sir Edward Harland, visited the *Teutonic* where he was received by Thomas Ismay. With the dignitaries conspicuously adorning the bridge the *Teutonic* proceeded to enter the new dock, where the Prince declared it open. On the following day Thomas's wife was introduced to the Prince at a luncheon in Liverpool Town Hall. The Ismays had reached the top of the social ladder.

Late in June T. H. Ismay was back in Belfast for the launching of the *Majestic*, which took place on the 29th. *Teutonic* and *Majestic* were the first new liners the company had bought for the North Atlantic route for a decade and a half. Almost a month later Thomas was off on his travels again, this time to Holyhead for *Teutonic's* trials.

On 1 July *Teutonic* ran aground and was stranded for six hours in Belfast Lough. She was changing anchorages before leaving for Liverpool to begin her service with White Star when the grounding occurred. Following her trials and spell aground, *Teutonic* sailed to the Mersey where eight 4.7in quick-firing guns were fitted in just 24 hours, demonstrating how quickly an innocent passenger vessel could be made to resemble a warship. The Queen's Golden Jubilee Review of the fleet had been arranged to be held at Spithead in August 1889, and *Teutonic* was to be one of the star attractions as the first armed merchant cruiser. Because of bad weather the fleet review was postponed for two days, until Monday 5 August. However, on the Sunday the Prince of Wales and his nephew, Kaiser Wilhelm II, visited the *Teutonic* to inspect her. The German Emperor was very impressed with the ship, and remarked to the Prince of Wales, 'We must have some of these.'

As soon as the Royal visit was over the *Teutonic* got under way, heading for Liverpool, which she reached at about 6.00 on Monday morning. Two days later, having had her guns removed, she was ready for her maiden voyage to New York. Aboard for the trip were all of the Ismays (except J. Bruce and Florence), the Pirries and Harland's chief designer, the Honourable Alexander Montgomery Carlisle (who would later play a leading part in the design of the *Olympic* Class liners for the White Star Line) and his family. The ship left Liverpool on 7 August.

On the following day *Teutonic* stopped to pick up mail from Queenstown in Ireland, where word reached the ship that a certain Mrs Maybrick had been found guilty of poisoning her husband James, a well-known Liverpool cotton broker with whom the Ismays were probably acquainted. Mrs Maybrick had been sentenced to hang for the murder, but the sentence was later commuted to life imprisonment. (More than a century later a diary was unearthed, supposedly written by James Maybrick, and showing him to have been 'Jack the Ripper', so it seems vaguely possible that Mrs Maybrick's custodial sentence might have been a little on the harsh side, but I somehow doubt it.)

Teutonic reached Sandy Hook in the early minutes of 15 August 1889, after a passage lasting 6 days, 14 hours and 20 minutes, during which she had encountered her fair share of rough weather. It also appears that Thomas Ismay had made a speech during the voyage, which had offended a number of passengers, although he thought it innocuous enough. Sadly, I have been unable to discover just what he said to cause so much displeasure.

The Ismays were in New York for a week while the *Teutonic* was turned around and prepared for the return journey. In the time available to them they met Florence's parents for the first time. This first meeting was especially notable in one respect because, while the Ismay family were being entertained at the Schieffelin home, Bower Ismay, Joseph Bruce's brother, met another of their daughters, Constance, whom he would later marry.

On 22 August the *Teutonic* left New York on the return leg of her maiden voyage, and arrived at Liverpool 6 days, 16 hours and 34 minutes later, on the 29th.

It was at about this time that James, the favourite son of the Ismay family, having completed his time at Oxford, finally joined the family business, working in his father's offices.

In July 1890 J. Bruce Ismay and his family returned to England aboard the *Majestic*, ostensibly for a holiday but there was business to be considered. While he was staying at the family home his father suggested that he and his brother James be made partners in the firm of Ismay, Imrie & Co with the object of Joseph becoming the head of the firm when Thomas retired. As usual Thomas wanted something in return. He would only make his eldest son his successor if he returned to live in England permanently, otherwise his younger, and favourite, son James would take over. At first J. Bruce wanted to stay in America, probably as much to spite his father as for any other reason, and anyway he had given his word to Florence's parents that he would live in the United States, and he liked the job he was doing, but there was the offer of the top job with the White Star Line to contemplate.

On 17 September J. Bruce Ismay left England to return to New York with his family. Once back in New York he set about persuading his father-in-law to release him from his promise. He had a powerful argument on his side in that it would increase Schieffelin's daughter's social standing if she were married to the head of a company rather than to a mere agent. No doubt Mr Schieffelin had already considered this eventuality before he ever gave his consent for his daughter to marry an Englishman. Anyway, he was persuaded, and gave his permission; after all, it was not as if the family would have any difficulty keeping in touch, and fares would not present a problem either. A year after leaving, J. Bruce Ismay and his family were once again in England, this time permanently.

On 1 January 1891 both Joseph Bruce and his younger brother James Ismay were made partners in the firm of Ismay Imrie, a clear indication of the high esteem in which Thomas Ismay held young James, and another slight on his elder brother. There can be no doubt but that T. H. Ismay had some reason to dislike his eldest son, a dislike that had, as it turned out, given him a clearer perspective than he might otherwise have had. After all, it was not James Ismay who would sell the family firm to an American financier whilst ensuring that he had a very well paid position in that financier's business empire while his siblings were pushed out of the company completely. At the time the brothers were made partners J. Bruce Ismay was still in America and would not return to Liverpool for another nine months.

Nomadic[1], the third White Star livestock carrier was launched at Belfast on 11 February 1891. At about the same time, while *Teutonic* was making her way from New York to Liverpool, she ran into gale force winds and heavy seas that lasted for two full days. During the storm her foresail was torn to shreds by the wind and the seas breaking over the ship poured into passengers' staterooms. When she finally arrived at Liverpool it was so foggy that trying to enter the port was out of the question so she had to wait for more than another day to offload her passengers. A little later in the year *Teutonic* would take the Blue Riband and hold it for just two months. This was the last time a White Star ship was to hold, or supposedly to attempt to take, the record for the fastest Atlantic crossing. Instead the company would rely on having the largest and most comfortable vessels to attract customers.

In 1891 T. H. Ismay served on the Admiralty Committee on the Royal Naval Reserves under Admiral Sir George Tryon. Two years later, when he single-handedly brought about the destruction of two British capital ships, the *Victoria* and *Camperdown*, Admiral Tryon was to do much the same for the Royal Navy's reputation for seamanship as Captain E. J. Smith was to do for that of the White Star Line.

Another livestock carrier built for the White Star Line, the fourth, was launched at Belfast on 12 March 1891. *Tauric* was a little lighter than *Nomadic* at 5,728 tons, but at 460ft long and with a beam of just over 49ft she was about the same size.

In April 1891 word reached Thomas and Margaret Ismay that Florence had given birth to a son, who was to be christened Thomas Henry Ismay after his grandfather. (Joseph Bruce and Florence would later have another son whom they would call Thomas Bruce Ismay, for reasons that will become apparent.). T. H. Ismay was delighted with the news that he had a grandson, and by the proposed name, although to avoid confusion the child would be known as Henry, or at least that was the plan.

Although T. H. Ismay was pleased, as always, to have got his own way when he persuaded his eldest son to return to live in England, he could not tolerate the idea that J. Bruce and his family might come to live with him at Dawpool. To avoid that possibility, in August he rented Wiston House, at Mossley Hill in Liverpool for his son, and Mrs Ismay sent one of the Dawpool staff, Ellen, to go and cook for Florence, for £30 a year.

As usual with J. Bruce Ismay, just when everything seemed to be going well, disaster struck. In the period prior to the Ismays leaving New York on the *Teutonic* the city was enduring a heatwave and the infant Thomas Henry was badly affected. The six-month-old child was suffering from chronic diarrhoea and the doctors believed that an ocean voyage might help, so rather than postpone their projected return to England, the Ismays decided to stick to their original timing and take the youngster with them.

As it happened, Mrs Florence Ismay was not a good traveller, or mother it seems, and for the entire voyage across the Atlantic she was confined to her bunk and unable to see to the welfare of her sick child. The baby was placed in the care of a young Irish nursemaid who was clearly not up to the task of looking after the afflicted infant sufficiently well.

When the *Teutonic* arrived in Liverpool it was met by T. H. Ismay, who took one look at the child and declared, 'That baby is going to die, he must see a doctor instantly.' Ismay senior was so concerned about the infant that before they left Liverpool he telephoned his wife to tell her, and also rang the family physician, Dr Russell, to arrange for him to be on hand when they reached home. They reached Dawpool at about 10am on 30 September, and both the doctor and Mrs Ismay expressed concern over the state of the child. During the day young Thomas Henry deteriorated steadily and by the evening the doctor was called again, and this time he stayed the night. On the morning of 1 October the baby was no better, and Mrs Ismay thought that he had become even worse, if anything. The doctor left at about 8.00 that morning, probably to see to his other patients, but he was back by 11.30 when he prescribed brandy and beef tea (a sure cure for chronic diarrhoea!). By 3.00 in the afternoon the infant had unsurprisingly become much worse, and he died an hour later.

T. H. Ismay was distraught and never even left the house on that, or the next, day. However, by 3 October he was sufficiently recovered to attend the funeral and rode in the carriage with Joseph, James, and young Thomas's remains when it left Dawpool for Anfield Cemetery that morning. J. Bruce Ismay never fully recovered from the death of his first-born son and always afterwards tended to avoid contact with children as much as possible, with the single exception of his eldest daughter Margaret.

On 1 January 1892 T. H. Ismay officially retired from the firm of Ismay, Imrie & Co, although he remained as chairman and took an active part in the running of the company; so active in fact that his decisions were still regarded as final. At about the same time he became president of the Liverpool Royal Infirmary, and started an endowment fund for the hospital with £1,000 of his own money. He was also made High Sheriff of Cheshire, and his whole family turned out to see him in his robes and carriage. Thomas H. Ismay also took an interest in the officer cadet training ship *Conway*, and he and members of the family were on hand for its prize givings, although he still took a greater interest in the boys from the *Indefatigable*, which he had helped to found.

With more time to himself Thomas could better look after the various charities he was involved with, such as taking 200 deaf and dumb children for a one-day cruise on the *Teutonic*. The children should have thoroughly enjoyed their cruises because there was always something exciting going on. For example, *Teutonic* was run into by the steamer *Indiana* as she tried to dock at Liverpool on 26 March 1892. Three of the *Teutonic's* hull plates were dented in the collision. Not at all satisfied with its performance so far, the *Indiana* rammed and seriously damaged a nearby collier.

Naronic, the fifth of White Star's livestock carriers was launched at Belfast on 26 May 1892. Although primarily intended as a cattle boat the *Naronic* also had a Board of Trade certificate allowing her to carry as many as 150 passengers. Just over a month later the *Bovic*, the sixth White Star livestock carrier was launched at Belfast, on 28 June. In most respects she was practically identical to *Naronic*. White Star's cattle boats were not to prove the luckiest class of ship ever built and, in common with many of the early liners built at Belfast, seem to have been predisposed to mechanical failure. For example, the *Nomadic* limped into Liverpool on 13 October 1892, having completed her journey on just one engine after the other had broken down.

It seems that luck had again turned against the Oceanic Steam Navigation Company in a big way by late in 1892. The *Tauric* ran into the Allan liner *Buenos Ayrean* in the Mersey on 11 November. The *Tauric's* bow was stove in and the Allan liner's stem was twisted. But things were destined to get worse before they got better. Just over a fortnight later, on 27 November, *Naronic* arrived at Liverpool from New York. During the voyage the exceptionally high number of 34 head of cattle had died aboard the ship.

Then came another of the major disasters that seem to punctuate the story of the White Star Line. *Naronic*, under the command of Captain William Roberts, sailed from the Alexandra Dock, Liverpool, for New York on 11 February 1893. The pilot, William Davis, was dropped off at Point Lynas, and *Naronic* was never seen again. About three weeks later, at 2am on 4 March, the steamer *Coventry* came across an upturned lifeboat with *Naronic's* name painted on it, drifting in position 44°02'N, 47°37'W. About 12 hours later the same ship came across another deserted lifeboat at 44°34'N, 46°25'W. This second boat was in good condition and its mast was floating close by, attached by the painter as if it had been used as a sea anchor. *Naronic's* name was painted on the bow, positively identifying the small boat as one of hers. It would appear that whatever happened to the *Naronic*, there was time to get at least one lifeboat away safely.

A Board of Trade Inquiry into the loss of the *Naronic* was held in St George's Hall, Liverpool, with a Mr Paxton appearing for the Board of Trade and Mr Dickinson, of Hill Dickinson, for the owners. Mr Paxton told how the ship had left the dock at about 6.00 on the morning of 11 February. There were 74 crewmen aboard, 14 of them cattlemen, as well as 3,572 tons of general cargo and 1,017 tons of Welsh coal. From the stowage plans it was ascertained that the vessel would have been drawing about 20$\frac{1}{4}$ft of water forward, and 6in more aft. Davis, the pilot, explained that it was because of heavy seas that he did not leave the ship at the Bar, as usual, but remained aboard until she was off Point Lynas, and that when he left her the vessel was behaving very well. *Naronic* had made her first three voyages under the command of Captain Thompson, who now commanded the *Bovic*, and the next three under Captain Roberts, who was still in command when the ship disappeared on her seventh voyage. Her Chief Officer, Mr White, held a master's certificate and had been with the White Star Line since 1874. As far as the court was informed there was nothing dangerous in her cargo and no ice had been reported within a hundred miles of where she seemed to have disappeared. After weighing up the facts it had been presented with, the Inquiry published its findings, which were that it had not got the faintest idea what had happened to the ship.

As usual with the White Star Line, *Naronic* and her cargo had been uninsured so the company would have to stand the loss of £121,685 for the vessel and £61,855 for her cargo.

Probably because of their accident record, which would have tended to push insurance premiums up, White Star ships habitually sailed either under-insured or not insured at all.

To help make good some of the money the line had lost in the *Naronic* disaster, and in keeping with its policy of selling ships once they began to show their age, the *Celtic*[1] was sold in 1893.

The run of bad luck was not over and after breaking her propeller shaft the *Ionic* had to be towed into Cape Town by the *Hawarden Castle* on 15 February. Then, two days later, on 17 February, the *Belgic* arrived at San Francisco from Hong Kong and Yokohama. As there were several cases of smallpox aboard, the ship was detained at quarantine until she had been fumigated. Just over a week after *Belgic* was quarantined, on 26 February, *Majestic* was forced to steam at reduced speed for several hours using just her port engine, the other having broken down.

Cevic, the penultimate White Star livestock carrier was launched at Belfast on 25 September. She entered service the following year, along with the 395-ton tender *Pontic*, acquired for use in the River Mersey.

Gothic, ordered the year before from Harland & Wolff, was handed over to her new owners in November 1893. Specially designed for the London–New Zealand trade she was the first twin-screw vessel to be used on that route, and the largest ship, at 7,755 tons, ever to enter the Port of London. Thousands of people came to see the new ship and wish her well when she set off on her maiden voyage to Wellington on 30 December. Within a short time she had broken the speed records for both the outward and return trips by averaging better than 14kt. Things seemed to be looking up.

In May 1894 T. H. Ismay and his immediate family took a trip to New York aboard the *Majestic*. The object of the trip was to see the Chicago Exhibition, which they did before going to Washington to meet President Grover Cleveland. On 29 May they left New York for Liverpool, aboard the *Teutonic*. On their return to England J. Bruce Ismay and his wife found the house they wanted, Sandheys, in Mossley Hill Road. It was a large and rather hideous Georgian-style house surrounded by its own 10 acres of ground. With the unerring Ismay eye, Joseph Bruce had managed to find another eyesore to buy, although not in the same league as his father's house, Dawpool.

In December 1894 *Germanic* was returned to Harland & Wolff to be modernised. Her funnels were lengthened, an extra open deck was added, and the original engines were replaced with new triple-expansion ones built by Harland & Wolff.

White Star still did not seem to have mastered the art of transporting live cattle. On *Cufic's* arrival in Liverpool from New York on 17 January 1895 Captain Edward John Smith reported that no fewer than 75 had died on the trip.

In 1895 the six-year-old *Runic*[1] was sold to the West India and Pacific Steamship Company, for £37,500 and renamed *Tampican*. She would win notoriety 22 years later when, as the *Imo*, she ran into the French ammunition ship *Mont Blanc* at Halifax. The French vessel exploded killing and injuring almost 10,000 people and flattening half of the town.

The *Adriatic* sailed for New York on 22 March 1895 but during the crossing she ran into a tremendous storm. Battling the heavy seas the ageing liner took a severe beating, arriving in New York after 10 days at sea. Many of her 834 passengers suffered minor injuries and the ship lost one lifeboat, torn away by the waves, with three more smashed to matchwood.

In May 1895 the *Germanic* re-entered service. On the 13th, two days before her scheduled departure for New York, Mrs T. H. Ismay and her daughter Ethel went to the docks to see what sort of a job the builders had made, and were very impressed. 'She has been beautifully done up,' said Mrs Ismay. The old *Oceanic*[1] was also in the Liverpool dock, for the first time in 15 years. Mrs Ismay had always regarded *Oceanic* as her favourite ship, but the ageing vessel seems to have lost some of her charm and even though Mrs Ismay had lunch aboard, she was disappointed in the ship. It is hardly surprising that after almost a quarter of a century of progress passing her by that the old *Oceanic* did not seem so impressive as she once had. The company's management agreed and *Oceanic*, White Star's very first liner, was sent for scrap in 1896. The 25-year-old vessel had not only pioneered the service to the New World but had also been the first ship on the Occidental & Oriental Line's Pacific service which began in 1875.

Georgic[1], the eighth and last of White Star's livestock carriers, was launched on 22 June 1895. The *Georgic* was intended to replace the lost *Naronic* and was a larger, improved version of the same general type. Towards the end of July the new ship completed her trials and, with both Thomas Henry and Joseph Bruce Ismay aboard, made the short run from Belfast to Liverpool, 'a most pleasant trip'. One small hiccup that T. H. Ismay appears to have neglected to mention on his return to Liverpool was the small matter of *Georgic* running aground as she left Belfast and having to be towed clear; a not terribly auspicious start to her career.

On 10 July Liverpool's new Riverside Station for Atlantic passengers was formally opened. The Mersey Docks and Harbour Board put on a celebratory luncheon, and the LNWR laid on a special train which brought several of its directors to the new station. The White Star Line's *Majestic* came alongside the landing stage, completing the link between the land and the sea; commanding the *Majestic* for the first time was Captain Edward John Smith, or E. J. to the men who served him (but only behind his back).

Belgic ran ashore at King's Point in Sateyama Bay, Japan, on 9 September 1895 while *en route* to Yokohama from San Francisco. Although not seriously damaged in the grounding, the *Belgic* was well and truly stuck and it took a month to get her off. Once refloated she was taken to the Yokosuka dry-dock so that the bottom of her hull could be repaired.

On 11 December 1895, soon after leaving Liverpool in dense fog, *Germanic*, under the command of Captain McKinstry, rammed the inbound 900-ton steamer *Cumbrae* in fog. The smaller vessel was almost cut in two in the collision and consequently foundered, although her 28 passengers and crew were rescued by the White Star liner. *Germanic's* bows were badly damaged and her voyage had to be cancelled. Her passengers and mail were transferred to the *Adriatic*.

The list of serious accidents, mechanical failures and fires throughout the early 1890s can have done little for the line's reputation, and must have adversely affected the numbers of passengers prepared to travel. The company's marketing literature unsurprisingly had other concerns. Around the middle of the decade White Star produced a series of brochures informing would-be American travellers who were thinking about 'doing' Europe that they could do so for as little as $500, all in.

On Christmas Eve 1895 word reached the Ismays, as they all gathered at Dawpool for the season, that Sir Edward Harland had died suddenly. Sir Edward's funeral was on 28 December and T. H. Ismay made the journey to Belfast in order to attend. Harland and Ismay had been friends for 25 years and the White Star Line owed a lot of its success, and a lot of its hardships, to the vessels that had come from the Harland & Wolff yard. Genuinely upset by the death of his friend, Ismay decided in 1896 to give £2,000 to the trustees of the Liverpool University College for a scholarship, to be called The Edward Harland Memorial Scholarship.

In a classic display of incompetence, *Gaelic* ran aground at Shimonoseki, Japan, on 15 August 1896. Company rules clearly stated that the sounding lead should have been used regularly while the ship was so close to land. Had it been, then the shallows would have been spotted in time to avoid the grounding of and consequent damage to the ship. The fore hold flooded to a depth of 12ft and the vessel was stuck for some days before she could be refloated and taken to Nagasaki for dry-docking, where she arrived on 28 August.

Mr and Mrs T. H. Ismay decided to visit Killarney races in Ireland in the summer of 1896, but the only convenient vessel calling at Queenstown was not a White Star ship, but a Cunarder. Nevertheless, the Ismays booked passage and at 5pm on 29 August they sailed aboard the *Campania*. Mrs Ismay was not impressed with the rival line's ship and wrote, 'had a nasty passage and a very small cabin'. She also complained that *Campania* 'rolled a good deal'.

For the return journey the Ismays decided against slumming and sailed aboard their own *Majestic*. 'The ship looked beautifully bright and clean,' she commented. The difference in standards of cleanliness Mrs Ismay had noticed were commented on again, many years later, when the Cunard and White Star lines were merged. However, cleanliness is not everything required by a shipping line; seamanship is a useful commodity as well. From their accident records it is relatively easy to see which line had the better record where seamanship and ship handling were concerned.

In January 1897 the man behind the creation of both the Oceanic Steam Navigation Company and Harland & Wolff's shipyard died at his home at 19 Kensington Palace Gardens, London, aged 88. Gustavus Schwabe had been retired for some years, but it should always be remembered that it was his idea that T. H. Ismay start a line of steamers running between Liverpool and New York, and his money that had allowed Edward Harland to buy and improve the Queen's Island shipyard. Despite this loss, 1897 was not a particularly bad year for the White Star Line in general, and T. H. Ismay in particular. The line accepted the new *Delphic*[1] from the builders, and Ismay senior was offered a most unexpected honour.

On 16 June he was summoned to the Foreign Office where he was informed that the Queen planned to confer a baronetcy upon him. For once unsure of what to do, Thomas wired Joseph Bruce to come and help him make a decision. J. Bruce Ismay arrived the next morning and he and his father discussed the proposed honour. Although as the eldest son he would automatically inherit the baronetcy on the demise of his father, J. Bruce put no pressure on his father to accept, but rather helped him to make up his own mind. On the 18th T. H. Ismay wrote to the Honourable Schomberg-MacDonnell CB, thanking the Queen for even thinking of conferring such an honour on him, but politely declining it.

Because 1897 was the 60th year of Queen Victoria's reign, another review of Her Majesty's ships at Spithead was scheduled. Once again *Teutonic* was armed to the teeth ready to appear as an armed merchant cruiser. With 170 guests aboard she sailed for Spithead. When the review took place on Saturday 26 June 1897, the weather was perfect.

The big hit of the review was undoubtedly the *Turbinia*. This rather unusual looking vessel arrived at Spithead uninvited and proceeded to pass back and forth through the lines of warships at incredible speeds, sometimes reaching 32kt. Although Admiralty launches and pinnaces gave chase they were soon left far behind the peculiar little craft. The reason behind the strange behaviour of the *Turbinia* was simple. The inventor of a new type of turbine engine, the Honourable Charles Parsons, was determined to show off its potential in a way that the Royal Navy could not ignore; the Navy was suitably impressed and Parsons' turbines soon began to find their way into warships, and the mercantile marine was not far behind. After its display of speed and agility the little *Turbinia* tied up alongside the *Teutonic* and Thomas Henry and J. Bruce Ismay were invited aboard, along with a guest, Sir George Baden-Powell, to take a demonstration run.

The tiny vessel steamed quietly away from *Teutonic* and was soon lost amongst the assembled might of the Royal Navy. When she reappeared she was moving at a speed that could only be described as 'terrific'. *Turbinia* sliced through the water at something like 37mph with flames belching from her funnel, and with a good third of her keel lifted out of the water. The Ismays were forced to hold on to whatever they could find in order to withstand the tremendous buffeting and slipstream that the boat's sheer speed produced. Parsons had given *Turbinia* her head in an effort to impress the Ismays, and had succeeded to the point where he had managed to give them a real fright.

Although the Ismays were impressed by the performance of the *Turbinia,* they were also well aware that high speed was expensive in coal, so they elected to stay with the tried and tested reciprocating engines in their ships. The Allan Line was the first to adopt turbine engines for use on the Atlantic. Cunard was also impressed enough to fit turbines into its top class liners within the next 10 years, and it was those vessels that led to the production of White Star's *Olympic* Class ships, which also featured a turbine engine combined with the more traditional reciprocating variety.

In the meantime the everyday business of the line continued and on 17 August 1897, as she backed out of her New York dock, *Teutonic* ran into and sank an ice barge which was being towed by the tug *Peter Nevins*. On the very same day the *Coptic* suffered a twisted stem and several stoved in plates when she collided with the Japanese steamer *Minitogawa Maru* in Kobe harbour.

On 31 December 1897 the Oceanic Steam Navigation Company moved offices from 10 Water Street to the new, purpose-built premises at 30 James Street, Liverpool. Norman Shaw had designed, and was overseeing the construction of, the new offices, which probably accounts for their marked similarity to New Scotland Yard. Mrs T. H. Ismay went to inspect the new offices on 29 January 1898, and did not altogether like what she saw. They were very businesslike, she thought, but they lacked the cosiness of the old Water Street building. She also disliked the way that William Imrie did not have an office to himself, but had to make do with a curtained-off alcove in the corner of one of the main offices.

On the last day of February 1898, after unloading her cargo, *Bovic* damaged her bows (yet again) by running into the entrance to the docks. And less than a month later the *Georgic* escaped serious damage when she caught fire while at Liverpool on 3 March, thanks to the prompt action of the fire-fighters. In other words, by the standards of the White Star Line, things were going along quite smoothly in 1898, and it was time for another new ship to join the line — the 12,552-ton *Cymric*.

Harland & Wolff had for some time been working on the design of two new super-liners for White Star. The first of these ships was to be called the *Oceanic*[2] and the second, which was not actually built, because of events beyond anybody's control, and the name not issued until 12 years later, was to have been *Olympic*. On 24 July 1898 Thomas Ismay and his wife travelled to Belfast to look over the interior decoration proposed for the new ships, and were not entirely happy with what they saw. Ismay called in Trollope & Co to assist in designing the interior decoration, and, not having learned his lesson with the house at Dawpool, he also turned to Norman Shaw for advice. All through 1898 the Ismays had consultation after consultation with Trollope & Co and Norman Shaw as they tried to perfect the interior décor of the new *Oceanic*, which was rapidly approaching launch day. As the new vessel would be the company flagship and bear the company name they especially wanted everything to be perfect.

The magnificent new *Oceanic*[2] was launched on 14 January 1899. T. H. Ismay and his wife had made the trip to Belfast for the launching and stayed with the Pirries. Mrs Ismay described the event in her diary:

'Mr Pirrie left for the yard at 6 o'clock, Thomas at 9 and Mrs Pirrie and I at 10. The *Oceanic* was safely launched at about 11.20 a.m. A most beautiful sight it was to see the noble ship, glide so gracefully into the water. May she be all that we could wish.'

During 1899 the *Afric*, *Medic* and the slightly larger *Persic* all came from Harland & Wolff, one after another. The new ships were specially designed for use on the Australian run. Although Harland & Wolff built the best ships it possibly could for White Star, it did not always get it 100% right. Following her maiden voyage in 1899, which was rather surprisingly to New York, *Afric* was returned to the builders for seven months of alterations and improvements.

Other White Star vessels also appear to have behaved somewhat erratically at times. Whilst they may have been amongst the most luxurious vessels in the world, and at times some of the fastest, these ever larger vessels designed by the Belfast shipbuilders do not seem to have handled particularly well. Of course that may have had nothing at all to do with the design of the ships but could have been the result of poor seamanship on the part of the officers and crews employed by the line, or perhaps of some unwritten rule that pushed men and machines beyond their capabilities. Most certainly there was something badly amiss.

Not long after the launching of the *Oceanic* T. H. Ismay began to complain of pains in his chest. He had always been a very active man, and had seldom gone down with any illness except perhaps the occasional cold, so his doctors took this new development seriously. Despite the best efforts of his own physician, and several others, Thomas's condition continued to deteriorate and concern for his health began to affect the company. As we have seen, there had been plans to built a second ship along the same lines as the new *Oceanic*, but because T. H. Ismay was so ill these were put on hold.

Even without this addition White Star planned to begin the new century with new, bigger and more luxurious liners. There would be no room in the new look line for the old *Adriatic*[1]. Normally a ship that had outlived its usefulness to White Star would be sold off to another line, usually a non-competitor, for a secondary career. Not so for the *Adriatic*. She left Liverpool, bound for Preston and the breakers' yard on 12 February 1899, just over one month short of having completed 27 years' service with the line.

In February 1899 Mr and Mrs Thomas Ismay were taking a break in Brighton when they read in the evening paper that the *Germanic* had sunk at her berth in New York harbour on the night of 13 February 1899. Owing to a combination of mistakes, none of which would have done much harm on their own, the White Star Line had, if only temporarily, lost another ship. While being coaled in the middle of a blizzard, the *Germanic* had iced up to the extent that she had listed so far that her coaling doors had sunk below the level of the water. The sea had rushed into the bunkers, and the ship settled onto the harbour floor. It was estimated that almost 2,000 tons of ice had accumulated on the vessel's sides, superstructure and rigging.

The structure of the ship was undamaged and salvage from such shallow water was relatively simple so it was not long before the *Germanic* was back in Belfast for drying out and repair, and by the end of June she was again in service. For some reason the ship's owners exonerated her officers and crew of all blame for the sinking, even though Captain McKinstry clearly should have set his crew to clearing the ship of ice long before it had accumulated to the extent that it endangered the vessel. The icing up of a ship at sea, in an arctic storm, is perhaps understandable, but to allow a vessel to ice up to the extent that it rolled over and sank in a harbour with the resources of New York takes a little comprehending.

The icing up of the *Germanic* had one quite interesting side effect. The ice had begun to accumulate before the ship actually reached New York. The ports that would usually be used to offload the mails at the quarantine station were blocked, with the consequence that the vessel avoided stopping there, as it would usually be obliged to do, and proceeded directly to its berth at Pier 45, a useful trick to know if one wanted to import anything into the United States without the bother of showing it to Customs.

Slowly T. H. Ismay's health seemed to improve. At the end of March, he and Margaret went to Windermere, where they had stayed 40 years before. While they were there Thomas was taken ill again 'with a violent pain at the bottom of his bowel'. Mrs Ismay got her husband into bed and summoned a doctor, who gave him a dose of morphine. By 6 March Thomas was feeling much better and the couple returned to Dawpool. However, he was far from recovered and during the next few weeks he suffered several more attacks of violent pain. The illness had first been diagnosed as appendicitis but as it progressed this diagnosis was changed to 'gallstones'.

By 26 April Thomas felt fit enough to travel down to London and stay at Brown's Hotel to attend a dinner of the Royal Academy. He seems to have been free of attacks during the spell in London, but they began again when he and Margaret returned to Liverpool, although not badly enough to stop him getting out and about. He travelled to London in May and June 1899 to attend meetings of the Oceanic Steam Navigation Company and the LNWR and in July he and the family went to Belfast to look over the almost completed *Oceanic*, and to receive the freedom of the city.

In August he collapsed again, and was confined to bed as the *Oceanic* steamed majestically into the Mersey. He was too sick to accompany the new vessel on her maiden voyage, even though he wanted to. However, he insisted on going aboard the new ship, and on 26 August he did so, remaining aboard for about three-quarters of an hour. The effort seems to have been too much for him and by the 28th he was seriously ill again.

Margaret Ismay thought that Thomas's trouble might be his liver so a specialist, Mr Mayo Robinson of Leeds, was sent for. Arriving at midnight, Mr Robinson examined the patient immediately and pronounced that an operation would be necessary. According to the specialist the required operation could only be performed under cocaine, and not under a general anaesthetic. Thomas Ismay agreed to the operation, which was carried out in his own home on 31 August. Thomas's wife, two eldest sons and his daughters all stayed at the house until the operation was over, and believed successful. Mr Robinson found a large abscess on Thomas's gall duct which he thought he had dealt with, but the patient did not begin to recover and a second operation became necessary on 4 September, this time under a general anaesthetic, and was carried out at 9.00 that evening.

The next day Thomas insisted that his daughters go aboard the *Oceanic* for tea, although they did not want to leave him. It seems quite likely that Thomas sent his daughters away for a while because he knew he was dying, and wanted to talk to his wife. He asked her to arrange that prayers should be said for him in church.

On 13 September 1899 T. H. Ismay had a heart attack, followed by several more occurring at intervals until 23 November. Mrs Margaret Ismay wrote in her diary for that night:

'A very quiet night having had a draught from which he is very drowsy. Moved into my bed, but was only awake at intervals, and took little nourishment. At 5.45 p.m. he had a severe tightness in the chest and my beloved one passed peacefully away at 5 minutes past six. I had his hand until they removed me.'

Mrs Margaret Ismay never fully recovered from the loss of her husband, who had been her whole world. The death of Thomas Henry Ismay also marked the end of an era as far as the White Star Line was concerned.

As the new century began, Joseph Bruce Ismay took control of the line, with the assistance of his brother James, and two of his father's oldest friends and partners, William Imrie and W. S. Graves.

Chapter 10
1899-1904

Before we go any further it might well be a good idea to look in a little detail at the man who had taken control of the White Star Line, for he was very different from his father. Joseph Bruce Ismay had a talent for administration, and was able, when occasion demanded, to think quickly. He was in many ways the ideal man to take over a company that had already been built up, but would, in all probability, have been incapable of building it up himself. T. H. Ismay and his son did have some characteristics in common. Thomas had always considered his shareholders in every decision regarding company policy, believing that as it was their money which had made the whole thing possible, they had a right to expect the company to look after them. J. Bruce Ismay adopted exactly the same attitude.

Because he was naturally of a shy and retiring disposition, not exactly an asset in the hurly-burly of business, J. Bruce Ismay had long since adopted a hard shell that gave the appearance that he was arrogant, sarcastic, brusque, dogmatic and critical. The constant humiliations his father had subjected him to had reinforced that shell to the point that one had to know him quite well before it became apparent that the real J. Bruce Ismay was not what he appeared. He was obsessive about punctuality to the extent that if a member of staff at 30 James Street had an appointment with him they would arrive a few minutes early and wait for the exact moment of the appointment before knocking on his door.

Despite the hard outer shell Ismay was quite capable of displaying a social conscience, even if he generally did so as unobtrusively as he possibly could, unlike his father. One day when he was taking a ride on the top of a tram, something he often did when he needed to think out the solution to a problem, he noticed a group of children playing on the flat roof of a building. When he returned to the office he asked Mr Shelley (later to become publicity manager for the company) what the flat-roofed building was. Shelley made a few enquiries and discovered that the building housed an orphanage. On hearing this, J. Bruce Ismay had him make out a cheque for £500, and had it delivered to them straight away.

Probably J. Bruce Ismay's greatest failing as managing director of White Star was his inability to handle publicity. This was particularly unfortunate since, as the head of a famous shipping line, he was a public figure, and his father had actively encouraged the attention of the press. J. Bruce hated talking to reporters, and if he was approached by them he usually pointed out that White Star had a publicity department which would answer their questions, which he would not. He also had great difficulty with public speaking, and never made a formal speech in his life. This inability to talk to the press left him at a considerable disadvantage following the loss of the *Titanic*, and led to a number of misapprehensions about why he resigned from the company at about that time, which persist in some quarters to the present day. Enough of Mr Ismay, for the time being. Let us return to the everyday operations of the White Star Line.

As we have seen, *Afric*, *Medic* and *Persic* were all specially designed for the Australian trade, with two more similar ships to follow, but it was *Medic*, the second to be built, which was the first to voyage to the antipodes. The new ships were a little unusual in that they carried only one class of passenger, third class, who would be at liberty to take advantage of all the facilities on offer. *Medic* left Liverpool on 3 August 1899 on her maiden voyage.

Also making his maiden voyage for the White Star Line aboard *Medic* as her fourth officer, was Charles Herbert Lightoller (a name almost synonymous with disaster). Describing *Medic's* arrival in Sydney, Lightoller said that she was the largest ship ever to visit the port, and that the Australians were so impressed that they 'gave us the time of our lives'. *Afric*, *Medic* and *Persic* were very successful, so plans for the next two ships went ahead, although they would be a little larger than the first three, by about 500 tons.

Britannic¹ left Liverpool on what was to prove her last voyage to America on 16 August 1899. In keeping with White Star's policy of beginning the new century with a fleet of large modern liners, the 25-year-old vessel was declared surplus on her return. However, instead of going to the breakers' yard *Britannic* was requisitioned by the British Government almost as soon as White Star had declared her surplus to requirements. The Boer War officially began in the second week of October 1899, but it had really begun some time before when, with the knowledge of the British Government, the infamous Jameson Raid had taken place. This raid into Boer territory by a band of cut-throats under the command of Cecil Rhodes' lieutenant, Doctor Jameson, was a major cause of the conflict.

The British Government held an inquiry into the raid, which whitewashed its involvement. On the board of inquiry was one Charles Bigham, who as Lord Mersey would conduct a similar inquiry into the loss of the *Titanic*, and another into the loss of the *Lusitania*, and yet a third into the loss of the *Empress of Ireland*, all of which are now generally accepted as whitewashes.

Under the designation Transport Number 62 the *Britannic* made her first trip from Queenstown to South Africa on 26 October 1899. Troops, horses and supplies were needed to maintain the British Army, as the might of the Empire was brought to bear on a few Dutch settlers. In all, *Britannic* made 11 trips to South Africa and back, mostly from Southampton.

Meanwhile everything continued as usual with the other ships of the line. On 11 June 1900 Captain E. R. McKinstry was forced to order his ship, *Teutonic*, to steam at half speed for 24 hours while the starboard engine, which had broken down, was repaired. Aboard the *Teutonic* at the time was the greatest American financier of them all, John Pierpont Morgan, and his daughter. Morgan maintained his usual calm demeanour and reassured passengers that there was nothing to worry about, while his daughter organised games to take nervous passengers' minds off what was happening and stop them worrying that something might be wrong with the ship, which, as it happened, there most definitely was.

Certain of the line's older vessels were still having trouble with their machinery. At position 51°34'N, 21°24'W on 16 December, the 12-year-old *Cufic¹* lost her propeller in heavy weather. The Bristol City Line's *Kansas City* came to *Cufic's* assistance but could not get a line on the White Star freighter for three days because of the rough seas. While trying to secure a line from the *Kansas City*, Mr Crosby, *Cufic's* chief officer, was drowned. Eventually another vessel, the *Throstlegarth*, joined *Kansas City* and between them they managed to get the *Cufic* to Queenstown. *Throstlegarth* later towed the White Star vessel to Liverpool for repair. For her part in saving the *Cufic* from destruction the *Kansas City* was awarded salvage of £6,800.

Less than a week after *Cufic* had dropped her propeller, on 21 December, in yet another display of dazzling seamanship *Germanic* ran into the pier head at Liverpool, damaging her port bow. The following day *Runic²*, the first of the two new, slightly enlarged vessels destined for the Australian run, was delivered to the White Star Line.

It was not only the line's older vessels that appear to have been unmanageable in confined waters. While *Cymric* was still in the Mersey, in the process of leaving for New York on 19 January 1901, she managed to collide with the British steamer *Caribu Prince*. Although *Cymric's* deck and several hull plates were damaged, she still left Liverpool on schedule, heading for New York.

On 22 January 1901 Queen Victoria died at Osborne House on the Isle of Wight. The Victorian age was ended, and the Edwardian had begun, not that a change of monarchs brought any improvement in the White Star Line's luck. In the four years from 1896 to the end of the century the line's vessels had been involved in at least nine serious collisions, one major mechanical failure and a fire, not to mention that one had sunk. From the beginning of 1900 until the end of 1904 White Star ships were involved in 11 serious collisions, there were six major fires aboard, five vessels suffered significant mechanical failures, and one ran hard aground.

The old *Cufic¹* was sold to the Dominion Line in 1901 and renamed *Manxman*. As if to fill the vacancy created by *Cufic*, the last of the five vessels specially designed for the Australian run, *Suevic*, joined the White Star fleet on 9 March. Before the line could make any use of the new vessel, however, she was immediately requisitioned for use as a troopship.

On 4 April 1901 the first of what are known as the 'Big Four' liners, the *Celtic²*, was launched at Belfast, the last ship T. H. Ismay had ordered before his death. The *Celtic* was another departure from the norm in the world of passenger travel. Until then the White Star Line had specialised in building ships that could carry very large cargoes as well as a great many passengers. They had also pioneered the large livestock carrier, and large freighters with accommodation for a small number of passengers. The *Celtic* was something new inasmuch as she was a passenger liner first and a cargo vessel second.

Although she could carry 17,000 tons of general cargo, this was really seen as ballast to steady the ship in rough weather. That the cargo could be charged for, off-loaded at its destination and a new one taken aboard, was a bonus. Because the ship was not meant for high speed passages the amount of coal she required per day was a mere 260 tons, whereas the *Oceanic²* used 400 tons daily to maintain a speed only 3kt faster than *Celtic²*. The *Celtic²* was an immediate success, many passengers preferring her extra steadiness to the slightly faster passages offered by other ships. The White Star Line promptly ordered another similar vessel, the *Cedric*.

By 1901 the number of emigrants heading for America via Liverpool had dropped and in order to attract passengers the shipping lines were reducing fares; a rate war had begun. Many shipping lines were struggling to make ends meet. Not only could they not afford to pay their shareholders a dividend but they had no spare cash to invest in new vessels, which in its turn affected the shipbuilders. Waiting in the wings for just the situation that had arisen was the American financier John Pierpont Morgan.

Some years before, while making an Atlantic crossing, a fellow traveller had asked Morgan if it would be possible to buy up all of the shipping on the North Atlantic. Morgan, who had already bought up all of the railway rolling stock on the North Eastern seaboard of the United States, and who controlled most of that country's steel production, answered in the affirmative. He had done nothing about it at the time but was now ready to make a move.

There was very little American shipping on the North Atlantic at the beginning of the 20th century, just the American Line, which had formerly been the Inman Line. Morgan began by buying up the American Line and then turned his attention to the Red Star, Dominion, Atlantic Transport and Leyland lines, buying them all and forming the combine, International Mercantile Marine. The ships of the IMM lines continued to sail under their own house and national flags because under American law only ships actually built in America could fly the Stars and Stripes.

Having swallowed up the small fry J. P. Morgan turned next to the big fish, Cunard, White Star, Hamburg–Amerika and Norddeutscher–Lloyd. The two German lines initially led Morgan to believe that there would be little or no opposition to his taking them over, but all the time they had absolutely no intention of selling out to any American financier. They used the time gained by misleading Morgan to consolidate their position and gain the backing of the German Government. The Cunard Line, under the guiding hand of Lord Inverclyde, somewhat underhandedly made the British Government an offer it could not refuse. In return for a government subsidy of £2.6 million Cunard would build two new super-liners that would be bigger, faster and more luxurious than any other ships afloat.

Taking a leaf from White Star's book, the new Cunarders would be constructed in such a way that they could easily be converted into armed merchant cruisers in the event of war. The ships, the first of which would not come into service for another five years, were the *Lusitania* and *Mauretania*, and they would shortly be followed by a third sister, *Aquitania*. The new liners, at more than 30,000 tons apiece, and capable of a sustained speed better than 26kt, more than lived up to Lord Inverclyde's agreement. Cunard also undertook not to sell out to the Americans for at least 25 years, in return for an additional subsidy of £150,000 a year. Of the big four North Atlantic shipping lines Mr Morgan had failed to gain control of three, although he had reached a trade agreement with the two German lines, so he tried a little harder with the fourth.

While J. P. Morgan was making his plans and putting them into practice, it was business as usual for the Oceanic Steam Navigation Company. The *Georgic* again demonstrated the high standards of seamanship required by the White Star Line when she ran into the dock at Liverpool on 5 August. Two days later the *Oceanic*[2] rammed and sank coastal steamer *Kincora* in the Irish Sea. *Oceanic's* bow was damaged in the collision, but it was not all bad news that day and half of the *Kincora's* 14-man crew were saved.

At 5.00 the same morning a fire broke out in a linen closet on *Majestic*[1] as she approached New York. In an attempt to control the fire a hole was cut in the deck above and water was poured in. Initially it was believed that the measures taken had been successful, but as the fire was probably electrical in origin then pouring water on it was perhaps not the cleverest of moves. Anyway, sometime around 10.00 that morning the fire flared up again and dense smoke filled adjoining staterooms. This time the closet was filled with steam, which effectively deprived the fire of oxygen and put it out. Curiously, although the fire had taken all morning to extinguish, not one of the *Majestic's* officers had thought to inform Captain E. J. Smith of the potential danger facing his command – and, as any seaman will tell you, there is nothing more dangerous at sea than fire.

Because of the demands made on the White Star Line during the Boer War the monthly service between Liverpool and Australia, envisioned about five years before, could not actually begin until 1902. On their outward voyages the one-class ships called at Las Palmas, Cape Town, Albany, Adelaide and Melbourne, before terminating at Sydney. On the return journey they added Durban to their ports of call.

It had always been a policy of Morgan's to offer more for a company than it appeared to be worth when he moved to take it over. His approach to the Oceanic Steam Navigation Company was no exception to this general rule. He offered White Star's shareholders 10 times as much as the line earned in 1900. White Star, maintaining the character of the company as established by T. H. Ismay, was extremely secretive about its earnings so Morgan probably had no idea just how much he would have to lay out if his offer was accepted. As it happened, 1900 had been an exceptionally good year for the line because the British Government had been obliged to charter so many ships to transport the army to South Africa to defeat the Boers.

Initially J. Bruce Ismay resisted the takeover for a number of reasons. Although his father had been a millionaire when he died, his fortune had been split up between members of the family, as had been his shares in the White Star Line. One of the stipulations in his will was that his daughters would invest only in the Oceanic Steam Navigation Company, which meant that if IMM bought the White Star Line then they would have to relinquish their shares. However, 75% of the shareholders were for accepting Morgan's offer as it would give them a substantial profit on their original investment. Even William Pirrie, J. Bruce Ismay's friend, was for selling out, if only because he confidently expected all of the lines making up IMM to come to him for any new vessels. Still Ismay resisted selling out, so Morgan began a rate war, pushing fares down to the point where nobody could make a profit. The financier was in a position to keep his ships working at a loss for longer than the White Star Company so J. Bruce Ismay was forced to reconsider his position. Morgan really clinched the deal when he offered to keep Ismay on as managing director and chairman of the White Star Line.

Other partners in the Oceanic Steam Navigation Company were to retire. James Ismay became a farmer, working several thousand acres of land in Dorset. W. S. Graves bought a small estate near Horsham, and William Imrie retired to his home at Mossley Hill where he died five years later. By the time the takeover was agreed only two of the original partners in the Oceanic Steam Navigation Company were to remain with IMM and White Star: Joseph Bruce Ismay and Harold Sanderson. Ismay and Sanderson had met when Ismay had been in America in 1886, and had become friends. In 1895 Ismay had invited Harold Sanderson to join Ismay, Imrie & Co, and he was made a partner in 1900.

Of course, there was a public outcry about the sale of the line to an American owner, not least over what would happen in the event of war. However, once it was explained that because the ships had not been built in America they could not sail under the Stars and Stripes but would continue under the British flag, the public complaints were somewhat mollified. Morgan also guaranteed that should there be a European war then the ships would serve Britain in whatever capacity was required, and so the last obstacle was overcome.

By May 1902 agreement had been reached and on the 17th the last Annual General Meeting of the Oceanic Steam Navigation Company took place. Five days later the agreement between John Pierpont Morgan and the White Star Line was signed. The line would become part of IMM in December provided that Mr Morgan had paid the shareholders by then. All of the shareholders in the old OSN Company had been paid by

1 December 1902 and the agreement handing over control of the line to J. P. Morgan's International Mercantile Marine was signed. The White Star Line belonged to J. P. Morgan.

In 1902 radio (then usually called wireless) was still in its infancy, although not as primitive as is usually believed. The first patent, number 129,971, for a viable wireless telegraphy system was issued to Mahlon Loomis by the United States Patent Office on 30 July 1872. The first temporary wireless installation aboard ship was fitted to the American Line's *Saint Paul* in 1898, by the inventor Guglielmo Marconi and his company. German shipowners were so impressed by this demonstration that the first permanent installation aboard a first-class liner was fitted to the *Kaiser Wilhelm der Grosse* in 1900. Wireless first proved its worth on 3 March 1899 when it was used to summon lifeboats from shore to assist the *R. F. Mathews*, which had collided with the East Goodwin lightship. Then, on 1 January 1901, the *Princess Clementine* reported by wireless that the sailing barque *Midora* was sinking. A tug came to the rescue and picked up the survivors. On 12 December 1901 Marconi established the first wireless link across the Atlantic, between the British wireless station at Poldhu, Cornwall, and Newfoundland; wireless had come of age.

In the early years of the 20th century the ability to send personal messages from a ship at sea proved very popular with wealthy passengers. Because of the tremendous amount of radio traffic that was generated by passengers and accidents the Marconi Company (which provided most ship's radio operators) evolved a series of codewords to replace much used phrases, a sort of shorthand. Some of these codewords are quite enlightening, such as, 'Awatcha' which meant 'Await my letter: it will explain matters', 'Mydavs' meaning 'My draft on you for the amount of — is returned unpaid. Why?', 'Rapido' which meant 'Sinking rapidly.' (hopefully referring to someone aboard rather than a ship), or 'Youthfully' which meant 'You have misunderstood my telegram.' Overall, this was a not particularly reassuring collection of messages that were required so often that it was worth while making up shortened versions to save time.

Britannic¹ was released from government service some months after the Boer War had straggled to an end and she arrived back at Southampton with her final load of troops on 28 October 1902. Having already survived into the twentieth century, White Star relented and sent the old *Britannic* back to her builders to have new engines and boilers fitted. She was also to be refitted ready to return to her old role as a transatlantic liner but when she was inspected at Harland & Wolff she was found to be too decrepit to justify the expense. Instead she would be sold for scrap. *Britannic* left Belfast for Hamburg, for her last voyage, on 11 August 1903. Having been condemned by her builders as not worth refitting, she was taken to the German port for demolition, under tow.

Even so, it had been a very good year for the White Star Line, at least as far as the number of passengers its ships had transported across the Atlantic was concerned. They had carried no fewer than 29,833 passengers while the two big German lines had taken 66,838 between them, and Cunard Line had managed 24,579.

The second of the 'Big Four' liners, *Cedric*, entered service on 11 February 1903. She was similar to *Celtic* in design and in the way she handled heavy seas, remaining steady in the roughest weather.

Throughout 1903 the previously independent shipping lines that had been merged to form IMM jockeyed for position within the organisation. Instead of working together they still competed with one another, with the result that the whole combine was in a precarious financial condition. IMM needed a strong hand on the tiller, but for that first year of its existence the president of the company was Clement A. Griscom, previously head of the American Line, and his health was failing. J. P. Morgan was well aware of what was happening to the company, and he also knew who he wanted to put it right — Joseph Bruce Ismay.

At the time Ismay was still chairman and managing director of the White Star Line, but he was also a director of the London & North Western Railway, the Liverpool, London and Globe Insurance Company, the Sea Insurance Company, the Pacific Loan & Investment Company, the Asiatic Steamship Company, and the Liverpool and London Steamship Protection Association. When Morgan approached him to take over as president of IMM more than halfway through the year, Ismay refused because it would curtail his railway work, though he had only become involved with the LNWR because he thought it would be a pleasant way to spent his time when he retired from the White Star Line.

As before, William Pirrie (of Harland & Wolff) worked on Morgan's behalf and brought as much pressure to bear on Ismay as he was able, in expectation of a larger assured market building ships for the whole of the IMM group. The other directors of IMM, among them Mr Charles Steele of New York and Sir Clinton Dawkins, head of the British committee of IMM, all did what they could to persuade Ismay to do as Morgan wanted as well. In the end Ismay agreed at least to talk to J. P. Morgan about the proposition.

In the meanwhile the bumps, scrapes and fires that were the everyday life of the line continued as usual. On 14 March 1903, while she was at Portland, Maine, fire broke out on the upper cattle deck of *Nomadic*. The ship was not seriously damaged but 73 bales of cotton had to be dumped because they were either damaged by the fire or the water used to put it out. Just over a month later, on 15 April, the *Celtic* was slightly damaged when she ran into the British steamer *Heathmore* in the River Mersey. *Celtic* had to return to her dock for temporary repairs to a hole in her plating amidships. On the same day, while about 150 miles east of Sandy Hook, White Star's *Armenian* signalled the *Finland* to inform her that she was 'not under command' but refused assistance while repairs were made. This appears to be a departure from normal practice inasmuch as White Star vessels seem to have spent a fair amount of their time out of control, without broadcasting the fact!

Germanic made her last voyage under the White Star flag on 23 September 1903, before being placed in reserve and then transferred to the American Line. Still within the IMM group of companies, *Germanic's* name was changed to *Ottawa* and she served the Dominion Line for a spell.

Much to the relief of the White Star Line *Cedric* arrived at New York on 26 November 1903. She had been reported as sunk with all aboard by the Lamport and Holt vessel *Titian*. White Star had been telling anxious relatives that the report was hardly believable 'because the *Cedric* is so built that she is practically unsinkable', a ridiculous claim that was to be repeated less than nine years later.

Following the takeover by IMM, and quite possibly as a gesture of goodwill towards his old company which might induce J. Bruce Ismay to accept the position as chairman and managing director of the combine, the White Star Line was allowed to take over highly profitable routes that had until now been the preserve of other lines. Notable amongst this poaching of other routes were the Dominion Line's Liverpool–Boston and Boston–Mediterranean runs.

Then, to make sure that White Star had enough ships to service the new routes, they were allowed to take over the four best ships in the Dominion Line fleet, and another two that were still being built for that company were also transferred. The Dominion Line's

New England became the White Star's *Romanic*, *Commonwealth* became *Canopic*, *Mayflower* became *Cretic* and *Columbus* became *Republic²*.

Knowing that Ismay would have a natural tendency to do all in his power to look after the White Star Line it is patently obvious that other shipping lines in the group were facing some very unfair competition. After all, J. P. Morgan had already expressed the opinion that the only man with the ability to make IMM a commercial success was J. Bruce Ismay, and he was playing hard to get.

On 24 January 1904 Ismay sailed for New York aboard the *Oceanic²* to discuss the possibility of his becoming president of IMM with J. P. Morgan. On his arrival in New York he was met by Clement A. Griscom and his son, and Jim Wright, another IMM official. Griscom told Ismay that he wanted to talk to him before he saw anyone else, so they retired to the former's rooms for a two-hour discussion. At that meeting Griscom told Ismay that he believed IMM should be run from Liverpool and not New York, and that there was only one person fit and proper to carry on the business in a satisfactory manner, Ismay himself. Griscom was also quite sure that Ismay could count on the support of all those working for IMM on the American side. There was little more that Morgan could do to persuade Ismay to join his company.

It did not take Ismay long to put his finger on the root cause of IMM's troubles, lack of adequate funding, a problem he discussed at some length with Griscom, who was in full agreement. During the meeting Ismay made it perfectly clear that unless J. P. Morgan was prepared to make more funds available, then he would not accept the position as president of IMM. The following day Ismay had an hour-long meeting with Morgan's right hand man, Charles Steele. The IMM executive had been ill for some time and, although his health had improved, he was still far from well. During the meeting Ismay asked Steele what condition he considered IMM to be in. 'Bad, and most unsatisfactory', he had replied. Steele confirmed that in the opinion of everyone involved in the management of the huge shipping combine he, Ismay, was the only person to save the situation, if only he would accept the presidency and assume full control of the company.

Ismay had enquired about the financial status of IMM, and been informed that it was wretched. He then made it a condition of his considering the appointment as president of the combine that J. P. Morgan & Co be prepared to put its hands in its pockets and help the IMM Company. Otherwise, he said to Steele, '… you might as well put up the shutters at once'. Steele had been a little dubious about Morgan putting up any more of his own money as he had already put in between $2,000,000 and $3,000,000. Steele then went on to explain that up until then a total of £50,000,000 had been invested in the company by IMM stockholders.

When they met on the day following his arrival in New York, Ismay and Morgan got on quite well, and the financier was very open about the problems he was experiencing with IMM. The American explained to Ismay that he did not mind losing money but that he objected to losing it because of poor organisation, and that he believed the White Star chairman was the only person in his organisation capable of sorting things out. Morgan offered to prop the ailing combine up for a period of three years by making good any shortfall in profits available to cover the fixed business charges, whatever they might be. He also suggested that any surplus profit should go towards helping Pirrie pay off his debts, and that Harland & Wolff should get preferential treatment when it came to paying creditors. It was quite obvious to Ismay that Morgan did not think much of William Pirrie, and the financier actually said that he believed the shipbuilder would have been bankrupt six months before if the merging of the shipping lines had not gone through. According to Morgan, Pirrie 'could not have carried the load he had on his shoulders' without the injection of American capital.

As a final incentive Ismay was offered the then substantial salary of £20,000 a year to take over as president of IMM, a powerful inducement. Ever the reasonable man, Morgan did not expect an immediate answer, but was prepared to allow the White Star chairman time to return to England in order to talk things over with his family and business associates.

Mrs T. H. Ismay and Harold Sanderson wrote to J. Bruce encouraging him not to regard the idea of spending time in America as a problem. They both suggested that if his other inclinations were to accept the job, then he should go ahead and do so. Ismay wrote back saying that if he were to consider only his own inclinations then he would have resigned before this, but that he was trying to do what was best for all concerned.

While he was still in America Ismay decided to take a trip to Boston to have a look at the *Republic*[2]; what he found gave him pause for thought. It was evident that the company's rules were not being adhered to. To begin with he did not think the wharf used by White Star vessels was ideal for a first-class passenger line, but his main criticisms were reserved for the ship and her crew. He dined aboard the *Republic*, where he found that Captain McAuley had invited three friends, and the ship's doctor had invited another two, which was strictly against company regulations.

Almost certainly unknown to her captain and crew, the head of the line was watching as the *Republic* left harbour at 8 o'clock the following morning, late, because some of the firemen had failed to turn up on time. The ship was absolutely filthy, covered in ashes from the ash ejector, though Ismay charitably assumed that the awful weather had made it impossible to clean the vessel before she left harbour.

More seriously he noted that there was no lookout on the bridge, the fog horn was not sounded to warn visitors of the ship's imminent departure, there was no United States mail flag flying from the mizzen-mast, a canvas save-all was hanging over the side, and the screens on the promenade deck were half up and half down when they should have been all down and stowed away. In all, he thought *Republic's* departure was most unsatisfactory, and most discreditable to all concerned. On top of everything else, there was no one from the office to see the ship on her way, 'in fact, the whole thing was as bad as it could well be'. The state of the ship, and the way company rules were being flouted, were probably critical when it came to making a decision about the future presidency of IMM for Ismay.

In a letter to Harold Sanderson, Ismay instructed him to write to Captain McAuley for an explanation of the disgraceful departure from Boston of his command. 'If he cannot maintain the discipline we must have, he is not the man we want.' he wrote. In the same letter to Sanderson, Ismay explained that if he were to take on the job as president of IMM, then much of the responsibility for running the White Star Line must devolve down onto his deputy. He also stressed that even though he would have too many other responsibilities to devote as much time to White Star as he had in the past, it was still the most important part of the IMM business, and must be maintained at its present state of efficiency.

By the middle of February 1904 Ismay had already identified another of the major problems besetting IMM. Mr Wilding, who controlled the Leyland Line, insisted on running it as an independent enterprise. While he was quite happy to work with the rest of the combine when doing so was in the best interests of Leylands, Wilding considered it his responsibility to protect the line when they were not. With this protection of the Leyland

Line's interests uppermost in his mind, Wilding refused to reduce the number of Leyland vessels operating on the Boston–Liverpool route. Despite being a part of the IMM cartel, he was in direct competition with it on this route. As Ismay observed to Sanderson, the situation made IMM look ridiculous to the steamship world generally. Unless the Leyland Line was brought to heel then Ismay would not accept the presidency of IMM, and he did not think anyone else would either.

Measures were being taken to bring Wilding and the Leyland Line to heel. Some of their best vessels were being transferred for use by the White Star Line, which would lead inevitably to a reduction in the number of Leyland ships on the Boston–Liverpool route. Wilding could not use ships that he no longer controlled to embarrass IMM.

On 21 February 1904 Ismay wrote to Charles Steele accepting the position as president of the IMM Company, with a note outlining the conditions of that acceptance. The 15 conditions were:

1) That Ismay would have the title of president and managing director.

2) That his management of the business of IMM would be unlimited, and his decision on all points other than financial matters would be final.

3) That the entire control of all the subsidiary companies of IMM should rest with him, and that his decision on all matters of policy and management of these companies would be final.

4) That he should have absolute power to appoint and dismiss, without any appeal, any person in the employ of IMM, or any subsidiary companies.

5) That all the companies in which IMM had an interest should be subject to his instructions.

6) That he would receive the support and co-operation of those interested in the welfare of the company.

7) That he would arrange to have a residence in New York, but the time that it was necessary for him to reside in America would be left to his own discretion.

8) That the business in America, Canada and the West Indies should be conducted as he thought best.

9) He should be at liberty to resign the position at any time, by giving six months' notice, and the board should have the right to call for his resignation on the same notice.

10) That he would be paid $50,000 per annum, in addition to whatever he was already receiving from the White Star Line, and as a member of the British committee and a voting trustee of IMM and White Star.

11) That J. P. Morgan was prepared, in the event of the earnings of the IMM Company and subsidiary companies not being sufficient to meet their fixed charges, to advance the monies necessary to make good any shortfall for a term of three years after 1 January 1904.

12) That Morgan would undertake the above liability on the understanding that the net earnings of the IMM Company and subsidiary companies would be used to pay such charges first.

Above: The Reading and Writing Room of *Adriatic*[2].
Robert McDougall collection

Left: Picture postcard advertising *Laurentic's* connections to Canada.
Robert McDougall collection

Below: Crowds watch the departure of an Atlantic liner from a Liverpool landing stage, circa 1910.
Robert McDougall collection

HANDS ACROSS THE SEA.

LAURENTIC.

Above: Republic² in the River Mersey.
Robert McDougall collection

Left: Jack Binns, the heroic wireless
operator of *Republic*.
Robert McDougall collection

Below: Adriatic². Real Photographs

Above right: Bow view of *Adriatic²* on the
stocks during construction.
Ian Allan Library

Right: Megantic in the Mersey.
Robert McDougall collection

Below right: Laurentic off a landing stage
at Liverpool.
Robert McDougall collection

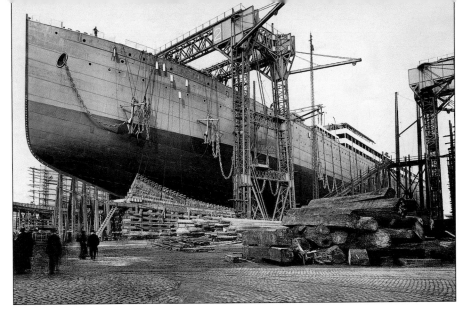

Above: The Arrol gantry, in the Harland & Wolff shipyard, Belfast, where many White Star ships were built. *Robert McDougall collection*

Below: Carpathia, the Cunard Line ship that rescued the survivors from *Titanic. Robert McDougall collection*

Above: Lapland, Red Star Line — the ship that brought most of *Titanic's* surviving crew home from New York. *Robert McDougall collection*

Below: The Titanic Engineers' Memorial as it was in 1915. *Robert McDougall collection*

Left: Mersey — believed to be the first sailing ship fitted with wireless.
Robert McDougall collection

Below: Guglielmo Marconi — pioneer of wireless telegraphy.
Robert McDougall collection

Above left: Chief Inspector Walter Dew disembarking from *Megantic* with the murderer Dr H. H. Crippen. Walter Dew's other claim to fame was that he was the first policeman on the scene of the fifth, and supposedly last, Jack the Ripper killing. *Author's collection*

Above: The entrance to Belfast Harbour, with Harland & Wolff's shipyard to the left. *Robert McDougall collection*

Right: A photograph taken aboard *Olympic* at Liverpool on 1 June 1911. *Courtesy of Prof Roy Storer*

Below: Olympic leaving Southampton. *Robert McDougall collection*

RMS "TITANIC" TENDERS
'AMERICA' AND 'IRELAND'
QUEENSTOWN 1912

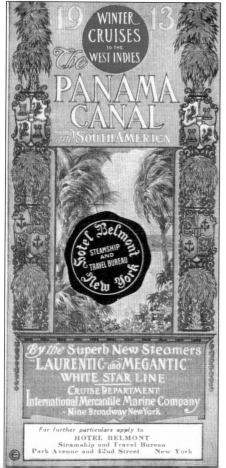

Above: White Star tenders *America* and *Ireland* at Queenstown, circa 1912.
Robert McDougall collection

Left: A 1913 brochure advertising White Star cruises to the Panama Canal and South America.
Robert McDougall collection

Right: Majestic².
Robert McDougall collection

Above: A postcard showing a view of a landing stage and the River Mersey before World War 1. *Robert McDougall collection*

HITE STAR
LINE

QUADRUPLE-SCREW R.M.S. "MAJESTIC."
56,621 TONS.
THE LARGEST STEAMER IN THE WORLD.

Above: Titanic. Robert McDougall collection

Below: Traffic — the tender built to service the new super-liners *Olympic* and *Titanic* at Cherbourg. *Robert McDougall collection*

Above: Arabic, which was later sunk after being torpedoed by *U24* in 1915.
Robert McDougall collection

Below: Calgaric. Robert McDougall collection

Above: Homeric. *Robert McDougall collection*

Below: The First Class Smoking Room of *Homeric. Robert McDougall collection*

Above left: The illustrated cover of a White Star Line passenger list.
Robert McDougall collection

Above right: White Star's James Street, Liverpool, offices today.
Robert McDougall

Below: The plaque outside 30 James Street today, reads 'Headquarters of the Oceanic Steam Navigation Company (White Star Line) Founded by T. H. Ismay 1869'. *Robert McDougall*

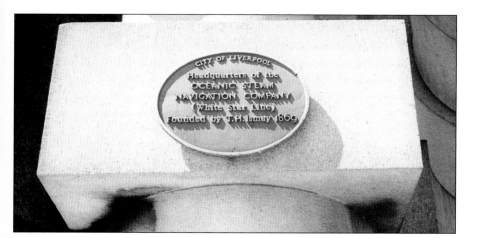

Above left: Ocean Dock, Southampton, in 1929, with Cunard's *Berengaria* (top right) and *Aquitania* (bottom right); White Star's *Majestic* (bottom left) and *Olympic* (top left) being eased into her berth by tugs. *Robert McDougall collection*

Left: Cedric, seen leaving Liverpool to be broken up on 11 January 1932. *Robert McDougall collection*

Below left: Doric². *Robert McDougall collection*

Above: Georgic. Real Photographs

Below: Regina. Robert McDougall collection

Left: Liverpool's *Titanic* Memorial outside the Liver building.
Robert McDougall

Left: A present day reminder of the once-great White Star name, a Liverpool public house.
Robert McDougall

13) That Morgan would be willing, in the event that the earnings of the IMM Company were in excess of the amount necessary to meet the fixed charges, for any surplus be used to pay off any debts owing to Harland & Wolff, before anyone else.

14) That the finance committee of the combine should not interfere with his running of the company.

15) That it be understood that the board of directors, the finance committee and anyone else that might control parts of IMM were to give complete control to Ismay in everything except financial matters. The only power left to the board was to call for his resignation.

Agreement was reached, and signed by J. Pierpont Morgan, P. A. B. Widener and Charles Steele. From the moment the agreement was signed J. Bruce Ismay was in almost total charge of everything that happened within IMM. Not only did he control everything but he would have been kept informed, one way or another, of everything that was going on within the company, and there was a lot going on.

On 24 February 1904 the new president and managing director of IMM and his wife left New York, bound for Liverpool aboard the *Cedric*.

Chapter 11
1904-1909

Joseph Bruce Ismay had never sought the position he now found himself in. In fact, had it been purely personal considerations that had influenced him he would never have taken the job on. On several occasions he made clear that it was only because so many people were relying on him to sort out IMM's problems that he had considered the post of president at all.

He had planned to retire in the near future to enjoy a life of ease, but now that would have to wait. Having taken on the job of turning the tottering shipping empire into a viable business enterprise, then Ismay would try to do just that. He had no illusions about the scale of the task confronting him, and he was by no means sure that the company could ever become a profit-making concern, but he was convinced that, provided everybody involved in the enterprise would pull together, it was worth a try. That Morgan was prepared to pay him $50,000 a year while he tried must also have influenced Ismay's decision to make the attempt.

At the time Ismay took control of IMM there was a worldwide slump in both passenger and freight business for the shipping lines to fight over, and fight they did. Ismay thought the whole shipping business was 'most discouraging'. One of his first tasks would be to persuade the other lines that a price war was good for none of them. The easiest way to accomplish this was to join in and push prices so low that it was in everyone's interest to call a halt and agree realistic prices. This strategy would have the extra benefit of getting rid of some smaller operators at the same time.

J. Bruce and Florence arrived home on 3 March 1904, but he had passed on the news of his acceptance of the post as president and managing director of IMM to William Pirrie in a letter written the day before. Pirrie wasted no time in putting the news to use and a letter was on its way to Ismay only two days after his return. That J. P. Morgan's assessment of the state of Pirrie's business was not far wide of the mark is clearly illustrated by the letter. He acknowledged receipt of the letter written by Ismay aboard *Cedric*, and expressed his relief, and that of his colleagues on both sides of the Atlantic, that it was the chairman of the White Star Line taking over as president of IMM. While accepting that Ismay had not sought the position, Pirrie, like Morgan, was convinced that with the correct man in control the combine could become a success.

Pirrie went on to say that the company's greatest problem at that time, and for the foreseeable future, was an acute shortage of working capital. Then, after assuring the new president that he would do all in his power to help the cash-flow problem, he went on to say, 'It must, however, be borne in mind that neither my own resources nor those of my firm are inexhaustible, and, as a matter of fact, they are exhausted at the present moment.' The shipbuilder, who had always in the past managed to conduct his business on a ready cash basis, was more than a little embarrassed by the confession that he was short of money. In fact he needed to obtain some of Morgan's cash from Ismay before he could complete the new *Baltic²*. Obviously there had not been the steady inflow of cash that Pirrie had anticipated when he helped persuade Ismay to sell out to J. P. Morgan.

From the time J. Bruce Ismay took over as president and managing director of IMM the efficiency of the company began to improve. Before long the giant combine was an effective business, and what had been substantial losses became a small profit. However, despite his position as head of IMM, Ismay retained his loyalty to the line his father had built up, and White Star always received preferential treatment from him, such as taking over the Dominion Line steamers in 1903 and 1904.

Clearly Ismay believed that the White Star Line could use all of the vessels that it could get its hands on. Not long after taking on *Canopic* the line also took over the 9-year-old 8,249-ton *American*. The vessel was renamed *Cufic²*, and she would serve faithfully for 20 years. Then the *European* was brought in and renamed *Tropic²*.

Of course, the fact that the line was receiving preferential treatment from the manager and chairman of IMM did not mean that its vessels fared any better once they were out of Ismay's sight. On 21 March *Georgic¹* ran into the British steamer *Kaliba* in St George's Channel. *Republic²* collided with the Canada Atlantic and Plant Steamship Company's vessel *Halifax* on 3 June, driving her ashore. Then, on 17 November 1904, as *Canopic* lay alongside her Boston dock, fire broke out ashore, threatening the vessel. On the following day *Oceanic²*, halfway across the Atlantic and running through rough weather, was damaged by a particularly large wave.

Baltic² was the third of the 'Big Four' White Star liners, and she entered White Star service in 1904. Like her sisters *Celtic²* and *Cedric* she was never intended to be particularly fast but was meant to provide a steady comfortable passage for those aboard her. Because Ismay had wanted the new *Baltic* to be the world's largest ship, her hull had been lengthened at quite a late stage in her construction. The alteration, of course, had its repercussions in that it increased the finished vessel's displacement by 2,840 tons, which meant that with the engines specified she was underpowered. By altering the valve settings on the engines her speed was increased to a point where she could just about keep pace with her sisters.

In 1905 Florence Ismay bought her first motor car, a large Mercedes. She was an enthusiastic motorist but her husband never took to it. J. Bruce Ismay chose, whenever possible, to travel by train, in a reserved compartment where he could work undisturbed. In later years he did purchase cars but employed a chauffeur to drive them. His attitude to chauffeurs was exactly the same as to his sea captains: they were in charge of their respective vehicles. Ismay often thought that his chauffeur drove too fast, and he complained of this to Florence. She advised him to have a word with the chauffeur but he replied, 'No, he is in charge, and if he thinks we should go so fast it is not up to me to interfere.'

This attitude illustrates how unlikely it would be for J. Bruce Ismay to have interfered in the running of a ship at sea, something he would be accused of in 1912, and would deny.

Although Ismay seems to have had complete confidence in his chauffeur, the same cannot be said of his children's driving abilities. He would never allow them to drive his car, and he would not ride in a car driven by any one of them.

March 1905 saw some particularly ferocious storms in the North Atlantic. On the 15th, while battling her way through one of these storms, *Cedric* was struck on her port side by two enormous waves at the same time. The huge mass of water crashing into and over the ship deformed the forecastle plating, splintered interior woodwork, smashed the Number 1 hatch cover, broke several portholes and carried away the ship's bell. *Cedric* was not having the best of voyages, for as well as having to endure atrocious weather, there were 21 cases of measles aboard. However, a baby boy being born in steerage, at the height of the storm, must have heartened crew and passengers alike; almost as much as arriving safely in port.

While she was at Liverpool on 28 May a minor fire broke out aboard *Majestic¹*. These White Star ships did seem a little prone to catching fire, particularly while they were at their home port or at New York. During the rest of the year fire damaged *Teutonic* on 28 July at New York, and *Oceanic²* on 23 August at Liverpool. The regularity with which these fires occurred must lead one to wonder if disgruntled dock workers might have had a hand in them.

Disgruntled dock workers were not the only problem the line faced. Dubious seamanship was another, and *Tropic²* was severely damaged when she went aground 15 miles north of Constitución, Chile, on 29 June 1905. Five days passed before the vessel could be refloated, and in that time both her second officer and purser were drowned. Once the ship was refloated it was discovered just how seriously she was damaged. The bottom of the hull had been pushed upwards, the deck under the engines had been bent. As the bottom of the ship had deformed, the engines and boilers had been moved on their mountings.

The fires, which had a nasty habit of breaking out aboard White Star vessels as they lay in their home port continued into the new year. On 6 January 1906 it was *Georgic's* turn. Luckily, the fire was not too serious and was soon brought under control, causing only slight damage. After all, White Star crew members must have been getting fairly proficient at fighting fires by this time, having had so much practice. Which was just as well!

For the first time under the command of Captain Charles A. Bartlett *Gothic* left Tenerife in the Canary Islands on 2 June on the last leg of a homeward passage from Wellington, calling at Montevideo and Rio de Janeiro, that had begun on 26 April. The ship was heavily laden with 118 first-class and 97 steerage passengers, and a cargo including 22,633 sheep carcasses, 44,031 lamb carcasses, 1,000 sheepskins, 1,446 bales of wool, 2,258 boxes of potatoes, 1,000 bags of bran, 1,364 bales of flax, 576 casks of tallow and 543 bales of hemp.

Late in the afternoon of Sunday 3 June passengers noticed smoke coming out of Number 4 hold, then, later in the evening a peculiar greasy smell in the air. As they were leaving the dining saloon they could not help seeing that the aft part of the upper deck was screened off. When asked what was going on stewards would only say that the cargo was being turned over. Captain Bartlett knew better. The ship's officers suspected that fire had broken out in the bales of wool in the hold. Bartlett ordered that steam be pumped into the hold to extinguish the fire by cutting off its oxygen supply, and that the hatch should then be sealed.

At breakfast time on 4 June the hatch on Number 4 hold was opened so that the damage might be inspected. As the hatch was opened smoke belched out of the hold. Clearly the fire was not quite out so crewmen descended into the hold to begin clearing the burning cargo away. Several smouldering bales were soon thrown overboard, and those that had been scorched were brought out and stored on deck, under canvas, where they were unlikely to present any further problems. By midnight everything seemed to be under control, but in reality the trouble had only just begun.

On the evening of Wednesday 6 June the smell of burning wool was again detectable, but it was thought probably to be coming from the scorched bales on deck. As laid down in the company's rules the chief officer began his nightly top to bottom inspection of the ship. All seemed to be well with Number 4 hold, but when he approached Number 3 the smell became noticeably stronger. When he reached the baggage room, directly above Hold 3 he found that the floor was hot; something was definitely wrong. Even as passengers slept soundly steam was pumped in, but to no effect. By morning smoke was coming out of the mainmast ventilators, high above the boat deck.

As the ship was only a few hours from Plymouth, Captain Bartlett decided to keep the hatches closed until the passengers could be taken off the ship. There was no panic; in fact the passengers were reassured to the extent that when the ship reached Plymouth half of them elected to stay aboard to watch the crew fight the fire. Only 101 passengers and the mail went ashore with the Great Western Railway's tender *Cheshire*.

The hatches were removed and clouds of smoke belched from Number 3 hold. Bartlett, realising that there was a serious fire aboard, immediately summoned help from the Naval Dockyard at Devonport. The remaining passengers were evacuated. By this time tugs were in attendance and they added their hoses to the fight against the blaze, pouring more than 100 tons of water into the hold. The fear now was that the fire might reach the tallow stored beneath the wool. As the crew struggled to move the cargo and the tugs poured in water, *Gothic* began to list heavily to port.

Because she had become a danger to other vessels in Plymouth harbour the tugs towed *Gothic* into the Cattewater, the inner harbour. Once there, Bartlett ordered the seacocks opened and the ship settled onto the harbour bottom. Still the fire raged unchecked, feeding on the untreated wool, tallow and frozen carcasses. Slowly the fire was brought under control and by 4.00 on 8 June it was out.

The *Gothic* was a picture of wretchedness as she sat forlornly on the harbour floor, her superstructure blackened by fire and smoke. Damage to the cargo alone was estimated at £200,000. However, things were not as bad as they first appeared and by 6pm enough water had been pumped back out of the ship to refloat her and she was towed out of the harbour into Plymouth Sound. By the following day her list had been corrected and most of the water had been cleared from the ship. In an astonishing example of just what determined effort could accomplish, at 4am on 9 June 1906, *Gothic* got under way to complete her interrupted voyage. She arrived at London's Royal Albert Docks on the 12th.

Gothic would require an extensive refit before she would be fit for further service and since Shaw Savill was already preparing to add *Arawa* and *Tainui* to the New Zealand service it ran with the White Star Line, she was no longer required on that route. She was transferred to the Red Star Line, who renamed her *Gothland*, and transformed into a third-class-only ship. Then *Coptic*, which had seen service with White Star on the New Zealand run from 1884–85 before being transferred to the Occidental & Oriental Line, and *Doric¹*, which had been transferred to the Occidental & Oriental Line 11 years before, were sold.

In 1906 the first of Cunard's new, government-subsidised, super-liners was launched, a vessel destined to become almost as well known as the most famous of White Star's own super-liners; she was the *Lusitania*. It was the coming of these Cunard vessels that spurred White Star on to construct even bigger and better liners of their own, just as T. H. Ismay had threatened to do 21 years before.

Ismay's old partner William Imrie died at home in early August 1906; his wife had died on 10 December 1888. The Imries had no children of their own but had adopted a daughter,

Amy, and it was to her that William left the major part of his fortune, in trust. Amy had no appetite for the business world of Liverpool and on the death of her father she entered a convent. When she died the Imrie fortune went towards the building of the new Liverpool Cathedral. Mrs Margaret Ismay had been in poor health for some time, suffering from Bright's disease. Late in 1906 she went to stay with her daughter Ethel at 29 Cadogan Square, London SW1. She died there on 9 April 1907, and was buried beside her husband.

Early in 1907 it was decided that the fastest ships of the White Star Line engaged on the North Atlantic routes should sail from Southampton instead of Liverpool. There were several reasons for the decision but the most important was simply that the Hampshire port was much closer to London than Liverpool was. That it was also closer to the continental ports, such as Cherbourg, and would reduce fuel costs and time spent on passage, was a bonus.

Even as the management of the White Star Line was planning the new express route from Southampton to New York one of the line's more remarkable episodes took place. *Suevic* left Melbourne on 2 February 1907 bound for Liverpool, calling at Cape Town, Tenerife, Plymouth and London, discharging her cargo on the way. In command was Captain Thomas Johnson Jones, who after 39 years at sea, 35 of them with White Star and the last 17 as a master, was making his last voyage before retirement. (As events little more than five years later were to show, the company could have done worse than retire their masters one voyage early.) There were 141 crew, 382 passengers, more than 80 of them children, and a couple of stowaways who finished up working their passage. In the holds was a cargo, including thousands of frozen meat carcasses, valued at about £400,000.

The ship left Tenerife for Plymouth, where she was supposed to land some of her passengers, on 13 March, a clear day, and with a following sea made good time, exceeding 13kt. At midday on 17 March *Suevic* was 138 miles from the Lizard Light on England's south-west coast and heading towards this well-known danger area. Captain Jones should normally have steered well clear of the area but because the weather had closed in and it had become foggy he wanted to use the light to fix his position, having been forced to rely on dead reckoning. The officers on the bridge finally spotted the light, low on the horizon, at about 10.15 that evening.

The officers thought the light was about 10 miles away, so ignoring company rules that clearly stated that the sounding lead should be used in shallow waters, they pressed on at full speed. At about 10.25 the lookout reported breakers ahead of the ship. The chief engineer, who happened to be on deck, suddenly made out the Lizard Light at the very moment the lookout raised the alarm. The engineer also saw breakers on the port side of the ship. The captain ordered the helm hard a-port but before the vessel could respond she crashed onto the Maenheere Rocks, a quarter of a mile from Lizard Point, still at full speed. The engines were put full astern to see if she might drag herself off, but the ship was hard aground and refused to move. Rather than risk damaging the ship even further the captain ordered the engines stopped and distress rockets to be sent up, although the vessel was in no immediate danger of foundering.

After about half an hour coastguards at Lizard Point noticed the frantic signals coming from *Suevic*, and the Lizard and Falmouth lifeboats went to the rescue. To be fair, there was a thick fog at the time which might well account for the ship's signals not being seen or heard immediately. In the meantime the ship's own boats were lowered, and the first passengers were ferried ashore to land at the tiny Cornish fishing village of Cadgwith. The Great Western Railway Company arranged for a fleet of motor cars to collect the passengers from Cadgwith and take them to Helston, a much larger town with the facilities to deal with them. It was after 7am before evacuation of the majority of the passengers could begin, and well after midday before it was completed. It had been quite a night for the local lifeboat service as the Elder Dempster liner *Jebba* had gone aground just a few hundred yards away from *Suevic* in the early hours of the morning, with 70 passengers on board.

Despite Herculean efforts to get her off, the *Suevic* was still firmly aground nine days later. Salvage ships from Liverpool came down to the Cornish coast but there was little they could do as the *Suevic* was too securely fastened onto the rocks. After some discussion it was decided that there were only two options open: either the vessel would have to be abandoned or the stern section would have to be cut from the grounded bow and salvaged separately.

White Star opted for the second alternative and several salvage firms were approached to see if they could do the job; all of them estimated that it would take more than a week to separate the stern from the rest of the ship. Then a young man called Fabian, who worked for the Liverpool Salvage Company, claimed that he could do the job in 24 hours.

Now this was not a simple matter of cutting the hull into two parts with acetylene torches or angle grinders. In 1907 the job would have to be done with dynamite. Hundreds of small charges would have to be placed where they would cut through the shell of the ship without causing damage to its structure, a very precise and skilled operation. The whole of the passenger accommodation, along with the engines and boilers were as yet undamaged, so the ship had to be divided immediately abaft the bridge and as much as possible salvaged intact.

Working without a break, under very difficult conditions, Fabian detonated more than 300 separate charges of dynamite to cut the hull into two pieces, the operation being completed on 2 April, the action of the sea finally separating the two sections. Fabian had done his work so well that the tugs which were standing by to take *Suevic's* stern to John I. Thornycroft's Southampton repair yard were only required to steer her and she was able to make the trip under her own steam, although she had to go all of the way in reverse.

The new forward hull section, 212ft long, was built at Harland & Wolff's Belfast yard and brought down to Southampton in the week following 19 October and moved into place on 4 November. The original ship and the new bow section had been so accurately built that no problems at all were encountered when the two halves were joined. Another two months were needed to join the hull sections permanently, connect up the electrical wiring and plumbing, sort out the ventilation system and do all the myriad other jobs necessary to repair the ship. On the afternoon of 8 January 1908 *Suevic* left dry-dock, moved to a coaling berth and began to take on fuel ready for her short trip to Liverpool, which began just two days later. All the effort involved in salvaging the *Suevic* proved worth while for she served the line well until she was sold off in 1928. Even that was not the end of the ship, for she sailed on into the early 1940s.

The Board of Trade Inquiry into the accident laid the blame squarely at Captain Jones' door. 'The ship was not navigated with proper and seamanlike care after 10pm of 17 March … The stranding and consequent damage to the *Suevic* was caused by default of the Master …' Captain Jones' master's certificate was suspended for three months, which would not have caused the captain too much hardship as he had retired some months earlier.

On 8 March 1907, as she prepared to enter New York harbour, the *Baltic* ran aground about a mile and a half outside Sandy Hook, where she remained for several hours before she could be refloated. The whole round trip was not one of *Baltic's* better efforts, for as she left the quayside for the return leg of the voyage she ran into, and sank, a fully loaded coal barge that was innocently under tow, a trick she would be quite happy to repeat on her next visit to the United States. Again as she was leaving New York on 13 April 1907 *Baltic* encountered another loaded coal barge, which she promptly ran into and sank.

On 7 May 1907 an arsonist set fire to the cargo in *Oceanic²'s* after hold while she was docked at New York's Pier 48. In all probability the fire was started by somebody in league with the striking longshoremen (dockers) who were not entirely happy with the employment of blackleg labour to load and unload ships. The fire destroyed much of the cargo in the hold, including the scenery of the noted actor Forbes Robertson, as well as bedding and fittings in the steerage quarters for women, situated at the stern of the ship. The fire did thousands of dollars worth of damage and delayed the ship's next scheduled departure by several days, even though it was brought under control after a couple of hours. Less than a fortnight later, on 20 May, while substitute labour was again being employed to unload a ship, fire broke out on the *Armenian* as she lay at New York's Pier 40.

A new era for the line began in May 1907 when *Celtic²* took the first experimental voyage from Southampton to New York. The voyage was a success and a month later a regular service began. The new Southampton–New York run would be maintained by the *Adriatic²*, which was the first vessel to sail on the new regular service, the *Oceanic²*, *Teutonic* and *Majestic¹*. The trend-setting *Celtic* returned to the old established Liverpool route.

Adriatic², the last of the 'Big Four', which entered service in 1907, was even larger than the *Baltic²*, at 24,540 tons, and as a result of the experience with her, more powerful engines were installed. Bigger, more powerful engines demand more steam so *Adriatic* was fitted with four extra single-ended boilers to provide it. Interestingly, *Adriatic* was the first ship to have a swimming pool and Turkish bath aboard. The 'Big Four' were one of the most successful series of liners ever built and they worked on the service to America almost constantly from 1907–28. For the earlier part of their careers they sailed mainly between Southampton and New York, although on occasion they operated out of Liverpool. They were known in their home port as the 'Pride of the Mersey'.

With Cunard's new *Lusitania* in service, breaking all records, and her sister *Mauretania* almost complete, it became apparent to the managers of IMM in general, and White Star in particular, that they were going to have to pull something special out of the hat if they were to continue to compete in the lucrative North Atlantic passenger service.

Cunard's new turbine-driven super-liners were impressive, at well over 30,000 tons apiece. They were as ornate as the best of the German ships and free of the vibration problems that these were prone to. The new Cunarders were also much faster than any other liners in the world, with a top speed significantly higher than 26kt. These vessels made all earlier ocean liners obsolete at a single stroke. Passengers flocked to the new leviathans to the mortification of other shipowners.

J. Bruce and Florence Ismay went to dine one night in 1907 with William Pirrie and his wife at their London home, Downshire House, in fashionable Belgrave Square. It was at this dinner party that, traditionally, the idea of the *Olympic* Class of White Star Liner is said to have been conceived; but this is entirely wrong. Because of the way that William Pirrie had already modernised his shipyard, so that it could build bigger ships than ever before, it is obvious that he, at least, had already considered the idea of building the world's largest liners. The conversation between Ismay and Pirrie in fact seems to have centred around the construction of three new giant ships. As originally conceived, the first two ships would be built side by side, one to be completed a few months before the other. Then a third would be built after the first two were in service, and their faults had shown up.

Initially Ismay liked the idea and he and Pirrie discussed the possibilities. Various layouts were considered, including five-, four- and three-funnelled designs. It is commonly believed that a three-funnel and four-masted layout was provisionally decided upon, but this configuration could and would be altered to suit the requirements of the owners and builders. Three-funnelled liners were not to become fashionable until almost the eve of World War 2, and five-funnelled ones never have been aesthetically acceptable. By the end of that evening the *Olympic* Class liners were still only an idea but they were destined soon to become a reality.

Harland & Wolff started work in earnest on preparing detailed drawing of the new ships. On 29 July 1908 a group of distinguished senior management members from White Star arrived at the Belfast shipyard. They had come to examine the plans of the proposed liners. The scale drawings, prepared under the watchful eye of Pirrie and his nephew Thomas Andrews, the manager of the drafting department, bore the legend

400 Plan – 29 July 1908 (Proposed General Arrangement)
SS No 400
850 x 92 x 64'6"
Design 'D'

The outline for the new ships included a great glass dome over the first-class dining saloon as in the new Cunarders. Electric lifts even in second class, a gymnasium, Turkish baths and a swimming pool were to be incorporated. Unlike the Cunard vessels the new 'Olympics' were planned with two reciprocating engines instead of the relatively novel turbines. They were expected to return a speed of 21kt on these engines alone.

The management of White Star simply would not believe in turbines until they had tried them for themselves. With this end in sight they commissioned Harland & Wolff to build *Megantic* and *Laurentic*. *Megantic* was fitted with traditional reciprocating engines, while *Laurentic* had a combination of turbine and reciprocating. The turbine-powered *Laurentic* would not be ready for her trials until well after construction of the first of the new 'Olympics' had begun. Although there was little difference in the overall top speed of the two vessels, *Laurentic* being slightly faster, there was a marked increase in fuel economy with the turbine-powered vessel. The results of the trials persuaded the White Star Line and the builders that turbine engines had some merit, and it was decided to add one to each of the new liners even though construction of the first had begun, and the keel would therefore have to be altered.

To make sure that an adequate supply of steel and the specialised forgings required would be available from firms controlled by John Brown, and to gain access to the new technology involved in producing turbines, Harland & Wolff combined with the famous Clyde shipbuilders. Together they would produce the low pressure turbine for *Laurentic*. At the same time another link was forged with White Star's great rival Cunard inasmuch as John Brown was that company's favoured builder.

As well as being more opulent than either the *Lusitania* or the *Mauretania*, the new White Star liners were to be half as large again as the Cunard flagships. They were planned to be the largest man-made moving objects in existence.

The party from White Star, which included amongst others Harold Sanderson and J. Bruce Ismay, were more than happy with the initial design. Two days later the contract letter (described as a sheet of quarto paper) was signed. Harland & Wolff's next step was to prepare working drawings from which the tradesmen in the shipyard would actually construct the ships. White Star did not lay down any specification for the *Olympic* Class vessels, leaving the design almost entirely in the hands of William Pirrie and his team. There was certainly no firm instruction about the number of lifeboats that were to be placed aboard, this being left to the discretion of the builders as long as they stayed within the bounds of the Board of Trade regulations. These regulations, set down in 1894 as we have seen, only allowed for vessels up to 10,000 tons and were hopelessly out of date by 1908.

The nominal chief designer at Harland & Wolff was the Honourable Alexander Carlisle, Pirrie's brother-in-law. He was nearing retirement and as a result the main design work was carried out by the chairman himself. Carlisle contented himself with most of the detail work such as decoration, fixtures and fittings and the life-saving equipment. Originally Carlisle wanted 64 lifeboats but this was considered extravagant and the numbers were reduced, against Carlisle's better judgement, first to 48, then 32 and finally to 16. As with *Atlantic*, this was far too few to accommodate the number of people that the ship could carry. This decision was made sometime in the week of 9–16 March 1910.

Eventually the plans for the first two of the new class of vessels were finalised. There only needed to be one complete set of drawings as both ships were to be identical at the time of their launch and could therefore be built from the same plans.

To raise some of the money to build the first of the new super-ships, White Star issued £1½ million worth of new shares in 1908. This sum, as it turned out, proved to be precisely how much each of these monsters in fact cost to build. The new vessels were intended solely for the Southampton–New York route, although at the time of their conception the American port did not have piers long enough to take them. The same thing applied to the two other regular ports of call on the North Atlantic route, Cherbourg and Queenstown, neither of which even had a harbour large enough for the new leviathans. As the new ships became available they were intended to replace the 'Big Four' on the Southampton service, along with the *Oceanic²*, while the *Celtic²*, *Cedric*, *Baltic²* and *Adriatic²* would transfer to operate out of Liverpool.

J. Bruce Ismay believed that it was beneficial to use officers who had been trained in sail to serve on White Star ships. With this in mind, in 1908 he bought the 1,713-ton, steel hulled *Mersey*, built by Connell's of Glasgow, for use as an ocean-going training ship. *Mersey's* greatest claim to fame, however, is that she was the very first sailing ship to be fitted with radio. Commanded by Captain Corner she sailed the oceans worldwide until the outbreak of the Great War when she was sold by Harold Sanderson.

It had been a little while since a vessel belonging to the Oceanic Steam Navigation Company had made a proper job of running into another vessel but then *Georgic¹* rammed the 2,600-ton American passenger liner *Finance* in the port quarter while off Sandy Hook, in dense fog, on 26 November 1908. Although the *Georgic* was supposedly travelling very slowly because of the weather conditions, within five minutes the *Finance* had taken on a 30 degree list. The American ship was clearly sinking so about 150 people aboard her were forced either to take to the boats or jump into the sea. Luckily only four lives were lost in the incident, although the *Finance* took her $300,000 cargo with her to the bottom of the sea.

The keel of the first of the new super-liners, *Olympic*, was laid on 16 December 1908. It was fabricated from a single thickness of 1.5in steel plating and a flat steel bar 19.5in wide and 3in thick. The ribs of the vessel were made of 10in steel channel spaced 2ft apart forward, 2ft 3in at the stern and 3ft apart amidships. The outer plating was of steel plates 6ft wide, 1in thick and usually 30ft long, each weighing 2.5–3 tons. A double bottom was incorporated which extended right out to the sides of the ship. The distance between the inner and outer skins was 63in over most of its length but this was increased to 75in beneath the main engine rooms, two-thirds of the way back from the bow. This double bottom was divided into 73 separate compartments to provide water storage for the boilers etc and trimming tanks.

The main part of the hull was subdivided into 16 separate compartments by 15 x $\frac{1}{2}$in-thick transverse bulkheads which reached, in most cases, to well above the water line. Forward Bulkhead A was closer to the bow than was deemed advisable and effectively reduced the useful number of compartments to 15. The bulkheads were stronger than was required by Lloyd's. Many of the main compartments were subdivided yet again, the hull containing no less than 29 supposedly watertight boxes. The bulkheads between the boiler rooms were backed by coal bunkers which again ran the full width of the ship. The bulkhead between Boiler Rooms 4 and 5 was exceptional in that it only reached $2\frac{1}{2}$ft above the waterline. It had been suggested to Harland & Wolff, while the ships were still at the planning stage, that the bulkheads should be extended up as far as Saloon Deck D. The suggestion was not adopted because it would have interfered with the layout of passenger accommodation and public rooms.

The bulkheads were fitted with watertight doors on the lower decks to allow communication between the boiler and engine rooms. These watertight doors would close automatically if the lower part of the ship was flooded. They could also be closed by simply flicking a switch on the bridge. The vessel was so subdivided as to be able to remain afloat with any two major compartments flooded. When one considers that an average boiler room on this class of ship was 57ft long and 90ft wide, one realises what an achievement this was.

The ship could also remain afloat with any four forward compartments flooded, which was only likely to happen as far as the designers were concerned in the event of the vessel ramming another ship or hard object, or going hard aground. If the vessel was itself rammed the worst that could be expected was the opening of two compartments to the sea.

Bulkheads 2, 3 and 4, numbering from the bow, were pierced by a watertight passageway on the lowest deck of the vessel (tank top). This passageway was protected at each end by watertight doors. At its nearest point to the outer skin of the ship it came within 5ft 3in of the bottom plating.

As planned, the new *Olympic* Class ships were to be 882ft 6in long and 92ft 6in wide. They measured 45,324 gross register tons but displaced (actual all-up weight) about 66,000 tons; by a comfortable margin, the largest vessels in the world.

Planning apart, 1908 was a fairly uneventful year for the line, with few collisions, rammings or fires worth talking about. Everything seemed to be going exceptionally well for White Star, but as we already know, that state of affairs seldom lasted long. *Republic*[2] left Genoa, under the command of Captain William Inman Sealby, on 30 December 1908 and headed southwards to Naples where she picked up more passengers for the trip to New York. Amongst the passengers were several survivors from a catastrophic earthquake that had recently destroyed the city of Messina, killing 85,000 people. However, although

Republic had a few earthquake survivors aboard many more had elected to leave Italy on the 5,118-ton Lloyd Italiano vessel *Florida*, which sailed from Naples on 10 January 1909, under the command of Captain Angelo Ruspini.

Republic arrived in New York on 14 January 1909 and left again for Italy on 22 January with about 650 tons of supplies and probably a quarter of a million dollars in gold for the naval fleet at Gibraltar, plus a cargo of potatoes, sugar, eggs, butter, smoked and fresh meat and turkeys – all relief supplies for the Italian earthquake victims. As she backed away from her pier the *Republic* ran into the steamer *Bermudian*, doing hundreds of dollars worth of damage. But this was merely the beginning of an unfortunate chain of events.

On 23 January 1909 the *Republic* was rammed, in fog, by the *Florida*. A huge hole was torn in *Republic's* side just aft of her funnel and 30ft of *Florida's* bow was crushed like a concertina. Photographs taken shortly after the collision show both ships with tarpaulin patches over their wounds. Sadly the canvas patch was not enough to save the *Republic* and she finally sank almost 40 hours after the collision. Three people died as a direct result of the collision, two almost instantly and another after reaching New York. The death toll would undoubtedly have been much higher but for the heroic behaviour of Jack Binns who operated the then novel wireless equipment.

The Marconi man, Jack Binns, working under almost impossible conditions and holding his equipment together with his bare hands, managed to summon another White Star liner to their assistance. More than 12 hours after the collision the *Baltic*[2] arrived on the scene, at about 7.30pm and four hours later had taken aboard all of *Republic's* passengers. Shortly before midnight she began to evacuate those passengers aboard *Florida*, taking no fewer than 1,650 from that vessel.

Binns remained at his post, repairing as best he could the wireless cabin which had been wrecked in the collision, and passing messages to other ships standing by. After almost 36 hours at his key the wireless operator abandoned the remains of his wireless cabin and the sinking liner at about 4pm. Shortly after 8.30pm *Republic* finally disappeared beneath the waves. With the loss of the *Republic* the White Star Line was able to claim another dubious record, that of owning the largest passenger ship to have foundered at sea. That record would stand until it was broken three years later by another White Star vessel, *Titanic*.

Jack Binns was lionised for his part in what was then one of history's greatest and most dramatic maritime rescue operations. Before the applause had died away he signed aboard another White Star ship, the *Adriatic*[2]. His new captain was E. J. Smith and when the skipper transferred to the new *Olympic* when she entered service in 1911 Binns transferred with him.

By 1912 Binns had left the employ of the Marconi Company and joined the staff of the *New York American* as a reporter. Originally planning to cross the Atlantic aboard *Titanic* to join his new employers, he was unable to contain his enthusiasm and transferred to an earlier steamer, the *Minnewaska*. He arrived in New York and started work for the *New York American* a matter of hours before the *Titanic* disaster. How very different things might have been had the hero of the *Republic* occupied the senior wireless operator's position aboard *Titanic*. Jack Binns knew the value of remaining in touch with any vessel in the immediate vicinity and might have been a little less dismissive to Evans of the *Californian*, but we will come to that a little later.

Chapter 12
1909-1912

A s we have already seen, 1909 did not get off to a particularly auspicious start and
things were slow to improve. During the first quarter of the year *Cretic* was
definitely having a bad time of it. She ran aground on Centurion Ledge, just inside
Boston harbour, on 23 February, having just arrived from the Azores with 1,100 passengers
aboard. After about half an hour she was floated off, but her rudder had been disabled and
the ship was unmanageable. Predictably, *Cretic* immediately ran aground again, this time
more securely. Red distress rockets were sent up and by the following morning tugs had
managed to pull her clear. Just over a month later, on 26 March, straw that had fallen out
of a mattress in her forward steerage accommodation caught fire. Clearly those aboard
were unfamiliar with the day-to-day running of a White Star vessel, where fire seems to
have been an almost constant companion, and panic ensued. 'A dozen men rushed from the
forward deck into the cabin accommodation, shouting and brandishing knives and causing
much excitement until they were subdued and sent below.' (That 'subdued' has the ring of
understatement about it.) The fire, which was hardly worthy of the name by White Star
standards, was put out without difficulty.

On 31 March 1909 the keel of the second *Olympic* Class vessel was laid. At the time
construction began, this ship, *Titanic*, was intended to be identical to *Olympic*, but minor
changes would be made after the maiden voyage of the first of the class making her about
1,000 tons heavier at full load than her sister. This increase would mean that *Titanic* would
be, for a short time, the largest ship in the world.

Not all of the collisions in which White Star vessels were involved were entirely their
fault. For example, while she was at Montreal on 27 May 1910, the *Megantic* was run into
by the lakes steamer *J. H. Plummer* and damaged slightly. However, the injury to the
Megantic was serious enough to delay her planned departure by a day.

Of course, the Oceanic Steam Navigation Company and its officers could be blamed for
some of the collisions in which White Star vessels took an active part. Almost 1,100 miles
east of the Ambrose lightship, on 30 June 1910, the *Baltic*[2] ran into the German-American
Petroleum Company's tanker *Standard*. The collision tore two holes in *Baltic's* bow, one of
which caused her hold to fill with water. Aboard the *Standard* one crewman had suffered
three broken ribs and internal injuries that required immediate surgery. The injured man
was transferred to *Baltic*, which carried a surgeon, and was operated on there. Both ships,
although quite seriously damaged, were able to continue their voyage, but when the
Standard reached Copenhagen, with a million gallons of petrol aboard, she caught fire and
was completely destroyed.

During June, attempting to avoid capture for poisoning and dismembering his wife,
Dr Hawley Harvey Crippen sailed for Canada on the Canadian Pacific Line steamer
Montrose. With Dr Crippen was his mistress, Ethel le Neve. The couple were travelling as

Mr Robinson and son. Had Dr Crippen not fled the country, then in all probability he would have escaped the consequences of his crime. Police had been alerted to the fact that his wife had disappeared but when Inspector Walter Dew interviewed Crippen he was satisfied by the explanation, that his wife had run off with another man to America. However, Crippen's hurried departure re-aroused Dew's suspicions and his house was searched. Mrs Crippen's remains were discovered, buried in the cellar and a world-wide search began.

Aboard the *Montrose* the captain had already noticed the unusually affectionate manner of Mr Robinson towards his son. On receiving a wirelessed description of the wanted doctor the captain began to suspect that Mr Robinson was none other than Dr Crippen, and sent a wireless message to that effect to Scotland Yard. Inspector Dew immediately took up the chase and sailed aboard the *Laurentic*, which was a considerably faster vessel than the *Montrose,* and caught up with the escapees at Father Point. Dew arrested Crippen and le Neve, and returned with them to England aboard *Laurentic's* sister ship *Megantic*. As we all know, Dr Crippen was convicted of murdering his wife and hanged, becoming one of the most famous murderers in English history, if only because he was the first to be caught with the aid of wireless. Walter Dew, nicknamed 'Blue Serge' from the suit he habitually wore, had played a prominent part in the hunt for another, even more infamous killer 22 years before. As a humble constable he had been the first policeman on the scene when the mutilated remains of Mary Jane Kelly were found, the fifth and final victim of 'Jack the Ripper'. Dew retired from the police force very shortly after the Crippen case, which had made him famous, and became a private investigator.

To get back to our account; firemen were a notoriously unruly element amongst the crews of White Star ships, often refusing to take part in such extra-curricular activities as lifeboat drills. On 8 August 1910 they carried things a step further when they mutinied aboard *Adriatic*, at Southampton. Mutiny was a very serious offence for which harsh penalties could be handed out, but probably because the ship was in harbour at the time the mutineers were dealt with quite leniently. This leniency might well have led the crews of certain White Star vessels to believe that they could get away with mutiny in the future. Anyway, less than a year on there would be another mutiny, this time aboard the line's flagship.

On 20 October 1910, her passage eased by 23 tons of soap and grease, *Olympic* slid stern first into the River Lagan. Fitting out, which would take another seven months, was begun, but not before damage caused by the vessel being blown against the quayside as she was being towed to the fitting-out wharf was repaired.

Constructed entirely along conventional lines the new ship only broke new ground in the extensive use of electricity aboard, and its sheer size. Over 200 miles of electrical wiring were needed to supply all her needs, including more than 10,000 light bulbs.

The finest craftsmen were employed in fitting out the first-class passenger accommodation, which was of a style and standard that would not have disgraced a luxury hotel of the time. Second- and third-class cabins and public rooms were also well above the standards of other lines, though they were not in the same league as first. The distinction between classes was even more pronounced during the early years of the 20th century than it is now. While first- and second-class passengers were treated with a certain amount of respect by crew members, steerage were definitely not.

Events aboard the *Canopic* on the night of 23 November 1910 are a classic example of the disregard for the safety of third-class passengers prevalent amongst senior officers on White Star ships. When fire broke out in the hold, directly below the ship's steerage accommodation, the crew fought the blaze for four hours, before getting it under control, without alerting the more than 1,000 passengers sleeping above. When the fire was eventually put out, the hatches above the hold were sealed and the decks washed down to conceal any evidence of the fire, and the terrible danger they had been in, from the steerage passengers. This cavalier attitude towards steerage passengers would show itself to even greater effect aboard the *Titanic*.

The line's vendetta against American coal barges continued. As she was leaving New York harbour on 23 November 1910 the *Oceanic²*, emulating *Baltic²*, ran into and sank the coal barge *Red Star No. 19*. The elderly captain of the barge and his wife were thrown into the water but luckily were quickly rescued by a passing tugboat.

In preparation for the new *Olympic* Class liners, which would be far too large to enter the port of Cherbourg, the line had commissioned two new tenders to carry passengers out to the leviathans. These vessels, which came into service in 1911, were the 1,273-ton *Nomadic* and the 675-ton *Traffic*. Both of these small vessels would have long and chequered careers, as we shall see.

In May 1911, after only two days of trials, *Olympic* was judged ready to be handed over to her new owners by Harland & Wolff. To gain extra publicity the second behemoth would be launched on the same day that the handing over ceremony took place, 31 May 1911. Amongst the prominent guests who made the trip to Belfast to witness both events were J. Bruce Ismay, his daughter Margaret, and John Pierpont Morgan. After seeing *Titanic* slip relatively uneventfully into the River Lagan, only one workman being seriously injured during the launching (he died later in hospital), *Olympic* left for Liverpool, with Morgan, Ismay, his daughter and the other dignitaries on board. Death and serious injury were no strangers in any shipbuilding yard on average one man died for every 10,000 tons of shipping that was built.

After leaving Belfast *Olympic* crossed the Irish Sea to Liverpool, where she was thrown open to the public, if they were prepared to buy a ticket, the proceeds from ticket sales going to local hospitals. The great ship lay in the Mersey, dressed for the occasion (her rigging festooned with flags), as the public peered into every nook and cranny. After a day in Liverpool *Olympic* left for Southampton to prepare for her maiden voyage, arriving there in the early hours of 3 June.

Not unusually, there was a certain amount of industrial unrest amongst the workers at the Hampshire port, including those who would normally have coaled the ship. This group decided to go on strike, bringing about the distinct possibility that *Olympic's* maiden voyage might be delayed. This potential delay was rather more than the White Star Line was prepared to countenance so it brought in its own people, including a large contingent of Yorkshire miners, to load the liner with coal in time for her scheduled voyage. As will become apparent, in times of unrest among its usual workforce the line regularly fell back on the Yorkshire miners to act as strike-breakers, sometimes making matters worse.

Under the command of Captain Edward John Smith, the White Star Line's new flagship sailed for New York on 14 June 1911, accompanied by the president and managing director of IMM, Joseph Bruce Ismay and his wife.

Ismay was not just along for the ride but to see for himself what details could be improved. He noticed, for example, that the promenade space on B Deck was underused, and could be better utilised as extra first-class cabin space. He made a note to have the alteration incorporated into the second vessel of the class, along with one or two other trivial items. The reception room was always too crowded after meal times and Ismay thought that another 10 tables and 50 cane chairs should be added to those already there. The after companionway on A Deck, between the Smoking Room and Lounge was hardly used at all and Ismay thought that this area, too, could also be usefully converted into first-class cabin space. Two more tables could be squeezed into the Saloon if service access was reduced to one door on each side. The mattresses were too springy, there were no cigar holders in the toilets, a potato peeler was needed in the galley, and a special bread oven was required if enough bread was to be available on a crowded ship.

J. Bruce Ismay was also extremely dissatisfied with the working of the new tenders, *Nomadic* and *Traffic*, at Cherbourg. Captain Beresford, the marine superintendent at Cherbourg, had been instructed as to precisely how passengers and baggage should be embarked, but for some reason Beresford had not followed his orders, and Ismay wanted to know why. He was also surprised that the superintendent had not remained at his post until all the baggage had been transferred from *Traffic*, but had left in *Nomadic*.

Yet another minor transgression had been brought to Ismay's attention. Some passengers, a Mr Van Eldon, two men with connections to a French line, and another, had been allowed to visit the engine room while the ship was heading for Cherbourg. This was strictly against company rules, and Ismay was a firm believer in rules.

Despite Mr Ismay's nit-picking the new liner performed very creditably, covering 428 miles on the first day, 534 on the second, 542 on the third, 525 on the fourth and 548 on the fifth day of the passage. She completed the voyage in 5 days 16 hours and 42 minutes, at an average speed of 21.7kt. Not bad for a ship only designed to make 21kt, and she managed that without benefit of her five single-ended boilers, which were not lit throughout the trip.

June 1911 was a troubled time for the shipping lines, labour relations being at a very low ebb. Much of the trouble was undoubtedly fomented by the new trade unions which were fighting for recognition by the shipping companies. J. Bruce Ismay was totally opposed to union recognition as it would mean the end of cheap, disorganised labour, but he knew that his position was a weak one because Cunard and others had already recognised the unions. On the 15th, firemen and ordinary sailors had to be promised an extra 10 shillings (50p) above their normal rate before they would sign aboard *Baltic²* and *Teutonic*. By the 16th, nearly a whole crew had been recruited, but only because the line was giving the extra 10 shillings as an advance.

By the 20th, the labour situation had deteriorated even further and stewards demanded £3 15s (£3.75) a trip. White Star and Cunard agreed to the demand, but it still was not enough to satisfy the militant crewmen. On the following day Southampton dock workers and crews alike stopped work. The dock workers wanted higher wages, and the crews larger advances, than their counterparts in Liverpool. Ismay and the White Star Line refused on the grounds that to agree would only cause more trouble at Liverpool. The recalcitrant crew were bluntly told that if they did not sign on at the rates on offer then the line would lay up the ships involved. The workers capitulated, at least for the moment, but the unions continued their struggle for recognition.

On 21 June 1911, at the completion of the outward leg of *Olympic's* maiden voyage, when she was temporarily under the command of New York harbour pilot Julius Adler to be eased into her berth by no less than 12 tugs, one of them was caught in the turbulence caused by her enormous propellers and dragged beneath the overhanging stern. About $10,000 worth of damage was done to the tug, the *O. L. Halenbeck*, while *Olympic* suffered only a few scratches and a dented plate.

At the beginning of the homeward-bound half of the voyage at midday on 28 June, soon after leaving New York's Pier 59, it was discovered that a passenger had forgotten his glasses. Another pair were quickly manufactured and the well-known aviator Tommy Sopwith attempted to fly them out to the ship while she was still in the narrows, and in full view of the press. Clearly the whole event was a carefully planned publicity stunt, but it all came to naught when the attempt to drop the glasses onto the ship failed, and the spectacles bounced overboard into the sea. Otherwise the return trip was quite uneventful and *Olympic* completed the crossing at an average speed of almost 22½kt.

Captain Smith's first round trip to New York and back as captain of *Olympic* could hardly be described as without incident, but there was more. As a general rule gambling in the ship's smoking room was prohibited, although it was tolerated as long as the stakes did not get out of hand. High-stakes games were carried on in private staterooms behind locked doors, and these were the haunts of the professional seagoing gamblers. During one such game 37-year-old Mr Barton J. Harvey had lost more than $10,000. Immediately after losing another substantial amount to a professional gambler on a single hand, he collapsed unconscious. The gamblers made themselves scarce with some alacrity upon Harvey's collapse. Mr Harvey, who had been drinking heavily for the previous two days, and may have been suffering from a weakened heart, died five hours later. Although White Star detectives boarded the ship as soon as she docked, they could not identify the gamblers.

White Star ship handling had not improved, and *Cedric* ran into a temporary pier extension as she attempted to dock at New York's Chelsea Pier on 22 June 1911. *Cedric* was undamaged, although the same could not be said of the new pier extension, which even if it had not been intended as temporary had certainly proved to be so.

June 1911 was not all bad news for the White Star Line. Agreement was reached with Albert Ballin's Hamburg–Amerika Line, the Allan, Dominion and Royal lines, in which they all agreed to set fares on eastern routes, and it was believed that there was a good chance the same sort of agreement might be reached over North Atlantic fares. Not that everyone who had ambitions to cross the Atlantic was prepared to pay the fare. As *Olympic* approached New York on 13 August her first two stowaways were discovered, Jeremiah Sweeney and Joseph Hipler. Nor were all those who were prepared to pay guaranteed to arrive at their destination. On the return half of the journey William Williams died aboard, and was buried at sea the following day.

On 20 September an incident occurred that, I believe, marked the beginning of the end for the White Star Line. As *Olympic*, with Captain E. J. Smith and the harbour pilot George William Bowyer on the bridge, was leaving Southampton Water at the start of her fifth westbound Atlantic crossing she was rammed in the starboard quarter by the Royal Navy's armoured cruiser HMS *Hawke*, 41-year-old Commander William Frederick Blunt in command.

The cruiser's armoured bow tore a huge hole in the relatively soft side of the liner, putting *Olympic's* starboard main and central turbine engines out of action at the same time. The badly damaged liner, the pride of the White Star fleet, would be out of commission for more than two months and repairs to the ship and lost fares in that time would amount to more than £250,000. An inquiry was held by the Royal Navy, supposedly to discover who was to blame for the collision. Unsurprisingly, this laid the blame on the White Star liner, even though she had been rammed and the *Hawke* had done the ramming.

Sir Rufus Isaacs, who took a prominent part in the inquiry into the loss of the *Titanic*, was a passenger on one of *Olympic's* voyages in early 1918. During the trip Captain Hayes asked him his opinion on the legal wrangle that had followed the collision, and how that case had been resolved in the Royal Navy's favour. Isaacs' answer does not seem to be recorded but Hayes summed the affair up masterfully when he commented, 'The Admiralty must have had the better lawyer as they certainly hadn't the better case.'

The only shipyard with a dry-dock large enough to take the *Olympic* was Harland & Wolff's main yard in Belfast so *Olympic* was sent there after being patched up in Southampton. *Titanic* was being fitted out in the dock at this time and had reportedly to be moved out to make way for the *Olympic* while parts and machinery intended for *Titanic* were also fitted to her sister.

At about 4 o'clock in the afternoon of 20 November 1911, after a day supposedly spent unnecessarily testing machinery that had already seen service on four round trips across the North Atlantic, *Olympic* quietly left Belfast. She reached Southampton on the morning of the 22nd. *Olympic* had been due to sail on her interrupted fifth voyage on 28 November but supposedly because of fog the departure was delayed by a full day.

The keel of the third *Olympic* Class vessel, *Britannic*², was laid, as far as we know, on 30 November 1911. There is no clear documentary evidence as to exactly when the keel was laid, but then lack of clear, reliable documentary evidence from the builders is nothing new, although it does not rival the White Star Line where a scarcity of reliable information is concerned. Even the original name for this third *Olympic* is not certain, but it is believed to have been *Gigantic*.

Whatever was happening with the line's ships, changes at the top were also afoot. In the autumn of 1911 J. Bruce Ismay offered the chairmanship of the Shaw Savill & Albion Company to his long-time friend, Harold Sanderson; the offer was accepted with certain reservations. In his letter of acceptance Sanderson made it clear that he had hoped to retire from White Star and IMM at the end of 1912, something he had already mentioned to Ismay, and discussed at length with J. P. Morgan's associate E. C. Grenfell. In a letter to Sanderson, of 10 January 1912, Ismay made it quite clear that he himself intended to retire from IMM on 31 December that year as well. He also told his friend that as he had never held the highest position in any of the companies they had been involved with, he should take the offer of the chairmanship of the Shaw Savill Line.

The news that the president and managing director of IMM planned to retire in a year seems to have caused no little concern to the owners and higher management of the company. After discussion with Morgan, and others concerned with the welfare of the giant shipping combine, Ismay was prevailed upon to postpone his retirement for a further six months, the new date for his leaving being 30 June 1913. He cabled news of his change of mind to Sanderson, who did not receive it graciously. Despite his avowed intention of resigning at the end of 1912, Sanderson was planning to step into Ismay's shoes as supremo of IMM at that time.

Over the next few days cables flew back and forth between the IMM president and his deputy. At first Sanderson was adamant that he would retire at the end of the year, and would only consider coming back to take over as president after six months if it then suited him. Ismay tried to explain his reasons for delaying his departure from the company. He also applied a little pressure to Sanderson by pointing out that if his deputy was doubtful about taking over six months later than he had anticipated then Ismay himself would remain in the position until other arrangements could be made.

Sanderson stuck to his guns and reiterated that he would retire at the end of the current year. In a transparent veneer of friendship and reasonableness he explained that retirement, even for six months, would give him a sorely needed break. Ismay, who of course recognised blackmail when he saw it, realised that if he allowed Sanderson to retire for six months and then return to take over the company on his own delayed retirement it would look as if he had attempted to carry on alone and had failed. He also recognised that when his deputy returned to take up the reins it would look as if he had not only been unable to run the company alone but that Sanderson had been brought back to sort it out. Some sort of a compromise would have to be reached.

Ismay and Sanderson finally settled on the president of the company resigning on 30 June 1913 while his deputy took a six-month leave of absence, returning to work on 1 June 1913 in order to familiarise himself with any changes before taking over from Ismay at the end of that month. On 26 February, Ismay suggested in a letter to Charles Steele, Morgan & Co's secretary, that the new arrangements should be kept secret so as to avoid any unrest within the company.

On 2 March Steele sent his reply to J. Bruce Ismay, agreeing to the revised arrangements. Steele went so far as to suggest that mental telepathy might have been at work because he had been about to suggest the very compromise that Ismay and Sanderson had agreed upon. Charles Steele concluded his letter with the line, 'There are a lot of things that may happen before the 30th June, 1913.' How right Mr Steele was. Just one month, to the day, after he sent the letter agreeing to the arrangements between Ismay and Sanderson the *Titanic* slipped out of Belfast Lough for her single short day of so-called trials.

At about 1.30pm on 14 January 1912, during her second voyage after repair following the *Hawke* incident, *Olympic* was struck by a huge wave while running through heavy weather. The ship's bows were lifted high in the air before the wave broke over them. A second monstrous sea broke over the bow, tearing off a five-ton steel hatch cover and knocking the steam winch and an anchor windlass off their mountings. The storm would have tested the mettle of a brand-new ship, let alone one that had been so recently badly damaged in a collision.

Olympic left New York on 21 February 1912, heading for Southampton. Three days out, while about 750 miles east of Newfoundland, she ran over what is believed to have been a submerged wreck, and broke a blade off her port main propeller. Despite the loss of the propeller blade, and consequently the use of the port main engine, *Olympic* arrived at Southampton on 28 February. The loss of the propeller blade was not the only incident of note on the voyage. James Kneetone, a madman being deported from America, had disappeared two days later. After a thorough search of the ship he was reported as lost overboard.

Olympic departed Southampton for Belfast on 29 February, making for the only dry-dock in the world big enough to take her, to have a new propeller blade fitted. The job had been expected to take just one day but the ship did not leave Belfast again until 7 March. No satisfactory explanation for the delay in performing the simple repair to *Olympic* has been put forward by the builders even though that delay caused the vessel's next scheduled voyage to be cancelled, with the resultant loss of fares. The delayed voyage began a full week late, on 13 March.

On one of the *Olympic's* voyages between the *Hawke* accident and his transfer to *Titanic*, E. J. Smith was drawn into a conversation about the collision with a group of people, including one of his own officers. 'The commander of the *Hawke* was entirely to blame,' said the young officer. 'He was showing off his warship before a throng of passengers and made a miscalculation.' Captain Smith smiled at the officer's interpretation of the event, but said nothing to confirm or deny it. He did have something to say about the dangers inherent in such accidents to the new super-liners. 'Anyhow, the *Olympic* is unsinkable, and *Titanic* will be the same when she is put in commission. Why,' he continued, 'either of these vessels could be cut in halves and each half would remain afloat indefinitely. The non-sinkable vessel has been reached in these two wonderful craft.' He concluded, 'I venture to add that even if the engines and boilers of these vessels were to fall through their bottoms the vessels would remain afloat.'

On the evening before Captain Smith left New York to return to England and take command of the *Titanic* he had dined with Mr and Mrs W. F. Willis of Long Island. During the dinner, according to Mrs Willis, he was enthusiastic about his new command. He said he shared with the designers of the vessel the utmost confidence in her seagoing qualities, and he told Mr and Mrs Willis that it was impossible for her to sink. It would not be long before Captain Smith discovered that he had somewhat over-estimated the survivability of the new ships.

On 1 April 1912 fire broke out in Number 10 bunker aboard the brand-new *Titanic*, which was awaiting her acceptance trials at Belfast. The fire, if it ever really existed, supposedly buckled some of the plating forming Number 5(E) bulkhead, and might have had a bearing on what was to happen a fortnight later.

At 6am on 2 April 1912 the second of the White Star Line's new leviathans began what have been ludicrously described as her 'trials', which lasted a short working day, half of which was spent in a leisurely cruise up and down Belfast Lough. Aboard the ship were H. A. Sanderson, representing the White Star Line; Thomas Andrews, the managing director of Harland & Wolff and James Pirrie's nephew; and Captain Edward John Smith in command. In order to take command of the new *Titanic* Captain Smith had handed the *Olympic* over to Captain Herbert James Haddock, the line's youngest captain. Pirrie, who had intended to go along for the trials, was prevented from attending because of prostate problems. After the 'trials' *Titanic* headed directly for Southampton, without being opened to the public at Liverpool as her sister had been. Public inspection of the ship would also be denied at the Hampshire port.

As this book is intended to tell the story of the White Star Line as a whole, I will not go into detail over the loss of its most famous vessel, but perhaps a brief outline would be in order. (New evidence suggests that the iceberg that caused the sinking of *Titanic* could have been either a sailing ship, or an auxiliary steamer, or a steamer draped in wet canvas. Readers who would like to know more about this story are recommended to consult the author's book *Titanic: The Ship That Never Sank?*, published 1998 by Ian Allan Publishing.)

Titanic reached Southampton very early in the morning of Thursday 4 April 1912. The ship was due to sail on her maiden voyage less than a week later, on the 10th, and there was a lot of work still to do if she was to be anywhere near ready. Cabins were not properly fitted out, carpets were still to be laid, equipment had to be checked, coal had to be brought aboard, and worst of all, the ship was on fire. Why on earth the White Star Line accepted a ship from the builders with a fire raging in one of her forward bunkers defies reason.

Because of a major coal strike then in progress, harbours around Britain were rapidly filling up with ships which, once they had arrived, were unable to collect enough coal to leave again. Many owners took advantage of this enforced layover of their vessels to carry out routine maintenance, such as scraping the barnacles off hulls and painting the ships. Not so the White Star Line; because of the coal shortage *Olympic* had topped up her bunkers in America, and by carrying extra fuel in unoccupied cabins had managed to squeeze enough aboard to complete the round trip back to New York. She had left Southampton only hours before *Titanic* had arrived there, taking with her most of what small coal reserves existed.

In order to collect enough coal for *Titanic* to reach New York the bunkers of five other IMM ships laid up in Southampton were stripped bare of their remaining fuel, not one of them having enough to proceed to sea itself. In an act of unimaginable stupidity Captain E. J. Smith allowed tons of precious coal to be poured into *Titanic's* already burning bunker, Number 10. It was not as if Captain Smith was unfamiliar with the workings, and potential hazards, of coal-burning ships. He had commanded 17 White Star vessels in succession, all of them coal burners.

Because it was Easter and the Ismay children were home from school for the holidays, Florence Ismay decided not to accompany her husband on the *Titanic's* first voyage, so J. Bruce was to make the trip alone. Representing the builders, Thomas Andrews and an eight man group of skilled workers would sail with the ship in order to help put any minor defects right.

On 10 April 1912 the *Titanic* sailed from Southampton on her maiden voyage to New York, via Cherbourg and Queenstown. On the first stage of the voyage the lookouts complained that they no longer had binoculars in the crow's-nest. Binoculars had been available on the trip down from Belfast, but as these were the responsibility of the then second officer, who had since left the ship because of a last-minute crew reshuffle, they were now locked away in what had been his cabin.

The first four days of the voyage were relatively uneventful as far as the passengers were concerned but numerous wirelessed ice warnings were received by the ship. All the while, unknown to the fare-paying passengers, the fire still raged in Bunker 10, in the forward boiler room.

At 11.40pm on Sunday 14 April the lookouts reported ice ahead of the ship, which should not have come as any surprise. In addition to the numerous warnings that had been received by the ship it should have heard about events on the afternoon of 11 April, when the French liner *Niagara* ran into an iceberg when very close to the position now occupied by *Titanic*. *Niagara's* distress call was picked up by the Cunard Line's *Carmania*, which was about 20 miles to the north-west of the damaged French vessel, at 41°58'N, 50°20'W, surrounded by huge bergs.

Mr Murdoch, the first officer, ordered the helm hard a-starboard and the engines full astern, but it was no good. *Titanic* struck the iceberg a glancing blow on her starboard side. The impact, which it was calculated had a force of 13,500,000 tons, was apparently hardly noticed by most aboard. None the less the ship was mortally wounded, with five of her 16 watertight compartments open to the sea.

Thomas Andrews, of Harland & Wolff, inspected the damage and informed Captain Smith that the vessel was sure to sink. Captain Smith ordered the boats to be swung out and loaded, with women and children going first. The order was misconstrued by the second officer, Mr Charles Lightoller, to mean women and children only, with the result that many boats left the ship badly underfilled. As in any case the ship only had enough lifeboats to carry about half of the people who were on board at the time, this underfilling was a serious error.

At the same time as the boats were being swung out and loaded, distress rockets were being sent up in the hope of attracting the attention of another steamer which could be seen about five miles away, but without result. J. Bruce Ismay, who was aboard for the liner's first outing, saw the lights of a sailing ship from *Titanic*, but it was a flat calm, perfectly clear starlit night, so a sailing ship would be as helpless as *Titanic* herself. In the light of information which has become available only within the last couple of years it seems that the vessel seen by Ismay might well have been the *Lady St John's*. This little two-masted sailing ship was on her way to St John's, Newfoundland, with a cargo of salt.

In *Titanic's* wireless cabin the operators worked feverishly to try and summon assistance and after a couple of false starts managed to reach the Cunard liner *Carpathia*, almost 60 miles away. The Cunarder started towards *Titanic* without delay and Captain Rostron apparently worked his ship up to 17½kt as he raced to the rescue, 3½kt faster than she had ever been intended to travel. It would take *Carpathia* about four hours to reach the position of the *Titanic*, 41°46'N. 50°14'W, while it would take the White Star giant only 2½ hours to founder.

Shortly after 2am on 15 April *Titanic* buried her bows beneath the icy cold, black waters of the North Atlantic. Since soon after the boats had begun loading, there had been a certain amount of panic aboard and officers had been obliged to use their pistols to retain some sort of order, but now nothing could control the 1,500 people trapped on the sinking ship. The boats had gone and all that remained for the people to do in an attempt to prolong their lives by a few minutes was to fight their way towards the stern of the ship. Sometime about 2.10am the liner's huge stern began to lift out of the water. The ship's band heroically played right to the end, or at least for as long as it was possible to stand on the steepening decks.

In the wireless cabin the senior operator, Jack Phillips, aged 22, remained at his post still trying to find help; the last wireless signals came from *Titanic* at 2.17am. At the same moment the electrical generators failed, cutting off the power to Phillips's wireless, and the lights which had burned steadily until then finally flashed once and went out for ever.

Soon, according to eyewitness reports, the stern of the great ship was sticking vertically up out of the water, like a giant tombstone. Many of the 1,500 people aboard were now clustered like swarming bees at the very stern of *Titanic* as she began to slip away. At 2.20am the waters of the Atlantic Ocean closed over what has since been described as the 'Greatest of the Works of Man'.

Carpathia arrived at the scene of the disaster at about 4am and began to pick up the people from the lifeboats in the area. Four and a half hours later Captain Rostron had 705 named survivors from *Titanic* aboard his ship (and a substantial number of other named survivors [from somewhere else?]). As *Carpathia* was collecting the last of the survivors another ship came up to join them, the Leyland Line's *Californian*.

At the time *Titanic* had sent out her first wireless distress signals the *Californian* was lying, stopped by the ice, about 19½ miles away to the north, much too far away for the liner's rockets and Morse lamp to have been seen. Although the *Californian* might have been close enough to have rescued at least some of the lost, news of the accident did not reach her until the morning. Cyril Evans, *Californian's* wireless operator, after trying to warn *Titanic* of the ice and being told to stop because the liner's operators were busy with commercial traffic, had switched his set off at 11.30pm on the 14th, having worked the usual 16-plus hour day that was expected of Marconi employees.

During the night a series of white rockets had been seen from the *Californian's* bridge but they did not go high enough or make enough noise for the officers there to think that they might be distress signals. They believed that the rockets were merely one ship passing a message to another, a common practice, and anyway the rockets were all white and *Titanic's* were red, white, and green.

By the time *Californian* arrived at the scene of the sinking there was very little she could do to help. Captain Rostron of the *Carpathia* had decided to return to New York with his load of survivors and, so that he could leave the scene without delay, he asked Captain Lord of the *Californian* to search the area for any more people from the wreck. Captain Lord obliged, and in doing so took note of the lifeboats Captain Rostron abandoned, after taking 13 of *Titanic's* aboard his ship.

Lord noticed, amongst the floating ice, two upturned boats, one a collapsible that should have been there, and one a full-sized wooden lifeboat that should not. Captain Rostron also noted the capsized extra proper lifeboat. Curiously, if the official history is to be believed, all of *Titanic's* wooden lifeboats reached *Carpathia* and were relieved of their passengers. None of the liner's full-sized wooden boats was tipped over during the evacuation of the *Titanic*, or while they awaited the arrival of *Carpathia*, or during the rescue. *Californian* found no more survivors to rescue.

Since 1912 there have been those who believe the *Californian* to have been the ship seen from the decks of the foundering liner, despite the rather obvious evidence that it cannot have been so. The steamship seen from *Titanic* was under way, as was the rocket-firing ship visible to the officers on the bridge of the *Californian*. As neither the White Star liner nor the Leyland Line vessel moved during the relevant period then it follows that they were not looking at one another but at a third, still unidentified, ship.

Olympic had left New York at about 3pm on Saturday 13 April on the homeward-bound leg of an Atlantic crossing. At 1am on the 15th she picked up a wireless distress signal from the *Titanic*. At the time the signal was received *Olympic* was about 505 miles to the south, and a little to the west, of her sister. Minutes after receiving the distress call Captain Herbert J. Haddock was heading at full speed towards *Titanic*, but the distance was far too great for there to be any hope of reaching the stricken vessel in time to be of assistance. *Olympic* completed her voyage, arriving at Southampton at a little after midnight on 21 April. In the latter part of the trip a collection had been taken aboard to help *Titanic's* crew and their families. This raised about £1,500.

Once the survivors reached America an official Government Inquiry into the disaster was begun, at which selected witnesses were called to give evidence. Those members of the liner's crew not required by the Inquiry were held incommunicado aboard the Red Star Line's *Lapland*. The carefully selected witnesses gave their evidence, some of which was listened to while some was totally ignored. Exactly the same thing would happen at the official British Inquiry, which was held as soon as all of the required witnesses returned to their home shores.

While the American Inquiry was going on, a member of *Californian's* crew sold his version of events to a newspaper. The story he told was so full of holes that it should have been laughed at, but it was accepted as gospel truth by those looking for a scapegoat. Strangely enough, some people still accept Donkeyman Gill's statement as accurate, even though a cursory examination of the available evidence shows it to be a fabrication from beginning to end.

One of the few really useful pieces of information to come out of the American Inquiry emerged on 25 May when the chairman, Senator William Alden Smith, visited *Olympic*. While he was there he had one of the liner's lifeboats lowered fully loaded. The whole operation, loading and lowering, took 18 minutes.

The American Inquiry was best described by *Titanic's* senior surviving officer, Charles Herbert Lightoller, as 'a farce'. The British version was little better, being a rather obvious and relatively successful cover-up. Geoffrey Marcus, in his book *The Maiden Voyage* covers the British Inquiry in a chapter entitled, 'Lord Mersey and the Whitewash Brush', which is an excellent description of the Board of Trade proceedings.

At both of the inquiries J. Bruce Ismay refused to divulge the circumstances of his escape from *Titanic*, saying only that as there were no more passengers around as Boat C was being lowered, he got into the boat himself. A long time later he told the truth to his sister-in-law: that he had been told to get into the boat by Chief Officer Wilde because his testimony would be needed at the inevitable inquiry, to exonerate Captain Smith. Ismay's later statement is supported by the sworn affidavit of ship's barber, Weikman.

Before *Olympic* was allowed to sail again after the *Titanic* disaster, Ismay issued specific directions ordering that enough lifeboats be provided for every person aboard. White Star's superintendent at Southampton, Captain Benjamin Steele, was at first directed to put an extra 16 lifeboats on the liner, then his instructions were changed and he was told to put 40 extra boats aboard. By the time 35 extra boats had been placed on the ship the instructions were altered yet again, to provide lifeboat spaces for 2,500 people. Eleven of the extra boats had to be taken off again. Ten of the extra collapsible lifeboats left aboard the ship were 10-year-old ones taken from HMS *Soudan*, which had seen better days.

Why the somewhat scruffy boats were left aboard while better looking ones were removed is not known, but 276 firemen, greasers and trimmers of *Olympic's* crew thought the boats unserviceable and refused to sail with the ship. The striking seamen were arrested as mutineers and put on trial at Portsmouth Magistrates' Court, where after a three-day hearing they were found guilty. However, the court refrained from jailing or fining them, realising that in the light of the recent *Titanic* tragedy the men had some justification in refusing to sail without what they considered to be adequate lifeboat accommodation. Eventually the lifeboat problem was sorted out and the ship sailed with 43 lifeboats and collapsibles, a seat for every person aboard, and arrived at New York on 22 May 1912.

The new lifeboats were nearly put to use towards the end of the return passage from New York when the *Olympic* almost ran aground on the northern coast of Land's End when she should have been miles to the south in the English Channel. However, the sea breaking against the rocky shore was seen in time for disaster to be avoided. Because the *Titanic's* sinking had happened so recently the management of the White Star Line thought it best to keep quiet about this latest incident and it remained a secret for 75 years, despite there being a full complement of passengers and crew who witnessed it.

The only possible explanation for the near disaster was appalling navigation and seamanship, which as we have already seen was not uncommon with the line. White Star put another captain aboard *Olympic* to monitor the performance of Captain Haddock and his crew for the next couple of round trips, not that it made a scrap of difference to the way the ship was run. *Olympic's* next round trip began well enough and she arrived in New York without serious incident. As she was leaving again on 6 July, she turned to avoid the yacht *Viking* and ran aground on a sandbank to the east of Ellis Island, damaging her steering gear. It took six tugs to pull her off.

As a result of the *Titanic* disaster, work on *Britannic²* was suspended while the vessel was redesigned so as to be immune to the sort of damage that had sunk her sister at the cost of so many lives. One result of the alterations was the provision of eight pairs of large and unsightly gantry davits each capable of handling six 34ft lifeboats. Forty-eight such boats could support all 3,522 people that the ship was designed to carry. On 11 August 1912 White Star also announced that it was withdrawing *Olympic* from service in November for a complete overhaul, a decision influenced no doubt by the understandable reluctance of a travelling public to entrust their lives to a vessel whose type had so spectacularly demonstrated just how sinkable it was.

Chapter 13
1912-1921

W hile it is generally accepted that conditions aboard *Olympic* Class ships of the White Star Line were better than on vessels belonging to any other line, this mollycoddling of passengers could have serious consequences. The quality and quantity of food available in third class, aboard *Olympic* on 2 September 1912, proved too much of a temptation to Isaac Guttenburg and he ate himself to death. He was buried at sea that night, after all his fellow passengers were tucked up in bed.

In October J. Bruce Ismay changed his mind about retiring as president of IMM and wrote to Morgan & Company requesting that he be allowed to stay on. E. C. Grenfell wrote back refusing Ismay's request and saying that both J. P. and his son Junius Morgan thought it best if he left. Grenfell dressed the dismissal up by saying how difficult it would be for everyone who was expecting to be promoted at the time of Ismay's retirement if he did not retire. Ismay was understandably disappointed, but he must have realised that by surviving the loss of the *Titanic* he had become something of a liability to the company.

Olympic returned to Harland & Wolff in late 1912 to have her bulkheads raised and an entire inner skin fitted to her hull. As originally designed, like *Titanic*, she would continue to float with any two of her major compartments flooded, but after the work was completed she would remain afloat with six such compartments open to the sea. By the time the alterations to her safety features were complete, at a cost of £250,000, she was probably the safest large passenger ship in the world. The number of lifeboats aboard was increased from the original and wholly inadequate 20 to 68, four more than Alexander Carlisle had wanted to put on the ship when he first designed her lifeboat layout. In all, the improvements to *Olympic* took five months to complete.

Olympic completed her refit and left Harland & Wolff's yard on 22 March. She set out on her first Atlantic crossing on 2 April, and performed faultlessly. For the next year and a half she plied back and forth between Southampton and New York without any problems and soon began to lay the ghost of her departed sister, and gain in popularity.

As a direct result of the loss of the *Titanic*, in early 1913 the United States Government started the North Atlantic Ice Patrol to keep a check on icebergs. The patrol continues to the present day, and on every 15 April lays a wreath on the sea at 41°46'N. 50°14'W. Although the patrol was started by the US Government, it is paid for today by all the nations using the North Atlantic sea lanes.

While on a trip to Europe and Egypt J. P. Morgan, who had not been a well man for some little while, steadily began to deteriorate. Whilst cruising on the Nile in the *Khargeh* he seems to have lost his appetite completely and existed on a diet of egg, onion and crusts of dry bread. As the Nile cruise progressed so did his decline, and along with the loss of appetite he began to suffer from insomnia and indigestion – which is hardly surprising considering his diet.

As he weakened, his daughter summoned his own physician, Dr Dixon, to join them in Egypt, which he duly did. Dixon called in a specialist from Italy who confirmed that Morgan's blood pressure was much too high. The specialist, who appears to have been something of a nationalist as well, advised that the financier should have a complete change of scenery and spend a few days in Rome before returning home for a complete rest. While in Rome Morgan's decline continued until he lapsed into a coma, regaining consciousness only fitfully and having to be fed intravenously. He died in his sleep on the night of 31 March 1913.

Despite Morgan's decline and demise the everyday business of the White Star Line continued and the new, 18,481-ton, *Ceramic* entered service in 1913. At the time she was the largest vessel to frequent antipodean shores.

On 30 June 1913 J. Bruce Ismay retired from the presidency of IMM and the White Star Line. With him went the name of his father's old company — Ismay, Imrie & Co — which became his exclusive property. Upon his retirement from White Star he went to stay at a house he had bought a few months earlier, sight unseen, in Ireland. He had bought the estate because it offered exceptionally good salmon fishing, and Ismay thoroughly enjoyed hunting, shooting and fishing.

When he got there he found that the domicile was a little more basic than he had expected. To begin with it was not, by his standards, a large house, and it did not have a large garden either at the front or back. There was no bathroom, no electricity, and the only water supply came from a well. In its favour was the house's location with the river running by the garden and a view over the lough; it was out of the way, and the fishing was everything Ismay expected. The Ismays decided to rough it for the summer. However, as soon as they returned to London in the autumn, J. Bruce gave instructions for the house to be brought up to a more respectable level of habitability during the winter. The house never did come up to expectations, though. In the 1920s it burned down, and in 1927 Ismay had it completely rebuilt to his own standards.

On Ismay's retirement Harold Sanderson took over as president of IMM and reorganised the whole management of the White Star Line. The managers were A. B. Caunty, Henry Concannon, and E. Lionel Fletcher. The loss of the *Titanic*, which remained a subject for conversation long after it happened, had seriously damaged IMM's reputation, and the combine had been going downhill ever since. The managerial alterations did not help in the slightest, and the combine continued its downward slide. Perhaps understandably, the new president's tenure of office was a little on the brief side. It was decided that an American president for the company might help so, late in 1913, Sanderson was removed as head of IMM and replaced by Phillip A. S. Franklin. Sanderson stayed with the company as chairman of the White Star Line. This change in management did not help much either.

The third and last of the *Olympic* Class vessels, *Britannic*, was launched on 26 February 1914 but further work on the new liner could only progress very slowly because of difficulties in obtaining materials. Although Harland & Wolff had no new vessels on order from the Admiralty, many other yards did and, with the threat of war looming, these other yards were given priority. In fact the *Britannic* would never be completed as a liner.

The first week of March saw another two fatalities aboard *Olympic*. On the 5th a third-class Italian passenger died of tuberculosis, pneumonia and heart failure. He was buried at sea that same night. Then, two days later, Seventh Engineer W. Costley sustained a depressed fracture of the skull when he fell into Bunker Number 5. Although an emergency operation was performed in the ship's hospital, the unfortunate engineer died two days later. *Olympic's* next voyage was little better and another two people died aboard, one of them, an eight-month-old boy, from meningitis. On top of that, as the journey progressed, five stowaways were discovered lurking in various parts of the ship. Burial parties on *Olympic* had a relatively slack month in April, however, when only one first-class passenger died, as a result of tuberculosis.

Fatalities aboard White Star vessels during March 1914 were not confined to *Olympic*, although she does seem to have had her fair share. In the last few days of the month *Oceanic²*, which seems to have had the unhappy knack of finding bad weather, battled her way through four days of terrific storms as she headed for Plymouth. Several passengers were injured and one, driven mad by the continual motion of the vessel, leaped overboard and drowned.

Throughout the summer of 1914 tension grew between the countries of Europe. The coming of war had long been foreseen and international organisations had done their best to defuse the situation. Unfortunately, many of the more influential members of those organisations had been going to a special peace rally in New York aboard the *Titanic*, which, as they had not survived, had done very little for their cause. Of course, there were also those who stood to make a substantial profit from war, such as steel manufacturers, like the owners of IMM.

During an early summer passage in June coal trimmer Henry Savage died of inflammation of the kidneys aboard *Olympic*, probably brought on by over-indulgence. With Savage in the ship's hospital was Fireman Arthur McMullen. It appears that he had become involved in an argument with another fireman, who had made his point quite forcibly with a crowbar.

June 1914 was notable for bringing to a head international discontent, the settlement of which would involve the use of far more sophisticated weaponry than the crowbar employed on Arthur McMullen; the Austrian Archduke Franz Ferdinand and his wife were murdered at Sarajevo. A month later, on 28 July, Austria declared war on Serbia. The great European powers, Germany, France, Britain and Russia mobilised for war. Russia sided with Serbia, while Germany backed its old ally Austria. Germany was ready first and immediately launched an assault on France, through Belgium. Britain had a treaty with Belgium and so, on 4 August, declared war on Germany. The Great War had begun.

Olympic left Southampton for New York on 29 July. On hearing of the declaration of war Captain Haddock ordered wireless silence, and *Olympic* was blacked out. She was escorted into New York by the Royal Navy's cruiser HMS *Essex*. For the four days that the ship remained at New York the crew were kept occupied perfecting their blackout and painting *Olympic's* superstructure dull grey.

On Saturday 8 August 1914, without any passengers, cargo or mail aboard, *Olympic* suddenly left New York, again escorted by the *Essex*. At her best cruising speed of 23kt the liner was well able to outrun any enemy warships she might encounter and so she left the *Essex* behind at Sable Island and crossed the Atlantic alone, zigzagging to confuse any shadowing enemy. As she approached the Irish coast she was met by another cruiser, HMS *Drake*, which escorted her into Liverpool on the 15th.

No sooner was war declared than Southampton was abandoned as a major port and the White Star Line went back to using Liverpool. It was considered that, for the time being, ships entering and leaving the confines of Southampton Water, the Solent and Spithead were simply too vulnerable to any enemy raider or submarine operating in the Channel. However, *Olympic* was too large for the facilities on offer at Liverpool to accommodate so she was temporarily transferred to Greenock. As it turned out she made only one voyage from there, leaving on 9 October for New York where she arrived seven days later after a passage spent zigzagging at high speed. Because of the difficulties in finding a safe berth for the giant liner, and the fact that she presented a prime target for the enemy, it was decided to lay her up. On 21 October she left New York, heading first for the Clyde and then Belfast where she would be safe, but a lot could happen between America and Northern Ireland.

On the morning of 27 October, six days after leaving New York and by now off the Irish coast, *Olympic* went to the rescue of HMS *Audacious*, one of the Royal Navy's newest and most powerful battleships. *Audacious* had struck a mine and was sinking by the stern. Due to concerns about the safety of the fleet base at Scapa Flow in the Orkneys from enemy action the British Grand Fleet had been transferred to Ireland's Lough Swilly until the regular base had been made more secure. Quite clearly the Germans were well aware of the fleet's move, and to emphasise the point the liner *Berlin* had laid a minefield across the British ships' route into and out of the lough. Without knowledge of this minefield the 2nd Battle Squadron of the Grand Fleet had decided to exercise in the area.

At 8.50am on 27 October the 23,000-ton *Audacious* had come across one of the *Berlin's* mines, off Tory Island. The British commander, Admiral Jellicoe, mistaking the explosion for a torpedo, ordered the rest of the squadron with the exception of the light cruiser *Liverpool* and some smaller vessels to clear the area. At about 10.30am *Olympic* was spotted by the captain of the *Liverpool* and ordered to assist in the evacuation of the stricken battleship. *Olympic* lowered her own boats to take off some of the crew of the crippled warship, and in less than two hours all but 250 of her people had been rescued and the liner had recovered her boats.

A destroyer, HMS *Fury*, managed to pass a cable from *Audacious* to *Olympic* and an attempt to tow her into shallower water began. Unfortunately the battleship's steering gear was out of commission and she sheered off to windward, breaking the towline. Although further attempts were made to get the warship under tow, they were unsuccessful and at about 5.30pm it was decided to remove the rest of the crew from the sinking ship. One and a half hours later everyone had been evacuated, either to *Liverpool* or *Olympic*. It was quite a shrewd move to take everyone off the battleship because at about 8.55pm her forward magazine blew up with an enormous explosion, and *Audacious* rolled over and sank. There had been only one casualty, Petty Officer William Burgess, of the *Liverpool*, who was standing on the deck of his ship when he was struck by a 2ft by 3ft piece of armour plate torn from the battleship as her magazine exploded. As the decks had been crowded with people watching the spectacle of the vessel's foundering at the time it was miraculous that nobody else was killed or injured.

Olympic then proceeded to Lough Swilly to drop off the Royal Navy personnel she had aboard, arriving there late on the evening of the 27th. As there were a number of German-born Americans aboard the liner she was ordered to drop anchor out of sight of the fleet, so that those with German sympathies could not gather any information of a sensitive military nature. (As if their witnessing the sinking of a British battleship was not of a sensitive military nature.) In the event, the loss of the *Audacious* was kept secret from the British public quite successfully, although the Germans soon published postcards commemorating the event. Accordingly *Olympic's* passengers, with the exception of one American, were not allowed to leave the ship for almost a week after she docked. The ship finally left the naval anchorage for Belfast on 2 November, arriving there the following day.

Instead of the planned lay-up the *Olympic* was now to be converted for use as a troopship. Her luxurious fittings were removed, or they would almost certainly have been turned into souvenirs by the soldiers who were to sail on her. Two guns were fitted, a 4.7in aft, and a 12-pounder forward. The conversion to a troopship took 10 months. The vessel's new role, White Star believed, demanded a new skipper and Captain Bertram Fox Hayes was appointed to the post on 16 September 1915.

Because of the outstanding way that Captain Haddock had handled his ship and co-operated with the Navy during the *Audacious* incident he was appointed by the Admiralty to command a squadron of merchant ships that had been converted to resemble British warships, based at Belfast. The function of Haddock's squadron was to confuse the enemy into believing that certain elements of the British fleet were not where they might otherwise have thought them to be.

The war brought other problems to White Star, and soon after the outbreak in August 1914 the training ship *Mersey* was sold, her officers and captain being needed for more important work. The Admiralty took over the *Oceanic²*, *Celtic²*, *Cedric* and *Teutonic* for use as armed merchant cruisers very shortly after hostilities began. Towards the end of the Great War the *Teutonic*, in company with *Celtic²* and *Cedric*, specialised in transporting troops between Egypt and Britain.

With its fleet reduced and the inevitable wartime reduction in passenger traffic, White Star was soon in serious financial trouble. By 1915 the Public Receiver in Britain had taken control of the company and it was only his skilful management, and the tremendous demand for merchant vessels to supply Britain's war economy, that kept the company afloat.

Justicia had been launched by Harland & Wolff on 9 July 1914 as the *Statendam*. Originally intended for the Holland-America Line the new ship was 740ft 6in long, 86ft 5in in beam, and displaced 32,232 gross tons. Well before she was fitted out the British Admiralty offered the owners £1 million for her as she was. After discussion it was decided that the Admiralty would complete the vessel to suit its requirements and charter her for the duration of the war, but at the end of hostilities the ship would be returned to the Holland-America Line.

When it took over the ship the British Government intended that she would sail under the Cunard flag, as is evidenced by the vessel's name. By the time *Justicia* was ready to enter service both *Lusitania* and *Britannic* had been sunk, but the *Lusitania's* crew had been dispersed while that of *Britannic* was still largely intact. Consequently the new vessel was handed over to the White Star Line.

Inevitably the war would bring losses to all major shipowners, including White Star. On 8 September 1914, the *Oceanic²*, while serving with the 10th Cruiser Squadron along with *Teutonic* and patrolling the North-West Approaches, ran aground on the Shaalds of Foula. The accident was probably attributable to there being two captains aboard the ship, her regular merchant skipper, Captain Henry Smith, and another from the Royal Navy, Captain William Slayter.

The unusual command structure would undoubtedly have caused a certain amount of confusion, with merchant seamen tending to prefer the devil they knew, in the shape of the merchant captain, while Royal Navy personnel would automatically obey their own senior officer. In this instance the naval captain, notionally the senior of the two, had insisted that the ship pass through the narrow waters between the island of Foula and the Shaalds, against the advice of the merchant skipper who was reluctant to risk his vessel in such confined seas. Luckily the ship was not seriously damaged in the grounding, and there were no casualties. However, it turned out that the ship was so hard aground that no amount of effort could refloat her. The crew was taken off and most of the armaments were removed before the *Oceanic* was abandoned to her fate. For nine years the vessel remained, pounded by the waves, before she was finally destroyed in a great storm.

Curiously, at the time she ran aground *Oceanic's* navigating officer was none other than David Blair who, until a last-minute crew reshuffle, had been second officer of the *Titanic*, and whose departure from that ship had caused the vital binoculars to be removed from the crow's-nest. It appears that it was a miscalculation by the ex-*Titanic* officer that led to the destruction of the *Oceanic*, although he was ably assisted in this by the two captains. Enemy action was not always a prerequisite for disaster, even in wartime.

Cevic was requisitioned by the Admiralty in 1915 and converted into a dummy battle-cruiser, the *'Queen Mary'*. The early part of her war career was somewhat marred by her tendency to run aground at regular intervals, but eventually she joined the North Atlantic patrol. The presence of what was believed to be the battlecruiser *Queen Mary* off New York was the principal reason for the surrender, and internment, of the German liner *Kronprinz Wilhelm* when the US joined the war in 1917.

On her way to New York from Liverpool, on 19 August 1915, *Arabic²* under the command of Lieutenant Will Finch RNR who had also commanded the vessel for White Star, was off the Old Head of Kinsale, at the southern tip of Ireland, when she was torpedoed by *U24*. Although at that time German submarines were under orders not to torpedo passenger ships without warning, Lieutenant-Commander Schneider, believing that *Arabic* was trying to ram his boat, felt justified in ignoring those orders. *Arabic* sank in just 11 minutes, taking 44 of the 253 crew and 181 passengers board with her. As 25 of the passengers aboard the *Arabic* were Americans the sinking caused something of a diplomatic incident, coming as it did only three months after the sinking of the *Lusitania*, and only an exchange of diplomatic notes prevented America from entering the war then and there.

At 10am on 24 September 1915 the *Olympic* left Liverpool on her first voyage as a troopship, bound for Mudros. As the war went on she would switch from carrying troops to the Dardanelles theatre to bringing them from Canada and then America to England, earning a nickname that remained with her for the rest of her long working life, 'Old Reliable'.

On that first trip as a troopship, with about 6,000 troops aboard, soon after passing Malta, *Olympic* came across a drifting lifeboat from the French steamer *Provincia*. The newly promoted Captain Bertram Hayes, who had been a lowly second officer on the *Georgic* only nine months earlier, stopped to rescue the sailors from the lifeboat before it was sunk by a machine-gun crew on the liner. Hayes was later reprimanded for his trouble, on the grounds that he had put his vessel at risk by stopping in submarine-infested waters. The French took a somewhat different view of the incident and awarded Captain Hayes the Gold Life Saving Medal. As in most things, it is all a matter of viewpoint. Adding a little weight to the naval viewpoint, while she was off Cape Matapan in November, *Olympic* was shadowed by an enemy submarine, but discretion being the better part of valour she made off at high speed, outrunning the hunter.

The organisation at Mudros was not all it might have been and it took eight days to disembark all of the troops from *Olympic*. However, the chaos there was nothing compared to what happened when *Olympic* reached Spezia (now La Spezia), in Italy, on her return passage. The pilot, who should have been on hand to guide the large ship into port, was missing. With no option but to attempt to make her own way, *Olympic* steamed slowly towards the harbour. Suddenly an Italian destroyer came racing out of the harbour, firing her guns as she went, to warn Captain Hayes that he was steaming into a minefield. No thanks to the Italian pilot, *Olympic* managed to avoid the mines and was guided into harbour by the destroyer. The pusillanimous pilot was waiting there to guide *Olympic* to her berth. The complications continued when it was discovered that the port's coaling arrangements were totally inadequate to cope with a vessel of *Olympic's* requirements. As a result, the liner was held up for eight days while her bunkers were filled before she could resume her voyage. By the time she reached Liverpool, on 31 October, because of all the delays, her supplies of drinking water had become foul and many of her crew were sick with stomach complaints. They recovered satisfactorily once supplies of fresh drinking water became available.

Britannic², the third and last of the *Olympic* Class ships built for the White Star Line, was taken over by the Admiralty on 13 November 1915 and was fitted out for use as a hospital ship. Her construction had been held up by the *Titanic* disaster and the ensuing inquiry, and again by a shortage of available materials once the war began. As the last, and best, of her class she was slightly larger than her two more famous sisters, 5ft longer and displacing almost 2,000 tons more.

Britannic's one day of trials were carried out on 8 December 1915. After those trials she was taken back to the builders for final adjustments and outfitting before sailing for Liverpool on the 11th. She arrived in the Mersey on 12 December 1915 and was handed over to the Admiralty, who commissioned her His Majesty's Hospital Ship *Britannic*. Command was given to Captain Charles A. Bartlett, who had been with White Star for 21 years, and had been their marine superintendent since 1912. *Olympic* was still at Liverpool when *Britannic* arrived. It was the penultimate time that two of the three vessels envisaged by J. Bruce Ismay and William Pirrie, and intended to work with one another on the North Atlantic, would be together. *Britannic* left on 23 December and *Olympic* 12 days later, on 4 January 1916, both for the eastern Aegean.

Towards the end of January 1916, while close to the south side of Lemnos Island, in the Aegean Sea, *Olympic* managed to avoid two torpedoes fired from an enemy submarine. A month later she was attacked by an enemy aircraft, but again escaped injury. Captain Hayes was to show, time and again, his understanding of just how a large liner like *Olympic* could be handled, usually without mishap. *Olympic* arrived back from the voyage on 12 February and was immediately sent to Southampton to pick up a load of troops from there. *Britannic* had arrived at the Hampshire port, with her second load of wounded, three days earlier. She was still there when *Olympic* sailed for Mudros on the 17th; the sisters would never meet again.

At the beginning of the war the *Baltic²* and *Adriatic²* had continued to operate between Liverpool and New York, but as the war progressed they were pressed into service as troopships. The *Adriatic* acquired the nickname 'Queen of the Munitions Fleet' and It was the *Baltic* that brought the very first American troops to Britain when the United States, somewhat belatedly, declared war on Germany in 1917. She carried a plaque commemorating the event for the rest of her working life.

Olympic arrived at Spezia on 1 March 1916, homeward-bound on her fourth and last trooping run to Mudros, and the long-winded business of coaling at the Italian port began. Normally coaling a ship, a universally hated operation, would have involved the entire crew but for some reason on this occasion a stock check was carried out at the same time. The check revealed a serious shortfall in the stores for the forward canteen. A thorough search discovered nothing, but the prospect of a further, more exhaustive, examination of the ship clearly unnerved some of the pilferers. On the following day, the 5th, much of the missing material, including 60 pairs of drawers, 72 singlets and 600 cigarettes, was found stacked in a main companionway. However, none of the missing food was ever recovered, and it is fairly safe to assume that sales of tobacco aboard fell alarmingly as 42lb of it were unaccounted for.

There had been some disagreement between White Star and the Admiralty for a little while over the cost of feeding troops aboard the line's vessels. After *Olympic's* first trip with a load of troops it had been found that they appeared to have consumed no less than £9,667 worth of food. The amount previously negotiated with the Admiralty had been only £6,953 for the same numbers. White Star seemed to be losing close to £3,000 per trip. In late January Harold Sanderson had suggested to the Admiralty that the daily allowance to cover food should be raised to 6 shillings and 6 pence (32.5p) for officers, 3 shillings (15p) for NCOs, and 1 shilling and 9 pence (9p) for ordinary soldiers. The Admiralty turned the suggestion down out of hand, which is hardly surprising if White Star crew members were helping themselves to almost £3,000 worth of stores per trip.

Olympic had never been the ideal vessel for use as a troopship between Britain and the Aegean simply because she had never been designed for such long voyages. She had been created for use on the North Atlantic, and her coal bunker capacity had been limited to just enough to make such voyages comfortably. In March 1916 the Canadian Government chartered her to ferry troops from Halifax to Britain, a task for which she was tailor-made. *Olympic* left Liverpool at the start of her first Atlantic crossing for a year and a half at midnight on 22 March, and arrived at Halifax on the 28th.

Before her first voyage loaded with Canadian troops began, Captain Hayes discovered that *Olympic* was expected to sail with an escorted convoy, which meant that she would only be allowed to steam at about 12kt. Understandably, he was not exactly overjoyed to learn of this and promptly protested. After he had explained that at 12kt his ship would provide a very tempting and almost unmissable target for a German submarine, and that his best defence against enemy surface craft and their underwater marauders lay in his ship's high speed, the Canadian Government relented. Captain Hayes was allowed to make his own way across the Atlantic without an escort and at his best speed. He set out with his first load of Canadian troops at about 9.15am on 5 April 1916. Not unusually, the voyage began badly when *Olympic* collided with a patrol vessel as it attempted to come alongside the liner to take off the pilot. Numbers 24 and 26 portside lifeboats were carried away by the patrol vessel's masts, and a davit was damaged. Luckily no one was hurt in the incident and *Olympic* was able to continue her journey without waiting for repairs. She arrived at Liverpool with her first contingent of Canadian soldiers six days later.

From the fourth week in March 1916 until the beginning of 1917 *Olympic* sailed across the Atlantic, ferrying Canadian troops from Halifax to Liverpool no less than 20 times, almost without incident. In that time, of the more than 50,000 troops carried, there were only two fatalities aboard. On 5 May, Private J. G. Stephen of 1st Battalion Canadian Expeditionary Force died and was buried at sea. On 7 June, Private Oswald Peto of the 88th Battalion died but his body was brought into Liverpool on the completion of *Olympic's* third round trip.

While at anchor at Halifax, at about 8am on 29 October 1916, *Olympic* swung round and went hard aground. She was refloated after four and a half hours amid fears that her hull might have suffered catastrophic damage, but the fears proved to be unfounded. Inspection revealed that the liner's hull had sustained no appreciable injury in the grounding. Just a week after the grounding a serious fire broke out in the flue of the third-class galley. The blaze took more than two hours to control and 18 barrels of flour were destroyed amid a considerable amount of structural damage. As *Olympic* was scheduled to return to Harland & Wolff for a refit after one more voyage, only temporary repairs were done to tide her over until then.

Because the numbers of casualties from the Mediterranean theatre of war had dropped, thanks to the evacuation of the Dardanelles in January 1916, *Britannic* was withdrawn from service on 12 April 1916, but retained by the Admiralty as a naval hospital for five weeks. She was discharged on 21 May, and after off-loading her medical staff and supplies, returned to Belfast to be refitted for civilian service. The government paid £76,000 for this refit, which never actually took place.

Not all White Star vessels were as lucky as *Olympic* when it came to encounters with the enemy. At about 4pm on 8 May 1916 *Cymric*, on her way to Liverpool from New York, was hit by three torpedoes fired from *U20*. Commander Walter Schwieger had, a year and a day earlier, sunk the Cunard liner *Lusitania*, which sank in 16 minutes after being hit by only one torpedo. *Cymric* remained afloat for almost a full day following the attack. There were no passengers aboard the White Star ship although she was capable of carrying 1,418, but four of her 110-man crew were killed by the exploding torpedoes and a steward was drowned as the ship was abandoned.

During the summer of 1916 heavy fighting flared up in Egypt and Palestine. The dramatic increase in the number of casualties requiring transport back to England meant that there was a shortage of available hospital ships. Before her planned conversion back into a liner had really begun, *Britannic* was recalled for use as a hospital ship. She sailed for Mudros to evacuate wounded on 23 September 1916.

Contrary to the rules of war, from time to time *Britannic* carried completely fit soldiers of the Royal Army Medical Corps who were not aboard to tend the wounded but were merely being taken out to, or returning from, the areas where the war was being fought. This meant, of course, that sometimes *Britannic* was serving as a troopship, not a hospital ship, and was therefore a legitimate target for the enemy.

On the morning of Tuesday 21 November 1916, while actually serving as a hospital ship, although luckily devoid of patients at the time, the *Britannic* struck a mine in the Aegean Sea. She sank with the loss of 21 lives, most of them victims of the vessel's own propellers, which were turning even as the lifeboats were lowered. Captain Bartlett, realising that his ship was sinking beneath him had decided to try to beach her. It was this decision that caused the casualties. There can be no doubt, with the benefit of hindsight, that Captain Bartlett's decision was wrong. *Britannic* took only 50 minutes to founder, not entirely as a result of the damage caused by the mine but also because of the coal bunker explosion that followed it. These combined explosions tore a huge hole in the ship's port bow, which was discovered when the wreck was explored in 1975 by Jacques Cousteau.

The 21-year-old *Georgic¹* was sunk by the German surface raider *Moewe* on 10 December 1916. *Moewe*, an armed merchant ship operating as a cruiser, was one of the more successful of the German ships selected for that role. While heading for Brest and

Liverpool from Pennsylvania with a general cargo of wheat and oil, and with 1,200 horses aboard, *Georgic* was intercepted by the raider about 590 miles east-south-east of Cape Race. The White Star vessel failed to respond to *Moewe's* order to heave to, so the German vessel opened fire, killing a member of her crew. The rest of the crew were taken off before the ship was sunk by torpedo.

Early in 1917 *Laurentic[1]*, under the command of Captain Reginald A. Norton, sailed from Liverpool for Halifax with £5 million in gold aboard. On 25 January, off Malin Head on the north coast of Ireland, she struck two mines and sank. The crew of 722 officers and men all managed to get into 15 lifeboats before the ship foundered, but eight of the boats never reached safety; 354 lives were lost. Most of the gold would be brought up from the wrecked vessel when the war was over.

While *Olympic* was being refitted Captain Hayes was given temporary captaincy of the *Celtic[2]*. While she was under his command, on 15 February 1917, *Celtic* struck a mine off the Isle of Man and had to be towed back to Liverpool, which she had left only the day before. The explosion had torn a 30ft hole in Number 1 hold but the vessel refused to sink. Luckily, despite her obvious damage, the ship was not too badly knocked about by the mine and she was back in service six weeks later.

After her winter refit, which had proven quite extensive, *Olympic* was officially commissioned as one of His Majesty's Transports on 9 April 1917, three days after America declared war on Germany.

As *Cretic* was homeward-bound from the Mediterranean on 26 October 1917 fire was discovered in a cargo of Turkish tobacco in Number 1 hold; which leaves one wondering just what a White Star ship was doing with a cargo of Turkish tobacco at a time when the British Empire was at war with Turkey. The hold was flooded, which put the ship down by the head, but the fire continued to burn. *Cretic* stopped off at the Azores to have the fire dealt with there, but even though more water was pumped into the hold the fire flared up again soon after the vessel put to sea. The fire was eventually put out after *Cretic* reached Liverpool.

The United States was taking an active, if belated, interest in the war by 1918. On 11 January *Olympic* left New York with her first complement of American troops, but there was still need to take care as German submarines were still active. *Justicia* was attacked by a U-boat while in the southern Irish Sea on 23 January 1918, but escaped unscathed by taking the sensible course and running away.

New York was still a hazardous port of call for White Star. While *Adriatic[2]* was there on 26 January 1918 fire broke out among some barrels of oil on her deck. New York City firemen flushed the decks, sweeping the burning oil into the North River, thus minimising damage to *Adriatic* but maximising it to the environment. Fire aboard *Adriatic[2]*, *Baltic[2]*, *Cedric* and *Celtic[2]* was exceptionally dangerous as during the war they not only served as troopships but also as auxiliary tankers carrying fuel for Royal Navy ships. They could each carry between 2,500 and 3,500 tons of fuel oil and between them brought in no less than 88,000 tons between August 1917 and the end of the war.

In a brief return to prewar practices, on 29 January 1918, when only 14 miles from the Mersey Bar, *Celtic[2]* ran into the Canadian Pacific Line's vessel *Montreal* which sank the next day. Other losses were less blameworthy. Soon after leaving Liverpool on 31 March the *Celtic[2]* was torpedoed by a German submarine. The torpedo killed six people and damaged the ship so badly that she had to be beached to prevent her from sinking. *Celtic* was eventually refloated and taken to Belfast for repairs.

The years of practice put in by White Star captains in the fine art of ramming and sinking other ships finally paid dividends on 12 May 1918. On her 22nd voyage as a troopship, and with a full complement of American troops aboard, *Olympic*, while being escorted by four American destroyers through the hazardous waters of the English Channel, was attacked by the German submarine *UB103*. Displaying just how nimble this class of ship could be when occasion demanded, *Olympic* not only managed to avoid the German torpedo but turned on her attacker so rapidly that she managed to ram the submarine and sink it. The bow of the *Olympic* was bent a couple of feet to port in the ramming but no water entered the ship.

The attempted attack on *Olympic* had been part of a German strategy to target troopships wherever possible. It was a strategy that was to prove a little costly on the morning of 6 May. About 150 miles ahead of *Olympic*, and directly on her intended route to Southampton, the *UB72* also lay in wait. Well before the liner reached her the German submarine was detected, and met the same fate as her commander had planned for *Olympic* when she was destroyed by torpedo.

Having been delayed for 30 hours while mines and enemy submarines were supposedly cleared from her intended route *Justicia*, under the command of Captain John David, left Liverpool on 18 July 1918 accompanied by eight other merchant ships and an escort of six destroyers. Shortly after 2pm the following day she was torpedoed by the *UB64*, a torpedo striking the port side, flooding the engine room and another compartment. The crew prepared to abandon ship in the normal fashion, but discovered that the bulkheads were holding and so set about doing what they could to save the vessel.

The rest of the convoy scattered and the destroyers began dropping depth charges around the crippled ship, forcing the U-boat to break off the attack. *Justicia* was taken in tow, but about two and a half hours after the first attack two more torpedoes were fired at her. One torpedo missed and the other was destroyed with gunfire from *Justicia's* crew. By 8pm the rescue tug HMS *Sonia* and another had the tow in hand and were heading for Lough Swilly, where it was hoped that *Justicia* could be beached. Even as they got under way a fourth torpedo was fired at the troopship, but was again diverted by gunfire from the crew.

It was now clear that the Germans were fairly serious in their intention to sink the *Justicia* so some of the ship's crew were evacuated before the tow was resumed. At 4.30 the following morning another torpedo just missed the White Star vessel's bow but this was to be the last escape. At 9.30am *UB54* fired a salvo of torpedoes at *Justicia's* port side. One struck Number 3 hold and another Number 5. The ship was doomed and the remaining crew were ordered to abandon her. *Justicia* sank stern first at 12.40pm on 20 July 1918. The third engineer and 15 other crew members, killed in the first torpedo attack, were the only casualties.

There was one more major casualty for White Star before the war came to an end. While still 200 miles from the English coast, and with almost 3,000 American troops aboard, the *Persic* was torpedoed on 12 September 1918. The escorting warships attacked the German submarine and it was apparently sunk. No lives were lost aboard the *Persic*, although the ship had to be beached to prevent her from foundering. She was eventually refloated and repaired and would remain in service until 1927.

IMM had never been the commercial success that J. P. Morgan had envisaged and by the closing stages of the World War 1 the company let it be known that it was prepared to sell its interests in non-American shipping lines. Great curiosity was aroused, particularly among British interests who were anxious to regain control of what had been British companies, especially White Star. Negotiations were soon under way between IMM and a syndicate headed by William Pirrie and Sir Owen Phillips (who was to become Lord Kylsant). After several months of talking the syndicate made an offer of £27 million for all the tonnage then sailing under the British flag, and for other assets including a cash accumulation of £11 million. IMM was delighted with the offer and promptly agreed to sell, but even as the papers were drawn up, American President Woodrow Wilson stepped in and vetoed the transaction. For the time being at least the matter was closed.

With the Great War over, the management of White Star began to restore the line to its prewar glory. One major problem that beset them was a serious shortage of vessels suitable for the Southampton–New York express run. Only *Olympic* remained of the three ships specially commissioned for this service, so they decided to order a new 40,000-ton ship from Harland & Wolff, to be called *Homeric*.

The 'Big Four', as they had always been known, had all survived the war but because of their limited speed they were now considered unsuitable for the prestige route to New York. After refitting, the *Adriatic²*, *Baltic²*, *Cedric* and *Celtic²* would resume their old role, operating out of Liverpool. In the meantime the service from Southampton would reopen with the *Adriatic²* and the Red Star Line's *Lapland* making do. They would be joined in 1920 by the refurbished *Olympic*. Between voyages the *Adriatic²* also made several cruises to the Mediterranean.

With the war's end, vessels ordered by the Shipping Controller, and just being completed, came onto the market. One such vessel was the *War Priam*, an 8,000-ton cargo ship. White Star promptly bought the vessel in an effort to make good some of the losses its fleet of freighters had suffered. They took over the vessel on 13 March 1919 and renamed the ship *Bardic*. She sailed on her maiden voyage for the line on the 18th.

Toward the end of 1918 the *Vedic* joined the White Star fleet. She was a one-class ship with no first- and second-class accommodation aboard, just third. But before she could begin to operate there was the serious business of bringing British troops home from overseas to be seen to, so *Vedic* was put to work at that. On one such voyage *Vedic* was returning from Archangel with 1,000 British troops aboard who had been fighting alongside tsarist forces in an attempt to support the Russian monarchy against the communist revolutionaries. On 20 September 1919, she ran aground on the Orkney Islands. She was pulled off by tugs and warships and was able to continue her journey, no doubt much to the relief of the soldiers.

Olympic returned to Liverpool on 21 July 1919 at the end of her last voyage as a troopship. For the past six months she had been engaged in repatriating thousands of Canadian and American servicemen. During her war service she had steamed over 184,000 miles, burned 347,000 tons of coal and carried almost 150,000 troops, hardly losing any, and without a serious mechanical failure. It was time for the ship to be converted back into a civilian liner and resume her interrupted career.

During her refit at the Gladstone Dock following the cessation of hostilities some minor damage to *Olympic's* hull plating was discovered, indicating that she was indeed a lucky ship. An 18in dent with a 6in crack was found 14ft below the waterline amidships. As there was no record of his ship being involved in any collision that might have caused this damage since her last overhaul, Captain Hayes could only conclude that his vessel had been struck by a torpedo which had failed to explode.

Olympic's immediate postwar refit was something of a landmark in the history of North Atlantic passenger liner history as she had her coal-fired system converted to oil, making her the first large Atlantic liner to be oil-fired. The refit took 10 months and cost more than £500,000 but at the end of it the liner was as good as the day she first left the builder's yard. The conversion to oil firing meant that fewer stokers were now required and consequently the black gang was reduced from 350 men to just 60.

Not long after, as *Olympic* was approaching New York, she was met by an American destroyer. Even as Captain Hayes was wondering just who he had aboard to warrant such attention, a signal from the destroyer was received enquiring as to whether or not a certain young lady was on the liner. The captain sent a reply confirming the presence aboard his ship of the young lady. The destroyer then followed *Olympic* to quarantine and anchored close to her. Within minutes a young officer from the destroyer was hurrying up *Olympic's* gangplank towards the young lady who was running towards him. When she was only halfway down the final flight of steps the young woman took a flying leap into the American officer's arms. The event was reported in all of the New York papers and the publicity was exactly the sort that White Star wanted, and had probably arranged.

Although White Star had run one-class ships on other routes before, *Vedic*, not one of White Star's more famous vessels, was the pioneer of this concept in Atlantic travel and was extremely popular for a while. People liked being able to go where they pleased on the ship instead of being confined to a few spartan areas, mostly deep within the bowels of the vessel, while first- and second-class passengers enjoyed the more spacious and airy parts of the ship. However, changes in the American immigration laws soon made the scheme impracticable and it was abandoned.

Before returning to service, as she lay at Belfast the reconditioned *Olympic* was opened to the public at half-a-crown (12.5p) a head. Between four and five thousand people paid up and tramped over the ship, admiring the opulence of an age that, although they did not know it at the time, had ended in the mud of Belgium. After two days of public inspection *Olympic* weighed anchor and sailed for Southampton. Aboard the pride of the White Star fleet was a large party of guests, among them Harold Sanderson and William Pirrie. At dinner Sanderson expressed his satisfaction with the ship, and his opinion that, because of world conditions, he could not see a competitor for such a large vessel being built for some time to come.

Even as the celebrations continued, the new propulsion system threatened the safety of all aboard. As an engineer in the forward stokehold tried to turn a valve regulating the flow of oil to the furnace, the top of it came off in his hand. The topless valve allowed oil that had been preheated to about 240° Fahrenheit to escape into the compartment at a pressure of 70lb to 80lb/sq in. As if that was not bad enough, just as the jet of hot oil sprayed into the room, another of the boiler room staff was in the process of lighting a burner. Inevitably, the escaping oil caught fire, seriously injuring John Hume of the oil supply company Brigham & Cowan. Because the supply of oil to the fire could not be stopped until the valves were closed in the next stokehold, the blaze took firm hold and took 15 minutes to bring under control. Fortunately the conflagration did not spread to the rest of the ship and she was able to continue on her way, but it had highlighted a serious design fault. Even so, on her arrival at Southampton *Olympic* re-entered service, joining *Lapland* and *Adriatic* sailing between Southampton and New York.

Her first voyage as an oil-fired liner began on 25 June 1920, when she departed Southampton for New York. She would make many more round trips in the next few months without mishap before White Star's unfortunate predilection for becoming involved in collisions and groundings caught up with her again.

It was apparent to the managers of White Star that the ageing *Adriatic*[2] and the *Lapland* needed to be replaced with a liner of comparable size and speed to that of *Olympic*. While the new *Homeric* had been laid down it would be quite some time before she was completed and ready for service, but there was an alternative. At war's end the whole of the German merchant fleet had been taken over by the Shipping Controller as 'War Reparations' and amongst those ships was the incomplete, 34,000-ton, *Columbus*, lying at Danzig and intended for the Norddeutscher-Lloyd Line. IMM promptly bought the *Columbus* as a partner for *Olympic* and Harland & Wolff workers went to Germany to help complete the vessel in a manner suitable for White Star service.

The *Columbus* was renamed *Homeric* and work on the vessel of that name being constructed at Belfast was terminated. As it turned out, the new *Homeric* was not suitable for White Star's express service at all. She was a record breaker in two respects, both of which should have alerted the managers of the White Star Line to her unsuitability. The German-designed ship was the world's largest twin-screw vessel as well as being the biggest ship in the world propelled solely by reciprocating engines. She was also a coal burner. Consequently, *Homeric* was found to be too slow, with a top speed of only 18$\frac{1}{2}$kt, to work alongside *Olympic*. Later conversion to oil firing raised the top speed by 1kt but even that was barely enough to make her a viable proposition.

Albert Ballin, the head of the Hamburg-Amerika Line, had ordered three huge new ships as an answer to White Star's *Olympic* and Cunard's *Lusitania* Class vessels shortly before the war. The first two of the new ships were taken over by the Cunard Line and the United States Line, the *Imperator* becoming the *Berengaria*, and the *Vaterland* becoming the *Leviathan*. White Star looked to the third, *Bismarck*, which was still incomplete when the war ended, the huge vessel lying in the River Elbe at Hamburg. To avoid any unnecessary competition between them, the two major British lines, White Star and Cunard, agreed to buy both the *Imperator* and *Bismarck*, split the cost and operate one each. As Cunard already operated the *Imperator* as *Berengaria* then White Star would take the *Bismarck* and rename her *Majestic*[2]. In a foretaste of what was to come, the ships were operated under joint ownership for 10 years.

After a long legal battle with the German owners the British lines finally gained ownership of the *Bismarck* and workmen from Harland & Wolff again made their way to Germany to help in the completion and fitting out of the vessel. When Captain Hayes took over the *Bismarck* her funnels were still painted in Hamburg-Amerika colours and the original German name was still on the bows and stern. In a demonstration of just how easy it was to change the identity of a ship the funnels were repainted in White Star colours, the German name was painted out and the new name *Majestic* was painted in.

Some time in 1920 the 16,821-ton Norddeutscher-Lloyd vessel *Berlin* was taken over by White Star for use on the Liverpool–New York route and renamed *Arabic*[3]. She had been built by Blohm & Voss 12 years before. *Arabic* would be transferred to the Red Star Line in 1925, and would finally go to a breakers in Italy seven years after that.

August 1921 saw two mysterious disappearances from *Olympic*. The first was on the 17th when first-class passenger Julius Smolin, who was travelling with his son Nathaniel, vanished from A Deck in the afternoon. He had been sitting with his son in the open air after lunch. Nat had dozed off, and when he awoke at about 3.30 his father was nowhere to be seen. He searched for his father for the next three and a half hours or thereabouts without success and finally reported him missing at 7pm In the ensuing enquiries it was found that Lift-Attendant Leslie Brown recalled taking Julius Smolin up from C Deck to A Deck sometime between 5.30 and 6.00. A first-class passenger remembered seeing Smolin near the crane at the aft end of A Deck at about the same time, but noticed nothing unusual about his behaviour. Julius Smolin was never seen again, and it has never been established whether he fell, jumped or was pushed overboard.

At about 8pm on 30 August, on *Olympic's* voyage following the Smolin incident, Annie Thompson, a second-class passenger, found the purse, ring, pen and knife belonging to her fiancé Thomas Brassington lying on her bed. With Brassington's effects there was a letter, which as far as Miss Thompson could recall read, 'I Thomas Brassington leave all my personal belongings to Annie Louisa Thompson, 635 Haight Avenue, Alecueda, California. My troubles at home and the thought of Ellis Island are more than I can bear.' Miss Thompson was understandably alarmed by the letter and went in search of her fiancé, and found him up on deck. During the conversation that followed Miss Thompson fainted, and when she recovered consciousness she was alone. A search of the ship was carried out but Brassington could not be found. Steward W. Girard later reported he had seen him at about 8.45, when he had asked him for some baggage tags and, just before 9.00, Brassington was seen in his cabin by a Mr D. Pratt, who was sharing with him. Mr Pratt thought that he looked disturbed and tried to speak to him about it, but Brassington ignored him and left the room. He was never seen again.

Amongst the passengers aboard for *Olympic's* return trip from America was Charlie Chaplin. The great entertainer did his best to avoid public attention while on the ship, but he did agree to appear in a ship's concert in aid of a seamen's charity, where he was the star attraction.

While heading for Cherbourg on 12 December 1921 *Olympic* ran into some extremely heavy weather and was forced to reduce speed. At about 3.45am she was struck by exceptionally large waves that smashed five galley ports, causing yet a further reduction in speed while the damage was patched up. Five hours later another giant wave shattered the starboard ports of the reception room, and damaged the falls of the Number 1 emergency boat. What was to come another five hours later is difficult to credit. We already know that the North Atlantic is capable of producing enormous waves, but only rarely does it bring forth anything like the seas that struck *Olympic* at 2.05 that afternoon. The giant liner was rolled back and forth so violently that the locks holding some of her watertight doors open failed. Third-class passenger John Onsik had his left leg shattered above the ankle and suffered serious cuts and bruising as Watertight Door 33 slammed shut on him. The leg was so badly mutilated that it was amputated three days later. Door 28 slammed shut on another third-class passenger, Domenico Serafini, who was killed instantly. The impact of the door had displaced a vertebra and caused a compression of the spinal column. The battered liner reached Southampton on 17 December. In another violent storm, as she was making a westbound crossing in the same year, two crew members were fatally injured.

When the war had ended it was decided that an attempt should be made to salvage the gold from the *Laurentic*, which had sunk off the north coast of Ireland after striking a mine in 1917. The wreck was found in 1921, badly battered by the sea, lying at an angle of 45 degrees in about 120ft of water. Because of the exposed position of the wreck the Admiralty divers could work on it only in good weather. It took the divers the better part of three years to recover most of the bullion (£4,958,708) in one of the greatest salvage operations undertaken to that time.

Chapter 14
1922-1932

T he White Star Line's financial problems were mounting steadily and, as we have already seen, it had been found advisable to sell off some the older vessels in order to raise enough money to buy in anything new. The old *Bovic* was another of those vessels judged to be surplus to requirements and was sold in 1922, becoming the *Colonian*. However, it seems that White Star overdid it on the cutting down and was obliged to buy a couple of ships to fulfil its obligations. These were the ageing *Poland* which was brought in from the Red Star Line and the *Pittsburgh*, which had been built by Harland & Wolff for the American Line. The *Pittsburgh* was taken over before she entered service with the American Line, another member of the IMM combine. Very early in her career with White Star, on 30 March 1922, a huge wave struck *Pittsburgh* when she was about 600 miles east of Sable Island on her way to New York from Bremen, via Halifax. The wave put her steering gear out of action and did a considerable amount of damage to her decks and fittings. Despite her rather unpropitious beginnings, this 16,322-ton ship was with White Star for three years until 1925, when she was transferred to the Red Star Line, and renamed *Pennland*.

The ex-German liner *Bismarck*, renamed *Majestic²*, joined *Olympic* and *Homeric* on the Southampton–New York route, her maiden voyage for the White Star Line beginning on 10 May 1922. At 56,621 gross tons, at that time she was the world's largest ship, and noticeably faster than anything else that White Star had ever owned. On her fastest Atlantic crossing she averaged 24¾kt. As a result of his sterling service on the *Olympic* Captain Bertram Hayes was appointed as master. At the same time Captain Hayes was made Commodore of the White Star Line, the first such appointment since E. J. Smith had been lost with the *Titanic* 10 years before. On 7 January, Captain Alec Hambleton of the *Adriatic²* was appointed captain of *Olympic* in Hayes' place, but he was soon to be superseded by Captain Hugh David.

By the time *Majestic* left Southampton at the start of her maiden voyage to New York, eight years had elapsed between her launching and her first voyage, which must be some sort of record. Although Albert Ballin is today recognised as one of the greatest ship designers of his age, *Majestic* was not one of his better efforts. Instead of the boiler uptakes passing upwards through the centre of the ship they had been split and rerouted up the sides of the hull, joining the funnels at boat deck level. This arrangement, although gaining space in the public rooms, seriously weakened the structure of the ship, with the result that on one voyage the ship cracked all down one side. Only superb seamanship and excellent trimming of the ship's ballast prevented the vessel from breaking in two.

The end of an era came on 1 July 1922 when the Dillingham Immigration Restriction Act, sometimes known as the 3% Act, began to come into force in America. The new legislation would reduce the number of immigrants allowed to enter the country to about

360,000 a year. As the huge liners belonging to the White Star Line had been designed with the passage of large numbers of immigrants in mind, they had become rather like dinosaurs; they had outlived their time.

During 1923 White Star took three vessels out of service and passed them to other lines within the IMM group, or sold them to foreign owners. *Cretic* was passed to the Leyland Line; *Cufic²* and *Tropic²* were sold to Italian owners. The new *Doric²*, specially commissioned for the Liverpool–Montreal route, entered service in the same year. She was the only vessel to be built for the White Star Line that was powered by geared turbine engines only. The otherwise unremarkable *Doric* sailed back and forth without serious incident for more than 10 years, before a collision with a French vessel caused so much damage to her that she was scrapped.

On 21 November Captain David of the *Olympic* was succeeded by Captain J. B. Howarth. The new commander would have only one voyage to familiarise himself with the ship before she was due to return to Harland & Wolff for overhaul. She arrived for the 10 weeks of work there on 10 December. The work was completed and *Olympic* returned to service, beginning her first voyage on 20 February 1924.

Collision, though serious enough on its own, was not the only difficulty encountered by officers and crews of the White Star Line; deliberate sabotage was another. On 24 February 1924 as *Majestic²* lay at Southampton, fire broke out aboard. The fire was believed to be the work of strikers and was quickly put out, doing little damage. Despite the accidents and sabotage that continually ate into the line's profits it was still making money, if only because there were so many Americans who wanted to visit Europe. On *Majestic's* last departure from New York in 1923 she had no fewer than 1,700 passengers aboard.

As *Olympic* was backing away from New York's Pier 59, on 22 March 1924, she ran into the Furness Withy liner *Fort St George*, striking her just aft of amidships on the port side. The collision was not wholly the fault of the White Star vessel as the *Fort St George* had just been racing with another ship, the *Arcadian*, which was a competitor on the Bermuda run. In the collision *Fort St George's* mainmast was snapped off at the base, 150ft of decking was caved in, ventilators, rails, lifeboat davits were destroyed, the hydraulic derrick was badly mauled and the ship's radio antenna was brought down. In all, the damage to the *Fort St George* was estimated at £35,000. It was believed at the time that *Olympic* had escaped serious damage and so she proceeded with her voyage, but in reality the collision had broken her immense cast stern frame. Later repairs to *Olympic* would involve replacing the entire frame, the first time such a repair had been undertaken with so enormous a vessel.

Another passenger was reported as having disappeared from *Olympic* on 27 April. George Garizio, travelling second class, had not slept in his bed the previous night according to his bedroom steward. A search of the ship, and penetrating enquiry, revealed nothing except that he had last been seen at dinner the evening before. His fellow diners had noticed that Garizio had seemed a little quiet during the meal but had noticed nothing else unusual in his behaviour. The ship was searched again the following day, with exactly the same outcome as before, so George Garizio was officially listed in the log as missing.

In 1924 the Royal Mail Steam Packet Company persuaded William Pirrie (by that time Viscount Pirrie) to make an inspection tour of the harbour facilities on offer at South American ports. He set out aboard the Royal Mail Steamer *Arlanza* but later transferred to the *Ebro*. It was on the *Ebro*, on 7 June 1924, that he collapsed and died, having been unwell for some time with prostate problems.

Mid-June 1924 produced a couple of incidents aboard *Olympic* that might or might not have been related. During the voyage on which these events took place the liner was bringing the body of William Pirrie home for burial. At about 10.50pm on 14 June, as Master-at-Arms E. A. Coward was making his rounds for the night he came across Seaman Connolly standing by the top of Number 4 hatch, on the aft well deck. Noticing that the grating had been removed and the locking bar forced, Coward asked what the game was. Connolly claimed that he was getting a trunk up, but Coward spotted another seaman, W. Shave, standing on a lower deck and called the boatswain's mate. To begin with, Shave claimed that they had the butcher's permission to borrow a barrel from the hold to make a drum but the excuse was patently untrue. When the men were brought before Captain Howarth two days later they admitted that they had no right to have been removing anything from the hold. They also admitted to trying to persuade assistant butcher Kellaway to tell the master-at-arms that he had given them his permission, but the butcher had refused.

The incident might possibly have been connected to the disappearance of 53-year-old Bedroom Steward Arthur Paul. Paul was reported missing at 7.45am on 17 June, the day after Captain Howarth had questioned Connolly and Shave. The steward had last been seen the previous evening at just before 11.30. He had been on C Deck, carrying a tray. Crew mates were questioned as to whether Paul had been behaving strangely but nobody had noticed anything out of the ordinary. However, a fellow steward who slept in a nearby berth reported that Paul had not turned in for the night by midnight and was not in his bed when the stewards were roused at five that morning. Despite a thorough search of the ship no trace of Arthur Paul was ever found and he was listed as missing in the ship's log.

In July 1924 the American immigration restriction, previously set at 3% of the foreign-born population was reduced to only 2% of those shown in the 1890 census. This meant that the number of immigrants had now fallen from more than a million a year before the war to a measly 160,000 a year, nothing like enough to support the various shipping lines engaged in the immigrant business.

As if that was not enough, *Bardic* ran hard aground in thick fog off Lizard Point, Cornwall, on 30 August 1924. At about 1am the ship ran amongst the Maenheere rocks, a few hundred yards from where *Suevic* had run aground 17 years before, and began to take water into Numbers 1, 2 and 3 holds, and the engine room. *Bardic* was unable to get clear of the rocks under her own power so a distress call was sent out. The Lizard Point lifeboat arrived and took off 80 of the freighter's crew, leaving the captain and several engineers aboard to operate the pumps.

Two local tugs tried to haul the stricken ship clear but failed. White Star then engaged the services of the Liverpool and Glasgow Salvage Association, who had successfully saved the *Suevic*, and their salvage ship *Ranger*, under Captain I. J. Kay, arrived the next day. For almost all of the next month the salvors battled to save the ship, despite several major storms that threatened to undo their work. Then, with another vessel, the *Trover*, lashed to *Bardic's* starboard quarter to provide extra lift, and with the assistance of several other vessels with the capacity between them, and using *Bardic's* own recourses, of clearing 1,160,000 gallons of water an hour from the grounded ship, it was time to try again.

At 3.45pm on 29 September 1924 *Bardic* was finally dragged off the rocks, badly down by the head and listing 11 degrees to port. She was taken to Falmouth to be beached so that emergency repairs could be carried out which would enable her to make it to the local dry-dock. It was discovered that 140 hull plates had been torn to shreds and a considerable amount of the ship's framing had been bent or destroyed. For complete repair *Bardic* would have to return to Harland & Wolff's Belfast yard, and she set off from Falmouth, under her own steam, on 17 October. By the end of the year she was back in service with White Star on the Australian run, but not for long.

There can be no doubt that William Pirrie played a large role in the fortunes of the White Star Line, particularly after the death of Thomas Henry Ismay. Had the shipbuilder not decided to use his influence to help J. P. Morgan gain control of the line, then there is every chance that J. Bruce Ismay would have held out against the takeover, and in all probability the White Star Line would be in existence still. Instead, Pirrie tried to capture a lucrative market by becoming shipbuilder to the IMM company, and in so doing handed the purse strings of the White Star Line to the American financier. We have already seen how ready IMM was to put money into an enterprise that would not show an immediate return. After the death of J. P. Morgan the new managers of his financial empire appear to have taken a much more modern approach to business than he had: take every penny you can, and put back as little as possible. It would be fair to say that from the moment William Pirrie intervened in the negotiations between Morgan and Ismay the outlook for the White Star Line was doubtful in the extreme.

As mentioned earlier, when Pirrie died his body was taken to New York and then shipped home aboard his favourite vessel, *Olympic*. He was buried in the city cemetery in Belfast, and on his tomb there is a plaque with a picture of *Olympic* and the legend: 'RMS *Olympic* 45,439 tons for the White Star Line, built by Harland & Wolff 1911'.

On 26 August 1924, as *Arabic*³ was making her first voyage from Hamburg to New York, via Southampton, Cherbourg and Halifax, she was struck by a hurricane. The ship was devastated by the storm. About 100 people were in the library when a huge wave smashed all the windows and flooded the room. The people in the room were thrown off their feet, to land amongst the wreckage of chairs and tables, and then to be washed back and forth as the ship rolled heavily. A lifeboat and four life-rafts were torn away completely and another nine boats were smashed to the decks, useless. Pillows were stuffed into broken ports and windows in an effort to keep some of the water out of the ship. One woman, inexplicably in a deck chair, was about to be washed overboard when she was saved by a seaman grabbing her by the hair. Other people, knocked off their feet by the violent motion of the ship, sat in corridors with their hands up to protect their faces from flying debris. One unfortunate passenger was actually thrown right through the wall separating his cabin from the next. All of the ship's 17 engineers, 40 firemen and 6 greasers were injured by coming into violent contact with the vessel's machinery. The lights and wireless failed and the cargo shifted, causing the ship to list to port. When *Arabic* arrived at New York she had more than 100 casualties aboard, being ministered to by the ship's surgeon and six doctors from among her passengers. Seven ambulances were awaiting her arrival. By the time she reached New York the *Arabic* had a 10 degree list to port, and the interior of the ship was a waterlogged shambles.

Homeric entered New York harbour close behind *Arabic*, having been caught in the same storm. She had been struck by an 80ft high wave that had carried away a lifeboat, smashed ports and windows, broken chairs from their mountings in the decks, and injured seven people – and she had missed the worst of the frightful storm. The weather was little better two months later when wind and tide pushed the Red Star liner *Finland* into the *Baltic*² as she was berthing at New York on 8 October 1924. Fortunately neither vessel suffered any serious damage. Still the weather battered away at ships sailing the North Atlantic. While on her way from Southampton to New York, on 14 November, *Adriatic*[2] ran into a hurricane that carried one lifeboat away and smashed three more.

We have already seen that close ties existed between White Star and Harland & Wolff whereby ships were built and heavy repair work carried out on a 'cost plus profit' basis. Similar ties existed between the builder and other shipping lines, notably those of Lord Kylsant's Royal Mail Group. Before William Pirrie died Lord Kylsant had gained control of Harland & Wolff, and upon Pirrie's demise he took over as chairman. Clearly Kylsant expected the long-standing arrangement between IMM and what was now his shipbuilding yard to continue, but he was mistaken. In common with other shipowners, White Star was becoming increasingly concerned at the rising cost of building new vessels and having older ones repaired. Cost cutting had become an essential part of the line's continued existence, at least as far as IMM was concerned.

With the coming of the new year the White Star Line resumed its practice of getting rid of vessels that it thought it no longer needed. The ex-Dominion Line's *Canopic* was scrapped, *Bardic* was sold off to the Aberdeen Line and *Pittsburgh* was transferred to the Red Star Line. With so many vessels being sold off, transferred to other lines within the group or scrapped, the line found it necessary to bring in extra ships during 1925. The *Delphic*[2] was one such vessel, and the *Regina* was another.

In February 1925 Captain Howarth of the *Olympic* was replaced by Captain William Marshall. The White Star Line was not only changing its ships and transferring captains but was planning to introduce a whole new concept into North Atlantic travel. As a result of the new American immigration regulations the major shipping lines held a conference to decide how best to deal with the situation. A new class of passenger was created at the conference, to be known as Tourist Third class. Passengers travelling in this new class would occupy either the very best accommodation available in the existing third-class areas of a ship, or the least desirable second-class cabins. They would be expected to pay a little more than normal third-class fares but would be treated very much as if they were full-fare-paying second-class passengers. Quite naturally this new arrangement brought a noticeable drop in the number of people travelling second class and less than three years later second class was done away with completely. From then onwards there would again only be three classes of passenger aboard White Star vessels: first, tourist and third.

Bad luck caught up with *Olympic* again on 24 May 1925 when Toefile Rechleuicen, a 52-year-old Lithuanian housewife, fell overboard. Captain Marshall had the ship's engines put astern as soon as the news reached him, in order for the liner to retrace her course as exactly as possible. About 15 minutes after Mrs Rechleuicen had gone overboard lookouts aboard the ship thought they spotted her floating with a lifebuoy. A lifeboat was lowered to attempt a rescue but the unfortunate woman could not be found. After a 20-minute search the rescue attempt was abandoned.

In the mid-1920s IMM again let it be known that it wanted to dispose of all of its foreign (that is non-American) holdings, including the White Star Line. This time nobody seemed very interested, possibly because by this juncture the fleet was getting a little antiquated. Round about this time the last ship for the Oceanic Steam Navigation Company was ordered from Harland & Wolff.

Instead of the usual 'cost plus' arrangement the new ship was to be built to a fixed price. The new *Laurentic*[2] was the only ship built by the Belfast shipbuilders for White Star on this basis, and she turned out to be disappointing in almost every respect. Even allowing for the fact that Phillip A. S. Franklin was determined not to spend a penny he did not have to on the new vessel that was soon to be sold, her obsolete coal firing still takes some explaining. On top of that her fixtures and fittings were well below the usual standards required by the line. *Laurentic²* was obsolete before she even went into the water.

The directors of the White Star Line had made up their minds that in future all orders placed with the Belfast shipbuilders would have to be on a fixed price contract. A couple of months after placing the order for *Laurentic* they sent a letter to Harland & Wolff giving the required six months' notice terminating the old 'cost plus' agreement. The new contract arrangement was not to the shipbuilder's taste, and the only reason they had accepted the *Laurentic* deal was because White Star had made it plain that if the ship was not built to a fixed price, then it would not be built at all.

By about halfway through the roaring twenties the White Star Line seems to have lost the ability, or perhaps the inclination, to maintain its vessels properly. This lack of preventive maintenance is clearly illustrated by the case of *Celtic²'s* starboard propeller which fell off as she was leaving Boston harbour on 27 October 1925. The ship was obliged to return to her berth and disembark her passengers who were sent to New York by train. The dropped propeller was recovered from the bottom of the harbour by divers and it was refitted in the Boston Navy Yard's dry-dock.

Arabic³ arrived at Hamburg on 9 November 1925 with a starboard bunker on fire. The fire, which could easily have caused a major explosion that would almost certainly have sunk the ship, fortunately caused little damage and was quickly put out. As far as the available records show, this seems to be only the second time that fire had broken out in a coal bunker aboard a White Star ship, the other, of course, being the *Titanic*.

Olympic underwent a major overhaul and refit during the winter of 1925/26 when her stern frame, damaged in the collision with the *Fort St George,* was completely replaced, the first time such a repair had ever been carried out. Almost immediately after that work had been completed some small cracks were discovered in the starboard side of the bridge deck that also required patching up.

News that IMM was ready to sell the White Star Line finally provoked a response and in 1926 a London syndicate, headed by Sir Frederick Lewis, the chairman of Furness, Withy & Co, began talks with the owners. The talks were held up when no agreement could be reached over New York terminals. Then the British General Strike happened and the negotiations fell through. Already alarmed by the fixed price contract to build *Laurentic²* and afraid that Harland & Wolff might be expected to build other ships for White Star and perhaps other lines as well without a guaranteed profit margin, Lord Kylsant then began negotiating for control of the Oceanic Steam Navigation Company. In the end, only a few months after the talks with Sir Frederick Lewis had broken down, it was announced that Kylsant, as chairman of the Royal Mail Steam Packet Company, had bought the White Star Line, for £7 million. His first act as chairman of the line was to withdraw the letter sent a few months earlier, ending the 'cost plus' agreement with his own shipbuilding company, Harland & Wolff.

Already the leading shipowner in Britain, Lord Kylsant also had interests in more than 50 companies including shipbuilding, oil installation and port development concerns. With the acquisition of the White Star Line the Kylsant Group of companies became, with more than two million tons of shipping, the largest shipowners in the world. The only real fly in the ointment was that Lord Kylsant, and the Royal Mail Group, did not have the necessary money to pay for the White Star Line. The attempts to raise the £7 million required came close to finishing the line off completely.

The first idea Lord Kylsant came up with was for the Royal Mail Steam Packet Company to issue more debentures, but his bankers insisted that, if he did so, then a substantial proportion of the money raised should go to reducing the amount the company already owed to them. Obviously that scheme would not do, so he next decided to form an entirely new company. In January 1927 the new company, White Star Line Limited was incorporated, with Kylsant as chairman and Harold Sanderson as deputy chairman. At first IMM objected to Kylsant's new company using the White Star name, even if it did take over the purchase of the Oceanic Steam Navigation Company. IMM, as the vendor, considered it unreasonable for the new buyers to make use of any goodwill attaching to the name until they had at least paid a reasonable part of the agreed price.

By January 1927 the difficulties between White Star Line Limited and IMM were largely resolved and Lord Kylsant's latest money-raising scheme went ahead. Two and a half million £1 preference shares were issued, which raised almost four times their face value. Encouraged by the response of the first share issue by the new company, a further issue of another £2.5 million worth was made six months after the first. Both of these share issues were guaranteed as to capital and interest by the Royal Mail Steam Packet Company, which put that company at risk because, as we have already seen, it did not have the necessary reserves to cover the guarantee.

The new shareholders were probably unaware that when White Star Line Limited was formed £4 million in ordinary share capital was issued, but this was all subscribed from within the Royal Mail Group, which paid only 2 shillings (10p) on each £1 share. Instead of raising the £4 million that outsiders might have expected, the company therefore had only £400,000 in capital. Not for the first time the fate of the White Star Line rested in the hands of Lady Luck, and this time she was not so ready to smile on it. Put simply, the new company's financial affairs were little more than a huge swindle.

No sooner had the Royal Mail Group taken over the Oceanic Steam Navigation Company than Lord Kylsant had himself installed as chairman. Without delay he began to siphon off White Star profits and channel them into Royal Mail's coffers, at a time when the only sensible thing to have done was re-invest those profits in bringing the White Star fleet up to date. To make matters worse there was already a drop in the numbers of passengers requiring passage across the Atlantic. Clearly, a bumpy road lay ahead of White Star and the Royal Mail Group.

On the very day that the White Star Line officially became part of the Royal Mail Group, ill luck again showed itself aboard *Olympic*. On 1 January 1927 third-class passenger James Kipila died of pneumonia in the ship's hospital. He was buried at sea at nine o'clock the following evening. During *Olympic's* annual winter overhaul some new cracks had been found, this time in the port side of the bridge deck. Again the damage was patched up, but inspectors from the Board of Trade were not entirely happy with the repairs. As a consequence the Board of Trade inspectors put *Olympic* on what was known as their Confidential List. This meant that the old liner would be carefully watched for any sign of further deterioration. Over the next few years there would be no shortage of deterioration to watch.

Arabic[3], which had been operating for the Red Star Line but still belonged to White Star and wore its livery, reached Antwerp on 12 January 1927 with a coal bunker fire aboard, the third such fire to show up in the line's history, and the second aboard *Arabic*. The blaze did some damage to the ship before it was extinguished. The fire and resultant damage to *Arabic* helped the management of the White Star Line to reach a decision about her future. They promptly transferred her to the Red Star Line.

Under Lord Kylsant's guiding hand the White Star fleet was increased by three extra ships in 1927. They were the 18,940-ton Royal Mail Steam Packet Company's *Ohio* which joined the fleet as the *Albertic*, the 19-year-old *Orca*, renamed *Calgaric*, and the new *Laurentic²*. As usual at the turn of the year it was time for the line to get rid of whatever ships appeared to be no longer necessary. Early in 1928 the *Persic* was scrapped, *Medic* was sold to N. Bugge of Tönsberg, and converted at Birkenhead into a whale factory ship and renamed *Hectoria*, and *Suevic* was sold to Yngvar Hvistendahl, Finnvhal A/S, Tönsberg, Norway, and renamed *Skytteren*. *Athenic* was also sold and became the *Pelagos*.

Captain Marshall was transferred from *Olympic* to *Majestic²* in September 1928. He was replaced by Captain Walter Parker from the *Homeric*. Although the transfer was a definite promotion for both men, Captain Marshall had become more than a little attached to his vessel. Captain Parker, upon seeing just how upset Marshall was, offered to take over *Majestic* instead but Marshall declined, saying, 'I suppose I ought to feel honoured. She is, after all, the largest ship in the world, you know, Parker – but I am leaving the best to you, for all that.'

Even though, in Captain Marshall's opinion, *Olympic* might be the best ship in the White Star fleet, she could not be described as lucky. On Captain Parker's very first voyage as master, on 25 September, Junior Second Engineer James Laidlaw died of blood poisoning in the ship's hospital. The unfortunate engineer's fatal condition had been brought on by a carbuncle on his knee. Two voyages later Bosun's Mate John Gravell died from a fractured skull after falling into the mail room from the bridge deck. He had been removing a ventilator from Number 3 hold when the accident occurred.

One prerequisite of a good commander is the ability to make a decision and then to stick to it. A lack of this ability was clearly demonstrated when *Celtic²* ran aground off Roches Point lighthouse near Queenstown at about 5am on 10 December 1928. Because of bad weather Captain Berry had already decided not to try putting into Queenstown on this voyage, although he was scheduled to do so. However, after bypassing the port and almost reaching Liverpool he had changed his mind and turned back.

Although the weather had been rough, visibility was still relatively clear and the lighthouse, marking the harbour entrance, had been in full view for some time when *Celtic* went aground on the Cow and Calf rocks, less than a quarter of a mile from it. Captain Berry immediately had the ship's whistle sounded to alert the lighthouse keeper, F. Hill, who notified the authorities and shore-based lifeboats. Despite several attempts to get her off, the *Celtic* was stuck fast and began taking water in at least one of her holds. As the vessel listed it began to seem as if she might capsize, so Captain Berry sounded six blasts on the whistle, the signal to abandon ship.

With the daylight came the tugs *Gelezee* and *Morsecock*, and the tender *Failte*. The tugs tried unsuccessfully to drag the stranded liner off the rocks before the tender began to take off her passengers. All of the passengers and crew, with the exception of those needed to continue the salvage attempt, were safely evacuated from the *Celtic*, but by the time that had been accomplished Number 3 hold and the boiler rooms had flooded. Without steam the ship was helpless, her engines and pumps unusable, so the passengers' luggage was transferred to the other vessels standing by. By the following morning the German salvage tug *Seefalke* and the Liverpool and Glasgow Salvage Association's *Restorer* had also arrived on the scene to assist in trying to pull the liner clear, while HMS *Sesame* and HMS *Scythe* stood by. It was all to no avail, and the *Celtic* remained firmly aground.

On 13 December another tug, *Ranger*, (a veteran of the *Suevic* incident) arrived to assist, but it was already becoming apparent that something fairly dramatic would have to be done if *Celtic* were to be saved. By this time the *Celtic's* hull was holed in a number of places including beneath the engine room and Holds 2, 3, 4, 5 and 6, and the ship had taken on a 7 degree list to port. The vessel would have to be lightened before she could be refloated, and the first thing to do was to discharge her cargo into lighters.

On 16 December two officers and several salvage men went aboard *Celtic* to assess the damage. The ship was insured only for £230,000, and it was rapidly becoming obvious that the costs of salvage and repair of a 27-year-old liner would exceed this sum. On 19 December White Star decided to salvage as much as it could from the vessel and then abandon her to her fate and the shipbreakers. *Celtic's* masts, funnels and some of her superstructure were cut away because the authorities were worried that they might obstruct another vessel's view of the Roches Point lighthouse. Then she just lay rusting on the rocks for a while until the hulk was bought by the Danish shipbreakers Petersen & Albeck, and dismantled where it lay.

Since buying the White Star Line Lord Kylsant had continued to expand his marine empire, despite the economic downturn that was soon to become the worldwide Great Depression and the fact that other lines were struggling for their very existence. In 1928 he spent £1,900,000 buying the Australian Commonwealth Line in White Star's name, and a further £994,000 on purchasing the Shaw Savill Line, even though he already owned a controlling interest in it. In the same year, although already desperately over-extended, Kylsant ordered a new 60,000-ton *Oceanic³* from Harland & Wolff, for £3.5 million. It could not last.

During her 1928/9 overhaul it was found that *Olympic's* new stern frame, fitted only four years before, was badly corroded. Clearly the newer forging was not up to the standard of the original, which had not been as badly pitted after 15 years under water. William Pirrie might not have been the most successful businessman ever to have dealings with the White Star Line but he was certainly the best shipbuilder. Various tricks were tried to prevent the corrosion getting any worse, such as coating the frame in magnetic cement, but nothing seemed to work. Eventually the stern frame was coated in white metal in a last-ditch attempt to prolong *Olympic's* life.

The Royal Mail Steam Packet Company owed quite substantial amounts of money to the Treasury and the first repayment became due in 1929, and another in the next year. Lord Kylsant was unable to find the cash, so he asked the Treasury for an extension on the loans. The Treasury's Advisory Committee, under Lord Plender (an accountant) decided that as the Royal Mail Group of companies was so intertwined, and as there was so little information available as to its true financial status, that an independent report was needed.

Sir William McLintock (another accountant) was instructed to look into the affairs of the Kylsant group. McLintock's report to the Treasury, in 1930, led them to conclude that an extension on the loans would not help, and that a consultation involving all those with a financial interest in the Royal Mail Group was required. As a result of this consultation the Treasury agreed to extend the loans, but only if control of all the companies within the Royal Mail Group, including White Star, was put into the hands of three trustees. It was not enough, and as the Depression continued, the fortunes of the White Star Line sank ever lower. Things could not get much worse. Because of the desperate shortage of funds, construction of White Star's new 60,000-ton *Oceanic³* was abandoned in 1929.

The shortage of funds began to manifest itself in other ways, notably a lack of preventive upkeep to the line's vessels. While *Albertic* was at Cobh (as Queenstown had been renamed) on 21 May her rudder failed and emergency steering gear had to be employed. A tender was sent from Liverpool to escort the crippled vessel back to the Mersey where she could be dry-docked for repair.

During the afternoon of 18 November 1929 a massive earthquake shook the ocean floor off the Grand Banks, causing a huge underwater landslide that for many years afterwards was believed to have buried the wreck of the *Titanic*. When the earthquake struck, the *Olympic* was just passing over the area, at latitude 42°12'N, longitude 56°56'W. The ship was violently shaken for two minutes and Captain Parker, who was in the chartroom at the time, had to be convinced that she had not collided with something. The fact that the engines were still running smoothly was enough to tell the officers that the ship had not dropped a propeller blade. Except that the lights in the mail room had failed, the ship appeared to be undamaged and proceeded on her way. It was only after *Olympic* had reached New York that her crew learned the true explanation. After just one more voyage Captain Parker retired along with his Chief Engineer J. H. Thearle, who had served on *Olympic* throughout her working life until then. Command of the ship was taken over by Captain E. R. White, who had previously been on the *Adriatic²*.

By the end of the 1920s *Olympic* was getting a little old-fashioned, despite having her facilities modestly upgraded over the years. However, she was still popular, if only as a reminder of a more elegant bygone age and many passengers remained faithful to her, but the general Depression was rapidly diminishing their numbers.

When *Olympic* was surveyed during the winter of 1929/30 the cracks in the bridge deck first noticed in 1927 were found to be spreading alarmingly. It was at first thought that to repair the ship effectively it would be necessary to replace most of the plating to her upperworks. As this would, however, cost somewhere in the region of £100,000 it was out of the question. Instead the cracks were welded up and steel doubler plates welded over them. The Board of Trade was satisfied enough to allow the ship to return to service, but she would remain on its Confidential List.

In the late 1920s the British film industry produced the *Atlantic*, starring Madeleine Carrol and Adolf Menjou, a film that now appears to be lost. The film, which was based loosely on the loss of the *Titanic,* caused worldwide consternation amongst the owners of the major shipping lines and their governments. The German newspaper *Bayerische Staatezeitung und Bayerischer Staatsanzierger* in its issue of 1 and 2 December 1929 reviewed the film. The general manager at the White Star Line wrote to the Mercantile Marine Department of the Board of Trade, saying, 'I understand that this paper is an official Government paper, that is a newspaper for Bavaria in which the Government publishes its official announcements. The damage that such an article is doing to the British Shipping prestige in Germany is beyond estimation.' The *New York Herald* of 5 January 1930 said, 'I do not know whether the film has actually been released in America yet, but I fear that there is every reason to anticipate that this will happen.' Clearly the film was not particularly complimentary about the British mercantile marine.

In his letter the White Star manager pointed out the very prejudicial effect that this 'very deplorable film' would have on the reputation of British shipping. Mr Caunty even pointed out that, although the film was based on a disaster which had befallen one of his line's ships, the name of that vessel or of the White Star Line were not mentioned, tarring all British lines with the same brush. Practically all trace of the film has since been erased.

In 1930, for the first time, the White Star Line operated at a loss, which is hardly surprising when one considers the number and severity of the accidents that occurred in the period. The writing was on the wall, and the line would never recover from its involvement with Lord Kylsant, showing a loss for 1931, 1932 and 1933 as well.

By the beginning of 1931 *Olympic* was really looking her age and deteriorating rapidly. Rivets and frames as well as shell plates were showing the strain of 20 years' service. Even after the ship had been repaired, the Board of Trade was so unsure of her continued seaworthiness that it would only grant a certificate for six months, instead of the usual year. At the end of the six months *Olympic* was inspected again, and as the repairs seemed to be holding up well, a second six-month certificate was issued. She was then granted a certificate of seaworthiness for a full year, although as we shall shortly see, she was not really up to the required standards.

Concern over White Star Line Limited's finances brought about a government inquiry into its affairs early in 1931. The inquiry discovered at least some of the irregularities that had occurred in 1926–28. On 13 May 1931 Owen Phillips, Lord Kylsant, was charged with falsifying the 1926 and 1927 annual reports and issuing false statements in the 1928 stock prospectus. Kylsant's accountant, John Morland, was charged with 'aiding, abetting and instigating Lord Kylsant in issuing false statements'. Kylsant took full responsibility for the goings-on and, having been found guilty of 'making, publishing and circulating' a misleading prospectus, was sentenced to one year's imprisonment. Upon his release Lord Kylsant retired from public life, except for occasional appearances, to his home in Carmarthenshire, Wales. He died on 5 July 1937 at the age of 74.

For a while, in order to make better use of some of its vessels, the White Star Line began running two- and three-day cruises from British ports, using *Homeric*. These cruises were so popular that they were continued the following year and the concept was enlarged: four- and six-day cruises from New York to Halifax or Nassau were added to the itinerary, using *Olympic* and *Majestic*[2]. *Olympic* took two cruises to Halifax on 6 and 27 August 1931 before the Depression made even cruising unprofitable. Because there was now so little money to be made, even from cruising, *Olympic* made just two three-day trips from Southampton in 1932, one at Whitsun and the other on August Bank Holiday.

During an examination while *Olympic* was at Southampton on 14 October 1932, a fracture in the high pressure journal of her port engine was discovered. Closer inspection revealed a number of other faults needing correction, such as cracks in the engine bed plates. When the engine thrust blocks were lifted it was discovered that a substantial part of the hull required re-riveting so it was decided to cancel any more planned voyages for 1932 and give the ship a complete overhaul. The work, which was expected to take about three months, would be carried out at Harland & Wolff's Southampton yard. In fact the work would take four months, but once completed by the end of April 1933 the ship seemed to be as good as new. A Board of Trade inspector reported, 'Everything went very satisfactorily, there being practically no movement of the bed plates.' Even the ship's chief engineer commented that engines and bed plates had never before been so free of movement. The future looked bright for the old *Olympic*, but looks can be deceptive.

Chapter 15

1932-1934

The brand-new *Georgic²* arrived in Liverpool on 13 June 1932, and on 25 June the 27,793-ton vessel sailed on her maiden voyage to New York, via Cobh. As Hull Number 896 she was the last ship to be constructed by Harland & Wolff for the White Star Line. By the time she was built the shipping line was in such dire financial straits that the new ship could only be completed with the aid of loans guaranteed by the government of Northern Ireland, aimed at preserving jobs in the shipyard.

So great had the line's difficulties become by 1933 that the company began to break up into its original component parts. The Shaw Savill Line ceased to be a part of White Star Line Limited and became an independent company once again. Then Shaw Savill joined forces with P&O and formed the Aberdeen and Commonwealth Line.

When the Australian Government demanded the money it was owed for the Commonwealth Line, the owners of White Star were compelled to sell the ships of that fleet to the Shaw Savill and P&O combine for £500,000. As the monies owed amounted to almost £2³/₄ million the sale of the ships did not help a great deal. Effectively, White Star Line Limited was bankrupt.

The 33,876-ton *Baltic²* and the 14,500-ton *Megantic* were sold to Japanese shipbreakers, and the 8,006-ton *Delphic²* was sold as a going concern in an effort to raise a little capital.

White Star's losses between 1930 and 1933, coupled with the fact that the fleet was obsolete and in desperate need of modernisation or replacement, meant that the line was in great danger unless new finance was secured. J. Bruce Ismay (now over 70 years old) was approached by Colonel Frank Bustard, a White Star manager, to take over as chairman and attempt to rescue the company. Ismay agreed to try, and a new board of directors was appointed, but it was already too late. The only way that anything could be saved was with the help of His Majesty's Treasury.

The depression had also caused one or two problems to the White Star Line's great rival Cunard. John Brown's Clydebank shipyard had laid down a new ship for Cunard late in 1930, the 81,000-ton liner later to be called *Queen Mary*, but known to those who lived in the area by her builder's number 534. Shortage of funds had meant that work on the 534 had been suspended at the end of 1931, and nothing had been done for a couple of years. Luckily, the new Cunard super-liner had caught the public imagination and this put a certain amount of pressure on the government to help finance the completion of the vessel. The Treasury finally agreed, but with conditions.

The government would advance the money to complete the *Queen Mary* only if Cunard and White Star merged. Naturally, those with a financial interest in White Star were opposed to the union and IMM even tried to get an injunction to prevent it, but without success. The directors of both companies agreed to the merger on 30 December 1933. In 1934 the two lines combined. The Treasury, under the conditions imposed by the newly passed North Atlantic Shipping Bill, then advanced £9.5 million to the newly united companies, £3 million for the completion of the *Queen Mary*, £5 million to build the *Queen Elizabeth*, and £1.5 million as working capital. Royal assent to the merger between the two shipping lines was granted on 28 March 1934 and Cunard White Star Limited was formed on 10 May, with £10,000,000 in capital. Of this 62% was allocated to Cunard, and the rest to White Star.

The Cunard White Star fleet consisted of 25 vessels. Fifteen of these were Cunard ships with an overall tonnage of 329,257, or an average of 21,950 tons per ship. The other 10 were White Star vessels displacing overall 285,680 tons, or averaging 28,568 tons each. Before many years had passed, all of the White Star ships would be disposed of, either sold or scrapped. Hundreds of White Star employees would be thrown out of work. Within a relatively short time practically all trace of the White Star Line's involvement with Cunard would disappear as the latter company disposed of anything associated with the former. The merger meant the end of the Oceanic Company and its assets, along with its interests in the Australian and New Zealand trade, its ships, its property, even the office furniture. In fact everything that could be sold to raise a little money was sold.

Almost all of what remained of the White Star fleet was disposed of in 1934. The 16-year-old *Vedic* was scrapped at Rosyth; *Ionic*² was sold to Japanese shipbreakers; *Albertic* was sold for scrap, in Japan, in August 1934; *Adriatic*², last survivor of the 'Big Four' was sold to Japan for scrap and sailed for Osaka in December 1934; *Calgaric* was sold as scrap, leaving for a Scottish breakers at Rosyth the day after *Adriatic* sailed for Japan. The little tender *Traffic*² survived, sold to the Société Cherbourgeoise de Remorquage et de Sauvetage, Cherbourg, and renamed *Ingénieur Riebell*; and *Ceramic* was sold to the Shaw Savill Line.

As well as Cunard vessels might have been looked after, this was nothing like as well as White Star looked after theirs, at least as far as keeping them clean and bright. When Cunard and White Star were merged an incident occurred that illustrates this as well as any can. As the 27-year-old *Adriatic*² lay alongside the Prince's Landing Stage in Liverpool, two Cunard Officers went aboard her. They were amazed at the condition of the old ship and one of them said that she looked as if she had just come from the builder's yard. The other replied, 'Oh, well, she'll look just the same as the others when we've had her for a little while!' How right he was!

The year 1934 turned out an eventful one for the Nantucket lightship, moored 41 miles south-east of Nantucket Island, about 200 miles from New York. On 4 January the lightship was sideswiped by the 24,500-ton American liner *Washington*, taking away her lifeboat davits and wireless rigging. On the night of 14 May two passing ships nearly ran her down in the fog. This was nothing unusual for the lightship's crew who had taken to swinging lifeboats out in fog, just in case.

At about 11 o'clock on the morning of 15 May, less than a week after the official formation of the Cunard White Star Line, another huge dark shape loomed up out of the fog, the *Olympic*. Although the liner had already reduced speed three times during the night, first from 19¹/₂kt to 16kt, then to 12kt, and finally to about 10kt, there was still no time to avoid a collision. The liner's rudder was put hard a-port and her port engine full astern. The huge bow began to swing clear as *Olympic* slowed still further until she was doing no more than 2-3kt when she crushed the lightship. As soon as he saw the lightship Captain Binks of the *Olympic* had his port emergency boat manned and lowered and the starboard one quickly followed, but the *Olympic's* boats still only managed to rescue four of the lightship's 11-man crew. Three bodies were recovered, but the other four men were never found. This costly collision heralded the demise of the line.

White Star's head offices at 30 James Street, Liverpool, closed down on 1 September 1934. It is a commonly held belief that the vast majority of the line's records were also disposed of at this time, but there is some evidence to show that this might not be quite correct. The possibility exists that at least some of the company's records were simply deposited in the cellar at 30 James Street to remain until the Luftwaffe dropped incendiary bombs on the building during World War 2, slightly damaging the roof. It seems that the records might then have been moved to a damp, rat-infested Liverpool warehouse for safekeeping. At least a part of the paperwork from this warehouse was apparently sent to a northern paper mill for destruction in the late 1960s or early 70s. The whereabouts of the remainder is a question that still requires an answer.

On 25 January 1935 Cunard White Star announced that *Olympic* would be retired at the end of the spring. She completed her last transatlantic voyage, arriving at Southampton on 12 April. Among her crew for that last round trip to New York by an *Olympic* Class vessel was none other than Frederick Fleet, the lookout aboard *Titanic* immediately before her fatal collision 23 years before. The old liner was then towed to the new Western Docks where she was laid up for the summer.

Even as 'Old Reliable' was making her last Atlantic crossing, on 8 April 1935, White Star Line Limited was wound up by High Court order. In just eight years the preference and ordinary shareholders, along with other creditors, had lost over £11 million, and this was at a time when £11 million was a huge sum of money!

Laurentic[2] left Liverpool on a 14-day 'North Cape' cruise to Scandinavian and German ports on 17 August 1935, under the command of Captain William Sewell Quinn. Slightly after 2.30 the following morning, when the ship was south of the Isle of Man, she was rammed in the starboard side, forward of the bridge, by the Blue Star Line freighter *Napier Star*. The freighter's bow penetrated 15ft into the side of the White Star liner, killing 6 crewmen and seriously injuring 5 more. Some 38ft of the *Napier Star's* bow was crushed in the collision. The Blue Star vessel was making no more than 7½kt at the time of the accident.

Although quite seriously damaged, *Laurentic* was still able to move under her own steam and slowly made her way back to the Mersey. Before the ship could cross the Mersey Bar an eight-ton length of *Napier Star's* port anchor chain, which had become wedged with the anchor in the damaged side of the White Star ship, had to be removed. At about 3pm on Sunday 18 August 1935 *Laurentic* tied up at the Gladstone Dock in Liverpool. Several passengers who had been aboard for the *Laurentic's* cruise, which was of course now abandoned, transferred to the *Doric*[2], commanded by Captain Greig, for a 13-day Mediterranean excursion. They could have made a luckier choice of ships to sail on.

All went well with *Doric's* cruise until she was on her way home. On Thursday 5 September while off Oporto, Portugal, *Doric* encountered thick fog and so reduced speed. At about 3.30am history repeated itself, at least as far as some of the passengers were concerned, when the Chargeurs-Reunis steamer *Formigny* loomed up out of the mist and rammed *Doric* in the starboard side, just forward of the bridge, tearing a 10ft by 5ft hole in her hull. The *Laurentic* veterans aboard should have been getting used to this scenario by now.

Although the ship immediately began to list to starboard, there was no panic aboard and women and children began to fill the lifeboats. Two hours after the collision the first rescue ship, the P&O liner *Viceroy of India*, arrived on the scene and the transfer of passengers began. Just an hour later, at about 6.30, the Orient Line's *Orion* came up and also began to take *Doric's* passengers aboard. With the passengers out of the way, the crew of *Doric* could set about nursing their battered vessel into Vigo for emergency repairs. She arrived back at Tilbury on 15 September when it was decided after an inspection of the damaged ship to lay her up as being beyond economic repair. Shortly afterward she was sold for scrap, for £35,000. *Doric²* set out on her last journey, to Sir John Cashmore's scrapyard at Newport, Monmouthshire, on 9 November. The ship was only 12 years old when she went to the scrapyard, a sorry testimonial to Cunard's determination to be rid of all of its former rival's fleet.

On 20 August 1935 Cunard White Star announced that prospective breakers could inspect *Olympic* on the following Monday. She was bought for £100,000 by Sir John Jarvis, who quickly sold her on to Thomas W. Ward Ltd of Inverkeithing, with the stipulation that she should be broken up at Jarrow, an area badly affected by the Depression. On 11 October she left Southampton for the last time. *Olympic* arrived at Jarrow on 13 October and dismantling of what had arguably been the most successful of all the ships to have sailed for the White Star Line began on 6 November; it would take almost two years to complete. Fixtures and fittings from the ship were auctioned aboard her in 4,456 lots by Knight Frank and Rutley. The last lot was sold on 18 November 1935, a sad end for a great ship.

The Royal Mail Steam Packet Company, the parent company to White Star Limited, failed in February 1936, with a deficit of over £22,000,000.

The 14-year-old *Homeric*, which had begun life as the German *Columbus*, was sold as scrap to Wards and broken up at Inverkeithing. *Majestic²* was also sold to Wards for scrapping in May 1936, but this was not the end for the ex-German *Bismarck*. In June Wards sold her to the Admiralty and she was converted into the training ship HMS *Caledonia*. On 29 September 1939 she was destroyed by fire while at Rosyth, Scotland, and sank at her berth. In March 1940 she was sold back to Wards and in July 1943 she was towed to Inverkeithing for final demolition.

On 14 September 1936, after almost a year's lay-up, *Laurentic²* was pressed into service as a troopship, making a single voyage carrying British soldiers to Palestine.

By the time Cunard had finished weeding out the White Star ships it did not want, only two remained, the *Britannic³* and the *Georgic²*, and these could hardly be described as trouble-free. Problems with her engines delayed *Britannic³* for three-quarters of an hour in quarantine at New York on 4 January 1937. After temporary repairs she was able to reach her dock, and the next day she was dry-docked for more permanent repairs to be effected.

On 19 September 1937 *Olympic's* hull was taken from Jarrow and towed to Wards of Inverkeithing for final demolition, arriving there the following day. The first of the three giant ships Ismay had planned, and arguably the named ship of possibly the most famous class of ships ever, was soon to be followed by the man who had been most responsible for her creation. On Sunday 17 October 1937 Joseph Bruce Ismay died at his London home three days after suffering a stroke that had taken his sight and speech. A year before he had lost his right leg below the knee. The following day, flags in Liverpool were flown at half-mast, as they had been for his father and mother. When Colonel Bustard turned up for work in the Cockspur Street office of the Oceanic Company he was amazed to discover a mirror, which J. Bruce Ismay had given him many years before, had inexplicably shattered.

By the close of 1937 all that remained in Liverpool of the once great Oceanic Steam Navigation Company was the small office in Cockspur Street. Even that was eventually closed when the last of its furniture and carpets was sold at auction. In all but name the White Star Line had ceased to exist. The Oceanic Steam Navigation Company was wound up on 21 August 1939, less than a fortnight before the outbreak of World War 2.

For some reason Cunard White Star had kept the nine-year-old *Laurentic²* in reserve since 1936, instead of scrapping her. Finding a home for the idle ship had presented some minor problems and she had been moved from Liverpool to Southampton in May 1937, and then to the River Fal in Cornwall in April 1938. The decision not to scrap the vessel was justified when, on 24 August 1939, *Laurentic* was taken over by the Royal Navy as an armed merchant cruiser. Armed with several 5.5in guns the converted cruise liner was sent to patrol off Iceland to intercept German blockade runners. On 3 November 1940 she was torpedoed by U-boat ace Otto Kretschmer's *U99*, to the north of Ireland. *Laurentic* foundered at about 4am the following day after being struck by four torpedoes, taking 49 men with her.

Even though now only two of the old White Star Line fleet remained in service, they could still make their presence felt in their home port, and indeed elsewhere. Arriving at Liverpool on 15 March 1940 *Georgic* collided stern first with a sea wall. Her next sailing to New York had to be postponed by three days to allow for damage sustained in the collision to be made good. Shortly after her contretemps with the Liverpool sea wall *Georgic* was requisitioned for use as a troopship. She was equipped to carry over 5,000 troops, more than three times her peacetime capacity, and painted battleship grey. She was mistakenly reported as having been severely damaged by German bombing on 19 September 1940.

On 14 July 1941, as *Georgic* lay anchored in Port Tewfik, at the southern end of the Suez Canal, she was attacked by German bombers. For a while it looked as if she might escape unscathed as bomb after bomb missed. Then the sixth bomb aimed at her struck her port side plating before bouncing into the water, where it exploded causing severe damage forward of the bridge. Number 4 hold began to flood. Then a second bomb struck the ship on the after deck, passing through five decks before exploding and damaging the engine room bulkhead and causing serious fires aft. Ruptured fuel tanks fed the flames and within 20 minutes the fire was out of control. Explosions rocked the ship as the fire reached obsolete ammunition in Numbers 7 and 8 holds, and the magazine for *Georgic's* 6in stern gun.

Obviously the ship was doomed but Captain Greig was faced with something of a dilemma. Should he evacuate the 800 men, women and children aboard, or should he move the ship to somewhere where she would not obstruct the vital seaway when she foundered? Captain Greig elected to move the ship before evacuating the personnel, whose safety he was responsible for. *Georgic* was beached on North Reef, the passengers and crew taken off, and the ship was allowed to burn herself out, which took two days.

The burned-out shell of *Georgic* was raised on 27 October and towed to an anchorage. On 29 December, as an unmanned hulk, she was taken in tow by the Clan Line steamer *Clan Campbell*, and being steered by the Ellerman Liner *City of Sydney*, set off towards Port Sudan where she could be patched up. She arrived there on 10 January 1942. After seven weeks of patching at Port Sudan *Georgic* was again taken in tow, this time by the Harrison Line's *Recorder*. The combination steered by the tug *Sampson*, she set out for Karachi on 5 March, where quite extensive repairs could be effected. The tow, one of the longest ever attempted, did not go exactly according to plan inasmuch as the *Sampson* sank on 6 March. Other ships were found to help, such as the Bibby Line's *Dorsetshire* and British India Line steamer *Haresfield*, and the tow was eventually completed, having taken 26 days.

Georgic reached Karachi on 1 April, and before long about 400 Indian workers swarmed aboard. Displaying an incredible amount of ingenuity the Indian workmen soon had the ship's machinery operational and her own electrical generators on line. The badly twisted stem of the ship was straightened, not by dry-docking her but by flooding the after holds and double bottom to raise the bow, then building a fire in an iron cage around it and beating it out straight with sledge hammers. The Indian workers had achieved something that probably no other workforce would have even considered faintly possible. On 11 December the battered vessel sailed under her own power for Bombay and five weeks of repair work on her hull.

She arrived at Bombay on 13 December 1942, and during her stay there new hull plates were fitted to her port side, her rudder and propellers were inspected, and hull stiffeners were attached. Before leaving on 20 January 1943 5,000 tons of pig iron were taken aboard as cargo. After all her trials and tribulations *Georgic* arrived back in the Mersey on 1 March 1943 after breaking her journey at Cape Town. Her owners received the princely sum of £10,000 for transporting the cargo of pig iron.

After yet another inspection the Ministry of War Transport and the Admiralty decided to convert *Georgic* into a dedicated troopship. On 14 December 1944 she re-entered service. For the remainder of the war she worked carrying troops to India, Italy and the Middle East. Once the war was over *Georgic* was employed repatriating servicemen and ex-prisoners of war, which kept her occupied until 1948.

The company that had finally brought about the downfall of the line, White Star Line Limited, which had been wound up 10 years before, was dissolved on 16 March 1945.

Two years later the Cunard Steam Ship Company bought all that remained of Cunard White Star share capital. From then onwards the White Star Line was wholly owned by Cunard and the name was systematically phased out. In 1949 Cunard announced that it was taking over all assets and operations of the Cunard White Star Line Ltd, and dropping the White Star part of its name. However, the remaining White Star ships, *Georgic* and *Britannic*, were allowed to remain in their old company colours.

By this time the elderly *Britannic* was getting a little tatty but she was still very popular and regularly sailed fully loaded. One possible reason for this popularity might well have been the roaring log fires that blazed in the open fireplaces of her public rooms, and that dogs were allowed to sleep in front of them. On 28 January 1950 *Britannic's* engines broke down as she was leaving New York for a 54-day Mediterranean cruise. She had to return to her dock for two days of repairs before the cruise could begin. A little later in the year, as *Britannic* was again leaving New York in thick fog on 1 June, she collided head-on with the United States Line freighter *Pioneer Land*. The *Pioneer Land* returned to port with her bow smashed but *Britannic* continued her voyage.

On 20 November 1953 *Britannic* suddenly sprang a leak which delayed her departure from New York for one day while it was repaired. Such a sudden leak was an indication that the ship was long overdue for an overhaul, which of course she was. Arrangements were made for the vessel to be given a thorough going-over when she returned to her home port, but on 30 December 1953, while *Britannic* was duly being overhauled at Southampton, fire broke out aboard. Southampton Fire Service were called out again; they had only left the dockyard half an hour earlier after fighting a fire aboard the *Winchester Castle*. The ship's own sprinkler system controlled the fire and the fire brigade, using gas masks because of the dense smoke, traced the seat of the blaze to mattresses and life-jackets in a cabin. The firemen removed the burning material from the ship.

Georgic's penultimate voyage ended on 19 November 1955 when she arrived at Liverpool from Hong Kong with 800 soldiers aboard. The next time she left port it would be for a one-way trip to the breakers' yard. *Georgic* was sold to Shipbreaking Industries of Faslane, Scotland, and arrived there for scrapping by 1 February 1956.

During May and June 1960, while she was at New York, several transatlantic voyages scheduled for *Britannic* were cancelled because one of her diesel engines was out of commission due to crankshaft damage. Although repairs were attempted at New York, they could not be completed until replacement parts were flown out from England. After the two month enforced layover and the repairs, costing the owners £84,000, *Britannic* left the port on 7 July. In August of the same year, during a strike by British seamen which included those aboard *Britannic*, 52 passengers each managed to earn $3.15 a day, plus about $50 in tips, by working in the galley and as waiters. Cunard announced *Britannic's* retirement in August, the decision hastened by the unreliability of the ship's ageing machinery and the militant attitudes of her crew.

As *Britannic*, the very last White Star liner, was leaving New York for the final time, on 25 November 1960, one of the city's fireboats saluted her passing by sending up fountains of water from the hoses, a ceremony otherwise reserved for ships completing their maiden voyage. She arrived back at Liverpool on 4 December. Less than a fortnight after completing her last scheduled voyage *Britannic* was sold to Thomas W. Ward Ltd and set out on her last trip, to the breakers' yard at Inverkeithing, on 16 December 1960.

At the start of the third millennium one of two tenders specially built to service *Olympic*, *Titanic* and *Britannic* is still afloat as a restaurant on the River Seine in Paris. *Nomadic*[2] is all that remains of what was, arguably, once the greatest shipping line of them all: White Star.

Ship List

Vessels owned, chartered or loaded by White Star, including some of their movements, listed in the order they first operated for the line. Also included in the list are vessels owned or managed by T. H. Ismay prior to his gaining control of the White Star Line. Note: All tonnages, except where noted, are gross register.

The Early Days

Elizabeth, a small brig, was the first vessel advertised by Pilkington & Wilson for which they had procured a cargo. The ship sailed for Canada on 26 February 1846.

Desdemona, one of two vessels of about 1,200 tons for which Pilkington & Wilson acted as agents between 1846 and 1848. One of the first two emigrant ships loaded by the partners.

Thomas H. Perkins, the other of the first two emigrant ships loaded by White Star.

Iowa, an 879-ton ship, the first vessel bought by Pilkington & Wilson, in 1849. She had been built specially for them at St John, New Brunswick, Canada. The *Iowa* cost the partners £8,500, and was the very first true White Star ship. *Iowa* was sold to J. Steel & Co of Liverpool on her return from Australia in 1854. On her next voyage she disappeared without trace.

Windsor Castle, built by G. Black & Co of Quebec, was about 10 years old when John Pilkington bought her some time about 1850 to trade between Liverpool and Valparaiso. Command was given to Captain T. Rogers. *Windsor Castle* was sold in 1857, probably because of Pilkington's retirement, to Captain C. Bruce, who became her new master.

Argo was advertised on 20 May 1852, as sailing for the New Liverpool, Line of Australian Packets (Pilkington, Wilson and Baines).

Northumberland was advertised on 20 May 1852, as sailing for the New Liverpool, Line of Australian Packets (Pilkington, Wilson and Baines). Baines of the Black Ball Line was to buy her a couple of years later.

Maria was advertised on 20 May 1852, as sailing for the New Liverpool, Line of Australian Packets (Pilkington, Wilson and Baines).

Bhurtpoor was advertised on 20 May 1852, as sailing for the New Liverpool, Line of Australian Packets (Pilkington, Wilson and Baines). *Bhurtpoor* was a 978-ton wooden ship built by W. & R. Wright at St John, New Brunswick, in 1851 for Pilkington & Wilson It was originally intended that Captain George Bainbridge would take the ship from Liverpool to Port Phillip or Sydney on 15 or 20 August 1852, but the voyage was cancelled. *Bhurtpoor* was lost off the coast of Ireland, near Wexford and replaced with the *Ellen*.

Marco Polo was advertised on 20 May 1852, as sailing on 21 June for the New Liverpool, Line of Australian Packets (Pilkington, Wilson and Baines).

Ellen, a 397-ton barque built in 1834 at New Brunswick. White Star advertised this modest vessel, first on 1 June 1852 as a ship of 1,600 tons, under the command of Captain Phillips, bound for Port Phillip, Australia, on 20 June, and then on 23 July 1852, as a 1,800-tonner bound for Australia under the command of Captain Leighton.

Ellen, which according to *Lloyd's List* was owned by H. T. Wilson as distinct from the partnership, sailed to Prince Edward Island in 1853.

Earl of Derby, a 1,047-ton wooden ship (advertised by White Star as 2,000 tons) built in 1851 at Quebec. Chartered from Moore & Co of Liverpool, she sailed for Melbourne on 5 July 1852, under the command of Captain Tweedie. Again chartered from Moore & Co, she sailed for Port Phillip in 1853 under the command of Captain Slater.

Phoenix, an 801-ton wooden ship (advertised as 1,700 tons) built in 1851 by J. Fisher at St John. Chartered, probably from Maggee & Co of Liverpool, she sailed for Sydney on 20 July 1852, under the command of Captain Soley. *Phoenix* was bought by White Star from Maggee & Co about 1859. She sailed for New Zealand on 10 October 1860 under the command of Captain Henry and was sold by White Star in 1863 to M. I. Wilson & Co.

Dundonald, a 1,142-ton wooden ship (advertised as 2,000 tons) built in 1849 at St John, New Brunswick. Chartered from Wright & Co of St John, she sailed from Liverpool for Geelong and Port Phillip on 5 August 1852, under the command of Captain Gilles.

Blanche, a 966-ton wooden ship (advertised as 1,800 tons) built in 1850 at St John, New Brunswick. Chartered from Brown & Co of Liverpool, she sailed from Liverpool for Port Phillip on 25 August 1852, under the command of Captain G. Rudolph. The 1 June advertisement had her as sailing for Sydney on 5 September.

Jesse Munn was built in 1852. Partly owned by H. T. Wilson (56 shares) and partly by her master Captain J. Duckett (8 shares). *Jesse Munn* was transferred to the Australian run, still under the command of Captain Duckett, in 1857. She made her last voyage to Australia for the White Star Line early in 1863. Then she was sold to S. Cearns, who in 1868 sold her to foreign owners.

Colonist was bought in 1852. She was a 594-ton wooden barque, built by W. Crane & Co at Baie Verte, New Brunswick. *Colonist* was sold to R. Wilson & Company of Liverpool in 1864.

David Cannon, a 1,331-ton wooden ship built by W. & R. Wright of St John's, Newfoundland. Bought by White Star in 1852, when she was five years old, for the Atlantic trade. *David Cannon* was wrecked on Big Dover Head, near Halifax, Nova Scotia, in June 1854, close to where she had been built.

Tantivy, a 1,040-ton wooden ship built in 1851 at New Brunswick, was chartered from Robinson & Co of Liverpool in 1852. She sailed for Australia in 1852, under the command of Captain S. Brewster.

Lady Russel, a 907-ton wooden ship built in 1852 at St John. Chartered in 1852 from Dempsey of Liverpool, she sailed for Australia in 1852 under the command of Captain Sinnot. She was sold by Dempseys to Farnworth & Co of Liverpool in 1853.

Fitzjames was bought by the line in 1852, with a little financial assistance. The 1,195-ton wooden ship had been completed in 1852 by J. J. Jardine & Co of Richibucto, New Brunswick, and then bought by Jardine & Co of Liverpool. Jardines then promptly sold her to Messrs Halstead and Fletcher (40 shares), Pilkington & Wilson (16 shares) and John Chambers (8 shares). The *Fitzjames* was registered as a Pilkington (White Star) ship and put to work on the Atlantic routes. *Fitzjames* transferred to the Australian run for one trip to Melbourne in 1854, under the command of Captain Alex Lowe. *Fitzjames* left Liverpool for Melbourne, carrying emigrants, on 20 January 1866. A few days out she sprang a leak and had to put in to Lisbon for repairs. While at Lisbon *Fitzjames* was condemned as unseaworthy and the remainder of the voyage was cancelled.

Agnes, a 441-ton wooden ship built at New Brunswick in 1847, was chartered from Hanmer & Co of Liverpool, in 1853. She sailed from Liverpool for Australia in January 1853 under the command of Captain Lloyd.

Lochiel, an 863-ton wooden ship built in 1852 at Richibucto, New Brunswick. Advertised on 18 March 1853 by Pilkington & Wilson as bound for Australia within the next couple of weeks. Chartered from Jardine & Co of Liverpool, she was loading at the Salthouse Dock ready to sail for Melbourne and Port Phillip under the command of Captain Thomas Rogers. *Lochiel* was again chartered from Jardine & Co of Liverpool in 1854, sailing again under the command of Captain Rogers.

North Atlantic, a new coppered and copper-fastened clipper (partly owned by Hill & Co of Bank Chambers, Cook Street, Liverpool) was advertised as a 1,500-ton vessel. She was to sail for Australia on 24 March 1853, under the command of Captain Henry Cook.

Defense, a 606-ton wooden ship built in 1844 at Miramichi, New Brunswick. Chartered from Richards & Co of Liverpool in 1853.

Mooresfort, a 1,278-ton wooden ship built in 1853 at St John. Chartered from Moore & Co of Liverpool. She sailed for Australia under the command of Captain Calthurst.

Tasmania, a 1,187-ton wooden ship built in 1853 by Storm & King of St John. Chartered from Aikman & Co of Glasgow, she sailed for Australia under the command of Captain Lewis Rudolph.

Mobile, a 1,016-ton wooden ship built in 1851 at St John. Chartered from Bates & Co of Liverpool by both the White Star and Black Ball lines, she sailed for Australia in 1853 under the command of Captain Ponsonby.

Marion Moore, a 1,036-ton ship built in 1852 at Liverpool. Chartered from Moore & Co of Liverpool by White Star and the Black Ball Line. She sailed for New South Wales in 1853, under the command of Captain Tweedie.

Albatross, a wooden vessel of 1,030 tons built at St John in 1847. Chartered from Gibbs Bright, she sailed from Liverpool for Melbourne in January 1854, under the command of Captain W. Geeves.

Tayleur, a 1,997-ton iron ship built in 1853 by Mr Tayleur, at the Bank Quay Foundry, Warrington. Chartered in 1853 from Moore & Co, who had purchased the vessel specifically to charter it to White Star for the Australian emigrant trade.

Golden Era, a 1,556-ton full rigged wooden ship built in 1853 by Smith and Hawes of St John, New Brunswick for Mr Nathan Smith. White Star bought the vessel from Smith in January 1854, giving command to Captain J. T. Pray. *Golden Era* remained on the Australian run throughout 1855, but now commanded by Captain H. A. Brown. *Golden Era* was lost on 22 June 1858 while under the command of Captain Brown, before he took over the *Prince of the Seas*.

Red Jacket was a 2,305-ton wooden vessel of a type known as an extreme clipper ship, built in 1853 by George Thomas & Co of Rockland, Maine. Pilkington & Wilson bought the vessel for the then very expensive price of £30,000 late in 1853 or early in 1854. *Red Jacket* had been designed by Samuel H. Pook for Secombe, Taylor & Co of Boston. This famous ship was launched on 2 November 1853. *Red Jacket* was sold to H. Milvain of

Newcastle for the Quebec timber trade in 1866. Later owned by Turner & Co of London, *Red Jacket* was hulked at Cape Verde. She was wrecked in 1886.

Mermaid, a 1,321-ton wooden ship built in 1853 by McDonald & Co at St John, New Brunswick. Purchased early in 1854 by Pilkington & Wilson for £14,850 for use on the Australian and New Zealand routes under the command of Captain Samuel Reid, who owned 8 shares in her. *Mermaid* was commanded by Captains Reid, E. Devey and Rose until 1867 when she was sold to Temple & Co of London. *Mermaid* left Liverpool heading for Quebec on 13 December 1883 and was wrecked on the coast near Southport.

Shalimar, a 1,402-ton wooden clipper ship built in 1854 for White Star by J. Nevins of St John. *Shalimar* made many voyages to Australia and New Zealand under Captains Duckett, Amos Robertson, J. R. Brown, Allen and Deighton. *Shalimar*, under the command of Captain A. Robertson, returned to Liverpool at the end of her first voyage to the antipodes in June 1855 only 6 months and 14 days after setting out. She had been detained for 45 days during the voyage. Taken over by the Royal Bank of Liverpool in 1867, *Shalimar* was still afloat in 1877 under the Swiss flag.

Moira, an 820-ton wooden ship built in 1853 at Quebec, was chartered from Rose and Co of Aberdeen. She sailed for Australia on 27 January 1854 under the command of Captain S. Smart.

Mystery, a new 1,155-ton wooden ship built in 1854 at Boston, Massachusetts, was bought by Pilkington & Wilson some time in 1854. Next to nothing is known of this vessel between the time she was bought by the White Star Line and when she sailed from Liverpool, bound for Australia on 5 January 1863. Equally mysteriously, very little is known of the vessel after she set out on this voyage.

Emma, a 1,049-ton wooden ship built in 1853 by W. Bennett and Sons of Hopewell Cape, New Brunswick, bought by Pilkington & Wilson, with the financial assistance of others in 1854. She was put to work on the Liverpool–Melbourne route for two years, under the command of Captain E. Underwood. *Emma* transferred from the Australian run to Atlantic trade in 1856. She remained on the Atlantic for a couple of years until she was lost in June 1858.

Arabian, a 1,068-ton wooden ship built in 1852 by J. Nevins of St John, specially for the emigrant trade. In June 1854 Pilkington and Wilson each bought 32 shares in this vessel for £14,100, and took delivery later in the year. They gave command of the new vessel to Captain Duckett. *Arabian* was sold to the Company of African Merchants of Liverpool in 1866, who hulked her.

Annie Wilson (probably named after H. T. Wilson's wife or daughter), a 1,119-ton wooden ship built for the White Star Line in 1854 by W. & R. Wright of St John. She worked on the Liverpool to Australia route until about 1859 under the command of Captain Edward Langley. She was put on the route to India in early 1859, still under Captain Langley, and plied back and forth for about four years. *Annie Wilson* was transferred onto the New Zealand run in 1863, under the command of Captain Duckett. While still on the New Zealand run, she was abandoned in June 1867.

Golconda, a 1,087-ton wooden ship built in 1852 at St John for Anthony & Co of Liverpool, was chartered in 1854. She sailed under the command of Captain Kerr.

Anne Chambers, owned by John Chambers, sailed for Australia in July 1854 under the command of Captain Robertson. The *Anne Chambers* was named after John's daughter.

Blue Jacket[1], 1,790 tons, was built in 1854 by Robert E. Jackson of East Boston to the order of Charles R. Green & Co of New York. *Blue Jacket*, which had first sailed for the line in December 1854 was again chartered for the Australian run and left Liverpool bound for Melbourne in March 1855 and arrived in Australia 69 days later. Her best ever performance for both outward and return voyages was 67 days. H. T. Wilson bought all 64 shares in the ship, for White Star line use, in 1860. *Blue Jacket* served on the Australia run for more than 6 years, first under the command of Captain Kerr, then Captain White, then Clarke and White again. *Blue Jacket* sailed on 20 May 1866 from London to Melbourne. It was her last advertised sailing for the White Star Line.

Blue Jacket[1] now owned by H. T. Wilson & Co of Liverpool, although her original owners, including James Chambers, had a share in her, caught fire and was abandoned off the Falkland Islands in 1869.

White Star, a wooden vessel of 2,340 tons, was built in 1854 as a second *Blue Jacket*, by W. & R. Wright at St John, for White Star. Pilkington & Wilson owned 43 shares, while Richard Wright held the remaining 21. *White Star/Blue Jacket* was listed to sail under her original name for Australia, chartered from C. Moore and Co in January 1855 under the command of Captain O'Halloran, but her name was changed to *White Star* before she left Liverpool. *White Star* made many voyages to the Australian continent between 1855 and 1857 under the command of Captains W. R. and J. R. Brown. She sailed from Liverpool on her first trip to Australia on 30 April 1855 under the command of Captain J. R. Brown, arriving at Melbourne only 79 days later. *White Star* was still on the Australia run in 1857. In June of that year command of the vessel was taken over by Captain J. C. Kerr, who remained with the ship until she was sold to Hutchinson & Co of Liverpool in 1866. Sold on by Hutchinson & Co to the Merchant's Trading Company of Liverpool in 1868. *White Star* was wrecked in fog on the Tuskar Rock while homeward-bound from Calcutta, with 2,000 tons of jute aboard, on Christmas Eve 1883. No lives were lost.

Shepherdess, a 1,226-ton wooden ship built for Pilkington & Wilson in 1855 at Sackville, New Brunswick. Command was given to Captain John Rodgers, who owned 8 shares in the ship. Chartered from Aikman & Co of Glasgow, she sailed for Australia in September 1858, probably under the command of Captain Rodgers. *Shepherdess* foundered on 15 September 1860.

Tiptree, a 1,617-ton wooden ship built in 1855 for Pilkington & Wilson at St John, sailed for Australia in the summer of 1855, under the command of Captain Penreath. *Tiptree* was sold to Redfern Alexander & Co in 1860. She was condemned in 1877.

Earl of Sefton, a 1,126-ton wooden ship built in 1854 at St John. Chartered from Moore & Co of Liverpool, she sailed for Australia in 1855 under the command of Captain John Noble.

Mary Ismay was partly owned by T. H. Ismay in 1856. At the end of the year she was sold by his trustees Joseph and John Sealby.

Charles Brownell was partly owned by T. H. Ismay in 1856. At the end of the year she was sold by his trustees, Joseph and John Sealby.

Anne Nelson was in 1856 owned by retired Captain Philip Nelson and named after his wife. Nelson was to become T. H. Ismay's partner. A model of the *Anne Nelson* is preserved in the Liverpool Maritime Museum.

Spray of the Ocean, 996 tons register, 2,500 tons burthen, was chartered for a voyage to Melbourne beginning on 20 February 1856 under the command of Captain P. Slaughter.

Sir William Eyre, a 1,316-ton wooden ship built in 1856 at Quebec. A chartered vessel, she sailed for Australia in April 1856 under the command of Captain Jopp.

Miles Barton, a 1,034-ton wooden ship built in 1853 for James Beazley of Liverpool by W. & R. Wright at St John. Chartered from James Beazley of Liverpool, she sailed for Australia in 1856 under the command of Captain Kelly. *Miles Barton* was again chartered from Beazley and sailed for Australia on 27 June 1857, this time under the command of Captain Darlington. She was wrecked at Storring Bay, South Africa, on 8 February 1861.

Titan. Nothing appears to be known about this vessel except that she was advertised as a 2,360-ton ship, and that she sailed for Australia on 20 May 1856 under the command of Captain Seers.

Star of the East, a 1,219-ton ship built in 1853 for James Beazley, by W. & R. Wright of St John. One of the finest clippers ever built. Chartered from Beazley, *Star of the East* sailed for Australia in 1856 under the command of Captain Christian. She was again chartered from James Beazley in 1859, under the command of Captain Gaggs. Probably still under the 1859 charter agreement with James Beazley, she sailed for Australia again in 1860 under the command of Captain Gaggs, and probably still under charter from Beazley, again in 1861,once more under the command of Captain Gaggs. *Star of the East* was finally wrecked at Storring Bay, South Africa, not far from where the *Miles Barton* was also lost.

Merry England sometimes known as *Merrie England*, a 1,045-ton ship built in 1856 at Waterford for Beazley of Liverpool at a cost of £21,735. Chartered from Beazley, she made her maiden voyage under the White Star flag in the summer of 1856, commanded by Captain William Kelly. *Merry England* was sold in 1867 to Captain Kelly, who abandoned his ship the same year off Cape Horn, loaded with guano, while on passage from the Chincha Islands. (And who can blame him?)

Mindoro, a 1,334-ton wooden ship built in 1853 by W. & R. Wright of St John. Chartered from French & Co of Liverpool, she sailed for Australia in 1856 under the command of Captain Crowell.

Cyclone, a 1,199-ton ship built in 1856 at St John, on a long-term charter from Anthony & Co of Liverpool, made a number of voyages to the antipodes between late 1856 and December 1860 under the command of Captain George Kerr.

Anglo Saxon, a 1,233-ton wooden vessel built at St John in 1853. Chartered from Farnsworth (elsewhere Farnworth) & Co of Liverpool, she sailed from Liverpool for Australia in December 1856 under the command of Captain G. Welsh. *Anglo Saxon*, again chartered from Farnsworth & Co, sailed from Liverpool for Australia in October 1857, still under the command of Captain Welsh.

Sardinian, a 1,208-ton wooden ship built in 1856 for the White Star Line by T. Oliver & Co of Quebec, sailed to Australia in 1856 under the command of Captain Sheridan. *Sardinian* was sold to Potter & Co of Glasgow who used her on the Glasgow–Australia run in 1857. She was lost on 19 September 1866.

The Second Generation

Anne Royden, a one-year-old 1,175-ton ship owned and built by Royden & Co of Liverpool, was chartered and sailed for Australia on 20 January 1857 under the command of Captain J. P. Fox.

Salem, an 839-ton wooden ship built in 1852 at New Brunswick. Chartered from P. Maggee & Co of Liverpool, she sailed for Australia on 27 January 1857 under the command of Captain Flinn.

Algiers, a 1,002-ton ship built at Miramichi, New Brunswick, in 1856. Chartered from

Mitchell & Co of Alloa, she sailed under the White Star flag from Liverpool for Australia in March 1857 under the command of Captain W. S. Morris.

Samuel Locke, advertised as an 800-ton ship, sailed for Australia on 27 April 1857 under the command of Captain J. Sweetnam. Nothing else appears to be known about this vessel.

Monarch of the Seas, a 2,440-ton register, 5,000-ton burthen vessel. Chartered from Fermie & Sons of Liverpool, she sailed from Liverpool for Australia on 20 July 1857 under the command of Captain Burgess.

Shaftsbury, a ship of more than 1,000 tons, built in 1857 at St John, was chartered from Farnworth & Co of Liverpool. She sailed for Australia on 27 July 1857 under the command of Captain S. Smiley.

John Barbour, a 989-ton wooden ship built in 1853 at St John. Chartered from Reed & Co of St John, she sailed for Australia in August 1857 under the command of Captain E. J. Bell.

Guy Mannering, a 1,700-ton ship, sailed for Australia on 20 August 1857, under the command of Captain Dollard.

Shakespear sailed for Australia in 1857, under the command of Captain Norcross. Virtually nothing seems to be known about this vessel.

British Lion, a 1,457-ton wooden ship built in 1853 at Quebec, was chartered from Moore & Co of Liverpool. She sailed for Australia on 29 September 1857 under the command of Captain F. Harrington.

Negotiator, a 1,017-ton wooden ship built in 1856 at Miramichi, was chartered from Cannon & Co of Liverpool. She sailed for Australia in 1857, commanded by Captain E. Lawson.

Invincible was chartered by White Star and advertised as a 1,709-ton ship. She sailed for Australia in October 1857 commanded by Captain Johnson, under the Black Ball flag. She was back at Liverpool by 6 May 1858. *Invincible*, again chartered, this time by White Star alone, sailed for Australia on 20 June 1858, still under the command of Captain Johnson.

Chancellor, a 1,854-ton ship built in 1855 in the USA. Chartered from Cassell & Co of Liverpool, she sailed for Australia in October 1857 under the command of Captain Borland.

Merchant Prince, a 1,745-ton wooden ship built in 1856 by McLachlan of Carleton, New Brunswick. Chartered from Willis & Co of Liverpool, she sailed for Australia in November 1857, under the command of Captain M'Lay. On this voyage *Merchant Prince* carried no passengers. *Merchant Prince*, again chartered from Willis & Co of Liverpool, sailed for Australia in April 1859, still commanded by Captain M'Lay. *Merchant Prince*, once more under charter from Willis & Co of Liverpool, sailed for Australia on 20 January 1862 under the command of Captain M'Lay.

Angelita, an iron brigantine of 129 tons, was ordered in 1858 by Ismay and Nelson and delivered in 1859 from the well-known Scottish shipbuilder, Alexander Stephens. *Angelita* encountered a ferocious storm off the south coast of Ireland on 22 January 1862, and was wrecked on the rocks off Horse Island, Dunmanus Bay.

Senator, probably chartered from Rathbone & Co, sailed for Australia on 20 January 1858 under the command of Captain Shoffin.

Blue Jacket², a 986-ton wooden ship built by McLachlan & Co of Carleton, New Brunswick, in 1858 for Wilson & Chambers. *Blue Jacket* sailed for Australia in February 1859. On returning from this voyage the vessel was transferred to the India run. *Blue Jacket²* was lost on Saugor Island in 1863.

Columbia, a 539-ton wooden barque built by T. Oliver of Quebec, was bought in 1858. Advertised as being a vessel of 1,291 tons, she sailed for Australia on 26 February 1858 under the command of Captain M. Clarke. *Columbia* was sold by Wilson & Chambers to T. Anderson & Co of Christiania in 1864.

Northern Bride, an 853-ton ship built in 1855 in New Brunswick, was chartered from Stitt & Co of Liverpool. She sailed for Australia and New Zealand in February 1858 under the command of Captain Candlish. *Northern Bride*, again chartered from Stitt & Co, sailed for Australia and New Zealand in June 1860 under the command of Captain Candlish.

Americana, a 1,046-ton wooden ship built in New Brunswick in 1857. Chartered from Roberts & Co of St John, she sailed from Liverpool for Australia in February 1858 under the command of Captain W. Potts.

Sirocco, a wooden ship built in 1856 by J. Thompson of St John. Chartered first from Morriser & Co of St John (1858–60 approximately) and then from Gibbs Bright (1860–2) for the antipodean trade. She was commanded in turn by Captains Thompson, J. Flood and O'Halloran. James Baines bought the vessel for the Black Ball Line in 1862.

Gertrude, a wooden ship built in 1853 on Prince Edward Island. Chartered from Lodge & Co of Liverpool, she sailed from Liverpool for Melbourne on 20 April 1858 under the command of Captain Roberts.

Beejapore, built in 1851 at St John, New Brunswick. Chartered from Willis & Co of Liverpool, she sailed from there for Australia in May 1858 under the command of Captain T. Drenning. *Beejapore*, again chartered from Willis & Co of Liverpool, sailed in November 1859, still under the command of Captain Drenning.

Simonds, a 1,113-ton wooden ship built in 1854 at St John, sailed for Australia on 27 May 1858, under charter from Captain Leavitt of St John, who owned and commanded her.

Prince of the Seas, a 1,326-ton wooden ship built in 1853 by James Smith & Co of St John, was bought by Wilson & Chambers in 1858. Cearns & Brown and J. G. Brown also had shares in the vessel. The ship worked the Liverpool–Melbourne route January 1859–62 under the command of Captain H. A. Brown. *Prince of the Seas* was burnt at Melbourne on 10 January 1862.

General Windham, a 795-ton wooden ship built in 1856 at New Brunswick, chartered from M'Morrison of St John, sailed from Liverpool for Australia on 27 June 1858 under the command of Captain A. Wilson.

Tasmania, sailed for Australia in September 1858, under the command of Captain J. Nourse. *Tasmania* was bought by Milvain of Newcastle in 1863 and wrecked in 1882.

Dirigo, a 1,152-ton wooden ship built in 1854 at New Brunswick, chartered from Coltart & Co, sailed for Australia on 27 November 1858 under the command of Captain Jones.

Tornado, a 1,721-ton wooden ship built in 1852 by J. Williams at Williamsburgh, New York, was probably bought by White Star in 1859, although it is possible that she was only chartered then and finally purchased in 1863. She sailed to New Zealand in 1859 commanded by Captain Crighton. *Tornado* stayed with White Star until financial disaster overtook the company in 1867 and in that time she was skippered by Captains Crighton, Aikin and Underwood. She was sold to Hutchinson and Partners in 1867. She caught fire at New Orleans in 1875 but was still afloat, probably as a hulk, in 1880.

Telegraph, a 1,164-ton wooden ship, built in 1853 for Kirk & Co of Liverpool by Smith and Haws of St John, was bought by the White Star Line in 1859 for the Australian and New Zealand trade. She would remain with the line and on the same routes until 1862. *Telegraph* was sold off to Coltart & Co of Liverpool in 1862 and then sold on again to M. I. Wilson & Co.

Beechworth, a 1,266-ton vessel built in 1856 in the USA, was chartered from Willis & Co of Liverpool. She sailed for Australia in January 1859 under the command of Captain Thomas Frain.

Tudor, a 1,786-ton wooden ship built in 1854 at Quebec, was chartered from S. Graves & Co of Liverpool. She sailed for Australia in 1859 under the command of Captain Frederick Wherland.

Scottish Chief, a 1,053-ton wooden ship built in 1856, was chartered from Wright & Co of St John, who probably built her. She sailed on 15 March 1859 under the command of Captain P. Buchan.

Miriam, an 899-ton wooden ship built in 1854 at New Brunswick, was chartered from Miller & Co of Liverpool by Wilson & Chambers. She sailed for Australia on 1 April 1859 under the command of Captain Rhind.

Ida, a 1,075-ton wooden ship built in 1852 at St John, chartered, she sailed from Liverpool under the command of Captain J. W. Dunlop in May 1859.

Shooting Star, a 1,518-ton wooden ship built in 1853 at Quebec, chartered from Currie and Co of Liverpool, sailed for Australia in the summer of 1859 under the command of Captain E. J. Allen.

Argonaught, a 1,237-ton wooden ship built in 1853 in Quebec, was chartered from Graves & Co of Liverpool. She sailed in June 1859 under the command of Captain William White.

Herald of the Morning, a 1,459-ton wooden ship built in 1854 at St John, chartered from Fermie & Co of Liverpool, she sailed in the summer of 1859 under the command of Captain G. Rudolph.

Empire of Peace, a 1,540-ton ship built in 1859 in New Brunswick (probably by Wright & Co), chartered from Wright & Co, she sailed for Australia in 1859 under the command of Captain Baker. *Empire of Peace*, again chartered from Wright & Co in 1861, sailed under the command of Captain Calvert. This vessel was chartered to the Black Ball Line in 1864 and sold by Wrights to Fermie Brothers the following year.

Hilton, a 1,293-ton wooden ship built in 1853 at Quebec, was chartered from Halstead & Co of Liverpool. She sailed for Australia in September 1859 under the command of Captain William Thomas.

Greyhound, a 1,375-ton ship, built in 1854 as the *Euroclydon* at St John, chartered from the Black Ball Line, she sailed for Australia in 1859. *Greyhound*, again chartered from the Black Ball Line, sailed for Australia in 1863.

James Cheston, chartered from James Baines, sailed in the summer of 1859 under the command of Captain Bryans. Bought by Baines, for a song, as a derelict in 1855, the *James Cheston* had sailed twice to Australia for the Black Ball Line, in 1857 and 1858 under Captain Bryans.

David G. Fleming, a 1,314-ton wooden ship built in 1854 at St John, chartered from Wright & Co of St John, she sailed to Australia and New Zealand in 1859, and again in 1860, under the command of Captain Hatfield.

White Jacket, a 1,148-ton wooden ship built in 1859 (launched in July) at New Brunswick, was chartered from Rome & Co of Liverpool for two years, from December 1859 until 1861, under the command of Captain Flood.

Carntyne, a 940-ton wooden ship built in 1852 at Bathurst, New Brunswick, was bought from G. Fletcher & Co of Liverpool for use in the South American trade, in 1860. However, she sailed for Australia in February 1860 under the command of Captain J. Smith. *Carntyne* was lost in 1863.

S. Curling, nothing is known about this ship except that she sailed for Australia, under the White Star flag, on 20 February 1860 under the command of Captain Gilchrist.

Commodore Perry, a 1,964-ton wooden ship built in 1854 for James Baines of the Black Ball Line by Donald Mackay at East Boston, Massachusetts, sailed from Liverpool to Melbourne in 1860 under the flags of both the White Star and Black Ball lines, under the command of Captain Kiddie. *Commodore Perry* made a trip to Australia under Captain Kiddie in 1861 and again sailed for Australia in August 1863.

Great Tasmania, a 1,961-ton wooden ship built in 1855 by Donald Mackay at East Boston, Massachusetts, and owned by the Black Ball Line, sailed in April 1860 for Australia under the flags of both lines.

Saldanha, a 1,563-ton ship built in 1853 at Quebec, chartered from James Baines, sailed for Australia on 20 May 1860 under the command of Captain G. Dawson.

C. W. White, chartered, sailed for Australia in June 1860.

Elizabeth Ann Bright, a 1,430-ton wooden ship built in 1856 by W. Olive & Co of Quebec, chartered from James Baines' Black Ball Line, sailed for Australia in June 1860 under the command of Captain Stark. This vessel had been bought by Baines from Gibbs Bright that year, probably with the charter to Wilson & Chambers in mind. *Elizabeth Ann Bright* sailed for Australia under both White Star and Black Ball line flags in 1862, and for White Star in March 1863.

Samaritan, advertised as a 1,272-ton vessel, sailed for Melbourne on 1 May 1860.

Ocean Home, a 596-ton wooden ship built in 1858 at New Brunswick, sailed to Australia in 1860 under the command of Captain Noble. All 64 shares in the ship were bought by H. T. Wilson for White Star use in 1860. In 1861 she was chartered to the Black Ball Line and sailed to Australia, still under Captain Noble. *Ocean Home* was then sold to Currie & Co in 1863. In 1864 they sold her to Kellogg & Co of Liverpool. According to one account she was sunk on 5 September 1866 off the Lizard in a collision with the American ship *Chembim*. Alternatively, she was burnt on 2 January 1869 when off Spithead.

S. Gildersleeve, sailed for Australia in August 1860.

Electric, a 1,106-ton wooden ship built in 1857 by H. N. Jones at Quebec, was bought by G. Cooke and H. T. Wilson (32 shares each) for White Star service in 1860. She was put onto the Australia run, at first under the command of Captain Bell. *Electric* sailed to Australia in 1861 under the command of Captain Underwood. She was sold to Alfred Cleve & Co of Sydney and Dunedin in 1864 and was condemned at Bluff Harbour, New Zealand, (presumably later) in 1864 but seems to have been repaired and then sold again. She was lost on Barbary Island, in the St Lawrence, in 1870.

Lord Raglan, a 1,886-ton wooden ship built in 1854 at Quebec by Charles Jobin & Co for S. R. Graves & Co of Liverpool. Bought by H. T. Wilson for the White Star Line in 1860. The *Lord Raglan* had already seen considerable service, some of it as a trooper, and had had more than one owner. Graves had sold the vessel to Barcroft, Houghton & Carroll soon after receiving it from the builders. The ship had next passed to Carrol & Co of Cork, and it was from them that Wilson bought it for use in the Australian trade. *Lord Raglan* was still on the Liverpool–Melbourne route under the command of Captain Roper in 1861.

Presumably still under the command of Captain Roper, she sailed for Melbourne on 20 February 1863. She was seen at 2°N, 22°W on 23 March, but never again.

Green Jacket, a 1,088-ton wooden ship built in 1860 by King & Co of St John, chartered from Fermie & Co, sailed for Australia in January 1861 under the command of Captain Shaw. Later sold by Fermie, *Green Jacket* was still afloat in 1882, under the Norwegian flag.

Chariot of Fame, a 2,050-ton wooden ship built by Donald Mackay of East Boston in 1853 for Messrs Enoch Train, Benjamin Bangs, A. T. Hall and her first skipper Captain Allen H. Knowles. Bought for White Star in 1861 by H. T. Wilson for use on the Liverpool–Melbourne route, under the command of Captain Kerr. Captain Clarke took over as skipper from Captain Kerr in August 1864. *Chariot of Fame* was sold to Hutchins & Co of Liverpool in 1866. She was abandoned whilst on passage from the Chincha Islands to Cork in January 1876.

Star of India, possibly a ship of 1,690-tons (advertised as such) built in 1861 by W. & R. Wright of St John (and probably owned by them). Most likely chartered, sailed to Australia in 1861, under the command of Captain Buchanan. Probably chartered, she sailed for Australia in 1863, and almost certainly under charter again, to Australia in 1866, both times under the command of Captain Buchanan.

Morning Light, a 2,377-ton wooden ship built in 1855 by W. & R. Wright at St John. Although owned mainly by her builders, James Baines of the Black Ball Line also owned some shares in the vessel and she sailed as a Black Ball ship from the time she was built until 1861, under the command of Captain J. Gillies. In October 1861 *Morning Light*, under charter from her owners, sailed for Australia under the White Star flag. *Morning Light* was again chartered from W. & R. Wright of St John and the Black Ball Line in 1863 and would remain in White Star service until February 1866, making regular voyages between Liverpool and Melbourne.

Queen of the Mersey, a 1,227-ton wooden ship built in 1860 (launched October) by Macdonald & Co of St John, chartered from Henry Fermie & Co of Liverpool, sailed for Australia in March 1861 under the command of Captain Allen. Sister ship to *Mermaid*, *Tiptree* and *Queen of the Clyde*. *Queen of the Mersey*, again chartered from Henry Fermie of Liverpool, sailed for Australia in December 1865 under Captain Allen. She was sold by Fermie in 1875, and was still sailing as the Norwegian vessel *Johanne* in 1882.

Sovereign of the Seas, a 1,227-ton wooden ship built in 1857 by W. & R. Wright & Co of St John, was chartered from joint owners Wright & Co and James Baines. She sailed for Australia on 26 March 1861 under the command of Captain Cruikshank.

Empress of the Seas, a 2,197-ton wooden ship built in 1853 by Donald Mackay of East Boston, was bought by the Black Ball Line in 1860. Made her first voyage to Australia for that line in the summer of 1860 under Captain J. T. Bragg. Chartered from Baines, she sailed for Australia under the White Star flag in May 1861, still under Captain Bragg. She was to sail again for the White Star Line in April 1862 (as advertised in January 1862) but never got the chance. She was burnt at Port Phillip on 19 December 1861.

Lillies, a 1,665-ton ship built in 1855 at St John. Chartered from M. Seeley & Co of St John, she sailed for Australia in September 1861 under the command of Captain Bell.

Donna Maria, an 810-ton wooden ship built as the *Beaconsfield* by Valin & Co of Quebec, launched in May 1861. H. T. Wilson bought all 64 shares in the vessel in 1862. He gave command of this vessel to Captain Couth and set the ship to trading with South America, presumably under the White Star flag. She was sold to G. Stewart of Liverpool, then to Thompson of Shields in 1866, and sold again, to T. F. Tilley & Co. of South Shields in 1877. She was lost in the English Channel on 24 November 1877.

Duke of Newcastle, a 993-ton wooden ship built in 1861 by Lee of Quebec, chartered from James Baines & Co, sailed for Australia from Liverpool and Cork in 1862. *Duke of Newcastle* was again chartered from Baines during the summer of 1865, as the Black Ball Line teetered on the edge of complete collapse.

Morning Star, a 1,534-ton wood ship was built at St John. Owned by and chartered from Henry Fermie & Sons, she sailed in April 1862 for British Columbia under the command of Captain Mathews.

Mistress of the Seas, a 1,776-ton wooden ship built in 1861 (launched in July) at New Brunswick, chartered from Fermie & Sons of Liverpool, sailed for Australia on 20 March 1862 under the command of Captain Baker. *Mistress of the Seas* was abandoned, on 15 February 1880, while on passage from Philadelphia to Bremerhaven.

Great Australia, a 1,661-ton wooden ship built in 1860 at New Brunswick, chartered from Wright & Co of Liverpool, sailed for Australia in April 1862. *Great Australia* had sailed to Australia for the Black Ball Line in the previous year.

Royal Saxon, a 1,109-ton wooden ship owned and probably built by Wright & Co of St John, and launched in 1857. Chartered by White Star, she sailed for British Columbia in April 1862 under the command of Captain Hamm.

Silistria, chartered by White Star, sailed for British Columbia in April 1862.

Blanche Moore, a 1,837-ton wooden ship built in 1854 to the order of Charles Moore & Co of Liverpool by Donald Mackay of East Boston. Chartered by White Star, she sailed for Melbourne from Liverpool on 20 May 1862. The *Blanche Moore* was then sold to James Baines, who put her on the Melbourne run for two trips, in November 1863 and December 1864, under the command of Captain Middleton. Baines sold her to H. T. Wilson sometime in 1866, but for what purpose is unclear. She was not put on the Australian route, or any other established run as far as I have been able to discover. However, her career with the White Star Line was to be short-lived. *Blanche Moore* was lost on the coast of Ireland on 26 May 1867.

Excellent, a 1,212-ton wood ship launched in July 1859 by Baldwin & Co of Quebec, chartered from Henry Fermie & Sons, sailed on 10 June 1862 for British Columbia under the command of Captain Beadie.

King of Algeria, a 1,707-ton wooden ship built in 1856 at St John, chartered from Fermie & Co of Liverpool, sailed for Australia in June 1862 under the command of Captain Brown.

Queen of the North, a 1,668-ton wooden ship built in 1862 by McMorron & Dunn of St John, was bought outright for £13,500 when she was completed in 1862 by H. T. Wilson for the White Star Line. The vessel was used in the Australian and New Zealand trade 1862–66 under Captains Clarke and Forsyth. *Queen of the North* was transferred to the more remunerative trade with India in 1866. She was taken over by the Royal Bank of Liverpool in 1869. In December 1890 she was hulked by her then owners, Warmington & Crusoe of London.

Glendevon, a 954-ton wooden ship built in 1862 by J. J Jardine & Co at Richibucto, New Brunswick, owned by White Star and the Brown family, she operated on the Australia/New Zealand run until early 1866. *Glendevon* was transferred from the Australian to the Indian run in early 1866. She was sold to Bilborough & Co in 1867. *Glendevon* left Liverpool in December 1871 and was never seen again.

Rising Sun, a 824-ton wooden ship built in 1857 at St John, chartered from Wright &

Co of St John, who probably built her, sailed for Australia in December 1862 under the command of Captain M'Kinnon.

Pride of the West, a 382-ton iron barque built in 1859 (launched December), chartered from either Langley & Co of London, who built and owned her, or from Curwen & Co of Liverpool, who bought her in 1863, she sailed for New Zealand from London on 5 February 1863.

British Trident, a 1,555-ton wooden ship built in 1855 at St John, was chartered from B. Mozely & Co of Liverpool. She sailed for Australia in March 1863 under the command of Captain Haddock.

Southern Empire, a 1,142-ton wooden ship built in 1863 (launched in March) by Baldwin & Co of Quebec, probably chartered (but possibly owned by White Star), sailed for Australia in 1863.

Queen of the South, probably chartered, sailed for Australia on 20 May 1863.

Albert Williams, a 505-ton barque was launched by J. Laing & Co of Sunderland, for Wilson & Chambers in May 1863. She was taken over by the Royal Bank of Liverpool in 1867. *Albert Williams* was aground near Southport in January 1888, but was salvaged and re-rigged as a barquentine and renamed *Else*. *Albert Williams* was wrecked at Hamelin while on passage from South Africa to Britain in August 1900.

Lingdale, nothing very much is known about this vessel except that she was supposedly new, and she sailed for New Zealand in July 1863.

Vanguard, a 643-ton ship built in 1852 at Port Glasgow. Chartered from Nicholson & Co of Liverpool, she sailed from Liverpool for Melbourne in July 1863 under the command of Captain Connel.

Ulcoats, a 671-ton iron ship launched in 1863, and built for White Star by Jones, Quiggins & Co of Liverpool. Initially she was put on the New Zealand route, commanded successively by Captains J. Thomas and J. Chambers. Later she was transferred to the Indian trade under Captain R. Potts. *Ulcoats* was bought by Cearns & Brown of Liverpool (major shareholders in White Star) when the White Star fleet was sold in 1867.

Cecelia, a 612-ton wooden barque built by Mackern & Co of Preston for White Star. Wilson and Chambers each owned 32 shares in this ship, which sailed for New Zealand in September 1863 then changed routes. *Cecelia* was sold off to Swire & Co in 1866 and was finally lost off the coast near Sunderland on 3 March 1881.

Golden Sunset, a 628-ton iron barque built in 1863 by W. Doxford & Co of Sunderland, was bought by Wilson & Chambers in 1863 for the White Star Line on completion. *Golden Sunset*, sailed on her maiden voyage for White Star from London to New Zealand in February 1864. Her last advertised sailing for the line was in February 1866, as the sun really set on the first incarnation of the line. *Golden Sunset* was wrecked on Enderbury Island on 17 December 1866.

Gladiator, a 503-ton ship built in 1850 at Aberdeen. Chartered from Adamson & Co of Aberdeen, she sailed for New Zealand in November 1863 under the command of Captain J. Young.

Royal Standard, left Liverpool on her maiden voyage on 23 November 1863, bound for Melbourne. *Royal Standard* was sold to Swire & Co of Liverpool in 1866. Swires had the auxiliary screw and steam engine removed, converting the ship into a pure sailing vessel. She was wrecked near São Tomé, just north of Rio de Janeiro, Brazil, on 10 October 1869.

Santon, a 511-ton iron barque, built by Pile Hay & Co of Sunderland. Bought on completion, in 1863, by Wilson & Chambers for use in the Indian trade, under the command of Captain W. Balmeno. *Santon* was sold to Cearns & Co in 1866.

Pampero, a 558-ton iron barque launched in January 1864 by Royden & Co of Liverpool, was bought on completion by T. H. Ismay in 1864. She was used throughout her life on the route between Liverpool and Callao, on the coast of Peru. First commanded by Captain Lesley, she was later skippered by Captains Waller and Metcalfe. *Pampero* was sold to W. Gellatly, for scrapping, in 1874, after being taken out of service the preceding year.

Royal Family had already sailed under the Black Ball flag in November 1862 when she was advertised in 1864 by the White Star Line as a new ship of 1,750 tons. She sailed for Australia in January 1864 as a White Star vessel.

W. H. Haselden, an 897-ton iron ship built in 1864 for the White Star line by Pearse & Co of Stockton. Initially was she put on the New Zealand route but was soon transferred to the Liverpool–Melbourne run, where she remained until sold in 1867 to Hutchinson & Partners of Liverpool and sold by them in 1870 to Roxburgh & Partners of Glasgow. *W. H. Haselden* left Montreal bound for Glasgow in September 1870. She was seen and hailed on the 18th, but she was never seen again.

Napier, a 572-ton iron ship built in 1863 by Pile & Co of West Hartlepool. Chartered from Park Brothers of London, the *Napier* sailed for Melbourne and New Zealand in February 1864 commanded by Captain Petherbridge. She again sailed for Melbourne and New Zealand in February 1865 under the command of Captain Petherbridge.

Africana, a wooden ship of 1,557 tons, launched in October 1860 by Roberts & Co of New Brunswick, was chartered from D. & G. Roberts of St John. On 20 February 1864 she sailed for Australia under the command of Captain J. Hatfield.

Hartfield, a new ship, was also scheduled to sail for New Zealand in February 1864. Whether or not she actually did sail does not seem to be on record.

Industry was chartered and sailed for New Zealand in April 1864.

Envoy, a 389-ton barque built for Tongue & Co of Liverpool by Henderson & Co of Miramichi. She was launched in July 1860. *Envoy* sailed for Vancouver Island under the White Star flag on 10 April 1864.

Sam Cearns, a 1,422-ton iron ship built in 1864 (launched June) for H. T. Wilson, who held all 64 shares, by Scott & Co of Greenock. The vessel was named after a major shareholder in the White Star Line. She sailed for Melbourne in 1864 under the command of Captain Whinnery, and again for Melbourne in September 1865, still under Captain Whinnery. Immediately after this voyage she was sold to Lancaster Shipowners of Liverpool, but continued to be managed by White Star. *Sam Cearns* was lost on Tierra del Fuego or the Falkland Islands on 26 June 1871.

Star of England, a 1,544-ton wooden ship built in 1860 in America, sailed for Melbourne on 20 October 1864. Probably chartered by White Star, the *Star of England* had previously been used by the Black Ball Line in 1863, and would be again in 1866. By 1874 she was owned by Smith, Bilborough & Co of London.

Vernon, a 1,319-ton iron ship built in 1864 by Vernon & Co of Liverpool. Chartered from Alexander & Co, she sailed for Australia in December 1864 under the command of Captain Thornhill. Two years later *Vernon* also sailed under the Black Ball flag.

Sirius, a 620-ton iron screw brig, built by Earle & Co of Hull, was launched in February 1865. All 64 shares in the vessel were bought on its completion by H. T. Wilson, who then immediately sold the ship to G. Fleming of London, who promptly sold it abroad.

Wennington, an 882-ton iron ship built in 1865 (launched in March) for H. T. Wilson of the White Star Line by the Lune Iron Ship Company of Lancaster. She sailed to the antipodes in 1865 under the command of Captain Williams. *Wennington* again sailed for Australia and New Zealand in 1866 under the command of Captain Williams. Then the ship was transferred to trade between Liverpool and San Francisco, skippered by Captains Reade, G. Byron, Davis, J. M'Avon and Winder. After this stint *Wennington* was again transferred, this time to trade with the Orient, particularly Rangoon. *Wennington* was sighted in the Bali Straits on 30 January 1878. She was never seen again.

The Third Generation

Santa Lucia was a 642-ton iron ship launched in January 1866 by Evans & Co of Liverpool. Bought by T. H. Ismay on completion, *Santa Lucia* was put to trade with South America. In due course she was wrecked of the Chilean coast on 12 December 1882, while on a voyage from San Antonio to Liverpool.

Whittington, a 970-ton iron ship launched in 1866 for White Star by the Lune Shipbuilding Company of Lancaster. She sailed for Australia early in 1866 under the command of Captain Duckett.

Oliver Cromwell, a 1,112-ton wooden ship launched by Charland & Co of Quebec in April 1866, bought by Henry Wilson on completion and sold to R. Wilson & Co in the same year.

Western Empire, a 1,245-ton wooden ship built by Baldwin & Co of Quebec and launched in April 1862, was bought from Girvan & Co by Henry Wilson in 1866 and sold to Cearns & Co in the same year.

Fletcheroo, a 730-ton ship launched in May 1866 by Vernon & Co of Liverpool. Owned by T. H. Ismay, she was used by the White Star Line on the Liverpool–Australia route, 1866–69, under the command of Captain Hetherington. *Fletcheroo* was transferred to the American trade in 1869 under the command of Captain Waller. She ran aground and became a total loss in 1880.

Explorer, a 750-ton iron ship launched in January 1866 by Evans & Co of Liverpool. Not strictly a White Star ship at this time, *Explorer* was owned by T. H. Ismay and in 1866 she sailed to San Francisco under Captain Trumble, for her owner. *Explorer*, still owned by T. H. Ismay, was rammed and sunk in November 1888.

Arriero, a 167-ton vessel launched in October 1862 by Stephen & Sons of Glasgow, was bought by T. H. Ismay in 1866. She automatically became a White Star ship when Ismay purchased the line in 1869. *Arriero* was used for the trade between Liverpool and Vera Cruz until 1873 under the command of Captain Lewis and was then sold off to Harrison & Co of Liverpool, in 1873, after a spell lying idle. She was finally wrecked on Rathlin Island on 4 March 1876.

Arrowe, a 309-ton barque built in 1855 at Berwick. She was used on the South American run for a couple of years from 1866, under the command of Captain H. Hartley. *Arrowe* was 14 years old when she was sold at Valparaiso in 1869.

Delmira, a 338-ton iron barque launched in January 1864 and built by the Roodee Iron Works on the Dee at Chester. She was used in trade with South America for about six years from 1866, under the command of Captain W. Sherwin. *Delmira* was sold to Spence & Co in 1872. By now owned by Sumner & Benn, she was wrecked in December 1896.

Don Guillermo, a 599-ton iron barque launched in September 1866 by Evans & Co of Liverpool. She was used in the South American trade for 10 years from 1866, first under the command of Captain M'Murray and then Captain J. Ismay. *Don Guillermo* was sold to Paulsen & Co of Elsfleth in Germany in 1877. She was wrecked in 1882 in the Van Islands.

Castlehow, a 260-ton barque launched in April 1860 by Williams & Co of Harrington. *Castlehow* was put to the China trade for five years from 1866 under the command of Captain Trumble. *Castlehow* was sold to Davidson of Harrington in 1872. She foundered off Trinidad in 1892.

Esmeralda, a 730-ton ship launched in April 1866 by Vernon & Co of Liverpool, was bought by William Imrie in 1866. She sailed the Australian route in 1867 and 1868 under the command of Captain J. Beer. She was then transferred to the South American trade under Captains Nunn and Fordyce. She was sold to Danish owners in 1895 and sold again, to an Italian company, in 1909. This remarkable little vessel was still afloat and operating as a lightship in the River Plate as late as the 1950s.

Second Incarnation

Duke of Edinburgh, a 1,073-ton ship launched in September 1867 by Holderness & Co of Liverpool and chartered from her builders and owners. She sailed for Melbourne from Liverpool on 20 April 1868 under the command of Captain Balmana.

Woosung, a 729-ton iron ship launched in December 1863 by Stephens & Co of Glasgow. Chartered from Boadle & Co of Liverpool, she sailed for Melbourne on 20 May 1868 under the command of Captain Bourner. *Woosung*, again chartered from Boadle & Co of Liverpool, sailed for Sydney in the autumn of 1870, still under the command of Captain Bourner.

Duleep Singh, a 1,198-ton iron ship launched in December 1863 by Vernon & Co of Liverpool. Owned by Imrie, she sailed between Liverpool and Melbourne in 1868 and 1869 under Captains John W. Jennings and T. P. Follett. *Duleep Singh* was transferred to the run to India under the command of Captain Williams when William Imrie and T. H. Ismay became partners at the end of the decade.

British Statesman, a 1,262-ton iron ship launched in April 1867 by Royden of Liverpool, was chartered from BSO (British Shipowners) Company (Beazleys). Sailed for Australia in June 1868 under the command of Captain R. Tullock.

Bucton Castle, an 886-ton ship built in 1857 at Bideford, was chartered from J. Leech & Co of Liverpool. She sailed for Melbourne in July 1868 under the command of Captain McDuggan and in April 1869 under Captain Dodd.

Globe, a 736-ton iron ship launched in April 1867 by Bowdler and Co of Liverpool, chartered from Myers & Co of Liverpool, she sailed from there for Melbourne in August 1868 under the command of Captain T. Brimage.

Nereus, an iron ship launched in September 1868 by Bowdler & Co of Liverpool, was chartered from Myers and Co of Liverpool. She sailed for Melbourne on 28 October, under the command of Captain M. Duggan.

Philosopher, a 1,059-ton iron ship launched in 1857 at Liverpool. Chartered from Harrison & Co of Liverpool, she sailed from there for Melbourne on 20 November 1868 under the command of Captain Rose.

Borrowdale, a 1,197-ton vessel launched in November 1868 by Potter of Liverpool, chartered from J. Newton of Liverpool, made voyages between Liverpool, Melbourne and Sydney in 1868, 70 and 71, all under the command of Captain Robert Parr.

Weathersfield, a 1,051-ton iron ship launched in February 1863 by Duncan & Co of Port Glasgow. Chartered from Cowie & Co of Liverpool, she sailed for Australia in 1869 under the command of Captain A. Morris.

British Prince, a 1,282-ton ship launched in September 1864 by Clover & Co of Birkenhead, was chartered from BSO. She sailed from Liverpool for Melbourne in February 1869 under the command of Captain W. Christian.

Dallam Towers, a 1,499-ton ship launched in August 1866 by Clover & Co of Birkenhead. Chartered from Lancashire Shipowners Company, she was advertised as sailing for Melbourne in March 1869 under the command of Captain J. Rhind. She sailed in June 1869 under Captain J. Rhind.

Remington, a 999-ton iron ship launched in April 1863 by Smith & Co of Glasgow. Chartered from Cowie & Co of Liverpool, she sailed for Sydney in April 1869 under the command of Captain J. Fowler.

Hecuba, nothing seems to be known about the *Hecuba* except that she was advertised as sailing for Australia on 24 May 1869 under the command of Captain Walker.

Pride of the Thames, a 382-ton iron barque built in 1858 at London. Chartered from R. Curwen & Co of Liverpool, she sailed from Liverpool for Otago on 15 June 1869 under the command of Captain Tonkin.

Hoghton Towers, a 1,598-ton iron ship launched in May 1869 by Clover & Co of Birkenhead. Owned by T. H. Ismay, she sailed on her maiden voyage for White Star to Australia in June 1869 under the command of Captain Trumble. The vessel was then transferred to the South American trade. *Hoghton Towers* was transferred to the Liverpool–India route in 1873.

Warwickshire, a 679-ton iron ship launched in October 1862 by Vernon & Co of Liverpool. Chartered from Myers & Co of Liverpool, she sailed for Sydney in April 1869 under the command of Captain W. Mitchell.

Victoria Tower, a 1,563-ton iron ship launched in June 1869 by Evans & Co of Liverpool. Owned by T. H. Ismay, she sailed to Melbourne in June 1869 under the command of Captain John Kerr, who had until recently commanded the *White Star*. *Victoria Tower* was wrecked on Port Phillip Head on 7 October 1869. Aboard the ship was a valuable general cargo as well as her crew and passengers; luckily no lives were lost.

Hawarden Castle, a 1,101-ton iron ship built by Evans & Co of Liverpool, chartered from Richards & Co of Liverpool, sailed from Liverpool for Melbourne on 10 August 1869 under the command of Captain John Jones.

Vancouver, a 1,053-ton iron ship built by Boulder & Co of Liverpool, chartered from Myers & Co, she sailed from Liverpool for Sydney on 10 August 1869 under the command of Captain Dodd.

Castlehead, an 800-ton ship launched in August 1869 by Evans & Co of Liverpool. Owned by Ismay & Co, she sailed for Sydney (from Liverpool) in September 1869 under the command of Captain Armstrong.

Vandieman, a 1,051-ton iron ship launched in September 1869, chartered from Myers & Co of Liverpool. She sailed for Sydney on 20 October 1869 under the command of Captain Robinson.

Comandre, a 772-ton ship, was launched in August 1868 by Stephens & Co of Glasgow. Owned by Ismay & Co, she sailed from Liverpool for Sydney in October 1869 under the command of Captain J. Penrice.

Seatoller, a 558-ton iron ship launched in June 1866 by Evans & Co of Liverpool. Chartered from Gamble & Co of Liverpool, she sailed for Australia in October 1869 under the command of Captain D. Brown.

Casma, a barque launched in September 1869 by Potter & Co of Liverpool, chartered from Boadle & Co of Liverpool, sailed from Liverpool for Otago in New Zealand in October 1869 under the command of Captain McCulloch.

Compadre, an 800-ton ship launched in April 1867 by Evans & Co of Liverpool and owned by Ismay & Co, sailed from Liverpool for Sydney in 1869 under the command of Captain T. Downwards.

Bayard, a 1,319-ton ship launched in April 1864 by Vernon & Co of Liverpool, chartered from L. Young & Co of Liverpool, sailed from Liverpool for Melbourne on 20 November 1869 under the command of Captain John Jackson.

British Admiral, advertised as sailing to Australia in November 1869. Nothing seems to be known about this vessel. There was a later ship of that name, but it was owned by Fermies and not launched until 1873. The advertised vessel was probably replaced for the voyage by the *Bayard*.

Montrose, a 995-ton iron ship launched in October 1863 by Barclay & Co of Glasgow. Chartered from Cowie & Co of Liverpool, she sailed for Australia in December 1869 under the command of Captain McIntyre.

Ismay, a 422-ton iron ship launched in 1861 by Stephen & Sons of Glasgow, and probably owned and renamed by T. H. Ismay, sailed for New Zealand from Liverpool on 20 December 1869 under the command of Captain Sherwin. *Ismay* was sold to Robertson of Dundee in 1874 and abandoned off Valparaiso Bay on 1 June 1875.

Estrella, a 499-ton iron barque launched in January 1866 by Hedderwick of Glasgow. She sailed from there to Auckland in 1869 under the command of Captain S. Crowther.

Pembroke Castle, a 410-ton vessel launched in October 1863 by Stephen & Co of Glasgow. Chartered from Simpson & Co of Swansea, she sailed for Otago from Liverpool on 5 January 1870 under the command of Captain Reynolds.

Hausquina, a 428-ton barque launched in June 1864 by Fell & Co of Workington. Chartered by White Star, she sailed from Liverpool for Auckland on 10 January 1870 under the command of her owner, Captain W. Lowden of Whitehaven.

Rajah, a 1,257-ton iron ship launched in November 1864 by Hart & Co of Liverpool, chartered from Nicholson & Co of Liverpool, sailed for Sydney in January 1870 under the command of Captain Halliday.

British Navy, a 1,217-ton ship, launched in January 1869 by the Liverpool Ship Building Company. Chartered from BSO of Liverpool, she sailed for Melbourne in February 1870 under the command of Captain William Porter.

Cairnsmore, a 975-ton iron ship launched in January 1869 by Reid & Co of Glasgow, chartered from Nicholson & Co of Liverpool, sailed from Liverpool for Sydney, also in February 1870, under the command of Captain Kewley.

Santon, a 511-ton barque launched in March 1863 by Pile & Co of Sunderland, probably chartered, sailed for Auckland on 1 March 1870 under the command of Captain Moore.

Kirkwood, a 1,279-ton iron ship was launched in February 1869 by Boulder & Co of Liverpool. Chartered by White Star, she sailed for Australia on 30 March 1870 under the command of her owner, Captain Thomas Steele.

Delhi, a 675-ton ship, launched in November 1863 by Richardson & Co of Newcastle. Chartered from Holmes & Co of London, she sailed from Liverpool for Otago in April 1870 under the command of Captain Nichols.

Merwanjee Framjee, a 1,079-ton iron ship launched in May 1863 by Reid & Co of Port Glasgow, chartered from Johnston & Co of Liverpool, sailed for Sydney on 23 April 1870 under the command of Captain Bidwell.

Ravenscrag, a 1,263-ton iron ship, launched in January 1866 by Steele & Co of Greenock. Chartered from J. A. Allen & Co of Glasgow, she sailed for Melbourne on 30 April 1870 under the command of Captain J. Dunlop.

Cape Clear, an 853-ton ship launched in March 1869 by Boulder & Co of Liverpool, chartered from Myers & Co of Liverpool, sailed from Liverpool for Sydney in June 1870 under the command of Captain Landsborough.

Grace Gibson, a 540-ton iron ship launched in September 1867 by Stephen & Co of Glasgow. Chartered from Hewitt & Co of Liverpool, she sailed for Otago in July 1870.

Hannibal, a 1,198-ton iron ship launched in October 1862 by Smith & Co of Glasgow. Chartered from W. Dixon & Co of Liverpool, she sailed for Melbourne in July 1870 under the command of Captain J. A. Hill.

Cardigan Castle, a 1,200-ton ship launched in July 1870 by Evans & Co of Liverpool. Chartered from Richards & Co of Liverpool, she sailed from there for Melbourne in August 1870 under the command of Captain Davies.

Santiago, a 455-ton iron ship built in 1856, chartered from Balfour & Co of Liverpool, sailed for Auckland in August 1870 under the command of Captain Mills.

Jason, a 1,512-ton iron ship launched in August 1870 by Barclay & Co of Glasgow, was chartered from Carmichael & Co of Greenock. She sailed for Melbourne under the command of Captain McIntyre.

Oceanic[1], launched on 27 August 1870, the first of T. H. Ismay's new steamships. *Oceanic* entered the Mersey in February 1871, and began preparing for her maiden voyage, sailing from Liverpool, bound for Queenstown and then on to New York, on 2 March 1871. *Oceanic*, White Star's first true liner, was sent for scrap in 1896.

Ardgowan, a 1,283-ton iron ship launched in September 1867 by Steele & Co of Greenock. Chartered from Adam & Co, she sailed from Liverpool for Melbourne in September 1870.

Cornwallis, a 1,214-ton ship launched in June 1862 by Vernon & Co of Liverpool. Chartered from L. Young & Co of Liverpool, she sailed from Liverpool for Sydney in November 1870 under the command of Captain G. Brown.

Malleny, a 1,025-ton iron ship launched in June 1868 by Royden & Co of Liverpool, chartered from Alexander & Co of Liverpool, sailed for Melbourne in November 1870 under the command of Captain Scott.

Harvest Home, a 547-ton iron ship built in 1855 at Liverpool, chartered from Troughton and Co of Liverpool. She sailed from there for Otago in 1870 under the command of Captain Green.

Atlantic, launched by Harland & Wolff on 26 November 1870, the second of T. H. Ismay's new steamships. *Atlantic* was taken over by the line on 3 June 1871 and sailed from Liverpool on her maiden voyage on 6 June. She left Liverpool for her 19th voyage on 20 March 1873. On 1 April she was wrecked near Halifax, Nova Scotia, with 585 drowned.

British Peer, a 1,330-ton ship launched in January 1865 by Harland & Wolff. Chartered from BSO, she sailed from Liverpool for Melbourne in December 1870 under the command of Captain Davies.

British Sovereign, a 1,345-ton iron ship launched in October 1864 by Robinson & Co of Cork, and chartered from BSO Company (Beazley's), also sailed for Melbourne in December 1870 under the command of Captain Jackson. *British Sovereign* was sold to Gillison in 1880.

Otago, a 348-ton barque launched in October 1869 by Stephen & Co of Glasgow, sailed for Otago and Wellington in January 1871 under the command of her owner, Captain A. Cameron of Glasgow.

British Princess, a 1,291-ton ship launched in January 1865 by Clover & Co of Birkenhead. Chartered from BSO, she sailed for Melbourne in January 1871 under the command of Captain W. Brown.

Khandeish, a 1,004-ton iron ship launched in October 1864 by Duncan & Co of Port Glasgow, was chartered from Nicholson & Co of Liverpool. She sailed for Australia on 28 February 1871 commanded by Captain J. Sennett.

Aminta, an iron ship built by Jones & Co of Liverpool, and launched in February 1862. Owned by Thomas Ismay, she sailed from Liverpool for Melbourne on 20 May 1871 under the command of Captain W. Meyler.

Baltic¹, the third of the new liners, sailed on her maiden voyage in September 1871. She set a new record by averaging better than 15kt during an 1873 west to east Atlantic crossing. *Baltic* was forced to return to Queenstown, on 7 May 1888, for 10 hours of repairs to an engine when the low pressure cylinders failed. She was soon sold to the Holland-America Line, for £32,000 and renamed *Veendam*. She struck a submerged wreck and sank on 6 February 1898.

Adriatic¹, launched on 17 October 1871. Another of the *Oceanic¹* Class ships but slightly larger than the class leader at 452ft long. Also built by Harland & Wolff. Although more spacious than *Oceanic*, *Adriatic* only had a capacity of 1,150 passengers, 1,000 of them in steerage. The ship set a new east to west Atlantic record at 14.52kt in June 1872. *Adriatic* left Liverpool, bound for Preston and the breakers' yard on 12 February 1899, just over one month short of having completed 27 years' service.

Asiatic, Ismay Imrie bought this 2,652-ton ship from J. M. Wood for use in the South Atlantic trade in 1871. *Asiatic* was sold for £50,000 in 1873 to the African Steamship Company, who renamed the ship *Ambriz*. She was sold again in 1891 to Elder Dempster for New Orleans service and once more sold to Madagascar in 1895, becoming a coal hulk in 1896. *Asiatic* was wrecked in 1903.

Tropic¹, Ismay Imrie bought this 2,650-ton ship from J. M. Wood for use in the South Atlantic trade in 1871. *Tropic*, which had cost the partners £44,060 in 1871, fetched £52,500 in 1873, and was renamed *Federico*. She was broken up by Thomas W. Ward at Lytham in 1894.

Republic¹, the third of Ismay's new breed of liner, sailed on her maiden voyage early in 1872. *Republic* ran into the Cunard steamer *Aurania* when leaving New York on 20 September 1885, while under charter to the Inman Line. She was sold to the Holland–America Line for £35,000 in 1889. Her new owners renamed the ship *Mausdam*. Over the next 21 years the old *Republic* would become the Italian *Vittoria* and the *Citta di Napoli*. The 39-year-old vessel went to the breakers at Genoa under the name *Citta di Napoli* in 1910.

Celtic¹, having just been handed over to her new owners by Harland & Wolff, ran aground as she was steaming down Belfast Lough on 18 October 1872. *Celtic* made her maiden voyage for the White Star Line later the same month. She was an almost exact duplicate of her sister ship *Adriatic¹*. She was sold to a Danish owner and renamed *Amerika* in 1893 and scrapped in 1898.

Traffic¹, a 155-ton tender, built for the White Star Line by Speakman of Runcorn in 1873. *Traffic* was sold to the Liverpool Lighterage Company in 1896 and sold by them in

1898. *Traffic* was sunk on 5 May 1941 during a German air attack on Liverpool, finally being raised and broken up in 1956, 83 years after she had been built.

Gaelic¹, 2,652 tons, was bought on the stocks from the owners of the Bibby Line in 1873. On long-term charter to the Occidental & Oriental Company, she was engaged in trade on the Pacific Ocean in 1875. *Gaelic* was sold to new owners for £30,000 in 1883. She ran aground on 24 September 1896, after being sold again three years earlier to a Spanish owner and renamed *Hugo*. The ship became a total loss and was taken to Holland to be finally broken up.

Britannic¹, a 5,004-ton vessel, designed by Edward J. Harland, was launched at Belfast on 3 February 1874. The new ship was originally to be called *Hellenic* but the name was changed before she was handed over to the White Star Line. She sailed on her maiden voyage in June. *Britannic* left Liverpool on her last voyage to America on 16 August 1899 and was declared surplus on her return. She left Belfast for Hamburg on 11 August 1903. Her builders had condemned her as not worth refitting, so she was taken to the German port for demolition, under tow.

Belgic¹, bought in 1874. She had been built as the *Gaelic* but as the line already had a vessel of that name an alternative had to be found. As she was leaving Victoria Docks, London, on 24 November she ran into two barges, one unladen, the other carrying the rudder of an ironclad warship; they both sank. Later sold to Cia. de Nav. La Flecha, and renamed *Goefredo*. On 26 February 1884 she was stranded on Burbo Bank, near Liverpool, and broke her back.

Germanic, built at a cost of £200,000, entered service in 1875. *Germanic* was to become White Star's longest lived liner, lasting for no less than three-quarters of a century. *Germanic* set a new record for an eastbound crossing of the North Atlantic in February 1876 when she completed the trip in 7 days, 15 hours and 17 minutes, at an average speed of 15.79kt. She returned to Harland & Wolff to be modernised in December 1894 and re-entered service in May 1895 with new triple-expansion engines and new boilers fitted. She made her last voyage under the White Star flag on 23 September 1903, before being placed in reserve and then transferred to the American Line. *Germanic's* name was changed to *Ottawa* and she served the Dominion Line for a spell. She was sold in 1911 to Turkish owners and renamed *Gul Djemal* (*Gulcemal*). *Germanic* was demolished in Italy in 1950 when she was 75 years old.

Britannia, chartered for a voyage to Australia in March 1877. She had first sailed for the line 17 years earlier.

Arabic¹, entered service with the line in 1881. Although only nine years old, she was sold to Holland-America for £65,000 in 1890 and was scrapped at Preston in 1901.

Coptic, entered service with the line in 1881. She set out on the first trip of the new White Star service from London to Hobart. On 26 May 1884 *Coptic* transferred to the New Zealand route. She was sold in 1906, and renamed *Persia* and sold again in 1916 and renamed *Persia Maru*. She was scrapped in 1925 in Japan.

Ionic¹, handed over by the builders at Belfast on 26 March 1883. *Ionic* joined *Coptic* and *Doric* on the London–New Zealand route in December 1884, under the joint management agreement between White Star and Shaw Savill. She was sold in August 1900, for £47,500, to George Thompson & Co. They renamed her *Sophocles* and operated her for another eight years before scrapping her at Morecambe in 1908.

Doric¹, completed in July 1883. *Ionic* and *Doric* were chartered by the New Zealand Shipping Company as a stopgap measure until its own ships were ready. *Doric*, 4,744 tons, was on extended charter to the Occidental & Oriental Steamship Company, during 1896. *Doric*, which had been transferred to the Occidental & Oriental Line in 1896, was sold to the Pacific Mail Steamship Company (P. R. Schwerin) for £50,000, and renamed *Asia* in 1906. She was wrecked in fog close to Wenchau, near Shanghai, in South China on 22 April 1911.

Belgic², a vessel of 4,211 tons, entered service for the White Star Line in 1885. She was not intended for the North Atlantic passenger trade. She was sold off in 1899 and renamed *Mohawk*. As the *Mohawk*, was scrapped at Garston in 1903.

Gaelic², 4,205 tons, was the second vessel to come from the builders in 1885. She was not intended for the North Atlantic passenger trade. Sold in 1905, and renamed *Callao*. As *Callao* was broken up at Briton Ferry in 1907.

Teutonic, keel laid in March 1887, closely followed by that of *Majestic¹*. *Teutonic* was bought outright from White Star in 1915 by the Admiralty, supposedly for use as a troopship. She was returned to the line in 1918. Towards the end of the Great War the *Teutonic*, in company with *Celtic* and *Cedric*, specialised in transporting troops between Egypt and Britain. *Teutonic* went to the breakers at Rotterdam in 1921.

Cufic¹, the first of the White Star livestock carriers was launched at Belfast on 10 October 1888. She was chartered to a Spanish company in 1896 and renamed by it the *Nueva Señora de Guadalupe*. She came back to the Oceanic Steam Navigation Company the following year under her old name. As *Cufic¹* she was sold to the Dominion Line in 1901 and renamed *Manxman*. Sold on in 1915 to R. Lawrence Smith Ltd, of Montreal. Requisitioned by the British Government 1917–19 for use as an armed merchant cruiser, and then a troopship. She was then sold to the Universal Transport Company of New York. Still as the *Manxman*, she foundered in the North Atlantic on 18 December 1919 while on her way to Gibraltar, with the loss of about 40 lives.

Runic¹, a 4,833-ton vessel and the second livestock carrier, was launched on 1 January 1889. The ship would enter service with the line the following year. She was sold to the West India and Pacific Steamship Company, for £37,500, and renamed *Tampican* in 1895. She was then transferred in 1899 to Frederick Leyland & Co. Sold in 1912 to H. E. Moss & Co, of Liverpool, and then almost immediately sold again to the South Pacific Whaling Company of Oslo and renamed *Imo*. As the *Imo*, she ran into the French ammunition ship *Mont Blanc* at Halifax on 6 December 1917. The *Mont Blanc* exploded, killing about 1,500 people and injuring about another 8,000. A large part of the city of Halifax was destroyed in the blast. The *Imo* was badly damaged in the incident and had to be beached to prevent her from sinking. She was sold once again in 1920 to Norwegian owners and renamed *Guvernoren*. Ran aground at Port Stanley in the Falkland Islands in thick fog on 30 November 1921 and declared a total loss.

Majestic¹, launched on 29 June 1889. *Teutonic* and *Majestic* were the first new liners the company had bought for the North Atlantic route for 15 years. *Majestic* was scrapped at Morecambe in 1914.

Nomadic¹, 5,749 tons, was the third White Star livestock carrier, and was launched at Belfast on 11 February 1891. *Nomadic* was sold to the Dominion Line for £64,960 in 1905 and renamed *Cornishman*. As *Cornishman* she was broken up by T. W. Ward at Lelant in 1926.

Tauric, 5,728 tons, the fourth livestock carrier, was launched on 12 March 1891. *Tauric* was sold to the Dominion Line in March 1903, for £61,816 and renamed *Welshman*. Sent to the breakers at Bo'ness in December 1929.

Magnetic, a 619-ton tender specially built to serve the *Teutonic* and *Majestic¹*, joined the White Star fleet in 1891. Withdrawn in 1932. *Magnetic* was sold in 1933 and renamed *Ryde*. Arrived at the breakers at Port Glasgow on 21 August 1935.

Naronic, the fifth livestock carrier, was launched at Belfast on 26 May 1892. Under the command of Captain William Roberts, she sailed from the Alexandra Dock, Liverpool, for New York on 11 February 1893 and was never seen again.

Bovic, the sixth White Star livestock carrier, was launched at Belfast on 28 June 1892. The ship was sold in 1922, becoming the *Colonian*. *Bovic* was scrapped at Rotterdam in 1928.

Cevic, the penultimate White Star livestock carrier was launched at Belfast on 25 September 1893. She entered service the following year. *Cevic* was requisitioned by the Admiralty in 1915 and converted into a dummy battle-cruiser, the *'Queen Mary'*. Now called the *Pyrula*, she was broken up in Italy in 1933.

Gothic, completed in November 1893, for the London–New Zealand trade. She set off on her maiden voyage to Wellington on 30 December 1893. *Gothic* was transferred to the Red Star Line in 1907 after an extensive refit. Renamed *Gothland*, she was transformed into a third-class-only ship. *Gothland* ex-*Gothic*, set off on her first voyage for Red Star from Antwerp to New York on 11 July 1907. *Gothland* returned to White Star service in 1911, renamed *Gothic*. She ran onto the Gunner Rocks off the Scilly Isles while on her way back from Canada on 23 June 1914. After 3 days she was towed off, badly damaged, and had to go to Southampton for months of repairs. Sent to the breakers at Bo'ness in 1926.

Pontic, a 395-ton tender acquired for use in the River Mersey, entered service in 1894. Sold to Rea Tugs in 1919 and sent to the breakers in 1930.

Georgic¹, the eighth and last of White Star's livestock carriers was launched on 22 June 1895. *Georgic* was sunk by the German surface raider *Moewe* on 10 December 1916 about 590 miles east-south-east of Cape Race.

Delphic¹, 8,273 tons, entered service in 1897. *Delphic* was torpedoed and sunk 135 miles south-west of Bishop Rock in the Scilly Isles on 16 August 1917 while on her way from Cardiff to Montevideo with a cargo of coal. Five lives were lost.

Cymric entered White Star service in 1898. In 1900 she served as a troopship, HM *Transport 74*. On 8 May 1916, while on her way to Liverpool from New York she was hit by three torpedoes from *U20*, and sank the following day. Four of the 110-man crew were killed by the explosion and a steward was drowned as the ship was abandoned.

Oceanic², built by Harland & Wolff, was launched on 14 January 1899. *Oceanic, Celtic²*, *Cedric* and *Teutonic* were taken over by the Admiralty for use as armed merchant cruisers very shortly after hostilities began in 1914. *Oceanic* ran aground on the Shaalds of Foula on 8 September 1914.

Afric, entered service in 1899. Following her maiden voyage she was returned to the builders for seven months of alterations and improvements. *Afric* was torpedoed, five miles south-south-west of the Eddystone lighthouse in the English Channel, while returning from Australia on 12 February 1917.

Medic, entered service in 1899. Sold to N. Bugge of Tönsberg in 1928 and converted at Birkenhead into a whale factory ship, and renamed *Hectoria*. While operating as a tanker for the British Government, she was torpedoed and sunk in the North Atlantic on 11 September 1942.

Persic, 11,973 tons, entered service in 1899. *Persic*, while 200 miles from the English coast, with almost 3,000 American troops aboard, was torpedoed on 12 September 1918.

Remarkably, no lives were lost, although the ship had to be beached to prevent her from foundering. *Persic* was sent to Holland to be broken up in 1927.

Runic², the first of the two new, slightly enlarged, Australian-run vessels, was delivered to White Star on 22 December 1900. Sold to the Sevilla Whaling Company of London in 1930, and renamed *New Sevilla*. Still operating as the whale factory ship *Sevilla*, she was torpedoed west of Islay, Scotland, on 20 October 1940.

Suevic, joined the White Star fleet on 9 March 1901. Before the line could make any use of the new vessel, however, she was immediately requisitioned by the British Government for use as a troopship. Seriously damaged in a grounding accident near the Lizard in 1907. Sold to Yngvar Hvistendahl, Finnvhal A/S, Tönsberg, Norway, in 1928 for £35,000, for use as a whale factory ship, and renamed *Skytteren*. *Skytteren* was scuttled by her crew on 1 April 1942 after being intercepted by German naval units while trying to escape internment and reach Britain.

Celtic², of 20,904 tons, was launched at Belfast on 4 April 1901. She was the last ship T. H. Ismay ordered before his death. *Celtic* struck a mine off the Isle of Man on 15 February 1917 and had to be towed back to Liverpool. She was torpedoed soon after leaving Liverpool on 31 March 1918. *Celtic* ran hard aground off Roches Point lighthouse near Queenstown, at about 5am on 10 December 1928. Stuck fast, she was bought by the Danish shipbreakers Petersen & Albeck, and dismantled where she lay in 1933.

Athenic, of 12,344 tons, joined *Gothic* on the New Zealand run sometime in 1902. She was sold in 1928 and renamed *Pelagos*. Was still afloat as *Pelagos* in 1961.

Corinthic, 12,231 tons, on the New Zealand route in 1902. *Corinthic*, sold for scrap to Hughes Bolckow of Blyth in 1931. She was broken up by Swan Hunter at Wallsend the following year.

Ionic², of 12,232 tons, joined *Gothic*, *Athenic* and *Corinthic* on the New Zealand route in 1902. Ionic was eventually sold to Japanese ship-breakers for £31,500 in December 1934.

Cedric, the second of the 'Big Four' liners, entered service on 11 February 1903. She was similar to *Celtic²*. *Cedric*, 28 years old and 21,035 tons was withdrawn from service in 1931 and scrapped the following year.

Victorian, an 8,825-ton ship built in 1895, was chartered from the Leyland Line in 1903 for the Liverpool–New York run, then transferred to cargo service. *Victorian* was renamed *Russian* in 1914. Torpedoed while in the Mediterranean on 14 December 1916.

Armenian, taken over from the Leyland Line in 1903. *Armenian* and *Victorian* were sister ships, and almost identical, as were their service lives. *Armenian*, which had been transferred to cargo-carrying duties, was torpedoed and sunk by *U38* while she was off Trevose Head on 28 June 1915.

Arabic², 15,081 tons, came into service in 1903. *Arabic* was torpedoed and sunk by *UB24* off the Old Head of Kinsale, at the southern tip of Ireland, on 19 August 1915.

Romanic, 11,349-tons, ex-*New England*, taken over from the Dominion Line and renamed in 1903. *Romanic* was sold to the Canadian Pacific Line in 1912, renamed *Scandinavian*. Scrapped in Germany in 1923.

Canopic ex-*Commonwealth*, 13,000 tons, built in 1901, taken over from the Dominion Line in 1903. *Canopic* was scrapped at Briton Ferry in 1925.

Cretic ex-*Mayflower*, ex-*Hanoverian*, taken over from the Dominion Line in 1903. *Cretic*, 13,507 tons, passed back to the Leyland Line in 1923, for whom she had originally been constructed by Hawthorne Leslie in 1902 but only made three trips before being handed to Dominion in 1923. Sent to the breakers at Bo'ness in 1929.

Republic² ex-*Columbus*, taken over from the Dominion Line in 1903. She sank on 24 January 1905 after a collision with the *Florida*.

Laurentic¹, the ex-Dominion Line *Albany* was taken over by White Star in 1909 and renamed. *Laurentic¹* struck two mines and sank off Malin Head, on the north coast of Ireland, on 25 January 1917, with £5 million in gold aboard. 354 lives were lost. The wreck was discovered in 1921 in about 120ft of water. In a three-year salvage operation £4,958,708 of gold was recovered.

Megantic, ex-*Alberta*, taken over from the Dominion Line in 1909. *Megantic*, 14,500 tons, sold to Japanese breakers in 1933.

Cufic² ex-*American*, 9-year-old, 8,249-ton vessel, taken over in 1904. *Cufic* was sold for scrap in 1923 to Italian owners who changed her name to *Antartico*, and later to *Marie Guilie*. *Cufic* was sold to another Italian company in 1924 and initially renamed *Antartico*, and then *Marie Guilie*. She was sold for scrap in 1932 and broken up in Italy.

Tropic² ex-*European*, bought and renamed in 1904. The 8,230-ton vessel, which had been built in 1896, would remain with White Star until 1923. *Tropic* was sold to an Italian company in 1923 and her name changed to *Artico*. Sold again in 1927, she was renamed *Transylvania* and as *Transylvania* she was broken up in Italy in 1933.

Baltic², 23,876 tons, the third of the 'Big Four', entered service in 1904. Sold to Japanese breakers in 1933.

Adriatic², the last of the 'Big Four', entered service in 1907, larger than the *Baltic*, at 24,540 tons, and the first ship to have a swimming pool and Turkish baths aboard. Last survivor of the 'Big Four', she was sold to the Japanese for scrap in December 1934.

Mersey, 1,713-ton, steel hulled vessel, built by Connell's of Glasgow, bought by J. Bruce Ismay in 1908 for use as an ocean-going training ship. *Mersey* was the very first sailing ship to be fitted with radio. *Mersey* was sold in 1914, her officers and captain being needed for more important work.

Olympic, keel laid on 16 December 1908, launched on 20 October 1910. *Olympic* was officially commissioned as one of His Majesty's Transports on 9 April 1917. *Olympic* was bought for £100,000 in 1935 by Sir John Jarvis, who quickly sold her on to Wards of Inverkeithing, with the stipulation that she should be broken up at Jarrow, an area badly affected by the Depression. On 11 October she left Southampton for the last time, heading for Jarrow, where she arrived two days later. *Olympic* was taken from Jarrow and towed to Wards of Inverkeithing, where her hull would be demolished, on 19 September 1937, arriving there the following day.

Titanic's keel was laid on 31 March 1909. *Titanic* sank at 2.20am on 15 April 1912, after supposedly striking an iceberg, with the loss of more than 1,500 lives. She had left Southampton for New York on her maiden voyage on the 10th.

Zeeland, 11,905 tons, was chartered in 1910 and 1911 from Red Star for the Liverpool–Boston service. She was renamed *Northland* in 1915 because *Zeeland* sounded too Germanic. She was chartered in 1914 and 1915 for Canadian service, then used as a trooper. Transferred to the Atlantic Transport Line in 1927 and her name changed to *Minnesota*. Scrapped at Inverkeithing in 1930.

Nomadic², 1,273 tons, built in 1911 to serve as a tender to the *Olympic* Class White Star liners, was still afloat in 2000 and serving as a restaurant on the River Seine in Paris.

Traffic², 675 tons, came into service in 1911. *Traffic* was sold to the Société Cherbourgeoise de Remorquage et de Sauvetage, Cherbourg, and renamed *Ingénieur*

Riebell in 1934. Scuttled by the French when the Germans invaded in June 1940, she was raised and used by the German Navy. Now sailing under the German flag, *Traffic* was attacked and sunk by British motor torpedo boats in the English Channel on 17 January 1941.

Britannic²'s keel was laid, as far as we know, on 30 November 1911. She was launched on 26 February 1914 but would never be completed as a liner, being was taken over by the Admiralty on 13 November 1915 for use as a hospital ship. She was withdrawn from service on 12 April 1916, though retained by the Admiralty as a naval hospital for five weeks. Later brought back into use, *Britannic* struck a mine in the Aegean Sea on the morning of Tuesday 21 November 1916, while again serving as a hospital ship. She sank with the loss of 21 lives.

Zealandic, a 10,898-ton freighter, came into service with the line some time in 1911. She was sold to the Aberdeen Line and renamed *Mamilius* in 1926. Sold on to the Shaw Savill Line, becoming the *Mamari* in 1932. Sold again in 1939, to the Admiralty, to become the dummy aircraft-carrier '*Hermes*'. While on her way to be converted back into a cargo ship she was attacked by German aircraft, ran aground on the East Anglian coast, near Cromer, and was wrecked on 4 June 1941.

Belgic³, ex-*Samland*, ex-*Mississippi*, joined White Star for two years in 1911, from Red Star. Returned to Red Star Line in 1913 and scrapped in 1931.

Ceramic, entered service with the White Star Line in 1913, on the Australian route. Sold to the Shaw Savill Line in 1934. Requisitioned in 1940, but continued to carry passengers. *Ceramic* was torpedoed and sunk on 6 December 1942; all but one of her crew were lost.

Justicia, had been launched by Harland & Wolff on 9 July 1914 as the *Statendam*, for the Holland–America Line. Bought by the Admiralty, she was handed over to White Star for the duration of the war. *Justicia* was torpedoed by *UB64* on 19 July 1918 but remained afloat. At 9.30am on the following day *UB54* fired a salvo of torpedoes at *Justicia's* port side, one struck Number 3 hold and another Number 5. *Justicia* sank stern first at 12.40pm on 20 July 1918.

Lapland, the 18,694-ton Red Star Line vessel, built in 1908, that had brought the majority of *Titanic's* survivors home from America, served with the White Star Line 1914–19. *Lapland* struck a mine off the Mersey Bar lightship some time in 1917, but survived the incident and was returned to the Red Star Line in 1920. She was broken up in Japan in 1933.

Southland, ex-*Vaderland*, transferred to White Star from Red Star in 1914 and renamed. She was torpedoed while serving in the Aegean Sea, on 15 September 1915, but survived. She was sunk by *UB70* on 4 June 1917, about 140 miles north-west of Tory Point, Ireland, with the loss of four lives.

Belgic⁴; it seems that the line acquired another freighter of this name some time in 1917. Nothing else appears to be known of her.

Homeric, a planned 40,000-ton ship, was ordered from Harland & Wolff very shortly after the war ended but was never built.

Vedic, joined the White Star fleet towards the end of 1918 and was scrapped at Rosyth in 1934.

Gallic², ex-*War Argus*, taken over by White Star in 1919. Sold in 1933. Sailed under various owners until sold for scrap in 1955. Broken up in 1956 in Hong Kong.

Bardic, ex-*War Priam*, an 8,000-ton cargo ship, was bought by White Star shortly after the cessation of hostilities in an effort to make good some of the losses the fleet of freighters had suffered. White Star took over the vessel on 13 March 1919 and renamed the ship. She sailed on her maiden voyage for the line on the 18th. She was sold off in 1925 to the Aberdeen Line who renamed her *Hostilius* but changed that to *Horatius* less than a year later. Later renamed *Marathon*, she was sunk by the German battle-cruiser *Scharnhorst* on 9 March 1941.

Homeric[2], 34,000 tons, intended for the Norddeutscher–Lloyd Line as *Columbus*, awaiting completion at Danzig and available as War Reparations, she was bought by IMM soon after the war's end as a partner for *Olympic* and renamed *Homeric* in 1922 and served for 14 years before being sold as scrap to Wards of Inverkeithing, for £74,000 in 1936.

Bismarck, awaiting completion in Germany, was taken over by White Star in 1920 after a long legal battle. See *Majestic*[2] below.

Arabic[3], formerly *Berlin*, this 16,821-ton Norddeutscher–Lloyd vessel was taken over by White Star for use on the Liverpool–New York route in 1920 and renamed. She had been built by Blohm & Voss 12 years before. Transferred to the Red Star Line in 1925, but brought back into White Star service for a short time in 1930 before returning to her usual work for the Red Star Line. Scrapped in 1932.

Haverford, bought for White Star use in 1921 by IMM. Damaged in a collision with the American steamer *West Arrow* on 19 September 1923. Scrapped in Italy in 1925.

Poland, 8,282 tons, bought from the Red Star Line in 1922. Sold in 1925 and renamed *Natale*. Went to the breakers in Italy in 1935, when she was 37 years old.

Pittsburgh, 16,322 tons, which had been built by Harland & Wolff for the American Line, another part of IMM, in 1922 was taken over before she entered service with them. Transferred to the Red Star Line in 1925 and a year later renamed *Pennland*. As *Pennland* was sold again in 1935 to Arnold Bernstein's Red Star Line. Sold again in 1939 to the Holland–America Line. While operating as a troopship, was sunk by German air attack in the Gulf of Athens on 25 April 1941.

Majestic[2], (ex-German *Bismarck*) joined *Olympic* and *Homeric* on the Southampton–New York route, her maiden voyage beginning on 10 May 1922. She was sold to Wards for scrapping in May 1936, but not broken up. In June Wards sold *Majestic* to the Admiralty and she was converted into the training ship HMS *Caledonia*. As *Caledonia* she was destroyed by fire while at Rosyth on 29 September 1939, and sank at her berth. Sold back to Wards in March 1940, raised and towed to Inverkeithing for final demolition in July 1943.

Doric[2], specially commissioned for the Liverpool–Montreal route, entered service in 1923. She was badly damaged in a collision with a French vessel off Portugal on 5 September 1935, and was scrapped at Sir John Cashmore's yard at Newport, Monmouthshire.

Delphic[2], bought during 1925. This seven-year-old, 8,006-ton ship had already seen service with other lines as the *Mesaba* and *War Icarus*. *Delphic* was sold in 1933, renamed *Clan Farquhar* and eventually broken up at Milford Haven in 1948.

Albertic, ex-*Ohio*, joined the White Star fleet in 1927. The 18,940-ton one-time Royal Mail Steam Packet Company vessel had been built in Germany by Weser of Bremen for Norddeutscher–Lloyd in 1923 but had been bought by Royal Mail on completion. She was laid up in 1933 and fetched £34,000 when she was sold for scrap in 1934. She left for Osaka, in Japan, in August.

Calgaric, ex-*Orca*, bought in during 1927 and renamed. This 16,063-ton vessel had been built in 1908 for the Pacific Steam Navigation Company. *Calgaric* was sold as scrap for £31,000. She left for the breakers at Rosyth in December 1934. She was finally demolished in 1936.

Laurentic[2], joined the line in 1927. Placed in reserve in 1936. *Laurentic* was torpedoed by Otto Kretschmer's *U99* to the north of Ireland on 3 November 1940. She foundered at about 4am the following day.

Oceanic[3], construction of White Star's new 60,000-ton ship, ordered in 1928, was abandoned in 1929 because of the desperate shortage of funds.

Regina, which was completed in 1918 as a troopship, joined White Star-Dominion Line service in 1922, after conversion. Sold in 1929, and renamed *Westernland*. She was sold to the Holland-America Line in 1935 and sold again to the Admiralty in 1943 before being scrapped at Blyth in 1947.

Georgic[2], arrived in Liverpool on 13 June 1932. She was the last ship built by Harland & Wolff for the White Star Line. On 25 June 1932 the 27,793-ton vessel sailed on her maiden voyage to New York. *Georgic* was sold to Shipbreaking Industries of Faslane, Scotland, and arrived there for scrapping by 1 February 1956.

Britannic[3], the last White Star liner, which had joined the line in 1930, passed to Cunard and left New York for the final time on 25 November 1960. On arriving home she was promptly sold to Wards, and set out on her last trip, to their yard at Inverkeithing, Scotland, on 4 December.

Appendix

MESS UTENSILS. SMALL STORES, &c.

For The Use Of The Passengers On Board

GOVERNMENT EMIGRANT SHIPS
May 1863

SCALE NO 1. MESS UTENSILS

NOTES

1. All the Tin articles mentioned in the following Scales are to be made of the best Double Block Tin throughout.
2. The Cooperage articles are to be made with stout seasoned Oak Staves and well and strongly hooped; and the Mess Kits, Water Breakers, Scuttle Butts, Cooks' Tubs and Harness Casks, to be filled with Water at least 48 hours immediately previous to being put on board.
3. Whenever the word 'Adult' occurs it means 'Statute Adult' as defined by the Passengers' Act.
4. If any other than Normandy's Water Distilling Apparatus be supplied, the Commissioners will, on application, prescribe the Stores that are to accompany the Machine.

MESS UTENSILS TO BE PUT ON BOARD FOR EVERY EIGHT STATUTE ADULTS AND ONE FIFTH IN ADDITION

1 Mess Kit with Iron Handles to hold 2 gallons.
1 Tin Oval Dish, with Colander and Cover, 14 inches long and 8 inches deep.
1 Quartern Tin Baking Dish for Bread.
1 Half Quartern do.   do.
1 Bread Tub, with Wooden Hoops and Cover, to hold 10lbs.
2 Tin Pots, to hold $3^{1}/_{2}$ pints each, with Covers and Bar Hooks for Boiling Water.
1 Water Bucket, to hold 3 gallons, with nozzle of Galvanized Iron and Plug attached by short Iron Chain.
1 Tin Mustard Pot to hold $^{1}/_{2}$ pint.
1 Tin Pepper and Salt Cellar, divided 1 in the centre.
1 Butter Dish 7 inches in diameter, 1 and 3 inches deep.
3 Sets of Tin Tallies, hung with Wire Lanyards.
Potato Nets to hold 10lbs, $^{3}/_{4}$inch Mesh.

These Articles to be marked with consecutive numbers from 1 upwards, with a line *Underneath* the figures.

1 Pudding Bag, 18 inches long, by 12 inches wide of No 8 Canvas.
2 Mess Towels 1 yard long by 1 yard wide.
Wash Leather.

These Articles to be marked in indelible marking ink, with consecutive numbers from 1 upwards, with a line *Underneath* the figures.

SCALE NO 2 — SMALL STORES

The figures in brackets denoting the numbers of each item required by vessels carrying 200, 300, and 400 respectively.

Birch Brooms No 4. (18, 30, 42)
Coir Brooms. (18, 30, 42)
Hair Brushes, with long handles. (16, 24, 32)
Hair Brushes, with short handles. (16, 24, 32)
Scrubbing Brushes. (16, 24, 32)
Swabs. (16, 24, 32)
Dust Pans. (8, 12, 16)
Scrapers (New). (16, 24, 32)
Pails (New) to hold 3 gallons each, with perpendicular sides. (6, 10, 14)
Combined brushes and squeegee, $10^1/_2$ inch. (4, 8, 12)
Shovels. (2, 4, 6)
Mops No 5. (16, 24, 32)
Holy Stones 7 inches by $3^1/_2$ by $3^1/_2$. (96, 144, 192)
— do. mounted. (4, 8, 12)
Rubbish Tubs, 6 gallons each with Rope Buckets. (4, 4, 6)
Coals for cooking hearth, tons (best Steam Coal), for Distilling apparatus. (16, 24, 32)
do. for crew. (5, 5, 6)
Charcoal bushels. (10, 14 18)
Coke do. (10, 14, 18)
Firewood (fms. of 630lbs) (6, 9, 9)
Sand do. ($3^1/_2$, 4, 6)
Whiting lbs. (12, 18, 30)
Swing Stoves (4, 5, 6)
Fire Buckets, complete, with Handles and Lanyards of 4 fathoms each. (12, 12, 12)
Oven for Bread (as described below) to contain not less cubic feet, internal measurement, than (20, 25, 35)

SCALE NO 3. COOKING APPARATUS AND
MISCELLANEOUS
ARTICLES FOR EACH SHIP.

1 Cooking Hearth, complete, with proper rails, bars, and heating surface for Hook Pots, Hot Plates for Boilers, Oven and Damper, Chimney, and 2 sets of Furnace Bars. The Boilers to be of wrought iron, not less than 8 in number, to be fitted with Brass Taps, $2^3/_4$ inch and 1 $1^1/_2$ inch. The Boilers to hold in all not less than 2 quarts and 10 per cent over for each adult, to fit securely on the Hot Plate, and 2 of them to be fitted with the best double Block Tin Steamers, with racks to hold Saucepans. The oven to be fixed, and to be not less than 16 inches in depth, so as to admit of a shelf, and afford Baking accommodation at the rate of not less than 8 square inches per Adult, for the whole number of passengers. The Cooking Hearth and Oven to be properly covered and protected from the weather as far as practicable. Ships carrying more than 250 Adults to have 2 Hearths, with fittings as above, if the Emigration Officer should deem them to be necessary.

Bakehouse, to be fitted with proper Kneading Troughs and Covers, and Shelves for the use of the Baker; with an Oven to contain not less cubic feet than mentioned in Scale No 2 and to be made of wrought or cast iron, and the inner casing to be of iron, or to be made throughout of Sheffield firebricks or tiles properly laid and secured with iron framing. If tile inner casing iron it must be double throughout, with sufficient space between the surfaces to admit of enough sand to prevent the too rapid heating or cooling of the oven. The doors are to be double. The oven is to be fitted with not exceeding 3 Iron Shelves, proper Funnel, Soot Holes Steam Valves, Blowers, Scrapers, Pokers, Shovels, Peels, and a double set of Furnace Bars. In cases where the Baker's Oven forms part of the Cooking Hearth care must be taken to accommodate the Cook and Baker, so as not to give rise to disputes between them.

1 Small Dumpy Stove with Saucepan and Teakettle to fit, sufficient Iron Piping from the floor of the 'Tween Decks up one of the Airshoots to the Poop, 1 Iron Stay and Strap for every 3 feet of Piping, 1 cowl and 2 elbows.

3 Scuttle Butts, to contain 100 gallons each.

2 Tubs for Cook, to contain 40 gallons each.

2 Harness Casks (half hogsheads), fitted with Padlocks.

1 Large water Cask, to be converted into a Bath for men.

Bath room for females to be fitted with a 3 inch combing well caulked and pitched all round. The floor to be made watertight, and filled with a Scupper, and 2 wooden Baths, lined with 6lb lead, with proper supply and 2 inch Waste Pipes, Brass Cocks, and Plugs Seats and Clothes Pegs, to the satisfaction of the Commissioners' Officer. Zinc baths cannot be allowed.

4 Pumps for Water, Copper.

1 Copper Hold Pump, with 60 feet of proper Hose to issue allowance of fresh water on upper deck. Hose to be in two lengths, with brass couplings and deck plates.

2 Tarpaulins No 3 canvas for each Hatchway, large enough to cover the Hatchways Tent fashion.

1 Main Deck and 1 Poop Awning of No 1 Canvas, with side Screen, complete.

Canvas Screens for each Hatchway to be made of No 6 Canvas.

3 Windsails.

4 Life Buoys.

Hexagonal Safety Candle Lanthorns with spring sockets, *according to patterns to be seen at the Government Emigration Offices.*

10 for the first 100 Statute Adults.

1 for every 20 Statute Adults, Additional.

2 Spare Plates of Glass for each Lanthorn.

1 Spare Spring for ditto   ditto.

Price's Patent Stearine Sperm Candles, in 4 different sizes, prepared expressly for the Commissioners' Ships, packed in proper quantities, in separate parcels, and duly labelled for use by Price's Patent Kandle Company. No broken packages will be admitted. Samples may be seen at the Government Emigration Offices.

40 of Size No 3, to burn 3 hours; 40 of Size No 4, to burn 4 hours; 40 of Size No 5, to burn 5 hours; for each Lanthorn. 500 of do. No 7, to burn 7 hours for each Ship. Three-fourths of these quantities to be supplied for Vessels to the Cape.

1 Candle Dark Lanthorn. 2 Reflector Hand Lanthorns to burn Price's Patent Candles. For each Lanthorn 5 packets of 32 Candles, to burn 4 hours.

2 Safety Candle Lanthorns for Cook and Baker, and 70 Candles, to burn 3 hours for each Lanthorn.

4 Knives for Cook, one 10in, two 8in, and one 6 in.

1 Steel, 2 Flesh Forks, and 2 Tormenters.

3 Ladles 1 quart with short handle and lip, 1 pint and a half, and 1 pint.

4 best Block Tin Saucepans to fit Steamers.

2 2-quart Enamel Iron Saucepans.

2 10-quart oval Iron Saucepans.

1 12-do.   do.

1 Meat Saw, large size.

1 Cleaver (large size), and 1 Hand Chopper.

2 Hatchets for chopping Wood, fitted.

3 Coal Buckets for $\frac{1}{2}$ cwt each.

1 Coffee Roaster.

1 Coffee Mill, best quality, with fly wheels, hand-cut steel cutting wheels, and tins to hold the coffee while grinding.

1 Rice Sieve, tin with brass wire gauze.

1 Cooper's Adze and Driver, fitted.

1 3-inch Bung Borer.

8 Lever Knives approved.

1 Grindstone, fitted in Trough.

1 Biscuit Mill, with flywheel.

2 Pepper Mills.

2 Sieves for sand, $\frac{1}{8}$ inch mesh.

1 Water Filter, Ransome's Patent, 60 gallons; and if there is no Water Distilling Apparatus on board 2 small filters of the same kind for Hospital and Dispensary.

4 Tin Water Funnels — One $\frac{1}{2}$ gallon, three 1 quart each, to fit Water Breakers.

2 Brass Lock Taps for Porter.

3 Corkscrews.

1 Set of pewter Measures, 1 quart, 1 pint, 1 half pint, 1 gill, one $\frac{1}{2}$ gill, one for Lime juice.

2 Sets of Tin do.— Half gallon, quart, and pint.

1 Set of Wood do — Quart, pint, and half pint.

6 Tin Scoops assorted sizes.

1 Pair of Flour Scales, with Stamped Weights, from $\frac{1}{4}$ lb to 14lbs inclusive.

1 Pair of Counter Balance Scales, with Weights, from $\frac{1}{4}$ oz to 4lbs inclusive.

12 Extra panes of plate glass for Skylights.

1 Set of Clothes Lines, With Clothes Stops, and blocks to be fitted between main and mizen rigging.

1 Accommodation Ladder, fitted with Landings.

6 Rope Mats, 6 feet 6in long by 2 feet wide.

2 Cots, for Hospital No 4 Canvas.

2 Nursery Lamps.

1 Portable Watercloset for each Hospital, with galvanized iron Slop pail.

2 Fire Engines complete, one to be fixed, the other to be portable. The working parts to be of Gun Metal, and each Engine to be supplied with 80 feet of Delivery Hose, Suction Hose with a Rose at the end, and Delivery Pipe, to discharge in a minute about 35 gallons for Small and 50 gallons for Large Ships. The Engine hose of the fixed Engine to reach over the tafrail.

3 Signal Lamps, as per Admiralty Notice, 1st October 1858.

2 Guns, 4-pounders, with sponge, rammer, worm, ladle, and priming horn for each, also with quoins, and stool beds, &c.

Ammunition, 50 round of 8oz each, in flannel cartridges, and 6lbs of powder in magazine.

2 Dozen Blue Lights.

2 Dozen Rockets.

1 Lightning Conductor.

24 Deal boards, 1 inch.

24 Do. do. $\frac{3}{4}$ inch.

50 Feet 3 inch Quartering.

2 Dozen Iron Staples and Hasps, assorted sizes.

12 lbs of Nail assorted.

6 Feet Lead Piping each size, used for Water closets, &c., on Board the Ship.

4 Square feet 6lbs Lead.

6 Spare Iron Padlocks. No two keys to be of the same pattern.

6 Spare Brass Padlocks, $2\frac{1}{2}$ inch. No two keys to be of the same pattern.

1 Soldering Iron, large, with 8lbs Solder, and 2lbs Rosin.

1 Soldering Iron, small.   ·

1 Hammock for each single man, and *one fourth* additional. All to be fitted with white Clews and Lashings.

1 Stern Pump and proper hose, for ditto.

4 Spare Levers for Water closets.

6 Cork Life Belts.

1 Fog Horn.

3 Thermometers for Surgeon.

Mercantile Code of Signals.

Marine Navy List.

Charts of all the seas the Ship is to traverse, published by the Admiralty or stamped by the Hydrographer as correct.

LIST OF ARTICLES AND STORES TO ACCOMPANY THE WATER DISTILLING APPARATUS

The Articles to be of a suitable size and description for the Machine.

1 Set Stoking Tools.	1 $^3/_4$-inch Bend.
1 Scaling Tool.	1 1-inch Bend.
1 $^1/_2$ x $^5/_8$ Spanner.	1 $^3/_4$-inch Elbow.
1 Shifting Spanner.	1 1-inch Elbow.
1 Float for Steam-trap.	1 Slide Rod for Donkey Pump.
Box for Steam-trap.	1 $^1/_2$ pint Pneumatic Oil Can.
1 Set of Fire-bars.	5lbs Spun Yarn.
1 14-inch Flat Bastard File.	10lbs. Cotton Waste.
1 14-inch half-round File.	2 Sets 1$^1/_2$-inch Patent Joints.
1 10-inch half-round File.	1 Deal Box, with iron handles, hasp and staple.
3 File-handles.	
2 Cold Chisels.	1 Padlock for ditto.
1 Hammer and Handle.	2 Gallons Machinery Oil.
1 Pair Patent Gas Tongs.	Can for Ditto.
1 Soldering Iron.	1 Oil Feeder.
10lbs Solder.	1 Small Vice.
2lbs Resin.	1 Ratchet Brace.
6 Gauge Glasses.	4 Drills.
24 India Rubber Gauge Glass Washers.	12 Sheets of Emery Cloth.
30 $^1/_2$-inch Bolts and Nuts.	12 $^3/_8$ Bolts and Nuts.
36 India Rubber Washers.	2 $^3/_4$ Connections.
2 1-inch Connections.	

By Order of the Board,
John Walpole,
Government Emigration Office, Assistant Secretary.
Park Street, Westminster, S.W.
May 1863.

Index